SHAKESPEARE SURVEY

SHAKESPEARE SURVEY

AN ANNUAL SURVEY OF
SHAKESPEARIAN STUDY & PRODUCTION

18

EDITED BY

ALLARDYCE NICOLL

Issued under the Sponsorship of

THE UNIVERSITY OF BIRMINGHAM
THE UNIVERSITY OF MANCHESTER
THE ROYAL SHAKESPEARE THEATRE
THE SHAKESPEARE BIRTHPLACE TRUST

CAMBRIDGE
AT THE UNIVERSITY PRESS
1965

PUBLISHED BY
THE SYNDICS OF THE CAMBRIDGE UNIVERSITY PRESS

Bentley House, 200 Euston Road, London, N.W. 1
American Branch: 32 East 57th Street, New York, N.Y. 10022
West African Office: P.O. Box 33, Ibadan, Nigeria

Printed in Great Britain at the University Printing House, Cambridge
(Brooke Crutchley, University Printer)

LIBRARY OF CONGRESS CATALOGUE
CARD NUMBER: 49–1639

EDITOR'S NOTE

The central theme of this, the eighteenth volume of *Shakespeare Survey*, is 'Shakespeare Then Till Now'. This completes the trilogy which began, in *Survey 16*, with 'Shakespeare Today', followed by the special Quatercentenary volume devoted to the subject of 'Shakespeare in His Own Age'. Among the articles printed in this volume, five—those by Charlton Hinman, Harold Jenkins, Kenneth Muir, John Russell Brown and Winton Dean—were originally delivered as papers at the International Shakespeare Conference at Stratford-upon-Avon in 1964.

The theme of the next volume, the nineteenth, will be *Macbeth*. This will appear under the care of Kenneth Muir, King Alfred Professor of English Literature at the University of Liverpool, who is taking over the duties of editor. To him the present editor, now resigning, offers all best wishes in the pursuit of an interesting but often arduous task.

The latest date for the consideration of articles in Volume 20, which will be a general volume without a central theme, is 1 September 1966. Contributions offered for publication and all other communications concerning editorial matters should in future be addressed to:

The Editor, *Shakespeare Survey*
Department of English
The University
Liverpool 3

All other communications, including books for review, should in future be sent to:

Shakespeare Survey
Cambridge University Press
The Pitt Building
Trumpington Street
Cambridge

CONTENTS

[Notes are placed at the end of each contribution. All line references are to the 'Globe' edition, and, unless for special reasons, quotations are from this text]

LIST OF PLATES

CHIDING THE PLAYS: THEN TILL NOW

BY

CHARLES R. CROW

'Shakespeare is a dead issue.' Thus T. J. B. Spencer concludes his 1959 British Academy lecture. 'The resistance to his magnificent tyranny is over....'[1] And Spencer would seem to be right on the grounds of his argument. Whether Shakespeare's work, taken as a whole, is worth the attention it has come to compel, the influence it has exerted is not now a matter for much disagreement. Even the long-fought war on Shakespeare's language, so tellingly reviewed by Spencer, has ended in something like our surrender. We hear, now, much about what Shakespeare's words are doing, little about their 'conceited' badness. Utter detraction on these and on the other classic grounds has gone, detraction, that is, of Shakespeare. But not of Shakespeare's plays.

The distinction is a just one. Issues of judgment on particular Shakespeare plays are not dead. Critics do not ordinarily go to 'Shakespeare'. They go to *Troilus and Cressida* or *Othello* or *The Winter's Tale*, and they still find fault. Often they find fault with interpretations of other critics, not the play. When they do, they may exhibit the 'shadow-boxing of rival bardolaters', as Spencer says.[2] But where they make judgments against the play, or something in the play, the boxing is real. They do make such judgments, and not only against the earliest plays. There are the standard issues still active: the rejection of Falstaff, the death of Cordelia, the moral ambiguities of *Antony and Cleopatra*. Such matters are widely defended, subtly interpreted, and yet not settled. Shakespeare's handling of them, and not merely some critic's interpretation of it, is still questioned. In an age that likes to hold off explicit critical judgment, cultivates interpretation, sees interpretation indeed as an act of judgment, we may be less aware that these adverse judgments go on. They do, and in tones and manners not notably different from those of past centuries.

To display some of these tones and manners, then and now, is the object of this paper: the manners of critics as they show an enduring human willingness to find fault where fault seems to be in a Shakespeare play. There will be no examination of critical arguments, no analysis of their justice. Such undertaking would be too vast, of course, if it were to mean anything, and anyway not to the present purpose. For to look only at the arguments is to watch for the answers to them by other critics and probably to support the impression, given by some surveys of Shakespeare criticism, that there is a grand progression towards seeing the Shakespeare plays as faultless. It is good to check this impression by looking at critical manners that keep alertness to the faults alive. That is what will be done here. A rough grouping of kinds of manners, of tones taken towards the 'fault' in the play, will serve to bring past and present critics together for what may be some interesting likenesses. All the critics are well known. To yoke them by their manners will be to violate not only the separations of time but of contexts, with much loss of discrimination. The manners may stand out instructively nevertheless.

We start at the bottom of a scale of willingness to find fault, and look at a hesitant critical manner. Among considerable critics of Shakespeare it is not easy to locate except in one conspicuous place. Surprisingly it shows up for a sentence or two, no doubt as a ceremonious gesture, in John Dennis, a critic not noted for timidity. He has found *Coriolanus* wanting in certain respects of 'poetical art' and is offering his own 'alteration' of the play: 'I humbly conceive therefore that this want of Dramatical Justice in the Tragedy of *Coriolanus* gave occasion for a just Alteration, and that I was oblig'd to sacrifice to that Justice *Aufidius* and the Tribunes, as well as *Coriolanus*.'[3] The humility is little more than perfunctory. It is perhaps genuine when Dennis turns to *Julius Caesar*, and, after suggesting improvements on Shakespeare's way of presenting Caesar, including a sketch for a scene that Shakespeare did not write, says: 'I will not pretend to determine here how that Scene might have been turn'd; and what I have already said on this Subject, has been spoke with the utmost Caution and Diffidence.'[4] Still, it *has* been spoken, and firmly. This countering of a firm objection by a gesture of humility turns dramatic when we find it in Swinburne as he looks at *Measure for Measure*:

In short and in fact, the whole elaborate machinery by which the complete and completely unsatisfactory result of the whole plot is attained is so thoroughly worthy of such a contriver as 'the old fantastical duke of dark corners' as to be in a moral sense, if I dare say what I think, very far from thoroughly worthy of the wisest and mightiest mind that ever was informed with the spirit or genius of creative poetry.[5]

Here we do need the context. Those words about 'the wisest and mightiest mind' are not in the vein of Rymer or Shaw: they are earnestly meant. The 'if I dare say what I think' is wrenched out against them. Yet Swinburne has said what he thinks.

Conspicuously it is Coleridge who hesitates, and on glorious principle. Shakespeare's judgment is equal to his genius. The organic poem obeys its own strict laws, not laws imposed upon it by the critic. The critic attends its unfolding into full growth. And when the critic is balked he turns, sometimes, upon himself. Coleridge's turns are remarkable. Of the Brutus soliloquy 'It must be by his death...' he says:

This is singular—at least I do not at present see into Shakespeare's motive, the *rationale*—or in what point he meant Brutus's character to appear. For surely (this I mean is what I say to myself, in my present quantum of insight, only modified by my experience in how many instances I have ripened into a perception of beauties where I had before descried faults), surely nothing can seem more discordant with our historical preconceptions of Brutus, or more *lowering* to the intellect of this Stoico-Platonic tyrannicide, than the tenets here attributed to him....What character does Shakespeare mean *his* Brutus to be?[6]

Reluctance to blame the play could hardly be more pronounced. The critic must distrust himself. His 'quantum of insight' may increase, or better, in an access of the organic metaphor to himself, perception may 'ripen' as it has done before. However inconclusive, the attitude is consistent with the Coleridge principles. And in the observation about Brutus it does give an airing to at least a provisional objection. We may be glad, nevertheless, that Coleridge on other occasions was more decisive about blemishes in the plays, even when, as with the Porter scene, we think his perception and his explanation dead wrong.

To go up the scale from hesitation towards deliberate appraisal of faults has not been hard for many a Shakespeare critic. There is a way to do it that has been a favourite from the eighteenth century until almost now: the way that expresses or implies regret but gets down to business. Thomas Whately remarks of the 'careless strokes' he has found in *Richard III*: 'After every reasonable allowance, they must still remain blemishes ever to be lamented....'[7] Joseph Warton laments and censures in one breath: 'I always lament that our author has not preserved this fierce and implacable spirit in Calyban, to the end of the play; instead of which, he has, I think, injudiciously put into his mouth, words that imply repentance and understanding....'[8] Even Johnson can take something of this manner. Of Enobarbus' final speech he says: 'The pathetic of Shakespeare too often ends in the ridiculous. It is painful to find the gloomy dignity of this noble scene destroyed by the intrusion of a conceit so far-fetched and unaffecting.'[9] Coleridge's pain is more intense, a very real thing, when he looks at *Measure for Measure*, and this time his aim is as quick and as direct as Johnson's:

This play, which is Shakespeare's throughout, is to me the most painful—say rather, the only painful—part of his genuine works....[T]he pardon and marriage of Angelo not merely baffles the strong indignant claim of justice (for cruelty, with lust and damnable baseness, cannot be forgiven, because we cannot conceive them as being *morally* repented of) but it is likewise degrading to the character of woman....Of the counterbalancing beauties of the *Measure for Measure* I need say nothing, for I have already said that it is Shakespeare's throughout.[10]

'Shakespeare's throughout': the repetition twists the regret.

Hazlitt laments more mildly but with direct hits at the same play. He finds it 'as full of genius as it is of wisdom'. Yet he must say that 'there is an original sin in the nature of the subject, which prevents us from taking a cordial interest in it...'. He cannot like Isabella's 'rigid chastity'. And he says why. 'We do not feel the same confidence in the virtue that is "sublimely good" at another's expense, as if it had been put to some less disinterested trial.'[11] This play has drawn notable strains of regret from the critics, whatever the defences of its 'genius' and its 'wisdom'. Alfred Harbage says of III, i, 152–261: 'What follows is less in need of explication than apology'.[12] Charles Williams ends a series of questions about the play's 'cessation of all concern' with Angelo by sighing, 'It was not to be'. And his sigh comes to this conclusion: '*Measure for Measure*, then, remains poetically, like *Troilus*, an abandoned play. There may be every kind of noble lesson in it, but they have not been discovered by poetry.'[13] Sir Arthur Quiller-Couch even manages to transfer the sigh to Shakespeare. He says of the Mariana scene, 'Is it extravagant to suppose that Shakespeare invented this remote and exquisite scene, with its sob of the lute, on realizing that Isabella had failed, and was henceforth issueless, to deliver the spirit of his dream?'[14]

There is little more sighing as we go up the scale of faultfinding and reach a manner that says 'Let's face these faults with aplomb'. It goes especially well with historical or vocational accountings for Shakespeare's lapses. Johnson devotes five paragraphs to an examination of witchcraft and enchantment as his first note on *Macbeth* and concludes thus: 'Upon this general infatuation Shakespeare might be easily allowed to found a play, especially since he has followed with great exactness such histories as were then thought true; nor can it be doubted that the scenes of enchantment, however they may now be ridiculed, were both by himself and his audience thought awful and affecting.'[15] With this attitude might be compared that recommended by Harbage: 'Gaunt's extended punning upon his name, and his stichomythic wit-combat with Richard, proves offensive to some readers, and understandably so. It is unnecessary to rationalize into a virtue every detail in these plays, which, like Renaissance art in general, sometimes lapse into the bizarre.'[16] Sir Walter Raleigh, turning to the facts of a busy writer's life at any time, decries the 'superstition which refuses to assign to Shakespeare any hasty or careless work'. And he urges a truer view:

Yet he was a purveyor to the public stage, and surely must have been pressed, as the modern journalist is pressed, to supply needed matter. Many authors who have suffered this pressure have settled their account with their conscience by dividing their work into two kinds. Some of it they do frankly as journey-work, making it as good as time and circumstances permit. The rest they keep by them, revising and polishing it to satisfy their own more exacting ideals. Shakespeare did both kinds of work, and the bulk of his writing has come down to us without distinction made between the better and the worse.[17]

Raleigh can then calmly face *All's Well that Ends Well* as presumably 'journey-work': 'The principal characters...are designed for their parts in the intrigue, but not even Shakespeare's skill can unite the incompatible, and teach them how to do their dramatic work without weakening their claim on our sympathies.'[18] In similar vein Quiller-Couch watches Shakespeare the workman, though now the earnest workman: 'Thus in *The Winter's Tale* the gap between Acts III and IV comes of honest failure to do an extremely difficult thing, yet a thing well worth doing, which Shakespeare essayed again and again until at length, in *The Tempest*, he mastered it.'[19]

Take away the extenuating air and we arrive at the cool 'There it is: no bones about it' manner, useful to critics who are summarizing in brief space or who want to get on to something else. Here Johnson is the grand exemplar. 'This play', he says of *Richard II*, 'is one of those which Shakespeare has apparently revised; but as success in works of invention is not always proportionate to labour, it is not finished at last with the happy force of some other of his tragedies nor can be said much to affect the passions or enlarge the understanding.'[20] Coming at the end of Johnson's notes on the play, this sentence may seem too curt a dismissal; but these manners are prized in Johnson. His 'General Observation' that ends the notes on *Hamlet* is of course more ample. Its final paragraph is an unperturbed enumeration of faults until it surprises with a flourish of feeling:

The poet is accused of having shown little regard to poetical justice and may be charged with equal neglect of poetical probability. The apparition left the regions of the dead to little purpose; the revenge which he demands is not obtained but by the death of him that was required to take it; and the gratification which would arise from the destruction of an usurper and a murderer is abated by the untimely death of Ophelia, the young, the beautiful, the harmless, and the pious.[21]

Nowadays our critics, when they like, manage a cool faultfinding without the Johnson edge. Derek Traversi rises from deep immersion in *Cymbeline* to look at what has seemed wrong:

Once more...we are faced with a discrepancy, frequent in *Cymbeline* and perhaps the fundamental problem of the play, between expression and effectiveness. The language, concise and compact, is that of the mature tragedies, and the sentiments expressed are related, by means of it, to that exploration of moral realities which is characteristic of Shakespeare at his best; but the themes stated are not adequately developed, fail to make themselves felt in the course of an action that remains basically conventional. Nowhere is the provisional quality of the inspiration of *Cymbeline* more clearly apparent.[22]

Here, to be sure, is no need for brevity, no temptation of that sort to be curt. Traversi has, presumably, all the space he wants and he uses it for careful discrimination. Given less space, Kenneth Muir, in an introduction to an edition of *Richard II*, makes a precise judgment without brusqueness:

Shakespeare was only just beginning to portray character by varying the verse. He did this brilliantly with Juliet's Nurse and in the contrast between Richard and Bolingbroke in the abdication scene. But his touch was still uncertain. The Gardener scene (III, iv) was admirably conceived as a commentary by the common man on the state of England, and as a parabolic statement, which links up with Gaunt's description of England as 'this other Eden'. But the execution of the scene falls far short of the conception. The Gardener, speaking in formal blank verse, indistinguishable from that used by royal and aristocratic characters, never really emerges from his role as a chorus. It would have been better, perhaps, to have written the scene in prose; but, for some reason, Shakespeare avoided prose altogether. Perhaps he was trying to please his new aristocratic friends.[23]

In this manner that subdues the critic to his task, much of the solid writing about Shakespeare has been done.

At its most helpful, the cool manner is scrupulous in getting things down exactly as the critic sees them. It need not do so in single-mindedness of judgment. There is an extension of it that becomes a dialectic of scruples. In finding fault it says, 'Here is a fault to be defined only by precise analytic argument against its being a virtue'. We expect such arguments in the more finespun efforts of modern criticism. In Shakespeare criticism they go back to Coleridge perhaps, and certainly to Bradley. To Bradley—and thus for some mockery these days. There are the smiles at Bradley's solemn scrupulousness. Is it that he looks at the wrong things rather than that his manner is wrong? For the manner is not only his, though he gives it his own serious vibration partly by direct reference to his feelings. Here it is:

When I read *King Lear* two impressions are left on my mind, which seem to answer roughly to the two sets of facts. *King Lear* seems to me Shakespeare's greatest achievement, but it seems to me *not* his best play. And I find that I tend to consider it from two rather different points of view. When I regard it strictly as a drama, it appears to me, though in certain parts overwhelming, decidedly inferior as a whole to *Hamlet*, *Othello* and *Macbeth*. When I am feeling that it is greater than any of these, and the fullest revelation of Shakespeare's power, I find I am not regarding it simply as a drama, but am grouping it in my mind with works like the *Prometheus Vinctus* and the *Divine Comedy*, and even with the greatest symphonies of Beethoven and the statues in the Medici Chapel.[24]

The problem in perception and in judgment is then drawn to its contradiction:

But (not to speak of defects due to mere carelessness) that which makes the *peculiar* greatness of *King Lear*...interferes with dramatic clearness even when the play is read, and in the theatre not only refuses to reveal itself fully through the senses but seems to be almost in contradiction with their reports.[25]

There follow the pages that poise the elements of the contradiction through Bradley's two lectures on *King Lear*. Whatever their value as criticism, they exhibit a manner of address (quite apart from the decried emphasis on 'character') that is still with us.

It is a manner that sees both sides and all around, that will not have things one simple way where the matter is not simple as a judgment of fault. What is 'faulty' about *King Lear* as drama is precisely its '*peculiar* greatness' from another perspective; but the flaws remain flaws from the dramatic perspective. The attitude and the manner are shown crisply by Harbage as he ends his scene-by-scene guide into *Othello*:

If there is a defect in this play, it lies not in the stature of the tragic hero. There is not the same thorough integration of theatrical fiction and dramatic vision, of action and idea, that there is in the other great tragedies. Although the proven effectiveness of the play on the stage renders somewhat irrelevant both attacks and defenses of its plot, the concession must be made that it is more 'plotty' than need be in respect to its great theme. The machinations of Iago, fascinating though they are to watch, give us too much of a good thing, with the excess at the expense of a better thing. There lacks a perfect balance of emphasis upon what Iago does and what he is: his mystery is submerged in the intrigue. Perhaps this was inevitable since Iago is, after all, nothing. His answering snarl *What you know, you know*...to Othello's incredulous *Why* is all we can ever expect to get when we ask Evil to explain itself.[26]

Carried to its utmost possibilities, the manner we are looking at needs much space to work itself out. Mary Lascelles devotes a whole book to *Measure for Measure*. At the end she summarizes the exactions the play has imposed upon the critic's impulses to find fault:

Indeed, any hasty interpretation of *Measure for Measure*, or any which hardens into formula, is likely to approach misconstruction. By nothing short of resolutely sustained attention can both these besetting errors be warded off: that which will make of every anomaly to be found in it a sort of treachery on the dramatist's part, and that which will remove every such anomaly out of sight. Neither representation gives a true portrait of this great, uneven play; for neither allows us to recognize that in its very complexity is to be found the proof of its integrity.[27]

This, probably, is as far as we can go up a scale of faultfinding manners, from the hesitant to the complexly deliberate, before critical patience explodes. Patience *has* been stretched in that last manner, stretched by fine critics over worthy dilemmas in perception and in judgment. If the problems seem not worthy at all, but affronts, the critic lets go. He may be a critic ungiven to restraint, or anyone in a moment of rebellion. He lets go and gives us the spectacular manners, the high jinks of detraction. Naturally we remember them. Is it more for what they tell us about the critic than about the play? Not always.

Distinctions of manners in these situations are not easy, but we can try. There is the 'In all honesty the thing deserves this drubbing' manner. It rings with earnest indignation. Johnson tries for one sentence to be charitable with *Cymbeline* and then gives up. 'To remark the folly of the fiction', he says, 'the absurdity of the conduct, the confusion of the names and manners of different times, and the impossibility of the events in any system of life, were to waste criticism upon unresisting imbecility, upon faults too evident for detection, and too gross for aggravation.'[28] We watch him do the predictable, let fly with one of his favourite indignations, when he says of *Romeo and Juliet*, 'His comic scenes are happily wrought, but his pathetic strains are always polluted with some unexpected depravations. His persons, however distressed, *have a conceit left them in their misery, a miserable conceit*.'[29] The italics are Johnson's, to press even that style of his beyond its considerable powers. Or is he laughing at his own fury? This manner runs to memorable quips. Mark Van Doren wraps a whole play into one blunt sentence: 'If Aristotle was right when he called plot the soul of tragedy, "Timon of Athens" has no soul.'[30] To follow a passage by Van Doren is to get the manner in full cry:

The style of 'Troilus and Cressida' is loud, brassy, and abandoned. The world which Chaucer had left so tenderly intact explodes as if a mine had been touched off beneath it, while a host of characters, conceived partly in doubt and partly in disgust, rave at the tops of their never modulated voices. All of them are angry, all of them are distrustful and mendacious; and the tone of each is hardened to rasping by some unmotivated irritation. One is tempted to suppose that the irritation was in the author before it was in them. For once he cannot write with respect either for his subject or for their styles.[31]

Here is eloquent evidence of a sensibility affronted, the critic's sensibility. The passage is an honest attempt to say just that, with apt aid from the art of rhetoric.

In other hands the manner shades into downright gusto: drubbing is a pleasure. We think of undergraduate essays in this vein, and we think of Thomas Rymer. The Rymer hilarity, at least about *Othello*, has, to be sure, met guarded approval in our time. Plainly it gave Rymer much satisfaction. Not his over-familiar words, however, but some recent ones of William Empson may bring the gusto of detraction into full view. Empson is writing of Shakespeare's last plays. He begins his essay with an anecdote of Hugh Kingsmill's epic laughter in the Blackwall Tunnel over the pious ejaculations of Cleomenes and Dion about the oracle in *The Winter's Tale*. Though Empson does not laugh heartily at that particular passage, he finds other targets quickly enough. There is the conversation of the gentlemen leaving the brothel in *Pericles*. 'Here', says Empson, 'we meet a thrilling extremity of bad taste; plainly it was screwed up by the hand of the master.'[32] And there is 'the delicious heroine herself, protesting her innocence'. She gets the full treatment: 'The narrator Esther in *Bleak House* arouses the same electric nausea; it is done by implying "I'm such a good girl that I don't even *know* how good I am". In short, this is tear-jerks at their most reeking; Dickens is the only other prominent author who can go so far too far.'[33] As it turns out, of course, the Empson laughter has method. It wants to clear the critical air, blow away what Empson thinks to be pretentious current readings by laughing not only at the critics but at spuriously solemn things in the last plays.

The gibes of George Bernard Shaw come to mind, though they carry far less responsibility to Shakespeare's meanings or none at all. Contempt professes to edge the raillery. 'How anybody over the age of seven can take interest in a literary toy so silly in its conceit and common in its ideas as the Seven Ages of Man passes my understanding.'[34] Of Orlando's 'If ever you have looked on better days', Shaw comments: 'I shall really get sick if I quote any more of it. Was ever such canting, snivelling, hypocritical unctuousness exuded by an actor anxious to shew that he was above his profession, and was a thoroughly respectable man in private life?'[35] 'Electric nausea' again! There is, to be sure, another side to such criticism in Shaw: his raillery claims to be distinguishing the gold from the tinsel in Shakespeare. The manner of distinguishing is drastic:

When a flower-girl tells a coster to hold his jaw, for nobody is listening to him, and he retorts, 'O, you're there, are you, you beauty?' they reproduce the wit of Beatrice and Benedick exactly. But put it this way. 'I wonder that you will still be talking, Signior Benedick: nobody marks you.' 'What!

my dear Lady Disdain, are you yet living?' You are miles away from costerland at once. When I tell you that Benedick and the coster are equally poor in thought, Beatrice and the flower-girl equally vulgar in repartee, you reply that I might as well tell you that a nightingale's love is no higher than a cat's. Which is exactly what I do tell you, though the nightingale is the better musician.[36]

The manner triumphs for its moment, until we catch our breath and ponder that word 'musician'. Still, the Shaw manners on this particular subject do not stand quite alone. Quiller-Couch, writing on *Much Ado* for the New Shakespeare edition, blasts away in earnest at Shakespeare's wit in general. 'If we could rid ourselves of idolatry and of cant when we talk about Shakespeare, we should probably admit that his "wit"...is usually cheap, not seldom exasperating, and at times...merely disgusting.'[37] And 'we advance the business of criticism by announcing the stuff for rubbish'.[38]

With these blunt words a review of faultfinding manners might stop. There is much else to say, and there are hundreds of other critics whose manners offer variations on what we have looked at. Some of these variations are not clear-cut. They may or may not suggest faultfinding. One of them is worth a final glance.

It is the manner that simply resorts to silence or relative silence. It may of course mean lack of interest or lack of space, but it may mean avoidance of trouble. What some critics do with Autolycus in *The Winter's Tale* is an example, and perhaps because Johnson has thrown down a challenge. His general observation on the play has essentially two sentences: 'This play, as Dr. Warburton justly observes, is, with all its absurdities, very entertaining. The character of Autolycus is very naturally conceived and strongly represented.'[39] The 'very naturally', the 'strongly', and the fact that the character gets fully one-half of Johnson's total attention in the comment, make it difficult to see how Autolycus could be avoided in anyone's account of the play. Yet there has been silence about him. Traversi, in the shorter of his two examinations of the play, makes not a single reference to Autolycus in the twenty-three pages of the chapter, and Autolycus does not show up in the index.[40] With other critics the silence is not quite absolute, but Autolycus gets a barest minimum of their attention. Van Doren's chapter on the play has one reference: 'the surpassing roguery of Autolycus'.[41] Baldwin Maxwell, in an introduction to the play that runs to eight pages, has two references, one incidental and one complimentary: 'That engaging rogue Autolycus is, as is also the Shepherd's clownish son, wholly Shakespeare's'.[42] Frank Kermode, also in an introduction, this one running to fifteen pages, mentions Autolycus once, and in parentheses. What he says is significant: 'The mood [of Act IV] is of innocence (even Autolycus contributes to this, partly by establishing rustic virtues as opposed to those of the court—an old pastoral theme, and one paralleled by the debates between Corin and Touchstone in *As You Like It*)....'[43] Here Autolycus is not seen or cherished as a character 'strongly represented' but as a contributor to the theme that Kermode names. Is there implication that Autolycus has been a bother in the play, that only the 'theme', when one looks hard at it, validates him? These critics, all of them except Johnson, find the serious movement of the play to be remarkably significant without Autolycus. They are not quite saying so, but they seem by their silence or their offhand remarks to wish that Shakespeare had not brought him so prominently into that fourth act for the diversions that delighted Johnson.

But it is only their manner of showing this, if it does show it, that is of concern here. Quiller-Couch uses a very different manner, and a familiar one, when he brings the problem into the open:

Next for Autolycus: He is a delightful rogue, as Dr. Simon Forman found him, and as we all like to recognize him. But as a factor in the plot, though from the moment of his appearance he seems to be constantly and deliberately intriguing, in effect he does nothing at all.... Possibly Shakespeare meant to make a great deal of him, carefully elaborated him to take a prominent and amusing part in the recognition scene, tired of it all, and suddenly, resolving to scamp the Leontes-Perdita recognition scene, smothered him along with it.[44]

However this may be, Quiller-Couch is not greatly bothered, as certainly Johnson is not. The bother comes with organic or symbolic critical approaches to the play. And as Kermode's remark indicates, these approaches have been working hard to fit Autolycus in. E. M. W. Tillyard was doing it just at the time of Traversi's first 'approach'. Traversi has since had second thoughts and has given due attention to the 'vivacious spontaneity' of Autolycus.[45] And there are the other handlings that easily come to mind. Yet those silences or relative silences about Autolycus do stand, possibly, among the faultfinding manners.

All these manners bring out only one small part of Shakespeare criticism, but a toughly enduring part. The faultfinding is not likely to disappear as long as critics are as honestly attentive as the manners here reviewed have shown, or as humanly rebellious. The rebellions can renew the impulses to honesty. Even some of the 'shadow-boxing of rival bardolaters', if it is that, can push bardolatry away. How long will it be before *Othello*, so differently seen by Johnson, Coleridge, Bradley, and Helen Gardner on the one hand, and by T. S. Eliot, Leavis, and Heilman on the other, is accused of impossible contradictions? Not only the manners of Rymer will be at hand to do the job.

NOTES

1. 'The Tyranny of Shakespeare', *Studies in Shakespeare*, ed. Peter Alexander (1964), p. 170.

2. *Ibid.* p. 170.

3. 'On the Genius and Writings of Shakespeare', *Eighteenth Century Essays on Shakespeare*, ed. D. Nichol Smith (1962), pp. 29–30.

4. *Ibid.* p. 37.

5. *The Complete Works of Algernon Charles Swinburne* (1926), I, 146.

6. Samuel Taylor Coleridge, *Shakespearean Criticism*, ed. Thomas Middleton Raysor (1960), I, 14.

7. 'Remarks on some of the Characters of Shakespeare', *Shakespeare Criticism, A Selection: 1623–1840*, ed. D. Nichol Smith (1946), p. 149.

8. 'The Tempest', *ibid.* p. 56.

9. *Samuel Johnson on Shakespeare*, ed. W. K. Wimsatt, Jr. (1960), p. 106.

10. *Shakespearean Criticism*, I, 102–3. The italics are Coleridge's.

11. *The Collected Works of William Hazlitt*, ed. A. R. Waller and Arnold Glover (1902), I, 345–6.

12. Alfred Harbage, *William Shakespeare: A Reader's Guide* (1963), p. 287.

13. '"Troilus and Cressida" and "Hamlet"', *Shakespeare Criticism: 1919–35*, ed. Anne Bradby (1936), pp. 198, 199.

14. *Measure for Measure*, ed. Sir Arthur Quiller-Couch and John Dover Wilson (1922), p. xxxiii.

15. *Samuel Johnson on Shakespeare*, p. 102.

16. Harbage, *op. cit.* p. 128.

17. *Shakespeare* (1907), p. 113.

18. *Ibid.* pp. 138–9.

19. *Notes on Shakespeare's Workmanship* (1917), p. 260.

20. *Samuel Johnson on Shakespeare*, p. 87.

21. *Ibid.* p. 113.

22. Derek Traversi, *Shakespeare: The Last Phase* (1954), p. 72.

23. *The Tragedy of King Richard the Second*, The Signet Classic Shakespeare (general editor, Sylvan Barnet), ed. Kenneth Muir (1963), p. xxv.

24. A. C. Bradley, *Shakespearean Tragedy* (1955; originally published 1904), p. 198. Italics are Bradley's.

25. *Ibid.* pp. 200–1. Italics are Bradley's.

26. Harbage, *op. cit.* p. 370.

27. *Shakespeare's 'Measure for Measure'* (1953), p. 164.

28. *Samuel Johnson on Shakespeare*, p. 108.

29. *Ibid.* p. 110.

30. Mark Van Doren, *Shakespeare* (1939), p. 288.

31. *Ibid.* p. 202.

32. William Empson, 'Hunt the Symbol', *The Times Literary Supplement*, 23 April 1964, p. 340.

33. *Ibid.* p. 340. Italics are the author's.

34. *Shaw on Shakespeare*, ed. Edwin Wilson (1961), p. 27.

35. *Ibid.* p. 28.

36. *Ibid.* p. 143.

37. *Much Ado About Nothing*, ed. Sir Arthur Quiller-Couch and John Dover Wilson (1923), p. xxi.

38. *Ibid.* p. xxii.

39. *Samuel Johnson on Shakespeare*, p. 80.

40. D. A. Traversi, *An Approach to Shakespeare* (2nd ed., 1956), pp. 261–84.

41. *Shakespeare*, pp. 320–1.

42. *The Winter's Tale*, The Pelican Shakespeare (general editor, Alfred Harbage), ed. Baldwin Maxwell (1956), p. 16.

43. *The Winter's Tale*, The Signet Classic Shakespeare (general editor, Sylvan Barnet), ed. Frank Kermode (1963), p. xxxi.

44. *The Winter's Tale*, ed. Sir Arthur Quiller-Couch and John Dover Wilson (1931), pp. xx–xxi.

45. *Shakespeare: The Last Phase*, p. 138.

'THE GREAT VARIETY OF READERS'

BY

ARTHUR BROWN

John Heminge and Henry Condell seem to have had no doubt in their own minds about the composition of the public for which the First Folio was designed. They address themselves to readers 'from the most able, to him that can but spell', and mingle their natural wish that the venture shall be a profitable one ('whateuer you do, buy') with exhortations to 'diuers capacities' that they shall do their best not only to appreciate the plays for themselves, but also to help others to a similar appreciation. 'Reade him, therefore; and againe, and againe; And if then you doe not like him, surely you are in some manifest danger, not to understand him. And so we leaue you to other of his Friends, whom if you need, can bee your guides: if you neede them not, you can leade your selues, and others. And such Readers we wish him.' An estimated edition of about 1200 copies and a price of one pound a copy[1] were no doubt limiting factors in its circulation, but its editors at any rate envisaged a wide enough market. More than 330 years later the publishers of an American paperback edition (one play per volume) echo basically the same sentiments, though in terms suggesting the influence of modern market research, for they offer Shakespeare 'for the price of a coke and a hamburger', in a form that will fit easily into the pocket, and anticipate a very high sale through book stores, news stands, drug stores, and railway stations.[2] The story of Shakespeare's publishers and readers for the years in between is a long and complicated one; William Jaggard's *Shakespeare Bibliography* (1911) devotes no fewer than 63 closely printed pages to listing editions of the complete works alone, and of course does not touch the modern popular market, and it is only comparatively recently that scholarly attention has been devoted to unravelling a number of mysteries surrounding editions of the eighteenth century in particular. It is clear, therefore, that the survey offered here can do little more than indicate the main lines of development in the publication of Shakespeare's plays, and it should be clear that even these may be subject to certain modifications in the light of research now in progress.

However great or small the 'variety' of readers of the First Folio, there must have been enough of them to satisfy the publishers, for a second edition was put out only nine years later, quite a short time for so large and expensive a book. There were two re-issues of this edition, dated 1632 but probably made around 1637 and 1640.[3] A third edition appeared in 1663, its later issue (1664) containing seven additional plays attributed to Shakespeare (of which only one, *Pericles*, is now generally accepted as his), and a fourth edition, also containing the additional plays, in 1685. It should also be noted that apart from the folios the seventeenth-century reader had some of the plays available in quarto form—*Hamlet* in 1676, 1683, 1695, and 1703; *Othello* in 1655, 1681, 1687, 1695, and 1705; *The Merchant of Venice* in 1652; and *King Lear* in 1655. These go back to the early quartos, but with much alteration, and their theatrical origin is clear from the statement on some of the title-pages that this is the play 'as it is now acted' (reminding one inevitably of the modern 'book of the play' or 'book of the film'). Two or three other plays (e.g. *Taming of the Shrew*, *Julius Caesar*, and *Macbeth*) were also available in quartos reprinted from the folio text. Of the later folios McKerrow has remarked that the alterations in their texts

are for the most part merely the kind of alteration generally made in reprinting a contemporary or definitely recent author. They consist almost entirely of two kinds. Firstly, the correction of such misprints as happened to be noticed—we need say nothing about the introduction of new ones, for these were presumably unintentional—and secondly, the normal modernizations in spelling and in various points of typographical practice which have at all times been usual in reprinting any book in which exact reproduction is not regarded as important.[4]

He adds that in all the folios there were a certain number of attempts 'to emend passages which appeared unintelligible', but none of these appear to be more than guesses, and no consistent principles are involved.

Until the end of the seventeenth century, therefore, the reading public had to rely almost entirely for their knowledge of Shakespeare on the four folios. Little or nothing was done to make their enjoyment or their profit easier to come by, and probably little or nothing was felt necessary in this respect. The turn of the century saw a change in the attitude of the publishers and in the habits of the reading public; the interaction of these, the growth of a scholarly interest in the text, the development of a more general critical interest in the plays, the increasing popularity of the plays on the stage encouraged by a series of excellent actors, all conspired to create a demand for editions which was met in a variety of ways. In 1916 George Saintsbury could speak of the early eighteenth-century tempering, 'very inadequately, a contemptuous disapproval of nearly the whole Elizabethan, Jacobean, and First Caroline periods by an almost equally conventional, a conditional, a rather puzzled, and a not unfrequently very dubious acceptance of Shakespeare and Milton. . . . To all but a very few the prince of drama and the grand duke of epic were in spirit what their works were a little later in fact—handsomely bound volumes to lie on a drawing room table.'[5] No doubt there is some justice in this comment, but Nichol Smith, writing thirteen years earlier, paints a very different picture, and apparently saw no reason to alter it when a second edition of his book appeared in 1963. He says that 'even those who are willing to give the eighteenth century its due have not recognized how it appreciated Shakespeare. At no time in this century was he not popular',[6] and he goes on to draw attention to the editions, the critical investigations, the coffee-house discussions reflected in the periodical literature, all of which 'must have been addressed to a public which knew him'. He quotes Theobald's remark that 'this author is grown so universal a book that there are very few studies or collections of books, though small, amongst which it does not hold a place', and suggests that although the 'critical interest in Shakespeare occasioned by Pope's edition may have increased the knowledge of him. . .he had been regularly cited, long before Pope's day, as England's representative genius'.

Before we look more closely at some of the eighteenth-century editions, we should bear in mind McKerrow's general description of their purpose. He draws a valid distinction between the few who *study* Shakespeare, and the many who read him solely for pleasure. The latter have, as a rule,

no need for the kind of edition which appeals to the modern scholar. What *they* require is rather what the eighteenth-century editors aimed at producing, and did in fact produce, a text which is easy to read and intelligible, without asperities either of grammar or of metre, and provided with all those helps in the way of stage directions, indications of locality, and the like which enable the lazy-minded to fathom the meaning without puzzlement and the lover of literature to savour the poetry without distraction.[7]

Nicholas Rowe's edition of 1709, commissioned and published by Jacob Tonson (who had purchased the rights in the folio text of Shakespeare from the publishers of the Fourth Folio), stands at the head of this tradition. He carries on the 'modernizing' process of the folios mentioned earlier, even to the extent of substituting modern *forms* of words for older ones; his revision of the text was extremely haphazard, but he did some valuable work in introducing uniformity into the designations of the characters, in adding lists of *dramatis personae*, in correcting stage-directions, in dividing the texts, where necessary, into scenes, and in adding locations. 'To read Shakespeare in Rowe's edition', says McKerrow, 'must have been a very different thing from reading him in the Fourth Folio, and we ought not, I think, to refuse to recognize that in all probability it was to Rowe and his publisher Tonson that the beginning of the world-wide recognition of Shakespeare was due.'[8]

It may well be, as McKerrow suggests, that one of the reasons for this edition was Tonson's determination to draw attention to his possession of the copyright, since there was a good deal of piratical printing going on, and considerable uncertainty about copyright law. In view, however, of Nichol Smith's opinion, quoted above, it does not seem unfair to suggest further that Tonson, a shrewd businessman, would probably not have bothered to insist on his rights in this way unless he suspected that there was already a growing demand for the plays, or that there was likely to be one in the very near future. At all events, he seems to have had notions of a popular market in mind, the seven volumes, with their 'Life of Shakespeare' prefixed, for which Rowe was paid £36. 10s., being sold for thirty shillings, and this despite their forty-five engravings. The format chosen was octavo (a few sets being printed in royal octavo), a choice to be followed by countless subsequent editions. What was generally thought to be the second edition of Rowe, but was shown to be the third (since there were in fact two editions of 1709),[9] appeared in nine duodecimo volumes in 1714, with certain revisions by a 'Mr. Hughes' who received £28. 7s. from Tonson for the work. Three editions in five years is clear enough evidence that the reading public was interested, and that Tonson was justified in his efforts to retain his rights in the plays.

With Rowe's editions, as McKerrow points out, we come to an end of the treatment of Shakespeare 'as a contemporary, or at any rate recent, writer, who can be understood without more elucidation than can be afforded by simply modernizing the spellings'.[10] It may be for this reason that we find little in Rowe's edition to give us any clear indication that he had a particular class of reader in mind; we may assume that he was addressing himself very largely to the intelligent theatre-goer of the time, who might be interested in reading the plays either before or after he had seen them, but this is as far as we can safely go. With Pope's edition in six volumes of 1725, the first to be printed in quarto, and also published by Tonson, it is perhaps possible to be rather more certain of the nature of the intended reader. Seven hundred and fifty sets were printed at £6. 6s. each, a much more expensive purchase than Rowe's edition, and a list of subscribers was included; it seems not unfair to conclude that Tonson, having invited the foremost poet and critic of the day to do the editorial work, was looking to a cultured and wealthy class of reader for support. There are indications in Pope's own preface, too, which point the same way. He pays due homage to Shakespeare's natural genius, but goes on to say that 'It must be own'd that with all these great excellencies he has almost as great defects; and that as he has certainly written better, so he has perhaps written worse, than any other'.[11] Many of these defects he is prepared to blame first on the audiences of the time, for

it must be allowed that Stage-Poetry of all other, is more particularly levell'd to please the *Populace*, and its success more immediately depending upon the *Common Suffrage*. One cannot therefore wonder, if *Shakespear* having at his first appearance no other aims in his writings than to procure a subsistance, directed his endeavours solely to hit the taste and humour that then prevailed. The Audience was generally composed of the meaner sort of people; and therefore the Images of Life were to be drawn from those of their own rank....[12]

Other defects resulted from the ignorance of the printers, from the cutting of plays or the addition of unauthorized material to them, and from their handling in general by actors who were a very different kind of people from what they were in Pope's own day. For, he says,

I think I ought in justice to remark, that the Judgement, as well as Condition, of that class of people was then far inferior to what it is in our days. As then the best Playhouses were Inns and Taverns...so the top of the profession were then meer Players, not Gentlemen of the stage: They were led into the Buttery by the Steward, not plac'd at the Lord's table, or Lady's toilette: and consequently were intirely depriv'd of those advantages they now enjoy, in the familiar conversation of our Nobility, and an intimacy (not to say dearness) with people of the first condition.[13]

Shakespeare, then, is to be rescued from his fellows and made fit for these 'people of the first condition', and it is this principle which guides Pope throughout. We need not concern ourselves here with the details of his work, except to notice that his claim to have proceeded 'with a religious abhorrence of all Innovation, and without any indulgence to my private sense or conjecture' can scarcely be substantiated. His aim was to make the plays readable and unobjectionable to people of good taste. Variant readings were placed in the margin for those interested; what he considered 'authoritative alterations' were 'taken notice of as they occur'; suspected interpolations were degraded to the bottom of the page; scene divisions were more carefully and consistently marked than they had been in Rowe's edition; obsolete and unusual words were glossed; and attention was drawn, by the use of commas or stars, to the more outstandingly beautiful passages. McKerrow has said all that need be said about Pope's editorial shortcomings, but no one would doubt the justice of his comment that the edition was 'the work of a brilliant amateur, a real lover of Shakespeare as he saw him'.[14] A second edition appeared in eight duodecimo volumes in 1728.

Little need be said for the purposes of this essay about the editions of Lewis Theobald (seven volumes in octavo, 1733) or of William Warburton (eight volumes in octavo, 1747). The story of their 'collaborations' and enmity has been fully dealt with elsewhere, and adds little to our knowledge of the kind of reader who was becoming interested in Shakespeare. One may say, however, that their work represents rather editing for the sake of the editor than for any particular kind of reader, and that they were much more interested in justifying their own readings and emendations than in making Shakespeare generally better known. In the same way one might be prepared to ignore the six handsome quarto volumes of Sir Thomas Hanmer, printed at the Clarendon Press in 1743–4, for his own comments on these do not suggest that he had the interests of the reading public at large very much in his mind:

As to my own particular, I have no aim to pursue in this affair; I propose neither honour, reward, or thanks, and should be very well pleased to have the books continue upon their shelf, in my own private closet. If it is thought they may be of use or pleasure to the publick, I am willing to part with them out of my hands, and to add, for the honour of Shakespear, some decorations and embellishments at my own expense.[15]

Hanmer's edition, however, and that published by Robert Walker in eight duodecimo volumes in 1734–5, raised problems and had consequences which were of the greatest importance for the growth of interest in Shakespeare.

An excellent account of Walker's activities, and of the troubles facing Tonson and other powerful publishers when the protection afforded them by the copyright statute of 1710 apparently came to an end in 1731, has been given by Giles E. Dawson, and need not be repeated in detail here.[16] Dawson points out how in the 1730's a number of 'small men, both in London and in the country, began to print and sell the very books which the trade regarded as their most valuable stock, such as *Shakespeare*, *Paradise Lost*, *The Whole Duty of Man*'. Intimidation, reprisals, and bluff were all used to deal with these threats, but the situation was not finally disposed of until 1774. Walker began by publishing *The Merry Wives* in August 1734. Tonson retaliated by publishing the same play the following month, telling us in his 'Advertisement' that Walker intends to print the plays weekly at a penny a sheet, 'which, one with another, will amount to fourpence each play'; he refers to the 'very Mangled, Imperfect, and Incorrect manner' of what has so far appeared, accuses Walker of violating copyright, and concludes 'That each Play so printed by the said *R. Walker*, or any other Person, will be forthwith printed by the Proprietors of the Copy of the same, and the Whole Play exactly Correct, and in all respects better printed, shall be Sold to all *Hawkers* for One Penny each Play, so long as this vile Practice goes on'. Attention is drawn here particularly to the element of very severe price-cutting, and to the reference to hawkers, both of which would undoubtedly have the effect of disseminating the plays on a wide scale. Recriminations continued on both sides. At the end of his *2 Henry IV*, Walker accuses Tonson in turn of carelessness and ignorance in printing, and goes on to justify his own activities: 'Mr. Tonson and his Accomplices having in an arbitrary Manner kept up the Prices of the Plays at the Price of one Shilling, Mr. Walker, sensible of the grand Imposition, undertook to free the Publick from the said Oppression, and to publish the Plays at Fourpence each, and without the Sale of a great Number he could reap no Benefit.' Tonson has not only been undercutting him, but has refused to have the matter dealt with by arbitration, and has threatened to go on undercutting him until Walker has been ruined. At no time, it seems, was Tonson prepared to take legal action, in spite of the fact that Walker challenged him to do so on several occasions. Dawson argues from the various states of Walker's first edition that his venture met with considerable success; at a later stage he increased his output to two plays a week, and finished the edition by the end of March 1735. Tonson began by keeping pace with him, play for play, but before long dropped this course, proceeded at his own speed, and finished well ahead of his rival. Walker promised delivery of one complete play every Monday, 'delivered at their own Houses, or any Place they shall appoint, if in Town, or in the Country, within sixty miles of *London*'; the plays were to be printed so that six could be bound up in a volume, for which 'a general Title in Red and Black shall be given Gratis'; and an engraved head of Shakespeare, and an account of his life and writings (Rowe's account, as it happened) were also to be supplied. Each play was provided with a copperplate frontispiece, all but six of these being taken from Pope's edition.

In tracing Walker's career Dawson shows clearly enough that Tonson's price war was in the end successful, and may indeed have resulted in serious financial embarrassment for his rival; his efforts to change the copyright position and to break the monopoly in the end came to nothing. But, Dawson adds, in another way

it is possible that indirectly and unintentionally he did affect the literary history of his time. By starting a price war and causing his great rival to pour out floods of cheap Shakespeare, Walker was responsible for putting the plays into the hands of many lowly readers who otherwise could not have afforded them. For though Walker's duodecimos may have appeared in comparatively small editions, there is good reason to believe that Tonson produced his in enormous numbers. Thus, for the first time any reader could acquire all the plays for a few shillings. This was in the mid-1730's. At about the same time the popular demand for Shakespeare begins to indicate a noticeable increase. Garrick began acting in 1741 and soon showed an awareness of a demand for more and better Shakespeare. That the Walker–Tonson struggle was responsible for this growth of interest is too much to claim, but it very probably contributed in some measure.

During the 1740's and 1750's reprints of Pope, Theobald, Hanmer, and Warburton seem to have held the field, usually in octavo or duodecimo format. It may be noted, however, that these years also saw the beginning of editions printed outside London. Between 1752 and 1757 Robert and Andrew Foulis used Pope's second edition as the basis of their own, in sixteen volumes, from Glasgow. The plays were issued individually at intervals with separate pagination and titles, possibly the most convenient method for the use of playgoers. Hugh Blair's edition in eight duodecimo volumes appeared from Edinburgh in 1753, and was also issued with a London imprint in the same year; a second edition was published eight years later. Johnson's edition, in eight octavo volumes, appeared in 1765 (although the proposals had promised its publication at Christmas 1757), and *The Gentleman's Magazine* for October of that year mentioned 'the rapid sale of the impression which has already made a second necessary, though it has not been published a month'. Johnson had proposed an edition in ten volumes, to be printed by Edward Cave, as early as 1745, but Nichol Smith tells us that it met with no encouragement, and indeed with opposition from Tonson, who was still claiming the copyright in Shakespeare's text, with 'all the emendations to this time'.[17] It may be significant that the intervening twenty years should see, apparently, so great a change in the demand for the work, much of it no doubt inspired by Garrick and others in the theatre audiences. McKerrow does not have much to say in praise of Johnson's text, but sees the merit of the edition, apart from the preface, as 'being largely in the illuminating common sense of his notes, and especially of the critical judgements which follow each play'.[18] From the point of view of the reading public, it may also be significant that Capell's edition, published three years later, suffered greatly, in

McKerrow's words, 'by being almost entirely without notes or various readings, and having merely a general explanation of how he had constructed his text'; it seems that he had intended these to be contained in supplementary volumes which were to appear at once, but which did not, in fact, appear until 1783, two years after his death, 'a fact which no doubt told strongly against the acceptance of the edition by his contemporaries'.[19] This opinion is confirmed by Alice Walker in her lecture, 'Edward Capell and His Edition of Shakespeare', delivered before the British Academy in 1960, and her citations from Samuel Pegge's references to his exclusiveness and unsociability suggest that he was not particularly in touch with what was shortly to be required from an edition of Shakespeare—if indeed it was not required already—an ability to adapt scholarly considerations to a more popular audience.

In the same year as Capell's edition appeared the first one from Warwickshire, nine volumes in duodecimo, based on Pope's text with notes from other authors, and printed by Robert Martin of Birmingham. The production of this, for sale at the Stratford Jubilee in 1769, was suggested by David Garrick, whose influence on the dissemination of Shakespeare at this time must have been enormous. Certain booksellers in London, Sherborne, Gloucester, Lichfield, and Wolverhampton are named on the title-page as selling the edition, but it is also to be available from all country booksellers. Martin, who was Baskerville's foreman, was able to issue the work monthly in blue paper wrappers at 2s. a volume. A similar venture seems to have been undertaken about the same time by Nicholas Boden of Birmingham, one of Baskerville's trade rivals, and the appearance of two such editions is a clear enough indication of the rapid growth of interest in Shakespeare, stimulated no doubt in particular by the stage performances of the plays. Only five years later, in fact, we find even clearer evidence of the influence of the stage, with the publication of Bell's edition of the plays 'as they are now performed at the Theatres Royal in London, regulated from the prompt books of each house'. Again there were nine duodecimo volumes, with forty copperplate engravings included 'prepared under the superintendence of F. Bartolozzi'. The volumes were offered unbound at 3s. each, and seem to have sold very successfully; the list of subscribers' names and addresses occupied twenty-three pages, and included such men as Garrick, Tate Wilkinson, Douce, and even an American, Benjamin Guarred of South Carolina. It is of interest to note, in connexion with Bell's edition, that

historically, the first important inexpensive reprints, made possible by the momentous decision in Donaldson *v.* Beckett (1774), which killed the legal fiction of perpetual copyright, were those of John Bell, John Cooke, and James Harrison, each of whom produced two or more series devoted to out-of-copyright poets, prose-writers and dramatists. The delight they brought to impecunious book-lovers in the last quarter of the eighteenth century and the early years of the nineteenth was celebrated by Leigh Hunt, Hazlitt, Henry Kirke White, and William Hone, among others.[20]

Harrison's edition, eight volumes in octavo, appeared in 1791. The last quarter of the century saw the appearance not only of these, but of Reed's revision of the Johnson–Steevens edition, Malone's edition, John Nichols' edition, the first one-volume edition published in 1784 by Stockdale, and edited by Samuel Ayscough, and the first American edition, eight duodecimo volumes, published in Philadelphia in 1795-6. These are only a selection, but clearly indicative of which way the wind was blowing.

Selection becomes increasingly difficult in the nineteenth century. Some notion of the variety of editions to be expected may be gained from the appearance, in the opening years, of the first from Berwick-on-Tweed, nine duodecimo volumes with vignette portraits, the first of a number of miniature editions, nine volumes in sextodecimo, the first Boston edition in serial numbers, two plays to a volume, at fifty cents a number, complete in sixteen numbers, and, at the other extreme, Boydell's edition of 1802, consisting of eighteen parts to form nine folio volumes, and containing a hundred large copperplates from paintings by leading English artists—Reynolds, Smirke, Northcote, Porter, Stothard, Hamilton, Bunbury, Opie, and Westall. According to the prospectus issued in 1786, a type foundry, an ink factory, and a printing house were all specially erected for the production of this edition, and work for it had begun serially in 1791. Printing in parts, a method soon to become extremely popular as the publishers fought for the support of a greatly increased reading public, is well exemplified by the edition from Rivingtons in 1805, containing the text from Steevens, Malone's *History of the Stage*, Johnson's, Pope's and Chalmers' prefaces, and engravings from the original designs of Henry Fuseli; this was published in forty parts to form ten octavo volumes. The year 1807 is remarkable in that it saw the production not only of Douce's reprint of the First Folio, but of four duodecimo volumes containing twenty-four plays expurgated by Thomas Bowdler; the Family Shakespeare first saw the light of day under the auspices of a London publisher (Hatchard) and a Bath printer (Cruttwell). Before the first ten years of the century were over, twenty-four of the plays had appeared in Mrs Inchabald's *British Theatre* (1808) and nine plays, 'from the best edition of Johnson and Steevens', had been published in Avignon (1809).

More than enough has already been written about Bowdler's work on Shakespeare, but two points are perhaps worth emphasizing here. The first is that the idea of a 'Family Shakespeare' came to him, as he tells us in the preface to the first edition, through his father's habit of reading to his family circle:

Shakespeare (with whom no person was better acquainted) was a frequent subject of the evening's entertainment. In the perfection of reading few men were equal to my father; and such was his good taste, his delicacy, and his prompt discretion, that his family listened with delight to Lear, Hamlet and Othello, without knowing that those matchless tragedies contained words and expressions improper to be pronounced; and without having reason to suspect that any parts of the plays had been omitted by the circumspect and judicious reader.

Bowdler, therefore, wished to do the same thing for the reading public as his father had done for his own family, and the measure of success with which he met a public demand may be gauged by the fact that his version had gone through eleven editions just after the half century had passed, and continued to be reprinted for a long time afterwards. The second point worth noting in Bowdler's preface is the distinction he draws between the theatre audience and the reading public: 'Those persons whose acquaintance with Shakespeare depends upon theatrical representations, in which great alterations are made in the plays, can have little idea of the frequent recurrence in the original text, of expressions, which, however they might be tolerated in the sixteenth century, are by no means admissible in the nineteenth', while in the preface to the fourth edition he defends himself against his critics by claiming that 'I have attempted to do for the library what the manager does for the stage'. The habit of family reading and the influence this must have had on the rising generation, the envisaging of readers who would find in plays things that they had never expected from stage performances, and the obvious popularity of the 'Family Shakespeare' throughout the century, all seem to be pointers to a continually growing demand for the plays in print.[21]

Reference has already been made to Richard Altick's article on the reprinting of English Classics during the period 1830–1906, and no more need be said here of the reasons he advances for the rapid growth of this phenomenon. The breakdown of the notion of 'perpetual copyright', the discovery of a mass reading public, the spread of education and literacy, the many movements for the improvement, moral and cultural, of the 'lower classes', the economic fact that it was cheaper to deal in out-of-copyright works than in the works of living authors—all these had their part to play, and have been well described by Altick. It is interesting to note that three of the men he names as pioneers in the cheap reprint movement—John Limbird, Thomas Tegg, 'the energetic scavenger of remainders and expired copyrights', and the Chiswick printer, Charles Whittingham, who collaborated with the bookseller William Pickering in the production of the Aldine edition of *The British Poets*—all had a hand in Shakespeare editions before the middle of the century. Altick refers also to what he calls 'the episode of the shilling Shakespeares' which recalls the earlier battle between Tonson and Walker.

In 1864, the year of the poet's tercentenary, John Dicks brought out the plays at two for a penny, and sold about 150,000 copies. Collecting them into a 2s. cloth-bound volume, he sold 50,000 more. Then, hearing that John Camden Hotten was planning a complete Shakespeare to sell at 1s., Dicks cut the price of his own edition in half, substituting wrappers for cloth, and sold 700,000 copies in the next three or four years. For his shilling the Shakespeare lover got 1,020 pages of closely packed text and thirty-seven woodcuts. In 1868 both Routledge and Warne issued editions at the same price.[22]

It should be added that from evidence adduced by Altick elsewhere it appears that Abel Heywood, the leading wholesale newsagent of Manchester, was, thirteen years earlier than this, selling penny numbers of Shakespeare at the rate of 150 a week.[23]

The more scholarly editions continued throughout the century, of course, the Boswell–Malone Variorum, for example, appearing in twenty-one octavo volumes in 1821. Against these we may place such oddities as the continuation of the miniature editions, begun by Sharpe in 1800, in William Pickering's nine volumes in trigesimo-secundo, set in diamond type and issued in thirty-six parts in 1822–3, and Kent's Miniature Library edition, also in thirty-six parts, issued in 1882, with which, for 3s. 6d. extra, 'one could buy a French morocco pocket book, complete with patent clasp, pencil, and compartment into which one could fit either a conventional engagement book or a miniature volume of Shakespeare'.[24] Bowdler's third edition of 1822 could be purchased either in eight volumes octavo or in ten volumes eighteenmo. Complete editions from the continent and from America stand side by side with the abortive edition planned by Sir Walter Scott and J. G. Lockhart, of which three volumes only were ever completed. Portfolios of engravings to illustrate the plays, in copper, steel, or wood, seem to find a ready market. The regular appearance of a limited number of publishers' names typical of the eighteenth-century editions gives way to a bewildering medley of names as almost every firm, of good and of ill repute, strives to have some kind of 'Shakespeare' on its list. While Johnson, Steevens, and Malone continue to be safe 'stand-bys' for reprinting, Collier comes on the scene with his notorious 'manuscript corrections' from a folio of 1632, and produces his nine octavo volumes between 1841 and 1853. Charles Knight ranges through the 'Library' edition, the 'Cabinet' edition, the 'National' edition, to the 'Pictorial' edition. The first 'Cambridge' edition, edited by Clark, Glover, and Wright, came from Macmillan in nine octavo volumes between 1863 and 1866, and formed the basis of their 'Globe' edition in a single crown octavo volume of 1080 pages in 1864; in the next six years 95,000 copies of the 'Globe' were sold. Dent's 'Temple Shakespeare', a forty-volume series published in 1894–6, was selling 250,000 volumes a year for some time afterwards, and totalled five million copies sold by 1934.

Opinions in the nineteenth century vary widely about the influence of this wide dissemination of good literature, and about its reception by the lower classes in particular. Altick quotes George Gissing, for example, as saying:

Hardly will a prudent statistician venture to declare that one in every score of those who actually read sterling books do so with comprehension of their author. These dainty series of noble and delightful works, which have so seemingly wide an acceptance, think you they vouch for true appreciation in all who buy them? Remember those who purchase to follow the fashion, to impose upon their neighbour, or even to flatter themselves; think of those who wish to make cheap presents, and those who are merely pleased by the outer aspect of the volume.[25]

He quotes further from the *Academy* of 1903: 'The constant flow of new editions of Great Authors is deceptive. They are regarded as part of the necessary furniture of the house, not of the mind; and having been duly and dutifully bought they are taught to know their place on the appointed shelf', a remark which is reminiscent of Saintsbury's on the eighteenth century, quoted earlier in this essay. Against these comments Altick places the testimony of such men as George Dawson, a mechanics' institute lecturer, who in 1849 spoke of the great amount of poetry not only read but written by the working class, and asserted that 'Shakespeare is known by heart, almost', and of Dickens who, addressing the Birmingham Society of Artists in 1853, believed that 'there are in Birmingham at this moment many working men infinitely better versed in Shakespeare and in Milton than the average of fine gentlemen in the days of bought-and-sold dedications and dear books'. Evidence from the readers themselves is notoriously difficult to find, and the full truth of the matter may never be known.

If the student is bewildered by the plethora of nineteenth-century editions, he will be no less so by that of the first sixty years of the present century. Familiar names begin early; the Arden Shakespeare, now being completely re-edited, started life under the general editorship of W. J. Craig in 1899. J. M. Dent, the publisher of the Temple Shakespeare, Temple Dramatists, and Temple Classics, began Everyman's Library in 1906, and in that year issued Shakespeare's plays and poems in three volumes at one shilling each. The New Shakespeare, from the Cambridge University Press, started in 1921 under the editorship of Sir Arthur Quiller-Couch and John Dover Wilson, the latter being still actively engaged in revising some of the earlier volumes. At a cheaper and more popular level was the Penguin Shakespeare of the 1930's, edited by G. B. Harrison, and selling at the now incredible price of sixpence a volume. 'Shakespeare for sixpence,' said the *Morning Post* on its first appearance, 'Hamlet for the price of ten Goldflake', a sentiment echoed in transatlantic terms by a later American paperback edition. The *Sunday*

Times, welcoming the Penguin venture, complimented those responsible on the care taken to adapt both production and content to 'Shakespeare for the million'. The 1950's saw the appearance of its American counterpart in the Pelican Shakespeare under the editorship of Alfred Harbage. Popular editions, semi-popular editions, school editions, scholarly editions, editions of all sizes and prices abound to such an extent that there would be no sense in beginning to list them. It is interesting to note that although this century has seen the development of an intensely critical attitude towards Shakespeare's text, and a swing between optimism and pessimism in this connexion which shows little sign of abating, there has been practically no check in the production of reading copies for the great variety of readers. Attempts have been made from time to time, with indifferent success, to apply the results of textual criticism and bibliographical studies to more recent editions. The trouble seems to be that the textual critics and the bibliographers still do not know enough, the results so far attained are too uncertain to be assured of ready or general acceptance; and the non-scholarly public, whether compelled to read Shakespeare at school or university, whether attracted to reading Shakespeare by seeing the plays in the theatre or on the television screen, or hearing them on the wireless, or whether interested in reading Shakespeare for general cultural reasons usually difficult to define, is quite prepared to accept not too critically any handy and reasonably well-produced volume of the plays. The scholars may raise their hands in sorrow and despair, but they are faced with a well-entrenched tradition which began with Heminge and Condell. They did their best with his texts, without, we may be sure, putting themselves to extraordinary pains, and exhorted their readers to buy him and read him. This, it seems, has been the way of most publishers in the intervening centuries, and at no time do they appear to have met with a discouraging response; their products, from the most sumptuous folios to the most scruffy duodecimos, have always found a market, and many a sharp battle has been fought to ensure that the supply should not dry up.

NOTES

1. Charlton Hinman, *The Printing and Proof-Reading of the First Folio of Shakespeare* (1963), I, 39–47.
2. The Folger Shakespeare.
3. W. W. Greg, *Bibliography of the English Printed Drama to the Restoration*, III, 1116. A few significant examples of Shakespeare's popularity with the reading public during the twenty-five years after his death are cited by Miss C. V. Wedgwood, 'The Close of an Epoch', in *Shakespeare's World*, ed. by James Sutherland and Joel Hurstfield (1964), pp. 190–1.
4. R. B. McKerrow, 'The Treatment of Shakespeare's Text by his Earlier Editors, 1709–1768', *Proceedings of the British Academy*, XIX (1933), 91.
5. George Saintsbury, *The Peace of the Augustans* (1916); cited from the World's Classics edition (1946), p. 4.
6. D. Nichol Smith (ed.), *Eighteenth Century Essays on Shakespeare* (2nd ed., 1963), pp. xii ff.
7. McKerrow, *op. cit.* pp. 89–90.
8. *Ibid.* p. 97.
9. See McKerrow, *Times Literary Supplement*, 8 March 1934.
10. McKerrow, 'Shakespeare's Earlier Editors', p. 101.
11. Nichol Smith, *op. cit.* p. 63.
12. *Ibid.*
13. *Ibid.* p. 55.
14. McKerrow, 'Shakespeare's Earlier Editors', p. 109.

15. Nichol Smith, *op. cit.* pp. li–lii.

16. Giles E. Dawson, 'Robert Walker's Editions of Shakespeare', *Studies in the English Renaissance Drama*, ed. by J. W. Bennett, Oscar Cargill, and Vernon Hall, Jr. (1959), pp. 58–81. See also Dawson's 'Three Shakespeare Piracies in the Eighteenth Century', *Papers of the Bibliographical Society, University of Virginia*, I (1948–9), 49–58, for earlier attempts by William Feales to break the stranglehold of 'the Proprietors'.

17. Nichol Smith, *op. cit.* p. lvii.

18. McKerrow, 'Shakespeare's Earlier Editors', p. 114.

19. *Ibid.* p. 116.

20. Richard D. Altick, 'From Aldine to Everyman: Cheap Reprint Series of the English Classics 1830–1906', *Studies in Bibliography*, XI (1958), 3–24.

21. It is not often appreciated just how much Bowdler represented a widespread feeling about the plays. One hundred years after the appearance of his first edition Robert Bridges could write, in an essay prefixed to the Stratford Town Edition of Shakespeare (1907), that 'Shakespeare should not be put into the hands of the young without the warning that the foolish things in his plays were written to please the foolish, the filthy for the filthy, and the brutal for the brutal; and that if, out of veneration for his genius we are led to admire or even tolerate such things, we may be thereby not conforming ourselves to him, but only degrading ourselves to the level of his audience, and learning contamination from those wretched beings who can never be forgiven their share in preventing the greatest poet and dramatist of the world from being the best artist.'

22. Altick, 'From Aldine to Everyman', pp. 9–10.

23. Richard D. Altick, 'English Publishing and the Mass Audience in 1852', *Studies in Bibliography*, VI (1954), 3–24.

24. Altick, 'From Aldine to Everyman', p. 19, n. 27.

25. *Ibid.* pp. 20–1.

SHAKESPEARE'S TEXT—
THEN, NOW AND TOMORROW

BY

CHARLTON HINMAN

Then, now and tomorrow! The past, the present and the future! You will agree that my title is tolerably comprehensive if nothing else. My aims, however, are less immodest than they may seem. I shall say something about the history of Shakespearian textual scholarship; yet I shall be chiefly concerned with aspects of that history which belong rather to today and tomorrow than to yesterday. And here I propose to limit myself pretty strictly to specific illustrations of three main points—one about compositors, one about printing-house methods, and one about the kind of copy from which some of the plays were—or may have been—first printed.

To be sure, all three of these subjects can be said to fall under the *then* of my title in this sense: all are concerned with the falsifications that Shakespeare's text suffered during his own lifetime and in the few years just after his death, especially 1622–3, during the printing of the Okes quarto of *Othello* and, of course, of the First Folio. And what lies closer to the heart of 'the textual problem in Shakespeare' than the question of how much and what kinds of corruption characterize the various substantive editions of the plays? But all three of these subjects also involve *now* in that not until now, or at any rate until very recently, have they been intensively studied. And I hope to persuade you, finally, that all three not only deserve further investigation but may have some bearing on future editorial practice—on our continuing efforts to produce hereafter more satisfactory texts of the plays than any we have so far achieved.

One further preliminary. As I have been concerning myself with the quartos rather than the Folio of late, I beg to be indulged in giving particular attention to the quartos today. Not of course to all of them; not, for instance, to the Good quarto of *Hamlet* or the 'doubtful' one of *Lear*; mainly to the substantive quartos of certain history plays.

The fortunes of Shakespeare's text from 1623 to the beginning of the present century are now very generally known. We are perhaps likely to forget that the three later folios of the seventeenth century (those of 1632, 1663–4, and 1685) are not merely imperfect reprints, wholly without value. Each of them shows editorial activity of sorts, and the earliest one especially (F2, that is) reflects a real concern for improving on its predecessor. Yet each was printed directly from the latest preceding folio; none of the changes introduced editorially can be said to have any substantive authority; and each produced an abundant crop of new errors. So the history of the text in the seventeenth century after the publication of the First Folio is essentially one of progressive deterioration. Of the eighteenth and nineteenth centuries—the period beginning with Rowe's edition of 1709 and culminating with the Old Cambridge text of 1863–6 —it would surely be supererogatory for me to speak at any length here. How mistaken were the principles, albeit how brilliant were some of the emendations of the earlier eighteenth-century editors; what remarkable advances were made by Capell and Malone; and, finally, how admirable was the achievement of the Cambridge editors, unaware though they understandably were of large stores of useful information that have become available since their time: these are familiar matters, and I have but two observations to make. First, while we are no doubt right in urging that the chief task of an editor of the twentieth century is to repair the damage done to Shakespeare's text in the eighteenth, we may be failing to give anything like adequate acknowledgement to the depth and permanence of our real obligations to our eighteenth-century predecessors; and, secondly, when we claim that only in our own time has the value of the early quartos been properly appreciated, we are allowing Edward Capell, especially, something less than his due.

Our own time, however, has indeed had its triumphs—and these too, or at any rate the greater part of them, have already been expertly sung. In 1945, you will remember, appeared a volume entitled *Studies in Retrospect*—a work also intended for a birthday (though hardly for a 400th one, or Shakespeare's), as it was published to commemorate the 50th anniversary of the Bibliographical Society, which was founded in London in 1892. The star piece in this book is an essay by the late F. P. Wilson called 'Shakespeare and the New Bibliography', which very effectively tells the story of that relatively small band of scholars (above all the great triumvirate of analytical bibliographers, Pollard and McKerrow and Greg) whose labours have so profoundly influenced the course of Shakespearian textual study since the appearance in 1909 of Pollard's *Shakespeare Folios and Quartos*.

For though these men were indeed bibliographers they were also textual critics for whom 'the editorial problem in Shakespeare' was a central interest. All of them—McKerrow and Greg more than Pollard, of course—were in fact editors. Some bibliographers, no doubt, are men who treat books simply as material objects and have no regard for their contents. But *Shakespearian* bibliographers characteristically operate in that murky area where the boundaries between analytical bibliography and textual criticism tend to overlap and merge—or, as Greg himself has put it, where they 'appear to interlock in a manner that makes it difficult if not impossible to separate their respective fields'. So the New Bibliographers were certainly not bibliographers merely: they were practitioners of what some like to call biblio-textual criticism—men who sought to bring to the study of Shakespeare's text whatever help bibliographical investigation might be able to offer.

Pollard's *Shakespeare Folios and Quartos* must be regarded as the real manifesto of the New Bibliography, if only for making that distinction between Good and Bad quartos which is now so fundamental a part of our equipment, so to speak. Of course much that Pollard only began has been carried a great deal farther since 1909. It was not until 1929, for instance, that Alexander made clear that *The First Part of the Contention* and *The True Tragedy* are bad-quarto versions of *2* and *3 Henry VI*; and it was not until 1949 that Duthie demonstrated the inadequacy of Elizabethan systems of shorthand for taking down plays during performance. Again, Pollard's views on a number of particular points have been found unacceptable. But in general our present opinions about the quartos, about the relationship between these and the Folio, and about much else too, had their genesis in *Shakespeare Folios and Quartos*. Pollard and his fellow New Bibliographers showed not only that very few of the quartos are really Bad but also that both the Good quartos and the substantive Folio texts are likely to be based, if not directly on Shakespeare's holographs, then on the transcripts of these that were used as prompt books; and they eventually went a long way toward determining which plays were first printed from the one kind of copy, which from the other, and which from combinations—from conflations which reflect various degrees of editorial care. They subjected the surviving dramatic manuscripts of the period to intensive scrutiny, especially the three pages of *Sir Thomas More* that appear to be by Shakespeare and in his own handwriting. They formulated principles of emendation and provided very detailed studies of particular texts—one of the most important of these being without doubt *The Manuscript of Shakespeare's 'Hamlet'* by John Dover Wilson. And they edited Shakespeare and others. In short they both initiated and energetically carried forward, enlisting disciples as they went, the rigorous and systematic study of the transmission of Shakespeare's text that was so well chronicled by F. P. Wilson.

Nor have their projects languished since—even though McKerrow's death shortly after the publication of his *Prolegomena for the Oxford Shakespeare* in 1939 brought a temporary halt to progress on one of these. The New Bibliography was still flourishing when Wilson was writing about it twenty years ago; and of course it is still flourishing today. Yet certain large changes have lately been taking place; and even before Greg's death in 1959, just fifty years after the appearance of *Shakespeare Folios and Quartos*, various shifts of emphasis were already becoming plain. Indeed, if we were obliged to give a specific date to the advent of what might be styled the Newer Bibliography, we should probably have to fix on 1953, which saw the publication of Dr Alice Walker's little book called *Textual Problems in the First Folio*.

The change which shows itself here, let us recognize at once, is not symptomatic of any radical alteration of our ultimate objectives. Bibliographers—whether old or new or newer—are still bent on contributing as much as they can to the task of clearing Shakespeare's text of the corruption it has suffered since leaving his hands. The final aim, now as before, is an ever more exact knowledge of what stood in his own manuscript versions of the plays. During the past decade or so, however, the desirability of new approaches has become apparent. We have found it necessary to deal seriously with certain problems that were not much considered by our predecessors; and, in attacking these problems, we have been obliged to develop entirely new methods of investigation.

Let me try to explain by referring once more to Greg. Already in 1945 Wilson was describing him as the hero of the New Bibliography—and rightly so, even then, when so much of Greg's great work was still to be done; for he remained highly productive until the year of his death, and no one else has done anything like so much to advance our knowledge of Elizabethan dramatic texts in general and of the text of Shakespeare in particular. Our debt to him is, and will remain, enormous. But Greg, notwithstanding the wide range of his interests and his extraordinary investigative talents, was not equally attracted to all kinds of bibliographical inquiry. His chief preoccupation was with the manuscripts, now of course all lost, which necessarily underlie the first printed editions of the plays; and I think it may fairly be said that, in his continuing efforts to determine the nature of the copy used by Shakespeare's first printers, he somewhat tended to neglect that other major concern of Shakespearian bibliographical (or should we say biblio-textual?) study: the determination of how much and in what specific ways this copy, whatever its nature, suffered modification during the printing process itself.

Please do not misunderstand me. I am not trying to mount an attack on the late Sir Walter Greg, whom I revere only this side idolatry. I seek only to provide a kind of historical apologia for devoting most of my remaining time to what seem to me characteristic aspects of today's bibliographical approach to Shakespeare's text—to kinds of investigation which tend to proceed from the assumption (an assumption made necessary by facts not available to Greg) that a good many of the textual imperfections found in the substantive editions of the plays perhaps have little or nothing to do with the peculiarities of the manuscripts on which these editions are based, but are of printing-house origin only. I shall be urging, in other words, that at least some of the textual problems which have long been mystifying editors may be quite satisfactorily resolved, or at any rate better understood than heretofore, in the light of information about printing-house personnel and printing-house methods that is only now becoming known.

First, then, to printing-house personnel. One of the primary concerns of the aforementioned book on textual problems in the First Folio, as well as much of Dr Alice Walker's other published work of recent years, is with determining how accurately different compositors can be supposed to have reproduced their copy. Nor is it surprising that this should be so, since it has recently become very clear not alone that the reliability of the substantive editions of the plays depends most importantly on how well these men did their work but also that some compositors were much more faithful to copy than others. The following observations about the two parts of *Henry IV* are meant to illustrate the relevance of this question of compositorial accuracy to editors both of these and a number of other plays for which the basic authority is not the Folio but a quarto edition.

Part I of *Henry IV* got into print within a year or so of its first presentation in the theatre. What we label Q1, a quarto printed by Peter Short in the latter part of 1598, is our basic textual authority for most of the play. For most but not quite for all. Recovered long since from the binding of an old Italian grammar was a full quarto sheet, signed C, containing some 296 lines of *1 Henry IV*; and bibliographical analysis shows (1) that this unquestionably represents the true first edition, or what we now style Q0, and (2) that Q1 was printed directly from it. Detailed comparison of the eight surviving pages of Q0 with the corresponding text in Q1 brings forth these further facts: there are about 250 differences between the two; these differences, however, are almost entirely in accidentals (spelling, pointing, capitalization and the like); there are but three substantive variants. In two instances Q1 corrects a more or less obvious, but trifling, Q0 mistake. Once Q1 leaves out a single short word (it reads simply 'rogue' for Q0's 'fat rogue' at the end of Act II)—plainly an error of omission. Now an Elizabethan play text which introduces but a single corruption in the course of reprinting almost 300 lines must be considered faithful indeed to its copy. And there is reason to believe that such fidelity is not confined to these lines alone. Since both spellings and various typographical peculiarities indicate that the whole of Q1 was set by the same compositor, we may reasonably suppose that it reproduces Q0 (which was apparently set from Shakespeare's own autograph version of the play) with unusual accuracy throughout. The modern editor of *1 Henry IV* is, textually, in a fairly happy position. Although the quarto on which he must base his edition is demonstrably only a reprint, he can place far greater confidence in it than in— well, than in the true first edition of the companion play, the quarto of *Henry IV, Part II* that was printed by Valentine Simmes in 1600.

You may recall that there were two issues of this. What we now know as Act III, Scene i, a passage of 108 lines, was omitted from the original printing. The missing material was supplied in the second issue by means of a cancel: the last two leaves of original sheet E were replaced by four new leaves in which the omitted scene properly appears. It appears, however, only after a reset version of the last 52 lines of Act II; and it is followed by a resetting of the first 113 lines of the second scene of Act III. So the cancel contains some 165 lines that are also to be seen in the original setting; and since these lines were evidently reset directly from the cancelled matter, we have precisely the same sort of opportunity for comparison as before. And how accurately was the copy reproduced this time? Well, in the course of resetting only 165 lines— not 300 this time, but only 165—the compositor made, in addition to hosts of non-substantive changes, not fewer than nine verbal alterations: one correction (not necessarily right) of an obvious error, four additions, two omissions, one transposition, and one substitution. He would appear to have corrupted his copy more than ten times as often as the compositor who set Q1 of *1 Henry IV*. And if he was no more accurate in setting from manuscript than from printed copy, he must have introduced something like 180 unauthorized changes—corruptions—into the text of *2 Henry IV*; for there is abundant evidence that the whole of the 1600 quarto (including the expanded as well as the original version of signature E) was set by the same man. Hence it may not be altogether irresponsible to suggest, if only tentatively, that the quarto of this play may need emendation a good deal more often than the 1598 quarto of *Henry IV, Part I*.

Of course the cancel may have been produced in circumstances especially likely to lead to compositorial error; 165 lines are not very many, moreover, and it would be imprudent to generalize too far on the evidence they provide. So we ought, if we can, to find out more about the quality of this man's work. It is not only in the 1600 quarto of *2 Henry IV* that we are obliged to deal with it. His hand, as it happens, can be identified with relative ease, by virtue of his very unusual method of dealing with speech prefixes;[1] and it turns out that to him fell the lion's share of the setting of dramatic texts printed in the shop of Valentine Simmes over a considerable period. This same man set, for instance, in addition to a number of non-Shakespearian plays, both first editions and reprints, the whole of the Good first quarto of *Much Ado* (1600) and at least most of the Bad quarto of *Hamlet* (1603). He was in Simmes's employ for at least six years, for he was also the man who set over 50 of the approximately 70 pages of the Good first quarto of *Richard II* (1597). And since he appears also to have set the second quarto of the same play, the 1598 reprint of Q1, not to mention the greater part of Q3 (also 1598), there is plenty of opportunity for a much more extensive investigation of his accuracy. Now in progress, in fact, is such an investigation—and I hasten to say that preliminary reports rather strikingly confirm the testimony provided by the cancel in *2 Henry IV*: in resetting Q2 of *Richard II* from Q1 our compositor made approximately 160 substantive changes. This is not very comforting; it hardly bolsters our confidence in the substantive quartos of either *Richard II* or *Much Ado* (to say nothing more of *2 Henry IV*). Which is a pity; some bolstering would be welcome. For facts recently brought to light about the printing of one of these quartos have a distinctly opposite tendency—as we shall now see.

We shall see best, however, if we begin with a few observations about the First Folio. Until quite recently it was universally supposed that this book, like any other first edition, was set into type by successive pages—1, 2, 3, 4, etc., in the same order as we read these pages. In fact McKerrow had assured us in his *Introduction to Bibliography* that no other possibility need even be seriously considered.[2] But then, in 1955, typographical evidence of a kind not previously exploited made it perfectly clear that the Jaggard volume was set throughout, not by successive pages, seriatim, but by formes. A compositor, that is, did not set pages 1, 2, 3, etc. (in this order) in the usual and expected fashion; for each 12-page gathering (or quire) he first set pages 6 and 7, then 5 and 8, 4 and 9, and so on ending with pages 1 and 12. Now setting thus by formes necessarily implies setting from copy that had been 'cast off' in advance. For if a beginning was to be made with page 6 before pages 1–5 were in type, it was first of all required to determine exactly where to begin page 6; and precisely how much text would later be set into each of the pages antecedent to 6—first page 5, then 4, and so on back to page 1—had to be calculated. And calculated exactly, to the very letter, of course, else at the ends of these pages the text would not run smoothly on, without either gaps or repetitions, in the finished book.

So it was very surprising to learn that the First Folio was, nevertheless, set by formes. Surprising but not inexplicable: analysis showed that in this particular instance there were excellent reasons for proceeding in this way. Reasons for setting a large, double-column folio by formes, however, hardly apply to quarto printing; and we have accordingly continued to assume seriatim setting the rule, not for reprints to be sure, but for any *first* quarto—set as it must have been from manuscript copy, from copy not easy to cast off accurately. Some doubts, it is true, have been raised about the validity of this assumption; but no first quarto has hitherto yielded such entirely conclusive evidence of setting by formes as the Folio does throughout, nor such clear examples of textual corruption that is patently the result of inaccurate casting off. Of unusual interest, therefore, seem to me the following facts about the good first quarto of *Richard II*.

Here, to begin with the typographical evidence, the same defective and so individually identifiable types sometimes appear twice in the very same sheet. More than a dozen, for instance, are to be seen twice in sheet B (once in each forme, that is); and about the same number appear twice in sheet C—an absolute physical impossibility, of course, unless the setting had been done by formes. Setting was by formes, then; and there is almost equally conclusive evidence that outer formes were regularly set before inner formes. In other words the eight pages required for a given sheet were not set consecutively but in the following order: first pages 1, 4, 5 and 8 (the four outer-forme pages, the four pages that were printed on one side of the still unfolded quarto sheet) and then 2, 3, 6 and 7 (the four inner-forme pages, those for the other side of the sheet). Thus both pages 1 and 4—as well as 5 and 8—were regularly in type before pages 2 and 3, before the two intermediate pages of the text as we now read it; and thus also both pages 5 and 8 were in type before the text for intermediate pages 6 and 7.

Now there must have been good reasons for proceeding in this way. Two, at least, might be suggested. But what I wish to stress at the moment is that whatever advantages this method may have had for the printer, it manifestly had its disadvantages too. It obviously entailed certain risks. For what if there were some miscalculation; what if it turned out, when the time came to set pages 2 and 3, or 6 and 7, that the text meant for these pages required rather more space than had been left for them? The answer is, of course, that the compositor would be in trouble. He would be faced with a problem; and it just happens that in sheet D of the Simmes quarto of *Richard II* we can see exactly how he attempted to solve just such a problem.

The inner forme of sheet D was demonstrably set after the outer. Its second and third and its sixth and seventh pages followed its first, fourth, fifth, and eighth pages; or, since we may as well refer to them hereafter by their conventional bibliographical designators, D 1ᵛ–2 and D 3ᵛ–4 were set after D 1, D 2ᵛ–3, and D 4ᵛ. At least somewhat interesting, therefore, is the fact that the '*Exit*' direction on page D 2 is distinctly abnormal. Elsewhere such a direction ordinarily appears by itself, in a separate line—as it does in both D 1 and D 3; as it does, that is, in the outer-forme pages of this very sheet. But here, in inner-forme page D 2, it is crowded into a line of the text proper—as it plainly had to be unless it was to be left out altogether, since there is no space for it elsewhere. Indeed the real oddity about this '*Exit*' is perhaps that it was *not* simply left out; for from crowded inner-forme page D 3ᵛ a much more important stage direction—'*Enter Green*'—was left out altogether; and another entry direction is wanting from D 4.

Again, in both D 1ᵛ–2 and D 3ᵛ–4, though not in the outer-forme pages, there are multiple instances of another kind of abnormality (and one that has given editors more trouble): considerably more than one line of verse is sometimes squeezed into a single line of type. Twice in page D 4, for example, we find grossly hypermetrical verse. First comes

> And with uplifted arms is safe arrived at Ravenspurgh

and then, only a little farther along,

> And all the household servants fled with him to Bullingbrook.

Shakespeare, we may be pretty sure, did not write *Richard II* in iambic heptameter. By means of these two seven-footed verse lines, however, two full type-lines in the quarto have been saved—as they evidently had to be if the whole of the text that was meant to appear on page D 4 was in fact to be got into it.

But what is above all remarkable about sheet D is that not all of the text that was supposed to appear in its inner-forme pages *was* originally got into them. More or less essential text *was* actually left out; and it is only by chance, as we shall presently see, that what was omitted was ever restored.

Four copies of the 1597 quarto of *Richard II* survive, and one of these shows the uncorrected state of the forme in question. Here—in the single copy, that is, which patently represents the original setting of inner D—here both D 1ᵛ and D 3ᵛ altogether lack a one-line speech that ought to be present. Let only the second of these two pages, D 3ᵛ, be used for illustration; and let the corrected state of its text be considered first. Here, in colloquy with Bushy and Bagot, Queen Isabel speaks of her conviction that 'some unborn sorrow...is coming toward me'. To which sentiment, in an attempt to comfort her, Bushy at once replies; and what we read is

> *Bush.* Tis nothing but conceit my gracious Lady.

The abbreviated speech-prefix *Bush.* is indented in the conventional manner, and in the speech proper the queen is assured that her unhappiness is purely imaginary, is 'nothing but conceit'. After which immediately comes (and again, of course, with the appropriately indented speech-prefix)

> *Queene.* Tis nothing less: conceit is still derived
> From some forefather grief....

This dialogue, this exchange between Bushy and Isabel, must have stood in the copy (else it could never have appeared in the corrected state of the quarto and so in all subsequent editions of the play). In what the compositor originally set, however, as is shown by the uncorrected Petworth House copy, Bushy's speech is absent. Absent as well, moreover, is the speech-prefix for Isabel's reply; nor is the beginning of the reply proper indented. On the contrary. There is no sign of Bushy's interruption of the queen's lament. Isabel appears to have a single long speech; there is nothing whatever to show that her words 'Tis nothing less...' represent a response to something just spoken by an interlocutor. The compositor, in short, did not simply omit a one-line speech through inadvertence. He knew perfectly well that he was cutting this speech; and he took some pains so to alter what immediately followed the omitted matter as to cover his tracks, as to conceal the fact that he had, indeed, left something out. In other words—nor in my opinion can the importance of this point be well overstressed—his falsification of the text was quite certainly not accidental but deliberate. Deliberate—and, though reprehensible, by no means unintelligent. For what above all else the evidence we have been reviewing shows is how a sensible if also a somewhat unprincipled man might proceed when obliged to get more into a given type-page than could, without some change, be accommodated there. Thanks to inaccurate casting off the man now in question found that, even after he had used other and less drastic means of meeting his problem—by tinkering with the versification and omitting a couple of entry directions, for instance—he still simply could not get everything that stood in his copy into the space allotted for it. So in page D 3ᵛ, exactly as he had done a little while before when setting D 1ᵛ, he went a step farther: he omitted part of the text proper. And he succeeded in producing an abridgement which, while not what Shakespeare intended, was at least not obviously corrupt.

In both these instances, it is true, his falsifications of the copy were discovered and condemned, for he was obliged to restore the true text even though the required changes made both D 1ᵛ and D 3ᵛ abnormally long pages, each with 38 instead of the usual 37 lines of text. But had a proof-reader not gone over the original setting with an uncommonly sharp eye, and certainly with more care than he gave to some other formes of this same book (as other variants show), we should now have a less satisfactory text of *Richard II* than we do.

Even so the quarto is far less satisfactory than we could wish. Overcrowded and patently mislined pages are common, many entry directions (to say nothing of exits) are wanting, and in a number of places there seems to be something missing from the text proper. Inaccurate casting off is not necessarily the culprit in every instance. Something else may be responsible for our difficulties after the seventeenth line of Act II, for example, where both rhyme and sense suggest the loss of a line, and where editorial attempts to produce a generally acceptable reading by emending line 18 have hitherto so signally failed. And what of the passage later in this same scene (II, i, 279–281) where Rainold Lord Cobham is said to have broken with the Duke of Exeter—and where editors usually follow Malone in supplying a line which may or may not be exactly what Shakespeare intended but which at any rate both scans and accords with historical fact? Political considerations, if not mere carelessness on the part of the compositor, may account for omission here. But it is interesting to note that not fewer than six of the quarto's pages besides corrected D 1ᵛ and D 3ᵛ now contain 38 instead of the normal 37 lines. Unfortunately not one of these six happens to be in one of the few formes of which both the uncorrected and corrected states are preserved. It seems probable, however, that some if not all six are now of unusual length for the same reason that three of the four surviving examples of D 1^v and D 3^v are. In any event there is plenty of evidence to suggest that the text of *Richard II* was deliberately misrepresented elsewhere than in inner D; and there is likewise good reason to think that at least some of the corruptions thus introduced, having escaped the proof-reader, are with us still. In some happy tomorrow perhaps a few of them can be identified and corrected—though for the present we need insist on no more than this: that the authoritative first quarto of Shakespeare's *Richard II* was unquestionably set throughout by formes, and that this method of working demonstrably rendered particular parts of the copy text especially liable to misrepresentation in certain specific ways.

I cannot forbear to add that I am now embarked on a very general investigation of setting by formes and that my preliminary studies indicate that the very first of the Good quartos, 1594 *Titus Andronicus*, was set in this manner, and that the 1622 quarto of *Othello* was too. Probably also the 1597 *Richard III*, and pretty surely the substantive quartos of both *1 Henry IV* and *MND*—though not, despite what is said in a recently published article, the 1600 quarto of *Much Ado*. The practice, in short, though not invariably adopted, was by no means uncommon. It is to be seen in first quartos that issued from many different printing houses, and over a wide stretch of years. And fuller information about it can hardly be a matter of indifference to future editors of the plays. For instance we badly need to know—but I must now hasten on to my final point. This, though it concerns compositors and is not entirely unconnected with the question of setting by formes, is primarily about copy—or rather, and more specifically, about what kind of copy is implied by the presence of anticipatory errors in a printed text. And the focus will once more be on *Richard II*.

The New Arden editor of the play of course recognizes that the 1597 quarto 'is likely to be fairly close' (as he puts it in his introduction) 'to Shakespeare's autograph';[3] yet he goes on to argue that it is 'no longer possible to overlook the evidence of memorial elements in the Quarto and hence the possibility that a transcript intervened between it and the foul papers'.[4] This evidence consists essentially of a number of errors which seem to represent anticipations of readings that appear some lines farther along; for Peter Ure, accepting an argument advanced by Dover Wilson in 1934, is persuaded that such errors cannot properly be attributed to a compositor. 'It is very unlikely', Ure writes of an error of which he says 'the obvious source' is a reading four lines later, 'that a compositor...would anticipate a word so far ahead of the line he is setting',[5] whereas a scribe familiar with the play (as, for example, the book-holder or prompter might be) might well be guilty of doing so. This, like Dover Wilson's argument about the twenty-odd anticipatory errors he found in Folio *Hamlet*, seems plausible enough. 'Compositors', wrote Wilson in *The Manuscript of Shakespeare's 'Hamlet'*, 'may repeat words, but they are exceedingly unlikely to anticipate.' Repetitions by them are understandable. 'Thus it is easy enough to see how a word or phrase', just set, 'might get substituted for something else in the next group of words to be picked up by the compositor's eye. But how can compositors, not endowed with the gift of prophecy, anticipate words in their copy upon which their eye has not yet lighted? Such a feat is clearly impossible.'[6] Without doubt. But what if the compositor's eye had already lighted on the words in question? What if, just before setting a given line, he had for some reason read ahead some 20 or 30 lines, say? In this case a reading that appears in line 12 (for instance) might indeed have a corrupting influence over the similar reading that appears—or should appear—in line 2. In this case, in other words, what may seem to be an anticipatory error would in fact be only a recollection. And it strikes me as perfectly reasonable to suggest that many supposed anticipations are really nothing more. For if compositors were obliged to punctuate the texts they set, as they evidently were, how *could* they do so without first reading this copy over to determine its sense? Shakespeare's own pointing, the *More* fragment shows us, was very light. The punctuation in the substantive prints, though it is by no means everywhere alike and may even show considerable variation in different parts of the same play, is generally much heavier. Moreover, it is in the main tolerably satisfactory—a good deal more so, I submit, than we could expect it to be unless at least some pains had been taken over it. To me, indeed, it seems almost impossible to suppose otherwise than that a compositor would normally, as a matter of course, read over a fairly sizeable block of text before undertaking to typeset it, if for no other purpose than to prepare himself to point it in an acceptable way. Hear the one bit of seventeenth-century testimony we have on this subject. In his Preface to the section of *Mechanick Exercises* called 'The Compositors Trade', Moxon tells us that

by the Laws of Printing, a Compositor is strictly to follow his Copy, viz. to observe and do just so much and no more than his Copy will bear him out for; so that his Copy is to be his Rule and Authority: But the carelessness of some good Authors, and the ignorance of other Authors, has forc'd Printers to introduce a Custom, which among them is look'd upon as a task and duty incumbent on the Compositor, viz. to discern and amend the bad Spelling and Pointing of his Copy, if it be English.... Therefore upon consideration of these accidental circumstances that attend Copy [viz. bad spelling and pointing], it is necessary that a Compositor be a good English Schollar at least; and that he know the present traditional Spelling of all English Words, and that he have so much Sence and Reason, as to Point his Sentences properly.[7]

And this statement he amplifies later—several times, indeed, though I shall quote him only once more. 'A good Compositor', Moxon explains,

is ambitious as well to make the meaning of his Author intelligent to the Reader, as to make his work shew graceful to the Eye, and pleasant in Reading: Therefore if his Copy be Written in a Language he understands, he reads his Copy with consideration; that so he may get himself into the meaning of the Author, and consequently considers how to order his Work....As how to make his Indenting, Pointing...etc. the better sympathize with the Author's Genius, and also with the capacity of the Reader.[8]

In short, then, to read over the copy 'with consideration', in order to make his own pointing 'the better sympathize' with the Author's meaning, is here described both as a custom and as a 'duty incumbent on the Compositor'. So when, in the *Richard II* quarto, we find old Gaunt saying

> My oil-dried lamp and time-bewasted light
> Shall be extinct with age and endless *nights*

—where *nights* (plural) is unquestionably wrong, where the singular *night* is required to preserve the rhyme with *light*—it cannot be declared an outright impossibility, I would maintain, that this error may reflect the influence on the compositor of a plural that rightly appears just six lines farther along, in the same speaker's words

Shorten my days thou canst with sullen sorrow,
And pluck *nights* from me, but not lend a morrow.

Nor, perhaps—to return to the textual consequences of setting by formes—is it altogether absurd to suggest that a corrupt reading at a given point may be compositorial rather than scribal, even though it seems clearly to anticipate something that appears several whole pages later. Suppose, for instance, an error in page E 1ᵛ that looks like an anticipation of a similar reading some six pages farther along, in E 4ᵛ. In this quarto, remember, E 1ᵛ was not set long *before*, but immediately *after*, E 4ᵛ. So the error in question may not be an anticipation on the part of a copyist familiar with the play; it may represent nothing more than a compositor's inadvertent substitution of the reading he had just set into E 4ᵛ for the similar but different reading that stood in his copy for E 1ᵛ. And thus, once again, we are not absolutely required to suppose that a scribal transcript of Shakespeare's autograph must have served as copy for the first printed edition of *Richard II*. It may well be that some of the substantive quartos of Shakespeare's plays were printed from manuscripts of the kind envisaged by Peter Ure— transcripts intermediate between the author's last draft and the copy of this that was prepared for use in the theatre as a prompt book. It may be that the 1597 quarto of *Richard II* was. In this instance, however, at least part of the evidence adduced in support of the intermediate-transcript hypothesis becomes highly suspect once we consider, if not the compositor's general obligation to point his copy intelligently, then at any rate the fact that he did not set his pages seriatim but by formes. Perhaps, moreover, this particular compositor will prove to have been especially given to errors of just the kind we have been discussing. So there is yet another reason for further study both of compositors, of the relative strengths and weaknesses of the men who first put Shakespeare's plays into type, and of the printing-house procedures they followed. Only a beginning has so far been made; only a beginning—and there is much to learn about these matters. And hence the last word of my title. For if, *tomorrow*, like power divine, he were himself here to look upon our passes, it is likely that our master, whom we love, would find us full of labours still.

NOTES

1. See Craig Ferguson in *Studies in Bibliography*, XIII (1960), 19–29.
2. See pp. 31–4.
3. Peter Ure, ed., [New] Arden *Richard II* (London, 1956), p. xv.
4. *Ibid.* p. xix.
5. *Ibid.* pp. xvi–xvii.
6. John Dover Wilson, *The Manuscript of Shakespeare's 'Hamlet'* (Cambridge, 1934), I, 54.
7. *Mechanick Exercises*, ed. Davis and Carter (Oxford, 1958), pp. 192–3.
8. *Ibid.* pp. 211–12.

'HAMLET' THEN TILL NOW

BY

HAROLD JENKINS

Many men have seen themselves in the hero of this play; and it is especially easy for me to do so at the moment, when I have a task assigned to me which I know myself unequal to performing. I do not expect to escape censure for my weakness, though I hope it will not be put down to a defect of will and that something may be allowed to me for the magnitude of the task itself. For well over a century almost every writer upon *Hamlet* has begun by remarking that more has been written on it than on any other work of literature, before adding his own ink to the ever-swelling flood. In 1877 the Furness *Variorum*, in order to keep up with the tide, needed two volumes instead of the one that still suffices for other Shakespeare plays; and beginning where Furness left off, A. A. Raven listed in his '*Hamlet' Bibliography and Reference Guide* (1936) over 2000 items between 1877 and 1935, while the *Classified Shakespeare Bibliography* of Gordon Ross Smith (1963), continuing the count down to 1958, added over 900 more items, ranging from Dover Wilson's *The Manuscript of Shakespeare's 'Hamlet'* (1934), which I suppose deals with *Hamlet then*, to 'Hamlet as Existentialist' (*Shakespeare Newsletter*, VII, 1957), which may conceivably be *Hamlet now*. As I approach this enormous task of tracing the critical fortunes of this play, my mind, like Hamlet's own in Hazlitt's phrase, sinks within me. Yet I am in one respect more favoured than my prototype; I am not isolated from the help of others. I acknowledge the assistance I have received from Paul S. Conklin's *History of 'Hamlet' Criticism* (1957) down to 1821, from the critical collections given by Furness, and, when I come to the present century, from the reviews of Clifford Leech in *Shakespeare Survey 9* (1956) and G. K. Hunter in *Critical Quarterly*, I (1959). When I think of this last part of my task, however, my resolution becomes still more sicklied o'er. The writers upon *Hamlet now* include most of my present audience. To all those whom time or bestial oblivion will compel me to neglect, whom necessity will cause me to over-simplify, or whom incapacity will lead me to misconstrue, I offer my apologies.

The principal difference between *Hamlet then* and *Hamlet now* will already be apparent. *They* saw *Hamlet* direct, fresh on Shakespeare's stage beneath a clear Elizabethan sky, *we* staled with custom and through a cloud of commentary. Yet if by some miracle in nature this cloud suddenly disappeared, I still could show you little of the Elizabethan *Hamlet*. I confess to a craven scruple about speaking with any confidence of what the play meant to its contemporary public. It is true that scholars *now* write books about *The 'Hamlet' of Shakespeare's Audience* (J. W. Draper, 1938), surmise how it was acted at the Globe, and assure us how the Elizabethans would have taken it. But this construct of scholarship belongs, I suggest, in what may or may not be madness, rather to *Hamlet now*. A scholarly argument about how the Elizabethans must have regarded the play is not quite the same as a record of how they did. Yet there are at least enough contemporary allusions to *Hamlet* to tell us that it was immediately liked and even famous. The way had of course been opened for it by an earlier play on the same subject, which Lodge remembered for the Ghost that cried 'Hamlet, revenge' (*Wit's Misery*, 1596). The immediate appeal of Shakespeare's play certainly owed much to the spectacular incidents it derived from its predecessor. When after 1600 the Elizabethans refer to *Hamlet*, we cannot always be sure which play they had in mind, and perhaps they could not either. It would be all the same to the spectators at *Westward Ho* in 1604 when they heard injured husbands advised to 'play mad Hamlet, and cry revenge'. But Anthony Scoloker in the same year specifically names Shakespeare when acknowledging that Prince Hamlet 'pleases all', and then slily adds that he declines to run mad himself in order to do the same (*Daiphantus*, 1604). The madness was already a legend, and, as Patrick Cruttwell has recently observed ('The Morality of Hamlet …', *Stratford-upon-Avon Studies 5*, 1963), it was evidently *then* a much more violent affair than the stage usually shows *now*. The lover in Scoloker's poem, when he goes mad, tears a passion and undresses to his shirt 'much like mad Hamlet'. The hero could not be thought of without his madness, nor could he without his encounter with the Ghost. Shakespeare's tremendous dialogue in this scene so impressed itself upon the mind that it was often echoed in plays of other dramatists. To take but one example, in Beaumont's *The Woman-Hater* (1607) a gourmet pursuing a delectable fish-head says 'Speak, I am bound to hear' and is told 'So art thou to revenge, when thou shalt hear the fish head is gone'. The jest seems to assume in the audience a knowledge of the original; and such travesties, as Dyce remarked, are the surest form of tribute. Nor were the echoes of *Hamlet* confined to the Ghost and mad scenes. D. G. McGinn (*Shakespeare's Influence on the Drama of his Age*, 1938) has counted almost five hundred echoes in plays before 1642; and even if we dismiss many of these as part of the general verbal currency, there is still evidence to suggest that this play lived in people's minds perhaps more than any other. And it did so, I suppose, not merely for its theatrical excitement but also, *then* as it has done ever since, for its wisdom unsurpassedly expressed in Shakespeare's memorable language.

This was surely the quality that Gabriel Harvey recognized in *Hamlet* from the first. In saying that it had it in it 'to please the wiser sort' (*Marginalia*) he may have meant no more by his epithet than to signalize that tragedy was grave. But what we have to notice is that Harvey joins this one stage-play with Shakespeare's already celebrated poems and lists it among the best literary works in English, along with the *Arcadia* and *The Faerie Queene* and the big historical poems of Warner and Daniel. Whether or not scholars are right to suppose Harvey made his comment before *Hamlet* was in print, he seems to have envisaged it as having a reading public.

It was on the stage, however, that *Hamlet then* made its greatest impact. Its leading role at once became a famous one. As early as 1605 the anonymous author of *Ratsey's Ghost* made his hero commend an actor by saying he would back him to play Hamlet. An elegy on Burbage in 1619 names Hamlet first among his celebrated parts; and before the end of the century this part was established in that theatrical pre-eminence it has never since lost. As Betterton performed it—to directions descending from Shakespeare, if Downes is to be credited (*Roscius Anglicanus*, 1708)—it was, to the impressionable Pepys, 'the best part, I believe, that ever man acted' (*Diary*, 31 August 1668). In estimating *Hamlet's* renown at this time, no doubt we should distinguish between the theatrical part and the character, and both of them from the play. As Shakespeare's most celebrated character Hamlet as yet yielded to Falstaff; and when Rymer chose to examine the one among all English tragedies which was 'said to bear the bell away'

(*A Short View of Tragedy*, 1693), it was of course *Othello* that he went for, which at least spares us from knowing what he would have said about *Hamlet*. G. E. Bentley tells us that in critical opinion both were outdone by Jonson's *Catiline* (*Shakespeare and Jonson*, 1945). Yet by the time we reach the centenary of Shakespeare's death his supremacy is assured and *Hamlet* has clearly emerged as his most famous play. That is why Theobald chose it for his editorial demonstration (*Shakespeare Restored*, 1726), and Shaftesbury believed it was, of all plays on the English stage, the one which had not only 'been oftenest acted' but 'most affected English hearts' (*Soliloquy, or Advice to an Author*, 1710; reprinted in *Characteristics*, 1711). Shaftesbury already thought of it as having 'but one character', and it is from accounts of how Betterton had acted this character that we get our chief impression of what *Hamlet* was to the early eighteenth century. For clearly Betterton gave it them as they thought it ought to be. Steele was impressed by his 'ardour' (*Tatler*, 71, 20 September 1709). Cibber said that in the meeting with the Ghost you felt Hamlet's terror with him (*Apology*, 1740). Betterton, in fact, helped them to realize the power which Dryden had praised in Shakespeare: 'When he describes anything, you more than see it, you feel it too.' Betterton's Hamlet, we are told, had the 'vivacity and enterprize' of 'youth', while he was at the same time 'manly'. Prince Hamlet at this date was vigorous, bold, heroic. There was no hint yet of brooding introspection, nor of a man who could not make up his mind. Nor was it yet discovered that his passion exceeded its object. What was valued in the play was its power to stir the ordinary human emotions by showing them raised to their highest pitch by *extra*ordinary circumstance.

This is the *Hamlet* described in 1736 in the first formal criticism of the play we have, *Some Remarks on the Tragedy of Hamlet*, once but not now believed to be by Hanmer. The author shows of course the limitations as well as the virtues of his age. He does not believe in mixing comedy with your tragedy: the grave-digger scene, though 'much applauded', 'is very unbecoming such a piece as this'. He is aghast at Hamlet's reasons for not killing the praying king. It did not occur to plain eighteenth-century sense that Hamlet could not have meant what he said. But in spite of reservations, the author has no doubt that this play shows unsurpassed Shakespeare's characteristic excellences; and these are truth to nature, sublimity of sentiment, and exalted diction. The scene with the Ghost, still the most momentous one, creates 'awe' beyond any other the author knows, yet the handling of it is 'entirely conformable to nature'. This is the note which is struck over and over again. The scene between Hamlet and his mother could not 'have been managed...more conformably to reason and nature'. 'The Prince's reflections on his mother's hasty marriage' it is interesting, in view of later perturbations, to find described as 'very natural'. Hamlet's delay, however, is another matter: 'there appears no reason at all in nature' for it. But it as yet presents no problem. 'Had Hamlet gone naturally to work..., there would have been an end of our play. The poet therefore was obliged to delay his hero's revenge; but then he should have contrived some good reason for it.'

Yet Hamlet's delay, at first seen as a necessary feature of the plot, gradually came to be considered in relation to his character. This is part of the remarkable shift in dramatic criticism when the priority which Aristotle gave to plot began to be disputed and the chief virtue looked for in a dramatist was the power to depict character. The admiration for Shakespeare's lifelike characterization had much to do with this; but paradoxically it led to a demand for a consistency in characterization which he was found not always to supply. In 1770 Francis Gentleman, while appreciating the 'great variety' in the character of Hamlet, lamented that he 'should be such an apparent heap of inconsistency' (*The Dramatic Censor*). Provided this could be blamed on Shakespeare, there were no very serious consequences; but once it was assumed that this inconsistent creature was what Shakespeare meant Hamlet to be, Hamlet himself became an object of puzzled study. The question was no longer why Shakespeare failed to account for Hamlet's not killing the king at once but why Hamlet failed to do it. In 1763 the actor Thomas Sheridan won the approval of Boswell (*Journal*, 6 April) for an account of 'the character of Hamlet' which described him as 'irresolute', wanting 'strength of mind', striving towards 'manly boldness' but 'in vain'. Here the heroic Hamlet disappears. Yet what redeems him for us in this new avatar is that his very irresoluteness belongs with a delicacy which springs from his 'fine feelings'. This was of course the age of sensibility. In Sterne's *Sentimental Journey* (1768) the marquis who reclaims his sword while letting fall a tear evokes the exclamation 'O how I envied him his feelings'; and the public which enjoyed this could envy Hamlet his. It was Henry Mackenzie, famed as the author of *The Man of Feeling* (1771), who was presently to explain the secret of Hamlet's appeal. In two notable essays in *The Mirror* in 1780 Mackenzie addresses himself to the task of discovering the basic principle which gives unity to Hamlet's 'variable and uncertain' character, and he finds it in 'an extreme sensibility of mind'. It is a sensibility 'so delicate as to border on weakness'; and Shakespeare has skilfully placed Hamlet in a situation where this 'amiable' quality can only 'perplex his conduct', so that his 'principles of action' become 'unhinged'. Hamlet's difficulties arise therefore 'from the doubts and hesitations of his own mind'; but it is precisely this that invests the 'sweet prince' with pathos and gives him his 'indescribable charm'.

The change in critical attitude is well illustrated by William Richardson. Inheriting an earlier eighteenth-century taste for moral disquisition, he presented Hamlet as an exemplar of virtue, and when he first wrote on him in 1774 (*A Philosophical Analysis and Illustration of Some of Shakespeare's Remarkable Characters*), he hardly perceived a fault. But ten years later, in answer to critical objections, Richardson made 'Additional Observations on Hamlet' (*Essays on Shakespeare's Dramatic Characters*, 1784) in order to excuse his virtuous hero for the 'frailties' he now had to concede. Thomas Sheridan had already supposed that Hamlet's wish to send the king's soul to damnation was really 'an excuse to himself for his delay', and this is what Richardson takes it on himself to assert: 'I will venture to affirm that these are not his real sentiments.' Hamlet is thus liberated from Shakespeare's text, and the door is open for the nineteenth century to supply him with all the motives about which the play is silent. For his part Richardson can continue to insist on Hamlet's 'exquisite sense of moral conduct', but in his later editions he combines it with those 'amiable weaknesses' which belong with 'extreme sensibility'.

The man of the exquisite feelings and the man of the exquisite moral sense appear together in the Hamlet made famous by Goethe, with rather more of the weakness but certainly no less charm. When Goethe gave this portrait to the world (*Wilhelm Meisters Lehrjahre*, 1795), it may not have represented his own conception so much as Wilhelm Meister's, but the distinction is not one which its admirers were apt to make. To Wilhelm at any rate it was 'clear that Shakespeare meant . . . to represent the effects of a great action laid upon a soul unfit for the performance of it. . . . A lovely, pure, noble, and most moral nature, without the strength of nerve

which forms a hero, sinks beneath a burden which it cannot bear, and must not cast away'
(Carlyle's translation).

Here then is the romantic Hamlet on the threshold of the nineteenth century—a virtuous
prince with a sensitive soul in a situation of great distress, which is aggravated by the very
fineness of his feelings, which undermine his resolution and so bring him to a failure which is
nevertheless a sign of his superiority. Once he is *in* the nineteenth century, he undergoes
modification early on at the hands of Coleridge, whose analysis of Hamlet's character (preserved
in reports of his Lectures from 1811, supplemented by his own notes) has been described by
T. M. Raysor as 'probably the most influential piece of Shakespearean criticism which has ever
been produced'. Coleridge was not the first to be attracted to the philosophic side of *Hamlet*.
The 'To be or not to be' soliloquy had been echoed by Shakespeare's contemporaries, it had
been got by heart by Pepys, and the author of *Some Remarks on the Tragedy of Hamlet* in 1736
had thought it too well known to need comment. But now that its meditations on life and
death had to be referred to Hamlet's character, it was necessary to attribute them to his own
speculative turn of mind. It was this that fascinated Coleridge, who was only too well aware
that speculative thought is wont not to issue in action. He finds in Hamlet 'an overbalance in
the contemplative faculty' and an 'overpowering activity of intellect', which produces 'vacil-
lating delays' and wastes 'in the energy of resolving the energy of acting'. Already Schlegel in
Germany (*Vorlesungen über dramatische Kunst und Literatur*, II, 2, 1811; translated Black, 1815)
was insisting that what defeated Hamlet's purpose was the propensity towards thinking which
crippled his power of acting. What these two did, and Coleridge especially, was to transfer
the interest in Hamlet's character from the sensibility to the intellect. Yet while Coleridge
delighted to watch the intricate processes of Hamlet's thought, he noted as a 'most important
characteristic' Hamlet's tendency to escape from his own 'individual concerns' to 'generaliza-
tions and general reasonings'. For Schlegel it was the unique power of this drama of thought
that it inspired its readers and spectators to meditate with Hamlet on the enigma of human
destiny and the dark perplexity of the events of this world. Hazlitt, a little more down to
earth, remarks that the play abounds 'in striking reflections on human life' (*Characters of
Shakespear's Plays*, 1817). Yet it would not have taken possession of the popular imagination as
it did if one had not been able to enter into the experience of an individual human being and
identify him with oneself. Hamlet, again in Hazlitt's words, transfers his own distresses 'to the
general account of humanity. Whatever happens to him we apply to ourselves.' 'It is *we* who
are Hamlet', says Hazlitt.

Through the nineteenth century Hamlet the prince became many things to many men. He
was each man and every man; he was a modern born out of his time; he was a mystery; he was
a genius; he was Shakespeare; and, a little more unexpectedly, at least to Shakespeare's country-
men, he was Germany, and especially the mind of nineteenth-century Germany in the plight of
nineteenth-century Germany, which Shakespeare had prophetically divined. But whatever he
was, always at the heart of the tragedy was the problem of Hamlet's character and with it the
problem of why he left his task undone. The way to an explanation had been opened up, as we
have seen, by Goethe and Coleridge, with whose views discussion would almost inevitably
begin. It was possible to debate between them, whether Hamlet was frustrated by the refine-
ment of his feelings or by his habit of thinking too precisely; but the two were not necessarily

incompatible, and many interpretations sought to include both. An early synthesis was provided by Nathan Drake (*Shakespeare and his Times*) in 1817: Hamlet's 'powers of action', he says, 'are paralysed in the first instance, by the unconquerable tendency of his mind to explore . . . all the bearings and contingencies of the meditated deed; and in the second, by that tenderness of his nature which leads him to shrink from the means which are necessary to carry it into execution'. How little orthodox opinion, notwithstanding many fluctuations, was to change in the course of the century we may see by a leap ahead which, after a glance at, say, Dowden (*Shakspere: his Mind and Art*, 1875) and Boas (*Shakspere and His Predecessors*, 1896), brings us to rest in the introduction to Verity's edition in 1904. Verity has absolutely no doubt that the greatness of the play is 'the characterization of Hamlet'; and after quoting of course Goethe and Coleridge he concludes, 'I hold, then, that at bottom the cause of Hamlet's failure to execute the duty laid upon him . . . is the overbalance of the reflective faculty, the effect of which is further intensified by his great imagination and excess of the emotional temperament'.

Sometimes, however, voices would be raised on another side altogether and declare that Hamlet did not procrastinate at all. They said that what prevented Hamlet from acting was not a paralysis of will but the circumstances that opposed him, the difficulty of the task itself. The loudest of these voices was Werder's (*Vorlesungen über Shakespeare's Hamlet*, 1875), proclaiming that Hamlet's difficulty was not to kill the king but to justify to men his doing so, which, in the absence of proof, meant bringing the king to confession. That this is not in the text Werder himself conceded. Hamlet never says this, he admits, but the state of the case says it for him. What else the state of the case might have said, and sometimes did, was that to fall on a defence-less man was dishonourable, to kill a king impracticable and possibly sacrilegious, and even that Claudius's death would widow Hamlet's mother. When in 1898 A. H. Tolman reviewed the whole controversy about Hamlet's delay, he was able to list, at the cost of a little hair-splitting, eighteen different reasons which had been put forward to account for it ('A View of the Views about *Hamlet*', *PMLA*, XIII; reprinted 1906).

We cannot forget that the play of *Hamlet* in the nineteenth century was first and foremost the character of its hero. We *must* not forget that it also was a play about the universal mysteries. But another of the things it also was, was a vast congeries of problems. Second only to the delay was the problem of the madness, on which there is a whole literature—by alienists and others. The psychiatrist, Isaac Ray, pronounced that Hamlet's case showed Shakespeare's profound understanding of the symptoms of insanity ('Shakespeare's Delineations of Insanity', *American Journal of Insanity*, III, 1847; reprinted in *Contributions to Mental Pathology*, 1873); to which a distinguished man of letters retorted, no less confusing fact and fiction, that if Shakespeare could create those symptoms without himself going mad, why could not Hamlet do the same? (Lowell, *Among My Books*, 1870). Feigned or real madness became a topic of debate; usually there was both, but just occasionally neither.

Other notorious questions arose in the nineteenth century to perplex criticism ever since. Why did Claudius wait for the second enactment of his crime and not blench during the dumb-show? What exactly had Ophelia done to provoke Hamlet's cruelty? Did Hamlet know she was a decoy and that her father was behind the arras? When could she have received that letter from Hamlet that she handed to her father? On all these matters the play tiresomely says nothing and the critics fill in its gaps.

Here we see, in one of its aspects, the nineteenth-century mind: consulting my copy of Sprague (*Shakespeare and the Actors*, 1944), I am not surprised to learn that it was in the 1820's that the stage began that naughty piece of business which makes Hamlet spot the eavesdroppers. But this mind is one we all inherit—it still strongly colours *Hamlet now*—and I am afraid it is a rather prosaic one. Its habits are encouraged by the novel, which its forebears had produced. The novel has of course more room to tell us what an Elizabethan play leaves out; but it also wants to tell it us, because it thrives on verisimilitude and has a strong psychological bias. The nineteenth-century critic adds to Shakespeare's dialogue the sort of commentary with which George Eliot intersperses hers. He supplies the emotional developments between scenes: observing that Gertrude's behaviour to Claudius is unchanged after her interview with Hamlet, he shows us how she only half repented and subsequently gave up the struggle (Horn in *Shakespeares Schauspiele*, II, 1825). And the critic is not satisfied with this. He likes to regard a fiction as if it were a fragment of history, to suppose that the characters have complete lives, and that the parts we are not told of can be recovered by logical deduction and skilled reading between the lines. To avoid extreme examples, I find it being argued that Polonius could not have stood well with the dead king: if he had, Hamlet would have known and would not then have insulted him (Von Friesen, *Briefe über Shaksperes Hamlet*, 1864). And did not Bradley argue the whereabouts of Hamlet at the time of his father's death?

This is an unworthy route by which to arrive at Bradley (*Shakespearean Tragedy*, 1904). If the attitude I have spoken of is particularly associated with his name, it is surely because he is more read than his Victorian predecessors and because no one can excel him in the careful summing up of evidence which bears on both character and story. But there is always a part of his mind which remembers that *Hamlet* is a drama shaping in Shakespeare's imagination. Bradley is the bridge which joins the nineteenth century with ours. The greatest of the character critics, he concentrates—how he concentrates—on Hamlet's delay, but he refines on the psychological analysis of his predecessors, attributing Hamlet's inactivity not to his native constitution but to an abnormal state of melancholy arising from shock. The importance he attaches to Hamlet's distress at his mother's marriage gives a new critical emphasis, the effect of which will be seen in a period familiar with Freud. But while apparently absorbed in the analysis of Hamlet's character, Bradley shares the philosophical interests of the nineteenth-century Germans. He is careful to note that 'the psychological point of view is not equivalent to the tragic'. For him of course tragedy is not simply a literary genre; it is a way of interpreting the universe. For all his concern with the matter-of-fact details, the play of *Hamlet* suggests to him, especially but not only through the Ghost, how 'the limited world of ordinary experience' is but a part of some 'vaster life'; and though he does not much develop this, he perceives in the action of the play a meaning greater than itself.

The first characteristic of twentieth-century criticism, however, is its reaction against the whole school of character criticism that Bradley is taken to represent. It was after reading Bradley on *Hamlet* that a dramatic critic, A. B. Walkley, said, 'If we want to understand the play of *Hamlet* we shall not do so by assuming that it is a piece of real life, lived by people who have independent lives outside it' (*Drama and Life*, 1907). On this point, if few others, there would seem to be agreement between such diverse critics as Stoll, Wilson Knight and Dover Wilson. The one thing that unites the extremely various twentieth-century studies of *Hamlet*, always excepting the psycho-analytical, is the wish to put the prince back into the play. An early group of scholars discussed how the play grew out of its Elizabethan sources. Robertson, chief of disintegrators, found in *Hamlet* relics of the old revenge play upon which he supposed Shakespeare had grafted the motive of the son's distress at his mother's guilt, inevitably leaving incompatibilities which are the cause of all our difficulties (*The Problem of 'Hamlet'*, 1919). But Robertson is important only because T. S. Eliot, in one of his less happy moments, seems to have swallowed him whole and hence pronounced this most famous of all plays 'most certainly an artistic failure' (*The Sacred Wood*, 1920). But the key word here is 'artistic', for if I understand him rightly, Eliot thought Shakespeare had convincingly presented a psychopathological case. It being the nature of the case that the sufferer's emotions have no 'objective correlative', the play was excluded from providing one, and Shakespeare had set himself an insoluble dramatic problem. The prince would not go into the play. He was, however, being firmly shut up in it by Stoll, who kept insisting that Hamlet's delay was a necessary part of the revenge plot and had nothing to do with his character (*Hamlet: an Historical and Comparative Study*, 1919; *Art and Artifice in Shakespeare*, 1933; *Shakespeare and Other Masters*, 1940). Stoll's insistence on Elizabethan dramatic conventions was a useful corrective; and he could show that Hamlet's horrible sentiments towards the praying king, which the romantic critics had explained away, had their contemporary parallels. Many other scholars have sought to restore the play to its Elizabethan context. We have learnt a great deal about melancholy, ghosts, Montaigne, conscience and much else. And it has all helped us to interpret the play—except when the play has been distorted to fit it. When Schücking tells us that Hamlet himself typifies the Elizabethan 'melancholic' (*Die Charakter-probleme bei Shakespeare*, 1919; translated, 1922), and Lily Campbell that the play gives a demonstration of 'excessive grief leading to destruction' (*Shakespeare's Tragic Heroes*, 1930), we wonder if these views of the play are possibly as lopsided as the ones they propose to displace. The political analogies which Dover Wilson draws between Hamlet's Denmark and Elizabeth's England are unsound, as E. A. J. Honigmann has persuaded me ('The Politics in *Hamlet* . . .', *Stratford-upon-Avon Studies 5*, 1963). Yet Dover Wilson's scholarship has illuminated many dark corners of the play, not least in the notes to his edition (1934). And although we may easily disagree with his account of *What Happens in 'Hamlet'* (1935), his brilliant book has, I think, more than any other, renewed one's sense of the play's sheer excitement. He and Granville-Barker (*Prefaces to Shakespeare: 'Hamlet'*, 1936) in the thirties re-introduced to a wide public a *Hamlet* that was a piece of superb theatrical art; and they had of course a considerable influence on stage practice. They did not, I take it, change the fundamental conception of the play, nor wish to. Though their notions of Hamlet the man were very different, they both regarded *Hamlet* the play as his personal tragedy.

By now, however, a critical re-orientation had begun. In 1931 A. J. A. Waldock, after a masterly review of previous critical approaches, came to the conclusion that Hamlet's 'doubts and hesitations', though 'they are in the design', 'are not the design' (*Hamlet: a Study in Critical Method*). Henceforth, I think, it is the larger design that is looked for. Delay recedes into the background. We hear far far less of the hero's character. What we do hear of are themes. Wilson Knight, writing on *Hamlet* in *The Wheel of Fire* (1930), tried, as he afterwards explained, to see the hero 'not merely as an isolated "character"' but in relation to his 'dramatic environment'. Presently C. S. Lewis invites us to attend less to the prince than to the poem (*Hamlet:*

The Prince or the Poem?, 1942). Maynard Mack speaks of 'the imaginative environment that the play asks us to enter', and goes on to an excellent description of 'The World of *Hamlet*' (*Yale Review*, XLI, 1952; reprinted in *Shakespeare: Modern Essays in Criticism*, ed. Dean, 1957). In Shakespeare's creation of this imaginative 'world', though the characters may contribute, much is ascribed to the imagery, which will also give a clue to the themes. In her investigation of *Shakespeare's Imagery* (1935) Caroline Spurgeon found the predominant metaphors in *Hamlet* to be those of sickness and disease, and she concluded that the play was not focused on a mind 'unfitted to act' but on the rottenness in Denmark, which reflects an inner corruption destroying the whole of life. Wilson Knight saw Hamlet himself as having a 'sickness in his soul'—of which his failure to revenge was merely a 'symptom'. He saw him by his very presence spreading a poison through the kingdom. So, from the thirties onwards, although we continue to read of the Bradleian 'shock' that Hamlet suffers, we read much more of disease, corruption, and infection. D. A. Traversi, for example, describes the action of the play as 'the progressive revelation of a state of disease' (*An Approach to Shakespeare*, revised 1957). Instead of the 'native hue of resolution' being 'sicklied o'er with the pale cast of thought', the image which never fails to be quoted is the one about the 'imposthume', the tumour, which 'inward breaks, and shows no cause without Why the man dies'. But the interpretation of imagery can be a tricky business. Something seems to have gone wrong for Wilson Knight to make Hamlet himself the source of corruption amid a 'healthy' court and to contrast him in his 'death-activity' with such 'creatures of "life"' as Claudius and Laertes (*The Wheel of Fire*; *The Imperial Theme*, 1931). Others suggest that the rottenness is really in the state of Denmark and see Hamlet struggling against it or being infected by it or both. With all the disease in the play and uncertainty in the critics, perhaps it is not surprising that *Hamlet* comes to be grouped among Shakespeare's problem plays, with *Troilus* and *Measure for Measure*. Traversi, Tillyard, D. G. James all, though for different reasons, dissociate *Hamlet* from what they call the 'mature tragedies', the 'undoubted tragedies', or the 'tragedies proper'.

What all these critics would seem to agree on is that the 'problem' in *Hamlet* is not to be found in the hero's character, but rather in the nature of the universe in which he has his being. Tillyard comments on Hamlet's awareness of 'the baffling human predicament between the angels and the beasts' (*Shakespeare's Problem Plays*, 1950). And this predicament of man crawling between earth and heaven is part of that mysteriousness which Maynard Mack sees as the first attribute of the 'world' of *Hamlet*. Its other attributes are 'mortality' and 'the problematic nature of reality'. The views of the various critics do not always coincide, but it is clear that by the middle of this century critical interest in the play has moved away from the theatrical towards the poetic and still more from the psychological towards the metaphysical. C. S. Lewis suggests that many of Hamlet's own speeches give us less an impression of the speaker than of the things he speaks of. Tillyard thinks it a mistake to regard 'the turnings of Hamlet's mind as the substance of the play rather than as the means of expressing another substance'. The prince has got so much inside the play that what he says is more important than he who says it. For Lewis the 'true hero' of the play is man—man, 'incapable of achievement because of his inability to understand either himself or ... the real quality of the universe which has produced him'. For some others Hamlet's inability to understand becomes the centre of the play. It is not a play about being but about knowing, or rather not knowing. This, I think, is how it appears to D. G. James (*The Dream of Learning*, 1951), L. C. Knights (*An Approach to 'Hamlet'*, 1960), and Harry Levin (*The Question of 'Hamlet'*, 1959), though their interpretations are, again, very different. James ascribes to Shakespeare the 'momentous and profound intention' of exploring 'a mind arrested in dubiety before the awful problem of life'; the play is concerned with the inevitable plight of modern man in face of great moral and metaphysical issues. Knights, on the other hand, regards Hamlet's inability to make any affirmation about his world as a sign and consequence of his own spiritual malady. Hamlet's 'inability to affirm', we notice, has taken the place of his old inability to act.

In some respects, at any rate as I see it, this is unfortunate. For as Hamlet's action or inaction leaves the centre of the stage, it seems to take with it the dramatic action too. Levin certainly makes a design out of the play, and a very interesting one, but it is composed of questions, doubts, and ironies. Though James is careful to guard against this, in much mid-twentieth-century criticism one cannot but observe a tendency to abstraction. We have seen *Hamlet* become a play about a 'condition', about life and death themes, about 'the Hamlet consciousness'. It sometimes seems a nexus of images; to Levin it is 'primarily and finally a verbal structure'. The prince has retired so far into the play that he is almost out of sight; and a *Hamlet* without the Prince of Denmark is no longer inconceivable.

The prevailing tendency, however, I think, is to bring him back into view. He is not often *now* the noble hero with a tragic flaw. To Knights he is all flaw, a man who fails in both being and knowing. To Peter Alexander he is all nobility, combining in Shakespeare's 'complete man' the active virtues of the heroic age with the wisdom of a civilized later day (*Hamlet, Father and Son*, 1955). In neither event is he quite that complex, enigmatic person, with feelings and intellect and self-defeated will, who so fascinated our forefathers and kept escaping from the play. His character is viewed, as Alexander puts it, 'as a function of the idea that gives its form to the play'. This idea is what most critics *now* look for; but the idea, or the theme, they are coming to believe, finds expression not *in* yet *through* the hero. Mack insists that Hamlet does not merely discuss the human predicament, he 'exemplifies' it; so that the play acquires an 'almost mythic status'. The words 'myth' and 'archetype' have become common. And the mythic or archetypal quality that has been discerned in the prince, while extending his interest in one way, inevitably limits it in another. For the dramatic action in which he figures is taken to exhibit not so much his personal fortunes as his enactment of a significant role. Thus John Holloway in his recent book, *The Story of the Night* (1961), maintains that Hamlet's role is more important than his character. There seems, however, no general agreement as to what exactly the role is. We must be prepared for symbolical interpretations; and some of them are very symbolical indeed. When Christ appears in the offing, my mind tends to withdraw. Francis Fergusson (*The Idea of a Theater*, 1949) sees Hamlet as a hero who is transformed into a scapegoat, a view which Holloway develops and would extend to other plays.

Whatever we may think of this, and I confess to thinking it unsatisfactory, it is part of the attempt which is being made to reveal in *Hamlet now* that large design, which we all believe to be present, which will give coherence to its structure and will also express its meaning. It does not seem unreasonable to approach this design by way of the play's action, rather than through the imagery, though the imagery and style will help us to interpret the action. Hence Francis

Fergusson examined the interweaving of the play's various but analogous plots in order to find the 'underlying theme, to which they all point'. But misled, as I think, by the recent emphasis on the disease imagery, he centred the play in the imposthume poisoning Denmark, which he saw all the characters as trying to locate and destroy. Like Alexander and H. D. F. Kitto, he compares *Hamlet* with the tragedies of the Greeks. Kitto, though he too may be thought to have the disease imagery out of focus, gives one of the most comprehensive and deeply perceptive interpretations of the play we have (*Form and Meaning in Drama*, 1956). He especially emphasizes how in Greek tragedy a human action is played out against a divine background. In *Hamlet*, too, he views the protagonist not merely as representative man but as a man in relation to some supreme world-ordering power. This is why, if I do not oversimplify him, he would call *Hamlet* a 'religious' drama, as Bradley himself, though he thought the term inapplicable in its stricter sense, was tempted to do. Several other critics in recent years have emphasized this aspect of the play. Roy Walker (*The Time is out of Joint*, 1948) saw the hero, after he had received the revelation of the Ghost, becoming the instrument of unseen powers. More specifically his role is often seen now as that of Heaven's 'scourge and minister'. These words, which Hamlet uses of himself after the slaying of Polonius, have been made the title of one study of the play (by G. R. Elliott, 1951), form the subject of an article by Fredson Bowers (*PMLA*, LXX, 1955), and are central in the interpretation of *Hamlet* in C. J. Sisson's *Shakespeare's Tragic Justice* (1962). The words do not always mean the same thing; Bowers holds that a scourge, as distinct from a minister, is one who has committed crime himself, while Sisson shows us a Hamlet who is God's righteous 'justiciar'. The nineteenth century, beguiled by Hamlet's character and his reasons for delaying his deed, rarely went on to consider how he eventually accomplished it, and paid but scant attention to those references to Heaven and Providence towards the end of the play which we hear much more of *now*. But on the significance of Providence in the play, again opinions differ.

To bring into harmony all these critical interpretations of the tragic action of Hamlet is impossible; and you will hardly wish to add to my task that of synthesizing such of them as are not actually incompatible. But perhaps, in conclusion, I may very tentatively suggest what seem to me to be some of the essential features of this action, with acknowledgments to all those, dead and living, who have helped me to perceive them. I have to agree with Goethe that Hamlet has a great deed laid on him. And whatever the truth about delay, I observe, with the nineteenth-century critics, that for a long time he does not do it. I cannot deny that the deed is one of revenge. I accept from C. S. Lewis the importance of its being commanded by a ghost, with all that this implies. But I hope I may also add that the ghost is that of Hamlet's father, who is not less important than his mother, and whom he sees in his mind's eye as his ideal man with the seal of the god upon him. I believe, with Levin, that fundamental to the structure is the opposition between this Hyperion figure and the satyr figure who has killed him and rules the kingdom in his stead. In company with Kenneth Muir (*Shakespeare: Hamlet*, 1963) I allow myself to connect *this* with all the imagery of disease. I note that the god-man and the beast-man are brothers, sprung from the same human stock, which has also produced Hamlet. I take it from Mack that Hamlet is not only aware of the dual nature of man but exemplifies it in himself. And whatever may be said about his character, I seem to see this duality in his role. For while charged with a deed of revenge, he also incurs vengeance. One of the things that puzzles me is that Hamlet's dual role, as punisher and punished, has received so little critical stress. Yet it is only when he has come to accept it that he achieves his deed—finally killing the king at the moment when he is himself killed, and forgiven, by Laertes, whom he also kills and forgives. And in accepting this dual role, he submits himself to what is called Heaven or Providence; so that with it he also accepts, though he does not comprehend, himself and his own part, so mysteriously composed of good and evil, in that universal design which 'shapes our ends'.

SHAKESPEARE'S IMAGERY—
THEN AND NOW

BY

KENNETH MUIR

My object, in this paper, is to consider the attitude, during the last three centuries, to Shakespeare's use of imagery. There is no evidence that any of his contemporaries were aware of what Caroline Spurgeon was to call 'iterative imagery'; and, although Beaumont, Fletcher and Massinger sometimes echoed Shakespeare's plays, they made no attempt to imitate his characteristic use of metaphor. Ben Jonson is reported by Dryden[1] to have said, in reference to some obscure speeches in *Macbeth*, that 'it was horror'. We do not know to which speeches he was referring, but there are many in which one metaphor evolves from another in a way which would offend a purist:

> And Pity, like a naked, new-born babe,
> Striding the blast, or heaven's cherubins, horsed
> Upon the sightless couriers of the air,
> Shall blow the horrid deed in every eye,
> That tears shall drown the wind.

The image of the new-born babe bestriding the storm, and of the cherubim riding upon the wings of the wind, leads on to that of the wind itself followed by rain which is compared with tears, tears which are also caused by the wind. Although modern readers regard the lines as superbly characteristic of Shakespeare, one can imagine that Jonson would not approve of them.

The next generation of poets regarded Shakespeare with the same kind of suspicion accorded by the poets of the 'Movement' (as I believe it is called) to Dylan Thomas's very different style. Dryden himself, in spite of his recognition of Shakespeare's greatness, complained[2] that his

whole style is so pestered with figurative expressions that it is affected as it is obscure...'Tis not that I would exclude[3] the use of metaphors from passions, for Longinus thinks 'em necessary to raise it: but to use 'em at every word, to say nothing without a metaphor, a simile, an image, or description, is I doubt to smell a little too strongly of the buskin.

Dryden's feeling against what he regarded as an excessive use of imagery is revealed even more plainly in his adaptations of Shakespeare's plays. The long speech of Ulysses on the power of time, which is not so much a logical argument as a series of brilliant images, was omitted altogether; and Troilus' farewell to Cressida, which contains twelve images in sixteen lines, is reduced by Dryden to a single weak image:[4]

> Our envious fates
> Jostle betwixt, and part the dear adieus
> Of meeting lips, clasped hands, and locked embraces.

Even when Dryden and other adapters preserved one of Shakespeare's images, they deliberately simplified the expression of it. In Davenant's version of *Macbeth*, for example, the famous lines

> Will all great Neptune's ocean wash this blood
> Clean from my hand? Nay, this my hand will rather
> The multitudinous seas incarnadine,
> Making the green one red

become deplorably tame and metrically wooden:[5]

> Can the Sea afford
> Water enough to wash away the stains?
> No, they would sooner add a tincture to
> The Sea, and turn the green into a red.

Davenant cuts out Neptune, mangles the great third line, and apparently misunderstands the fourth, thereby justifying his claim to be Shakespeare's illegitimate son.

Little was said in the eighteenth century about Shakespeare's imagery. Pope does remark[6] in his preface that all his metaphors are 'appropriated, and remarkably drawn from the true nature and inherent qualities of each subject'; Joseph Warton complained[7] that some passages in *King Lear* 'are too turgid and full of strained metaphors'; and Lord Kames briefly commended[8] him for the way in which his images were formed of particular objects rather than of generalities. Dr Johnson deplored[9] Shakespeare's quibbles but made only incidental comment on his images.

The only eighteenth-century critic who devoted himself to the study of Shakespeare's imagery was the Rev. Walter Whiter, a learned Cambridge scholar, who published *A Specimen of a Commentary on Shakespeare* in 1794. The first sixty pages consist of an intelligent, but unremarkable, commentary on *As You Like It*. The remaining two hundred pages are given a separate title: 'An Attempt to Explain and Illustrate various passages of Shakespeare on a new principle of criticism derived from Mr Locke's Doctrine of the Association of Ideas'. Whiter tells us in his preface:

I have endeavoured to unfold the secret and subtle operations of genius from the most indubitable doctrine in the theory of metaphysics. As these powers of the imagination have never, I believe, been adequately conceived, or systematically discussed; I may perhaps be permitted, on this occasion, to adopt the language of science and to assume the merit of DISCOVERY.

Whiter's boast was justifiable. Locke had pointed out[10] that

Ideas, that in themselves are not at all of kin, come to be so united in some men's minds, that it is very hard to separate them; they always *keep in company*, and the one no sooner at any time comes into the understanding, but its *associate* appears with it; and if they are more than two which are thus united, *the whole gang* always inseparable shew themselves together.

Whiter emphasizes that Locke's theory relates not to ideas which are naturally connected, but to 'those ideas, which have *no* natural alliance or relation to each other, but which have been united only by chance or by custom'.[11] He declares that commentators had displayed great learning in annotating Shakespeare's intentional allusions to the customs of his own age and to the objects of his satire, but they had neglected to mark[12]

those *indirect* and *tacit* references, which are produced by the writer with *no* intentional allusion; or rather they have not unfolded those trains of thought, alike pregnant with the materials *peculiar* to his age, which often prompt the combinations of the poet in the wildest exertions of his fancy, and which conduct him, unconscious of the effect, to the various peculiarities of his imagery or his language.... In the fictions, the thoughts, and the language of the poet, you may ever mark the deep and unequivocal traces of the age in which he lived, of the employments in which he was engaged, and of the various objects which excited his passions or arrested his attention.

Whiter proceeds to show[13] that 'a certain word, expression, sentiment, circumstance, or metaphor' leads Shakespeare to 'the use of that appropriate language, by which they are each of them distinguished', even where the metaphor is no longer continued; that 'Certain terms containing an equivocal meaning, or sounds suggesting such a meaning, will often serve to introduce other words and expressions of a similar nature'—in other words, Shakespeare's images are sometimes linked by unconscious puns; that the recollection 'of a similar phraseology, of a known metaphor, or of a circumstance, *not* apparent in the text' will lead Shakespeare to use language or imagery derived from these sources; and that an impression on the mind of the poet, 'arising from something which is frequently presented to his senses, or which passes within the sphere of his ordinary observation' will suggest to him 'the union of words and sentiments, which are not necessarily connected with each other'.

The rest of Whiter's treatise, apart from an unfortunate digression on the Rowley poems, is devoted to the presentation of evidence in support of his four propositions. He argues,[14] for example, that in Apemantus' lines in *Timon of Athens*

> What, think'st
> That the bleak air, thy boisterous chamberlain,
> Will put thy shirt on warm? Will these moist trees,
> That have outlived the eagle, page thy heels,
> And skip when thou point'st out?

the word *moist* should not be emended to *mossed*, since a moist shirt was an unaired one, and the epithet was suggested by the previous mention of shirt.

Whiter might, however, have taken this to be an example of the linking of images by unconscious quibbles: *mossed* could be the correct word, suggested to Shakespeare through the intermediary of *moist*. For he himself gives many examples[15] of such links, some of them based on the alternative meanings of weed and suit:

> That we should *dress* us fairly to our end.
> Thus we may gather honey from the *weed*.
>
> (*Henry V*, IV, i, 11.)

> Besides, forget not
> With what contempt he wore the humble *weed*;
> How in his *suit* he scorn'd you.
>
> (*Coriolanus*, II, iii, 229.)

> *Jaques.* I am ambitious for a motley *coat.*
> *Duke S.* Thou shalt have one.
> *Jaques.* It is my only *suit*;
>   Provided that you *weed* your better judgments.
>
>   (*As You Like It*, II, vii, 45.)

One interesting example is to be found in one of Whiter's notebooks.[16] The Sergeant describes how Macbeth

>   *carved* out his passage,
> Till he *faced* the slave;
> Which ne'er shook hands, nor bade farewell to him,
> Till he *unseam'd* him from the nave to th'chaps.

The link between *carved, faced* and *unseam'd* is that all three words are associated with tailoring.

Whiter was the first to point out the presence of image-clusters, including the famous one of flatterers–dogs–sweets, rediscovered in the present century.[17] He shows[18] that the imagery of Romeo's speech in Act I, before he meets Juliet, is repeated in his last speech in the tomb, where he uses the same sequence of stars–seal–dateless–bargain–bitter–bark. Elsewhere[19] he shows that in *Troilus and Cressida*, *The Merry Wives of Windsor* and *Romeo and Juliet*: 'a Wanton Female—a Punk—and the attendant on such a personage, a Pandar, is connected with a Vessel—sailing upon the seas'. He has many examples of the influence of the stage on Shakespeare's imagery, and he shows how the poet's language is sometimes suggested by words in his source, though used with a totally different meaning. He points out,[20] for example, that when the Duke in *Measure for Measure* discourses on the text 'Let your light so shine before men', the language he employs is influenced by the story, on the adjacent page of St Mark's Gospel, of the woman who had an issue of blood:

And there was a certain woman, which was diseased with an issue of blood twelve years.... When she heard of Jesus, she came in the press behind, and touched his garment.... And immediately when Jesus did know in himself the vertue that went out of him, he turned him about in the press and said... who did touch me?

>   Heaven doth with us, as we with torches do,
>   Not light them for themselves; for if our *virtues*
>   Did not *go forth of us*, 'twere all alike
>   As if we had them not. Spirits are not finely *touch'd*
>   But to fine *issues.*

Whiter even hints at the use of iterative imagery when he remarks[21] that there is scarcely a play of Shakespeare 'where we do not find some favourite vein of metaphor or allusion by which it is distinguished'. Although Whiter's book was sometimes cited in the notes to the *New Variorum Shakespeare*, it seems not to have been known to E. E. Kellett who discussed image-clusters and unconscious puns,[22] or to Caroline Spurgeon who rediscovered the use of iterative imagery.

One final example may be given of Whiter's perceptive comments. In one of his notebooks[23] he discusses the line in *Romeo and Juliet* (II, iii, 3):

>   And flecked darkness, like a drunkard reels.

He shows how

this strange imagery has been produced, in which the Dawn is connected with the Drunkard. The darkness of Night, we see, which at the Dawn become flecked with streaks of Light, is associated with the Drunkard, because the poet is impressed with one application of the term *flecked*, which is used to express the spots (or blotches) in the face of a drunken man. But what is more curious, another property is introduced belonging to the drunken man, which is that of reeling; and we shall acknowledge that this circumstance has nothing to do with the imagery of Night, flecked by the streaks of light, which it is only the business of the poet to illustrate. Darkness or night, as connected with the dawn, possesses in our mind no property, from which we should have associated its departure with the reeling of a drunkard. But here again the poet was spellbound; and this imagery was forced upon his mind by another influence of the associating principle. Night is described in this very play, according to the opinion of some, as a runaway, although the passage is obscure...and Warburton compares a line in *The Merchant of Venice*:   For the close night doth play the runaway.

Thus we see, that because Night or Darkness is flecked with spots, as a drunkard is, she is compared to a drunkard, and because night is described sometimes as running away, she is here depicted as reeling away.

Most reviewers of Whiter's book seem to have regarded it as eccentric and there is no evidence that the critics of the Romantic period were acquainted with it. Coleridge in his lectures seems not to have said anything directly on Shakespeare's imagery, but in *Biographia Literaria*, in his discussion of the 'specific symptoms of poetic power' as revealed in *Venus and Adonis*, he remarked:[24]

It has been before observed that images, however beautiful, though faithfully copied from nature, and as accurately represented in words, do not of themselves characterize the poet. They become proofs of original genius only as far as they are modified by a predominant passion; or by associated thoughts or images awakened by that passion; or when they have the effect of reducing multitude to unity, or succession to an instant; or lastly, when a human and intellectual life is transferred to them from the poet's own spirit.

The modification of imagery by a predominant passion is the cause of iterative imagery.

Most Victorian critics focused their attention on the characters, as Coleridge and Hazlitt had done, but there were one or two who showed some interest in Shakespeare's imagery. H. Elwin, who edited *Macbeth* in 1853 under the misleading title of *Shakespeare Restored*, calls attention to the deliberate ambiguity of some of his expressions, and in his preface, oddly entitled 'A Lamp for the Reader', he has some general remarks on Shakespeare's style, its 'significant peculiarities':[25]

These facts of phraseology, and achievements of expression, may appropriately be denominated *the illustrative mechanism* of his composition. Profusely employed throughout his wondrously-contrived dialogues, they are often treated as obscurities, because unappreciated; although, the principle of their application being recognized, they cast a brilliant and certain light upon his treasure-stored page.

Elwin proceeds to comment on Shakespeare's 'practice of continuing a metaphor to an unprecedented extent'. He illustrates this from the lines in *Macbeth* (I, vii):

> But here, upon this *bank* and *school* of time,
> We'd jump the life to come. But in these cases
> We still have judgment here; that we but *teach*
> Bloody *instructions*.

He then comments on the imagery of the passage:

Bank is used for *bench*, and *time*, for *mortal life*; which, qualified as *a bench and school of instruction*, is placed in antithesis to *the life to come*. Here the idea of calling this life *the school of eternity*, as preparing man for the part he is to perform there, is not only thoroughly in accordance with the truthful genius of Shakespeare, but it is beautifully sustained in the expressions that follow it, 'that we but *teach* bloody instructions'. The turn of Macbeth's thought is toward a comparison of the measured time in which, during childhood, we are fitted to fill well the indeterminate period of manhood; and the finite life of this world, in which we purchase for ourselves success or failure in an unlimited futurity. The feeling expressed is this: If here only upon this bench of instruction, in this school of eternity, I could do this without bringing these, my pupil days, under suffering, I would hazard its effect on the endless life to come....The term *bank*, was, possibly, anciently employed for the raised benches of a school; but the judicious selection of it here is, at all events, rendered evident, since it was used to indicate a bench occupied by many persons, placed one above another; as 'a *bank* of rowers'. And the world, with its occupants of various orders, is the *bank* here typified.

Not many critics would agree that *schoole* of the Folio should be interpreted as *school* rather than *shoal*; and Elwin's interpretation of *bank* is likewise questionable. But the passage illustrates his recognition of Shakespeare's use of continued metaphor.

One further illustration may be given of Elwin's method, derived, one suspects, from Whiter. Nothing, he suggests,

displays more largely how he luxuriated in plentitude of power, than his constantly-repeated practice of constructing his sentences in a fanciful allusion, altogether differing from their express purport. As when, in the upbraidings addressed by King Henry IV to that sleep that has become a fugitive from his couch, in order to indicate an involuntary association of ideas in the mind of the royal soliloquizer, whose repose is interrupted by the rebellion of his subjects, the phraseology is fashioned to the notion of a visitation of justice on a scene of tumult; *seizing* and *hanging* on high the ruffians of the riot:

> And in the *visitation* of the winds
> Who *take* the *ruffian* billows by the top,
> Curling their monstrous heads, and *hanging* them
> With deaf'ning Clamours in the *slippery* clouds.

The epithet, *slippery*, glances at doubtful agents of authority, who permit offenders to escape; whilst its direct reference is to the effect produced by the distant billows of a stormy sea; each one in succession seeming to be suspended for a moment in the clouds, from which it presently glides again into the deep.

In the last quarter of the nineteenth century, the New Shakespeare Society occasionally turned its attention to the question of imagery. On 10 January 1879, the Rev. J. Kirkman read a paper[26] entitled 'Animal Nature *Versus* Human Nature in *King Lear*', in which he not merely tabulated 133 separate mentions by twelve different persons of 64 different animals, but argued that 'Darwin would state on biological grounds precisely the same fact in nature as Shakespeare worked out on moral or psychological principles'. Kirkman ends by asserting that if man forgets his nobler qualities he falls back to his animal origins, the moral being (in Tennyson's words) that he should 'let the ape and tiger die'.

Three months later, on 25 April, Emma Phipson, writing on 'The Natural History Similes in Henry VI', maintained that there was no other 'dramatist to whom such constant use of animal metaphors can be ascribed as a special characteristic'.[27] Here, perhaps, we have the first example of imagery being used as a test of Shakespeare's authorship, though Whiter had tried to prove that the Rowley poems were genuine. On 22 April 1887 Furnivall read a paper[28] on 'Shakespeare's Metaphors' by Otto Schlapp, who pointed out the scarcity of mixed metaphor in the early plays and its frequency later. On 8 April 1892 Grace Latham examined 'Some of Shakespeare's Metaphors and his Use of them in the Comedies'.[29] Although her account is pedestrian, she does make a number of valid points about the dramatic function of imagery. She suggests that in *A Midsummer-Night's Dream* Shakespeare for the first time 'employs metaphor to supply the imagination of the audience with the scenery the Elizabethan stage did not possess'; that in the mature comedies the 'form of the metaphors is now employed more frequently to show character'; that the metaphor within metaphor is caused by Shakespeare's wish 'to display character, feeling, ideas'; that in *Measure for Measure* 'the metaphors are still further subordinated to the characters that speak them, and the situations to which they belong'; and that in *The Winter's Tale*

we get fragmentary metaphorical speech, instead of a succession of metaphorical pictures, as in the middle and early period, Shakespere having realized that if we require something more than plain, unvarnished speech to express feeling, it also needs a special kind of mind...to produce highly-finished metaphor, complete in all its parts.

In this paper we have the germ of later studies of imagery by Spurgeon, Clemen and Morozov.

F. C. Kolbe, not long afterwards, wrote a series of articles in a South African journal, *Southern Cross*, which he revised and collected many years[30] later in a volume entitled *Shakespeare's Way* (1930). His thesis was that Shakespeare repeated throughout each play 'at least one set of words or ideas in harmony with the plot. It is like the effect of the dominant note in a melody'. Kolbe showed, for example, that the idea of false-seeming occurs 120 times in *Much Ado About Nothing*, that *love* and *folly* are mentioned 140 times each in *Twelfth Night*, that words of mercantile import occur nearly 300 times in *The Merchant of Venice*, that the key words of *Macbeth* are *blood*, *sleep*, *darkness*, and that the play deals with 'one episode in the universal war between *Sin* and *Grace*'. Kolbe is not consistent in his explanation of this characteristic of Shakespeare's plays: at one point he speaks of it as deliberate artifice, but in general he seems to assume that it rather reveals the unconscious workings of Shakespeare's mind.[31] Kolbe's method has been adopted by several later critics as an adjunct to the study of imagery.[32]

E. E. Kellett, in his 'Notes on a Feature of Shakespeare's Style',[33] rediscovered, apparently without knowledge of Whiter, the association of ideas linking many of Shakespeare's images, and he provided a number of examples of the way in which consecutive ideas and images are linked by hidden puns. In *The Tempest*,[34] for example, the word *cast*, in the sense of 'thrown', suggested to Shakespeare the casting of a play and, in the following lines, a number of theatrical terms:

> though some *cast* again,
> And by that destiny, to perform an *act*,
> Whereof what's past is *prologue*, what to come
> In yours and my *discharge*

where *discharge* means 'performance'. It is but a step from Kellett to William Empson's *Seven Types of Ambiguity* and M. M. Mahood's *Shakespeare's Word-Play*.[35]

The concentration on imagery between the two wars may have been influenced by the rediscovery of the Metaphysicals and by the Imagist movement. In the twenties there was a whole series of books and articles which touched on the subject: Henry W. Wells' *Poetic Imagery* (1924), Stephen J. Brown's *The World of Imagery* (1927), George Rylands' *Words and Poetry* (1928), Elizabeth Holmes' *Aspects of Elizabethan Imagery* (1929) and essays by J. Middleton Murry and others. At the same time Caroline Spurgeon began to publish the results of her study of Shakespeare's imagery,[36] and the first of her projected books on the subject, *Shakespeare's Imagery and What it Tells us*, appeared in 1935. It must be confessed that the first part of the book, in which we are informed of the revelation of Shakespeare the man through the imagery, is not very revealing. That Shakespeare was sensitive, that he had remarkable powers of observation, and that he was intimately acquainted with nature, merely confirms what we knew before; that he 'is absolutely clear-eyed, but rarely bitter' can hardly be proved by a study of imagery; and we cannot legitimately deduce that he was a good carpenter because he admired good carpentry, or that he blushed easily because he noticed that people do blush.[37]

The second part of the book is more valuable. Miss Spurgeon proves her contention that many of the plays have what she calls 'iterative imagery', a group of images drawn from one special field. The limitations of her method have become apparent during the thirty years which have elapsed since her book was published. It has been shown, for example, that the iterative imagery can often be interpreted in more than one way; that her card-index leads to the ascription of equal significance to a conventional derived image and to a highly charged imaginative image; that at times the imagery may reflect the poet's personal feelings which may run counter to the theme of the play; that many plays have several strands of iterative imagery; that we ought not to consider imagery in isolation from character, plot and structure; and that, as Rosemond Tuve has pointed out,[38] 'the basis upon which images are now most frequently differentiated and classified, i.e. the area from whence comparisons are drawn because of personal predilections of the author' is 'an unfirm basis, if not indeed an aesthetically irrelevant consideration'. These are all serious criticisms but they do not, I think, render Miss Spurgeon's book entirely worthless. It is difficult to believe that the sickness imagery in *Hamlet*, the cooking imagery in *Troilus and Cressida*, and the clothing imagery in *Macbeth* are quite without significance, even if we disagree with Miss Spurgeon's interpretation of them.

Meanwhile G. Wilson Knight had begun his series of interpretations with a modest booklet entitled *Myth and Miracle* (1929), soon followed by *The Wheel of Fire* (1930) and many others. Although these books have been influential, I do not propose to discuss them here, partly because I have written of them elsewhere,[39] and partly because they are concerned with many other things besides imagery.

The next important book on imagery was W. H. Clemen's *Shakespeares Bilder* (1936), revised after the war as *The Development of Shakespeare's Imagery* (1951). He concentrated on the dramatic function of imagery, showing how Shakespeare used it as decoration in his early plays, and organically in his mature ones, both to reveal character and to create atmosphere. He also showed that the plays from *Richard II* onwards had interwoven patterns of imagery which contributed to their dramatic effect.[40]

Meanwhile, before the publication of Clemen's English edition, Edward A. Armstrong had analysed in *Shakespeare's Imagination* (1946) a number of image-clusters in Shakespeare's plays associated with various birds and insects (e.g. kite, goose, beetle) and he suggested—though this was incidental to his main purpose—that the presence of these clusters could be used to establish Shakespeare's authorship of disputed scenes. The evidence is striking; but it needs to be supplemented by a study of Shakespeare's contemporaries to make certain that the associations are peculiar to Shakespeare. An American correspondent has recently called my attention to one of the 'Shakespearian' clusters in Webster. As Armstrong himself points out,[41] the wider the net has to be cast in seeking the constituent parts of a cluster, the greater is the element of chance. The kite-cluster in *The Two Noble Kinsmen*, for example, which I have myself used as a test of authorship, is spread over 31 lines.[42] It would need a mathematician to work out the odds against this being fortuitous.

Donald Stauffer's excellent book, *Shakespeare's World of Images* (1949), despite its title, was not primarily concerned with imagery. Brents Stirling's *Unity in Shakespearian Tragedy* (1956) argued that the unity in six of the plays was provided, or at least reinforced, by the imagery. Meanwhile Robert B. Heilman in *This Great Stage* (1948) and *Magic in the Web* (1956) had analysed the patterns of imagery in *King Lear* and *Othello* and related them to the characters and the structure of the plays. He carried the study of the dramatic use of imagery to the limit and sometimes, as in his analysis of sight-imagery in *King Lear*, he went, perhaps, beyond the limit. But the interpretation of the two plays, and especially of *King Lear*, still seems to me of considerable value. The big guns of the Chicago school were called up to demolish *This Great Stage*.[43] W. R. Keast declared that it was 'in almost all respects a bad book'; that *King Lear* is 'strictly unintelligible on Heilman's assumptions'; that 'the effect of the play suggested by his interpretation is one which no one has ever attributed to *King Lear*, which is, moreover, inappropriate to tragedy, and which, finally, Shakespeare's text does not support'.[44] It seems to me, on the contrary, that the interpretation of the play which emerges from Heilman's book is perfectly intelligible, largely traditional, and supported throughout by continual reference to the text. It is a pity that Keast set out to make a speech for the prosecution, since the tone of his article makes one distrust even the valid criticisms he offers of Heilman's method.

One other book may be mentioned—Maurice Charney's *Shakespeare's Roman Plays* (1961)—which is a model of its kind. He does not make the mistake of discussing imagery apart from its dramatic context and he is fully aware that the plays were written to be performed. The book shows that in the hands of a sensitive critic the study of imagery can be illuminating.

Nevertheless, it must be confessed that in recent years the study of imagery has fallen into disfavour. It was not to be supposed that Stoll or Charlton would approve of the school of

Knight; but their criticisms have been reinforced by those of Rosemond Tuve, Helen Gardner and Roland M. Frye.[45] Even L. C. Knights, who began his career with an attack on Bradley and the proclamation that *Macbeth* was 'a statement of evil',[46] has come round, if reluctantly, to the admission that character is important.

Miss Gardner properly criticized[47] Cleanth Brooks for his comments on 'Pity, like a naked new-born babe' because he was 'more interested in making symbols of babes fit each other than in listening to what Macbeth is saying'. The critic's attention has been distracted

from what deeply moves the imagination and conscience in this vision of a whole world weeping at the inhumanity of helplessness betrayed and beauty destroyed. It is the judgement of the human heart that Macbeth fears here, and the punishment which the speech foreshadows is not that he will be cut down by Macduff, but that having murdered his own humanity he will enter a world of appalling loneliness, of meaningless activity, unloved himself, and unable to love.

Although this criticism is valid, I do not think it entirely disposes of Cleanth Brooks's essay. It rather emphasizes that imagery must be studied in relation to its context and to its precise function in relation to character and situation: and surely the images of breast-feeding, put into the mouth of Lady Macbeth, her reference to 'the milk of human kindness', and even Malcolm's mention of 'the sweet milk of concord', do in fact symbolize the humanity and natural human feelings which are outraged by the murderers.

It is not my business to estimate the value of the New Criticism and its contributions to the interpretation of Shakespeare, but perhaps I may, in conclusion, outline some of the ways in which the study of Shakespeare's imagery could be profitably pursued in the future. In the first place, a lot more needs to be done on the sources of Shakespeare's images: what little has been done suggests that many of them have a literary origin.[48] But although, for example, the cluster of flatterers–dogs–sweets may have a literary origin,[49] Shakespeare's continued use of it, especially in *Timon of Athens*, may have a personal significance. Secondly, it is desirable to have a comprehensive study of the use of imagery by Shakespeare's contemporaries, particularly the dramatists. It may be found that some of the image-clusters which are thought to be peculiar to Shakespeare may rather be due to some association shared by his contemporaries. At the same time, as many of the image-clusters discovered by Armstrong, who is an ornithologist, were connected with birds, it may well be that many others remain to be discovered. Thirdly, it is important to distinguish between kinds of imagery and not to lump together the prosaic, the conventional, the casual and the imaginative, as Caroline Spurgeon did, believing she was following an objective, scientific method. Fourthly, every image must be considered in its context, in relation to the speaker and to the situation. The images can, indeed, be studied scene by scene, rather than by the spatial method favoured by Wilson Knight. Several critics have noted how imagery is used to differentiate character and how Othello, after he is infected with Iago's jealousy, uses the same kind of imagery as his enemy.[50] Lastly, as Clemen has emphasized,[51] the study of imagery cannot be isolated from other branches of criticism. We need 'to correlate the separate methods of investigation and to show the interdependence of style, diction, imagery, plot, technique of characterisation and all the other constituent elements of drama'. It will often be found that the study of imagery reinforces, rather than supersedes, other methods. I found, for example, when I came to make a detailed study of the imagery of

Macbeth, twelve years after I had edited the play, that the resulting interpretation was identical to the one I had reached before; and this was not, I think, because I was already incubating the disease in 1948.

NOTES

1. J. Dryden, *Of Dramatic Poesy and other Critical Essays* (ed. 1962), I, 173.
2. *Ibid.* I, 257.
3. The editions I have consulted read 'explode'.
4. J. Dryden, *Works*, ed. Scott and Saintsbury, VI, 349.
5. W. Davenant, cited in the *Furness Variorum*, p. 515.
6. Cited in D. Nichol Smith, *Shakespeare Criticism* (1916), p. 48.
7. *Ibid.* p. 69.
8. *Ibid.* p. 72.
9. *Ibid.* p. 92.
10. Cited Whiter, *op. cit.* p. 64.
11. *Ibid.* p. 65.
12. *Ibid.* pp. 71, 73.
13. *Ibid.* pp. 69–71.
14. *Timon*, IV, iii, 222; Whiter, *op. cit.* p. 81.
15. *Ibid.* pp. 84, 87, 83.
16. For this I am indebted to Mr G. A. Over.
17. Cf. E. E. Kellett and Caroline Spurgeon discussed below.
18. *Op. cit.* p. 124. *R.J.* I, iv, 107; V, iii, 111.
19. In an unpublished notebook (cf. n. 16, above).
20. *Op. cit.* p. 254. Whiter does not cite the Geneva version, as given here, nor does he refer to the adjacent text.
21. *Op. cit.* p. 124.
22. See n. 17, above.
23. See n. 16, above.
24. Coleridge, *op. cit.* (ed. 1921), p. 169.
25. H. Elwin, *op. cit.* pp. iii, ix, x, xvii.
26. *N.S.S. Trans.* 1877–9, pp. 385–405.
27. *Ibid.* p. 365.
28. *Ibid.* 1887–92, p. 24*. The paper was written as a doctoral thesis for Strasburg University, and a copy of it has been traced by Terence Spencer.
29. *Ibid.* pp. 397–427.
30. *Southern Cross* apparently ceased publication in 1901; but Kolbe speaks of his essay on *Julius Caesar* as having been written 'some thirty years ago'. Elsewhere he speaks of an incident in his childhood sixty years before the time of his writing.
31. K. C. Kolbe, *op. cit.* pp. 87, 95, 71, 3 ff., 145–6.
32. E.g. W. Empson and Brents Stirling.
33. *Suggestions* (1923), pp. 57–78.
34. *The Tempest*, II, i, 242.
35. Cf. also K. Muir, 'The Uncomic Pun', *The Cambridge Journal* (1951), pp. 472–85.
36. *Leading Motives in the Imagery of Shakespeare's Tragedies.*
37. *Op. cit.* pp. 200 ff.
38. *Elizabethan and Metaphysical Imagery* (ed. 1961), pp. 254, 420.
39. *Shakespeare Survey* 4 (1951), p. 20, and *Penguin New Writing*, No. 28 (1946).
40. For *Richard II* see Richard D. Altick's article, *PMLA* (1947), pp. 339–65.

41. *Op. cit.* (ed. 1963), p. 203.

42. K. Muir, *Shakespeare as Collaborator* (1960), p. 118. Although I refer to words separated by fifty lines, the cluster is complete without.

43. W. R. Keast, 'Imagery and Meaning in the Interpretation of *King Lear*', *Modern Philology*, XLVII (1950).

44. *Ibid.*

45. Cf. p. 56, n. 38, above, and p. 57, n. 47, below. Roland M. Frye, *Shakespeare and Christian Doctrine* (1963), p. 41, remarks sweepingly that 'From the appearance of *The Wheel of Fire*...those who have followed Knight's type of analysis have proliferated in number and productivity, but they have contributed very little of any real worth to the understanding of Shakespeare'.

46. L. C. Knights, *How Many Children Had Lady Macbeth?*, reprinted in revised form, in *Explorations* (1946), p. 18. His later attitude can be seen in *Some Shakespearian Themes* (1959) and *An Approach to Hamlet* (1960).

47. *The Business of Criticism* (1959), p. 132. She was referring to Cleanth Brooks's essay, reprinted in *The Well-Wrought Urn* (1949).

48. See, for example, *Shakespeare's Poetics*, by Russell A. Fraser (1962), and *Shakespeare's Derived Imagery* (1953), by John E. Hawkins.

49. Cf. James L. Jackson, *Shakespeare Quarterly*, I (1950), p. 260.

50. E.g. S. L. Bethell's article, *Shakespeare Survey 5* (1952).

51. *The Development of Shakespeare's Imagery* (1951), p. 231.

THE STUDY AND PRACTICE OF
SHAKESPEARE PRODUCTION

BY

JOHN RUSSELL BROWN

I have chosen such a large subject because I have only one point to make with regard to it: that the study of Shakespeare production from then to now in England has too little acquaintance with the professional practice of Shakespeare production today. In some other countries this statement would not be true, but I am sure that English scholars are neglecting an important task.

Few would deny that scholarship should try to make the literature of the past alive in the present, as fully, and as accurately, as possible; and yet it is on these grounds that I would argue that we have left a great part of our work undone. The themes, meaning, relevance, art and artifice of Shakespeare have been studied; the printed text has been improved rather than ravaged with time; the Elizabethan theatres and their practices have been minutely studied; later productions, including those of today, have been recorded and evaluated: but this is insufficient. Shakespeare's plays live in the theatre, and it seems to me that scholars should ensure by active and practical assistance that they do so as fully and as accurately as possible. Of course many who write about Shakespeare hope that their work will be read by professional directors and actors; but the wish does not ensure the deed; nor that what is read is helpful. In the seventeen annual volumes of *Shakespeare Survey* since it was founded in 1948 there have been reviews and reports of productions; but among the more than two hundred articles that represent the original work of scholars throughout the world those in which a knowledge of Shakespeare's text or of the past is brought directly to bear upon the practical problems of staging the plays today number only five. *Shakespeare Survey* contains much that a theatre director or actor could use, but he would have to search, and research, in order to find it, and, in a sense, translate. Few scholars have first-hand experience of the director's problems; and there is probably a larger number who have no wish to know about them. Many of the authors of *Shakespeare Survey* are interested in the text of the plays and its background, and in the plays' action and sound in the theatre of their own minds, untrammelled by the physical, technical and temperamental facts of any one production. They write about the words and their meanings, the presentation of narrative, character or theme, and about an unlocalized, disembodied performance that satisfies their conception of an Elizabethan performance. Other scholars discuss Elizabethan acting or stage-equipment in order to establish Elizabethan practices, not to make suggestions about how the plays should be staged today.

I am not arguing, simply, that scholars do not write for professional directors, and therefore are not influencing in useful ways the presentation of Shakespeare's plays in our theatres. There is a further step to take: that the scholars lose as well as the directors. Unless an interpretation or criticism is presented with reference to actual production its author will often fail to realize half of Shakespeare's achievement, or get one element out of proportion to the rest.

A play reveals itself in rehearsal: verbal ambiguities, emphases, hesitations; the forcefulness of a silent figure; the dispersal of an audience's interest, or the relaxation of tension, due to the time taken for a song, or for a corpse to be laid in the ground; a sharpness or irrelevancy in the writing which tends towards humour. Modern productions are not like Elizabethan ones —they could never be wholly so—but the freedom of rehearsal will be closer to Elizabethan conditions, and it is in rehearsal that many practical implications of Shakespeare's writing reveal themselves briefly. And, no matter what shortcomings a single production may have, if the scholar has known it from its first rehearsal he may submit to a performance in a very full and critical way, to the continuous impression of the play and the physical presence of the actors. He also witnesses the results of each actor's sustained concern with the words of his part. There is, I believe, no short cut to such knowledge. Let Henry Irving speak for me, from a lecture he gave to Harvard University in 1885:

We are sometimes told that to read the best dramatic poetry is more educating than to see it acted.... There are people...who fancy they have more music in their souls than was ever translated into harmony by Beethoven or Mozart. There are others who think they could paint pictures, write poetry, in short, do anything, if they only made the effort. To them what is accomplished by the practised actor seems easy and simple. But as it needs the skill of the musician to draw the full volume of eloquence from the written score, so it needs the skill of the dramatic artist to develop the subtle harmonies of the poetic play. In fact, to *do* and not to *dream*, is the mainspring of success....

How can I fairly show that scholars writing today fail to write about the play as if it were in performance? Close your eyes for a moment and suppose that the last scene of *Antony and Cleopatra* is in rehearsal; before you are the actors and the stage.... What would you tell them?...Here is John Holloway on this scene, in his recent *Story of the Night*; try to use his words in your instructions:

Only just behind the stage spectacle of the queen of Egypt in all her glory, is the sense of an outcast from society—gipsy, felon, whatever it may be—baited as the victim of the common people....

And later:

Caesar's closing tribute to the nobleness of both queen and servants fuses with a sense of Cleopatra's having been brought to the level of humanity at its simplest and most primitive; to the bedrock of life. As near to an animal as a human creature can come, the victim is hunted by his own kind until, with whatever justice and whatever nobility, his life is taken. Death is no mere crowning misfortune; it is almost recognized, by protagonist and pursuers alike, as the stylized act which fitly closes a stylized sequence. (Pp. 119–20.)

How can the actress show 'death' is 'almost recognized' as a stylized act? How can the whole play be a '*stylized* sequence'? Indeed, what *is* a 'stylized *sequence*'? How does Cleopatra come to the 'bedrock of life'? How does a verbal tribute '*fuse* with a *sense*' of anything at all? Holloway is writing about the scene we are considering in rehearsal, and he may interpret it as we do; but could his words be used to control the enactment of that scene? At least they will need some translation. And might not his discussion be more meaningful if it could be used in part to tell actors about the scene in rehearsal or performance?

If Holloway wrote for the director of the actors, besides being, necessarily, more direct and precise, he would notice other elements. A 'stage spectacle' is not simple. Caesar's presence —a Roman within the Egyptian monument—speaks as well as his words. So does the still and silent body of Cleopatra: no longer answering with words or action, but a still object baffling our scrutiny. And the slow, silent involvement of the '*Exeunt*' would again revalue Caesar and Cleopatra: Caesar is now watching; Cleopatra is borne carefully aloft by soldiers moving, necessarily, together.

Let me take a second example from another particularly instructive and intelligent book, Mrs Anne Righter's *Shakespeare and the Idea of the Play* (1962), a recent study specifically concerned with theatrical matters. This is its passing comment on the concluding scene of *All's Well*; read it and imagine that you have to instruct the Helena:

When she reveals herself at the end of the play, her first words are to deny the King's 'Is't real that I see?'

> No, my good lord;
> 'Tis but the shadow of a wife you see,
> The name and not the thing.

As G. K. Hunter points out in the New Arden edition of the play, the word 'shadow', that familiar associate of the actor's, here signifies ghost and imitation together. Only Bertram's 'Both, both! O, pardon' (v, iii, 302) can confer a palpable existence upon Helena, freeing her at the same time from illusion and non-being. (P.176.)

Here the critic spends time to remind us of the exchange of words; but how much help will it give to the enactment of the scene to assert that 'only' Bertram's brief words can 'free' Helena? How shall the freedom 'at the same time from illusion and non-being' be conveyed? Has Shakespeare given sufficient scope for this? We may imagine, or 'sense', or (in Irving's word) 'dream', this change in Helena; but how is it to be effected? by what means? and how do those means compare with the rest of the dramatic context? And how important is the change in relation to the rest of the last scene? Quoting words and identifying verbal crises is not sufficient: criticism should relate to the complex visual, temporal and verbal content of each dramatic moment.

I suggest that scholars who wish to keep Shakespeare fully alive in his proper theatrical context cannot rely on their own, unrealized sense of what is theatrical. In the theatre of the mind a brilliant verbal crux can fill the limitless stage, and the actors, groupings, tempo, rhythm, focus, even the more literary qualities of narrative and exposition, can be completely eliminated: the appropriateness of the word is sufficient and no other problem remains. But in the tangible world of the theatre nothing can be forgotten. Everybody is there, and the stage is there, and time is passing always: a director cannot ignore any of these elements. It would be a suitable discipline for a scholar to write all the time for a director, the one practical and wholly engaged man whose experienced approval would be worth whole lecture-rooms of others. To write for him, the scholar would have to be in close touch with professional productions. He would learn most from producing plays himself. Something of this can be done with students or amateurs, but not enough. The scholar should work with artists who bring a mature experience and a professional engagement to their task, and in a theatre without the distracting pressures of amateur or occasional productions but with an ordinary, paying, non-academic audience. Scholars often deplore the fashions and expediencies of the commercial theatre; but so far, in this country at any rate, the commercial theatre is the only continuous and mature theatrical enterprise, and must therefore provide the basis of the scholar's knowledge.

Perhaps more practical scholarship would bring about better productions. But no one could promise this; it is still to be proved, in practical terms, that the scholars are better Shakespearians, more able to keep his plays alive, than the theatre directors. We can only be sure that they are different Shakespearians. Here is a description of scholarship by a director of the Old Vic Company, before he became Professor of Drama at the University of Manchester:

The approach of a producer to the text of a Shakespeare play differs from that of a scholar. Literary criticism is abstract and largely impersonal, for the scholar must base his assertions on fact and his conjectures must be hedged with authority. The producer, however, has not the benefit of footnotes; he can give neither authority for, nor explanation of, his assertions....However much he may and should use the scholarship of the literary critic to provide him with background and knowledge, it is his imagination and his judgement that will finally affect his interpretation. For the producer has to take into account a primary factor of the stage which is unnecessary and unbecoming to the scholar—the live performance of the play to a contemporary audience.[1]

The temptation is to cry 'A plague on both your houses!': surely the directors need not relegate facts to the background; and surely the scholars should take into account 'the live performance of the play to a contemporary audience'.

The lack of sustained acquaintance between scholars and practitioners affects more than the interpretation of individual plays; the general mode of presentation in our theatres is also in question. While directors experiment with new techniques, scholars should measure their innovations against past experience of Shakespeare production 'from then till now', and might sometimes suggest new experiments. But today, in England, this does not happen. Our directors experiment right enough; they lap up suggestions from Brecht, Beckett and Artaud, from the Royal Court (the theatre), films and television; and they are influenced by the past through the work of the Canadian Shakespeare Festival. And elsewhere—in another country, almost—the scholars write about the past and make hypothetical or small-scale reconstructions of a Globe theatre.

The present arrangements for producing Shakespeare are so different from the Elizabethan that it can seem unlikely that historical studies could ever be relevant to today's theatre practice. Buildings, both stage and auditorium, equipment (especially lighting and scenery), actors' training and conditions of work, the introduction of actresses, methods of rehearsal and organization, the large printed programmes with biographies of actors and directors and conflicting contentions about the plays, the importance of journalistic comment and of private or public finance, the influence of television and films, the times and places of performance, the composition of audiences, the pronunciation of English, current fashions and notions, are all new, and all apparently impervious to scholarly criticism. But the difficulty of a subject need not deter a scholar: he should gain first-hand experience of his material and, then, try to learn how to describe it. A few have begun the task, and write with scholarly responsibility about performing Shakespeare today. But more work must be attempted, and more practically than hitherto.

One aspect of Shakespeare production—the part played by the director—has recently been the subject of scholarly debate, by Alfred Harbage in his pioneering *Theatre for Shakespeare* (1955) and in an article in *Shakespeare Jahrbuch* of the same year, and by Clifford Leech in an article called 'The "Capability" of Shakespeare' in *Shakespeare Quarterly* (1960). In calling for a closer acquaintance between study and practice in Shakespeare production I would like to follow this debate and elaborate my argument by considering its important subject. I shall try to show that such problems require a rigorous historical study, a knowledge of the whole story of Shakespeare production 'from then till now'; and also that there is no substitute for first-hand experience of the practical task of rehearsal and production.

The two scholars agree that the director has today overstepped the proper bounds of his authority. 'Shakespearean production', writes Harbage, 'has become wildly experimental with the more aggressive directors as the master-minds.' Leech quotes him at length and with approval:

I believe that the great problem for the director is how to avoid imposing himself upon the play and the audience, and that his only safe course is to blank out from his mind any over-all critical conceptions....[His] concern should be only with each individual speech and action as it appears, and [his] guide only the script. To maintain that the production under such circumstances would have no coherence or unity is to deny that coherence and unity have been provided by the author....The presenters should stick to the writing and let us form our own conclusions.[2]

Of course there are today bad, impertinent, cheap, flashy productions: there have always been plenty of inferior artists in any art. But Harbage is arguing, from an historical and scholarly standpoint, that theatre directors are new functionaries who are mis-directing Shakespeare. In the *Jahrbuch* Harbage uses the scholarly ploy of comparing present practices with earlier conditions: 'Presumably when there were no producers [or directors] there were no views [about the plays], and the plays of Shakespeare were vital and persuasive in their own right, as well as self-interpretive.'

This is a challenging position and yet I think it has not received sufficient answer from scholars or directors. Besides reviews, I am aware chiefly of Leech taking the argument a step further by relating the problem more widely to Shakespeare's dramaturgy: 'I am not so sure as he is', he writes of Harbage, 'that the dramatic author will always provide "coherence and unity".' Yet he remains in agreement, arguing that where there is no unity and coherence, 'the director should not try to impose them but should allow the unresolved contradictions of the playwright to emerge freely in the performance'. Indirectly, of course, more has been said, notably among the scholars by Bernard Beckerman in his *Shakespeare at the Globe* (1962) and by David Klein in a note called 'Did Shakespeare Produce his Own Plays?' in *The Modern Language Review* of the same year. But both these writers are concerned with the Elizabethan theatre rather than actual practices in theatres today.

Klein's note is important for gathering evidence to support the German report of 1613 that in England 'even the most eminent actors have to allow themselves to be taught their places by the dramatists, and this gives life and ornament to a well-written play'. Especially relevant is his contention that besides Quince, Shakespeare's author-director, every other author of a play-within-a-play in the Elizabethan drama is shown directing the performance. 'Let me return to the original presenters', writes Harbage: 'They were craftsmen of the theatre, and happily nothing more.'[3] But if the author gave instructions to the players, this statement needs rephrasing; it should take account, for example, of the Restoration report, not quoted by Klein, that John Lowin 'had his instructions' for the role of Henry VIII 'from Mr. Shakespeare himself'.[4]

Directors who try to give coherence to productions may have found a new name—they have an increasingly onerous task in controlling the elaborate equipment of our theatres—but their function is not new; 'instruction' has always been necessary. Certainly by the eighteenth century, for which our documentation is much fuller, the director could have precise power. Here is the actress Kitty Clive on Garrick's methods:

I have seen you, with your magical hammer in your hand, *endeavouring* to beat your ideas into the heads of creatures who had none of their own—I have seen you, with your lamb-like patience, endeavouring to make them comprehend you; and I have seen you when that could not be done—I have seen your lamb turned into a lion: by this your great labour and pains the public was entertained; *they* thought they all acted very fine,—they did not see you pull the wires.[5]

Not perhaps the best method to direct; and in his own day Garrick was criticized for turning actors into images of himself. But clearly this director had his 'ideas'. Garrick wrote no criticism, did not express his 'ideas' in words—as Shakespeare and earlier practitioners did not —but, obviously, he had them. Our directors are not the first to think, and conceive. Garrick frequently devoted three to eight weeks to rehearsals of a new play, following his own study of the text. Despite the demands of a repertoire of Elizabethan proportions, he took two months for *Timon* in 1771, and exceptionally, for *Every Man In His Humour*, he rehearsed for a whole year. Such labour was required to get his own way with a more permanent company of actors than most of those performing Shakespeare today.

As scenery became more elaborate the director's task was increased. Here is Ellen Terry describing Irving's methods:

When he was about to produce a play, Irving did everything himself. Although he did not understand a note of music, he would, through intuition, feel what the music ought to be, and would pull it about and have alterations made. He was nearly always right. Irving's directions to the composer were sometimes very amusing. He would hum a few bars spasmodically, with action of the hands, in a very expressive manner, and then say, with an air of finality, 'Now, go and do that'....

It was exactly the same with the lighting and the scenic work.... 'So it was', Miss Terry said, 'with everything. The only person who did not profit by his talent for teaching was myself. I continually said to him, "But, sir, why don't we rehearse together?" and always he answered, "O, we're all right! What I've got to fear are those limelight men. They're the people we've got to rehearse".'[6]

Harbage professes special admiration for Granville-Barker's productions, as the work of a director not concerned with the display of his own notions. But, in his time, Granville-Barker was highly controversial, and his conception of the plays awakened considerable adverse criticism. They had fantastic and highly fashionable settings that took attention away from the actors, especially so in his most famous productions of *A Midsummer Night's Dream* and *The Winter's Tale*. It was argued that they spoke for themselves not for Shakespeare's play:

The fault of Mr. Rothenstein's colours [one considered account of the productions noted] is there is no vital reason for them. Like the columns and curtains and cottage [of Norman Wilkinson's setting], they do not spring from a vital necessity.

The same critic found fault with the director for his treatment of the text (as Harbage and others blame our directors), saying that the speaking lacked 'the essential sense of rhythm which Shakespeare's lyricism demands'. These comments are from a book on *The Theatre of Max Reinhardt* and are part of a comparison of two very individual directors.[7]

That Granville-Barker had a clear and unifying concept of a play has recently been illustrated by Sir John Gielgud's account of the production of *Lear* in 1940:

Barker refused to have his name officially announced as director, and only agreed to supervise some rehearsals, using his own preface to the play as a foundation. I went to see him at the Queen's Theatre, and nervously endeavoured to read the part through with him. When I got to the end he remarked: 'You got two lines right. Now we will begin to work.' He also said: 'Lear is an oak. You are an ash. We must see how this will serve you.'[8]

'Lear is an oak': this 'idea' must be accommodated to the talents of the actor.

In some way or other each production must be given a unity, even, remembering Leech's addendum, if that involves the audience in an unresolved moral or emotional response. Indeed a director cannot avoid an interpretation of his own. One of the main difficulties with rehearsing Shakespeare is that too much is discovered in the text; a speech of twenty-five lines will yield so many jobs for an actor to do that it would take five minutes to enact them all; and at that rate an average Shakespeare play will take 500 minutes to perform, or eight hours without intervals.

'Their concern should be only with each individual speech and action as it appears': as I read Harbage's words, I could swear that he has never directed a play, or attended any but single or youthful rehearsals. Any tolerably hardworking production of Shakespeare is liable to play too long when it is first run through; and with the subsequent cutting, if not before, the director must select; and for selection there must be some governing idea. Moreover, 'hey-dey, freedom': 'do what you can with each individual speech and action as it appears' is no Shakespearian recipe in the face of conflicting possibilities: it is Jack Cade and Caliban who are given that advice to speak, or, rather, shout. Free energy is dissipated energy. The rule of an engineer that energy must be contained and controlled if it is to do useful work is largely true of art; modern abstract painting may look uncontrolled, but the best of these painters work with greater, or more private, concentration than almost any other generation of painters. Shakespeare's plays may seem as if they should bloom as easily as leaves come to a tree, but such perfect ease will come through control, through a long gestation and co-ordinated operations. Authors or, failing them, directors—under some name or other—have always been necessary functionaries in the presentation of plays; for shaping, selecting, innovating, and allowing the full power of some aspects of the plays to be developed, now one aspect and now another.

Harbage suggests that a play should be 'self-interpretive', but no one can supply instant production. Leech asks for 'fidelity to the text', and says that the height of a director's ambition should be to let us hear its many voices, whether they make up a consort or jangle out of tune; but every voice of the text cannot be heard at any one time and different actors will be able to accomplish different aspects of the same role, limited by their vocal powers and their temperaments—if Lear is an oak, the actor may be an ash. How should Prince Hal say 'I do; I will'? In the 1964 Stratford-upon-Avon production, the second half comes after a pause of deliberation. At Edinburgh, in Joan Littlewood's production, the whole speech is said rapidly, as Hal hastily dismounts from his improvised throne because of knocking at the door; and here, in the mounting urgency before the Sheriff enters, it is Hal's later words that gain in edge, in rebuke of Falstaff: 'thou art a natural coward . . .', and of himself: 'Now, my masters, for a true face and good conscience.' Which of these two ways is correct? Can fidelity to the text help? Do the four monosyllables hold the secret to tell us which way is correct? It has been remarked that the knocking on the door following 'I do; I will' is intended to emphasize the dramatic force of Hal's speech; but the knocking was first marked in the text by the editor, Capell; neither the quarto, from foul papers, nor the edited Folio version has any sign of it. As far as Shakespeare's text goes Bardolph might enter to interrupt Hal in the middle of a sentence. Or another completely opposite interpretation is possible. It may *not* be 'I will' that speaks Hal's deeper consideration, or contains a threat; the text itself could accommodate a contrary reading: firmly, '*I do*'—that is, 'at this moment I most certainly do'—and then lightly, 'I will'—that is, 'no; not yet'. The text *needs* interpretation, and so actors need 'instruction', as the Elizabethans called it.

An actor is seen as well as heard. How shall Hal be dressed? He could wear some, or all, or none, of the marks of royalty in this scene. He could imitate the foolish charade-like costume of Falstaff with a cushion for a crown and a dagger for a sceptre. He could move around, or be quite still. Leech asks for a 'neutral' production; and Harbage for Shakespeare 'pure and undefiled'; but in performance there are no such things. Even the lack of special costumes or a minimum of stage movement speaks for the individual production, modifies its impact, according to what *sort* of non-special costumes, *which* minimal movements. Harbage suggests that stage-business should be left to individual actors; but this too would lead to idiosyncratic productions, and very difficult ones to act in or to watch. In short, there can be no neutral production; there must be guidance, and a suitable overall conception for the local conditions of the building, actors and audience; the director's task is to find the most useful and the most responsive to the text of the play as a whole, and this involves selection and 'ideas'.

Supporting his contention that productions should involve the minimum of business, Harbage refers to what he takes to be Elizabethan practice: 'reading Shakespeare and seeing Shakespeare in the theatre were, in his own times, less disparate experiences than they have been at any time since'.[9] His chief authority for this view is the observation that when plays were printed, their stage directions were rarely amplified, and that 'laconic though they certainly are, they were nevertheless deemed a sufficient guide to visualization'. But the brevity of stage-directions in printed editions might indicate that those who prepared the texts were aware that none could be adequate. There are a few indications, surviving almost by chance, that Elizabethan performances did elaborate on the printed text in much the same way as our own actors do. The most notorious are the players' additions to *Hamlet* occurring in the Folio text which have been examined by Harold Jenkins.[10] Almost certainly, after Burbage had spoken the last words that 'had been set down for him:

> he has my dying voice.
> So tell him, with th'occurrents, more and less,
> Which have solicited—the rest is silence.

he continued his performance; he added something represented in the prompt book as 'O, o, o, o.' By a chance survival from Shakespeare's foul papers in the Good quarto of *Hamlet* we know that the author intended Hamlet's first contribution to the play to be, not his first words: 'A little more than kin, and less than kind', but a piece of surprising stage-business—his silent entry after the King and Queen, the Council, and Polonius and Laertes, an appearance out of his proper place according to degree. Perhaps a good director or actor would have stumbled on this piece of business without the stage-direction; but we cannot be sure. In *Romeo and Juliet*, the heroine comes to Friar Lawrence's cell to find Romeo ready to marry her, and there is decorous speech before the lovers talk together:

> Here comes the lady. O, so light a foot
> Will ne'er wear out the everlasting flint.
> A lover may bestride the gossamer
> That idles in the wanton summer air
> And yet not fall, so light is vanity.

Juliet replies to the Friar before uttering a word to Romeo:

> Good even to my ghostly confessor.

The Friar replies:

> Romeo shall thank thee, daughter, for us both.

And she, speaking now of Romeo in the third person responds:

> As much to him, else is his thanks too much.

Then, at length, Romeo addresses Juliet directly. What sort of enactment do these words suggest? I think they suggest a careful control, a restraint and delicacy; after a quick entry, a halt, some formalities, and then the delayed meeting of the lovers. But the boy actor of Juliet or his 'instructor' had none of this; we know from the 'bad' quarto that what happened was '*Enter Juliet somewhat fast, and embraceth Romeo*'. All the other directions in this quarto with 'and' in them imply almost simultaneous actions, so the natural interpretation is probably right: the lovers embrace at once. The Friar's words cover and contrast with the embrace, and refer, at least in part, to both the lovers. There is more humour too, for Romeo has 'thanked' her, as the Friar describes their embrace, before this is talked of: thus the 'shall' would mean 'must' or 'inevitably will'. The privacy, impulsiveness, mutuality of the lovers' delight in each other is thus delicately presented in a way that the words alone could not suggest. Sometimes with Shakespeare's direction, and doubtless sometimes without, the Elizabethan actors presented more than the 'text'.

I have dealt at this length with Harbage's view of a director's task, because I believe that the study and practice of Shakespeare production should go hand in hand. I have tried to show that his point of view is limited by lack of knowledge about the actual processes of rehearsal.

And, by the way, I have interpreted some evidence about Elizabethan and later productions in a different way. This also makes an important point: that in the more obvious concerns of scholarship—the study of Elizabethan practices and of theatre history generally—there is much work to be done, indicated by wide disagreements. (Similar divergencies would be apparent if I had talked mainly of the acting styles of the Elizabethans, of their use of stage-space or of properties and scenic elements.) The small details that have survived need further study by scholars who are widely read, especially perhaps in textual studies, and who also are able to put their theories to the test of practical experiment.

An historical perspective on contemporary practice is a contribution that only the scholar can bring to the theatre; and one that, couched in practical terms, alive to the realities of production, could be a salutary influence. For example, an obvious reflexion on the present proliferation of experimentation, or on a manifesto like Peter Hall's *Crucial Years* (1963), is that innovation has *always* been part of the theatrical scene. Hall is unusual, most the innovator, in seeking experiment for its own sake: 'We want to be in a world of experiment', he writes (p. 18). In other times directors innovated in order to have a greater or a different impression of reality, or to show off the exceptional powers of an individual actor, or to conform to some critical presuppositions. In his fashionable way of speaking Hall has said that he does not expect 'final solutions', but wishes to 'keep open'. His concept might be described as 'Experimentation in Public'; this is what is new in what he has to say, and scholars should hail it as such and, from a study of production from Shakespeare's day to our own, offer a definition of its implications; and, perhaps, alternative suggestions.

Scholars should be able to see further than immediate practical problems, and in the complexities of Shakespearian production that could be an important asset. They should be able to identify important developments and comment on the general strategy of our theatres. For example, one considerable innovation of very recent years is not always recognized as fully as the history of Shakespeare in the theatre suggests that it should. This is the emergence of directors who are not, and often have never been, actors. When the author and then the principal actors or managers directed the players, they were also still engaged in their primary capacities. But Irving's trouble with the limelight men was a sign that their tasks were growing enormously, and of the need for a separate functionary known as a 'director'. At first these were recruited almost entirely from among the actors: Stanislavski, Gordon Craig, Granville-Barker, Reinhardt. But today in England directors start as directors, or are often recruited after very little acting experience: Tyrone Guthrie, Peter Brook, Tony Richardson, William Gaskill, Peter Hall. This is, I think, a great danger: for the history of Shakespeare in the theatre shows that all the most notable innovations—Garrick's, Kean's, Irving's—have been intimately connected with ways of acting, with the manner of giving life to individual roles. The director's theatre has brought new achievements, of course—Granville-Barker's, Craig's, and those of our own day—but it would be unfortunate if direction by non-actors should lessen the chance of further innovation from the individual, imaginative and skilful exploration of great actors. Special precautions should be taken so that the actor has scope for invention within a general control; he must be able to influence productions, for he alone can 'prove' an interpretation in action and speech, and *must* remain close to the text. Shakespeare's poetic and psychologically expressive plays need the actor's involvement—close, imaginative and humble.

Even when the director is an actor, he may in his directing capacity inhibit others. Sir Laurence Olivier speaks of his cast as a general of his troops:

The actor must be disciplined. He must be so trained that he automatically carries out the director's orders. I expect my actors to do exactly what I tell them to do and to do it quickly,...I believe the director must know the play so well that he grasps every important moment of every scene. He knows—and he alone—when the action should rise and where it should fall. He knows where to place the accents.[11]

Another way of speaking is to consider the director as a conductor of an orchestra; Harbage, for example, draws this analogy. But a Shakespeare play is not very like a symphony: all the actors do not speak, predictably, at once; often in Shakespeare only one person is on stage—an eighth of *Romeo and Juliet* is soliloquy and for large stretches of time—three-quarters of many plays —there are no more than four characters on stage. Moreover, an actor has a much greater scope for timing, pitch, tone, interpretation, than a musician; no one can positively prove an actor is out of key, or out of tune. A director is neither an old-fashioned military man, nor a conductor: he must choose, control and also encourage his actors; and it follows that he must know a great deal at first-hand about acting. Although a director's general 'idea' is necessary, a good production will bring surprises, even to the actor who may originate them. This was Garrick's view:

the greatest strokes of genius have been unknown to the actor himself, till circumstances, and the warmth of the scene, has sprung the mine as it were, as much to his own surprise as that of the audience. Thus I make a great difference between a great genius and a good actor. The first will always realize the feelings of his character, and be transported beyond himself.[12]

If directors do not respect this kind of engagement, but expect actors to carry out orders 'automatically', a kind of sensation for which the past tells us Shakespeare has well provided may be unnecessarily denied to our audiences.

Scholars do, of course, help directors in details: the meanings of words; the meaning of references to music, or of stage-directions for battle-scenes; the procedure for ceremonies; the ideas behind certain arguments in the plays. There are reference books and dictionaries which are immediately helpful, and in such details many directors *do* rely—as far as their time allows—on scholars. But such works illuminate 'then' rather than 'now'. There is far more detailed work to do, as well as general. Scholars can analyse and compare; and they have time—more time than directors, at any rate—to take pains. Hidden in the text, in single lines and throughout whole plays, there may well be secrets: how to speak a particular speech, whether a persistent rhythm is required, or loudness; where to indulge the modern actor's love of pauses, and where this should be resisted; what objectives the scene-designer should have; how important, and in what ways, is the crowd, in this scene or that. With very very few exceptions, scholars have not had the knowledge of practical production that can suggest what to look for, test their discoveries, and enable them to write in ways that theatre directors can immediately understand.

But here, as at the beginning of this lecture, I am presupposing that scholars should work with, and in, the professional theatre; that they should be familiar with the problems of production involving mature actors, a professional rigour, and an ordinary audience. Such a meeting is not practicable in this country at the present time; and, until it is, we can only theorize, look back to Granville-Barker, and argue that a close acquaintance would lead to a fuller and more responsible criticism—perhaps more comprehensible criticism; and also, perhaps, to more satisfactory ways of ensuring that each production realizes its full potential, in a way that answers, as well as may be, to the text as a whole and in detail.

I know music scholars who conduct orchestras, and also compose. I know students of art who administer galleries and also paint. I know scholars of English Literature who are novelists, poets, editors. But I do not know any Shakespeare scholar in this country or America who is able to work in a consistent way with the professional theatre. This is absurd; and could be remedied very easily.

Actors, and theatres in suitably non-academic environments, are available, especially in the summer months when scholars are comparatively free from teaching duties. £10,000 a year for seven years would enable a university department to complete a significant series of productions and studies.

NOTES

1. H. Hunt, *Old Vic Prefaces* (1954), pp. x and xi.
2. *Theatre for Shakespeare*, pp. 58–9.
3. *Ibid.*, p. 59.
4. J. Downes, *Roscius Angliscanus* (1708), p. 24.
5. Quoted, K. A. Burnim, *David Garrick, Director* (1961), p. 61.
6. M. Menpes, *Henry Irving* (1906), pp. 33–5.
7. H. Carter, *The Theatre of Max Reinhardt* (1914), pp. 292, 295–6.
8. *Stage Directions* (1963), p. 51.
9. *Theatre for Shakespeare*, p. 82.
10. Studies in Bibliography, xiii (1960), 31-47.
11 From an interview in the New York *Times*, 7 Feb. 1960; quoted in *Directors on Directing*, ed. T. Cole and Helen K. Chinoy (ed. 1964), p. 412
12. Letter to Sturz, quoted by F. Hedgecock, *David Garrick and his French Friends* (1912), pp. 244–5.

SHAKESPEARE ON THE SCREEN

BY

LAURENCE KITCHIN

Shakespeare's plays were written to be used by live actors in the presence of a crowd. It follows that all screen versions of them are subject to the limitations of the screen. Neither the actors nor their audience can conform to the conditions which the author had in mind. Instead of the text there will be a script; instead of the actor in person, there will be his image in two dimensions. Any situation in which the substitute looks like gaining ground over the original would have a vital bearing on Shakespearian studies, but today the screen, the substitute, has not only gained ground on Shakespeare productions in the theatre. Apart from a minority, it has superseded them; and the scholars and critics who make it their business to assess the plays and Shakespeare's intentions have scarcely begun to be aware of the fact. Yet around them is building up the pressure of a public, including scholars of the future, which draws its assumptions about Shakespeare from what happens on the screen.

This public far outnumbers anything heard of in the history of the theatre. For the B.B.C.'s *An Age of Kings*, the serial version of the history plays, the average viewing audience was three million; for its successor, the Roman plays titled *The Spread of the Eagle*, four million. These figures do not include audiences in the U.S.A. and elsewhere. If we bear in mind that the series were viewed in many places where there was little competition from the professional theatre, and in most places none at all, it means that the producer-director of these television versions, Peter Dews, is by a long way the most influential interpreter of Shakespeare in the English-speaking world. Granting the skill and freshness of Dews's approach, it would be a pity if his versions were taken to be definitive. For one thing, most of the star roles were inevitably undercast. Frank Pettingell's Falstaff was a jaded stereotype and Paul Daneman's Richard III was later to be seen at the Old Vic, with little success. For another, the small television screen is notably ill-adapted to Roman mobs. It may well be the wrong medium, anyway, for epic drama, whether Shakespeare's or not. But audiences in Canada or Bradford are not likely to have such reservations, and so a drastically limited image of Shakespeare gains enormous circulation, infecting audiences in particular with television's allergy to lyricism and rhetoric, in fact to any form of heightened speech. There is plenty of intrigue and horse-opera left in the histories, plenty of conflict and passion in the Roman plays, it is true, when they are taken as prose. We still need to be on the alert, however, when this has been done to a great manipulator of words who is also a dramatist. We still need to estimate the loss. What the new mass audience most obviously represents to Shakespeare scholarship is a pressure of semi-literate opinion. Inasmuch as it will not tolerate verbal artifice this is ill-informed opinion; and it is steadily mounting, conditioned in part by the notorious limitations of television as a medium for drama. For its version of *Hamlet*, starring Christopher Plummer, the B.B.C. expects a total audience of near to 100 million.

With television scraping the barrel for living script-writers, its recourse to Shakespeare is inevitable, quite apart from prestige reasons. We must learn to live with the results. Compared with the medium's routine output they are excellent; compared with a good stage production they are cramped and perfunctory, at their best, perhaps, when the camera can hold one character at a crisis of emotion or a group round a conference table. The first fits the groove of hysteria in close-up, a cliché of television plays. The second conforms to a familiar layout in discussion programmes. In many ways, you would think, the cinema screen is the better one for Shakespeare. And so it is. It has room for epic sweep, for the battle scenes you feel Shakespeare would have been the first to elaborate if he had had the means, not to mention big areas of colour. Also it has a slight but distinct tradition of verbal rhetoric—Laughton's delivery of the Gettysburg speech in *Ruggles of Red Gap*, Muni as Emile Zola, Carnovsky as Anatole France in the same film. The cinema audience is already more of a crowd, a target for rhetoric, than the family group watching television, and crowds are easily massed on the cinema screen. As the reactions of the screen crowd are predetermined, the two can never be synchronized, but the live audience sees a lot of people listening to a speaker and will join in. When epic breadth and formal rhetoric were combined on film with a popular actor, the result was very satisfactory Shakespeare. I mean Olivier's *Henry V*. The trouble is that Shakespeare on the cinema screen costs a great deal of money.

As soon as big money comes into the reckoning, students of Shakespeare find themselves up to the neck in showbiz at its most garish and capricious. You can no longer hope for statistics because 1944, the year of *Henry V*, is as remote as 1600 from the mind of any showman of the 1960's. Knowing that film to have been a breakthrough, you might expect half-a-dozen of Olivier's best roles to have been filmed in the twenty years between 1944 and Shakespeare's anniversary; instead of which there is only a splendid *Richard III* and, working against the grain of his temperament, *Hamlet*. A meticulously prepared version of *Macbeth* is still on the shelf. Similarly, you might expect a follow-up to Joseph L. Mankiewicz's very good *Julius Caesar* (1952). It came, all right, in 1963, as a rescue job by the same director on *Cleopatra*, using Shakespeare's sources but not his words and wasting a first-class heroic actor, Richard Burton. This too we must learn to live with, in the spirit of *Put Money in thy Purse*, a sardonic account by Michael MacLiammoir of his part in Orson Welles's *Othello*. Usually the history of cinema Shakespeare has more to say about showbiz, in its most bizarre Hollywood form, than about the Bard himself, but the most unlikely places can offer valuable documentation. I remember going to a Bradford cinema to see a Hollywood revue called *The Show of Shows* of 1929. Suddenly there was a grumble of gunfire, a glimpse of smoky battlefield and then the face of John Barrymore, a handsome vulture in close-up as Richard of Gloucester. He delivered the soliloquy about Richard's deformity from *Henry VI, Part 3*, using the identical phrasing and intonation and spitting consonants that you can hear in his recording on disc. It was every bit as good as Olivier's delivery of the same passage, with a notable difference in context. Barrymore's came between turns by Ted Lewis and Rin Tin Tin.

His unlikely intrusion on *The Show of Shows* is a good example for the double standard you can apply to Shakespeare on the screen. Here was a fine interpretation going the round of fleapits in an ephemeral revue, presumably with no other motive than to cash in on the actor's name. Barrymore had been a top star of the silent films. Every schoolgirl had swooned at his Don Juan; every schoolboy had gloated over the scene where they cauterized him after Ahab's leg was cut off in *The Sea Beast*, a silent version of *Moby Dick*. From one point of view his

Richard of Gloucester fragment is a variety act in an early sound film, a hunk of ripe melodrama linking the turns of a comic and a performing dog. From another it is, or was, a valuable document in the history of classical acting. For a few minutes those polar opposites, the needs of the box office and the needs of scholarship, happened to come together.

Unless we think the plays can be improved on by media which did not even exist when they were written, the cinema's only firm claim to importance in this field is as a storehouse of individual performances. Olivier's voice on the sound track of *Henry V* is a good deal less thrilling than it was at the Old Vic in 1937, his screen image a poor substitute for the living actor. What wouldn't we give, all the same, for a film of Irving or Garrick? If the cinema had been invented two hundred years earlier it would not, as I have heard suggested, supersede the critic. Hazlitt on Kean would still be worth reading, because he reports and transmits the unrepeatable live performance, the public 'happening' as distinct from the studio 'happening', fixed eternally by the camera. What the screen preserves is everything except whatever it is that keeps an audience quiet when a great actor comes in sight. The screen, in fact, conveys as much of his art as he is conscious of himself, plus any intuitive bits that can survive the flattening, the shrinking to an image in two dimensions. Having done so much, the screen becomes of great value to Shakespeare studies, because the plays offer more scope to the individual actor than we usually care to admit, and a dominating actor can influence the criticism of an entire generation. It is important to know as much as we can about him. Hence the frustration which goes along with the cinema's handling of Shakespeare, with a medium which records for posterity Olivier's Hamlet instead of Gielgud's, Maurice Evans' Macbeth instead of Olivier's, and from a crop of obvious candidates no Coriolanus at all. Some of the results have been so good that it is not much consolation to remember that this is showbiz, that posterity was rarely in anybody's mind.

Ironically enough the most determined efforts to pin down famous stage performers were made when the cinema was least able to deal with them, when it flickered hectically and had no sound. A collector's piece of around 1902 put Arthur Bourchier and Violet Vanburgh in front of a static camera as the two Macbeths. Although this ought not to be regarded as a reliable record, the performances are distinctly hammy, more so, I imagine, than later versions would seem with the sound track silenced. The movies take over when Macbeth's attackers camouflage themselves as Birnam Wood. One soldier raises big laughs by getting separated from the main body and scuttling back to them, still holding his branch. The Benson company's *Richard III* of 1911 is also portentously hammy, without any escape into comic relief. On the whole, one prefers the approach of the people who made a one-reel burlesque of *The Merchant of Venice*, one reel of *Othello*, as an animated cartoon. There was little point in tackling Shakespeare seriously until the movies could speak.

After the first primitive period, half piously theatrical and half frivolous, there was a lull until the talkies came, and with them Douglas Fairbanks senior and Mary Pickford in *The Taming of the Shrew* (1929). I escaped from an unusually dull day's cricket in Manchester to see this film, but all I remember of it is Fairbanks eating an apple in church with incomparable Elizabethan panache. The speech of that famous couple of silent days was never their strong point. During the thirties, however, there were a few carefully prepared battles between Shakespeare and the cinema, ending in stalemate. Although Barrymore's Mercutio and Edna May

Oliver's Nurse would be worth seeing again, Leslie Howard's Romeo and Norma Shearer's Juliet for M.G.M. never took fire. In England, Paul Czinner directed an *As You Like It* built round the elfin charm of his wife Elizabeth Bergner. As her accent and speech rhythms work against Rosalind's lines, the film is mainly important for its accurate and civilized recording of the diction and acting styles of Henry Ainley, Leon Quartermaine and the young Olivier. The classic of the period is Reinhardt's *Midsummer Night's Dream* (1935), a unique example of a top theatre director at work on Shakespeare with the full resources of Hollywood. Here the best sequences have more to do with Mendelssohn than Shakespeare. The music goes along with a mobile, gliding camera as they explore the woods. It is true cinema, in the same decade as early René Clair. But nobody except Ian Hunter (Theseus) has a clue about speaking the verse. The enduring successes are a matter of inspired casting. Instead of being a lyrical clown, Mickey Rooney's Puck is raucously earthy, a corner-boy of the forest. James Cagney's Bottom, the best I have ever seen, never forgets his local status. He is a craftsman; he sets up a play as if he were setting up a loom. This is twice as funny as the customary rural oaf, twice as poetic when the weaver grows a donkey's head.

Showbiz is only partly assimilated in the three big films of the thirties. Reinhardt has a Hollywood co-director, William Dieterle; the woods are alive with anti-poetic voices. M.G.M's Juliet is married to one of the firm's senior executives, Rosalind is the wife of her director. In relation to Shakespeare, that is what I mean by caprice. You have to remember the great performances which never found a place on the screen. When the breakthrough came, the Olivier films, it was a by-product of war. It began with *Henry V*, not seen as the crown of an epic series as we take it now, nor as G.C.E. fodder, but as propaganda, with audiences predisposed to swallow the rhetoric. Generals were actually urging their troops on in terms of sport. It was no time for distancing the King by having him make his first entrance holding a cricket bat. That happened sixteen years later at the Mermaid, in a different world. If *Henry V* arises from the war situation, so does Olivier's *Hamlet* of 1948. It has a morose, claustrophobic atmosphere, dulled by the heavy masonry and dark corridors of Elsinore. It reflects European compression, what Camus called 'the lyricism of the prison cell'. The three Olivier films are continually revived, and I only want to make three points about them here. First, their availability gives them a vast influence on interpretation, more than a stage version can exert. Secondly, they are examples of epic and compressionism, open and shut, the two main forms of modern drama. Thirdly, they are the result of an artist, that is a top actor-director, having full control of the means of production. The last of them, *Richard III*, dates from 1955, since when nobody of comparable authority has had the same costly facilities.

From the point of view of Shakespeare studies, foreign versions, even at the high level of Yutkevich's *Othello*, Kozintsev's *Hamlet* and Kurosawa's *Throne of Blood* (Macbeth), are limited because they discard the text. Even the stodgy *Macbeth* of 1960, with Maurice Evans and Judith Anderson, is more relevant, because it preserves acting of varied styles, including those of three recent Hamlets, in the same scene. But cinema versions depend once more on the industry's caprices, and television's far more enterprising approach is lamed by the visual poverty of the medium. The crucial fact is that neither of these handicaps inhibits the screen as a trend-setter. How far, for example, did Rooney's Puck influence the playing of this part in the theatre? Tom Courtenay's Puck in a recent Old Vic production was on the same lines. There may have been no connexion between them at all. On the other hand, ripples sent out from the film years ago or in revival may be active yet. Sooner or later it must be the business of scholarship to find an answer. Again, how far was the Royal Shakespeare's *Wars of the Roses* of 1964 sparked off by the success of *An Age of Kings* on television? And what was the significance of Brando's Antony in the film of *Julius Caesar*? The last question at least is easily answered. Brando's Antony has conditioned the playing of this role, in the theatre as well as on the screen, for more than ten years.

As I see it, the bearing of all this on Shakespeare scholarship is twofold. First, the screen provides a valuable form of documentation, securely based here on the National Film Archive. In using it, the researcher can expect surprises. Even the early primitive phase of the movies has a major contribution, that is, Hepworth's silent film of Forbes-Robertson's Hamlet of 1913. Few would have guessed that this actor, renowned for his intelligence and voice, had also a range of gestures as rhythmic and varied as those of Ruggiero Ruggieri. With slight allowances for the actor's old age and the medium's infancy, the Forbes-Robertson film is not only a document but an unforgettable experience. Of films aiming only at entertainment, one hopes that two adaptations of Compton Mackenzie's *Carnival* have been preserved, for comparison of Matheson Lang and Sebastian Shaw in the last act of *Othello*.

In its other capacity, that of trend-setter, the screen is potentially a menace. It has given Shakespeare his biggest audience. Up to a point it can lead that audience, but it is a mass audience which demands concessions. How far concessions can go we have seen in the theatre, where the meditative, the lyrical, the aristocratic and even the royalist and Renaissance aspects of the plays are toned down, 'rethought' or disregarded on the grounds that we do not see life that way now, or more likely from cowardice, from lack of confidence in the plays themselves. The air of apology, whenever they are put on today, owes a good deal to moving pictures. 'This', we were told at the beginning of Olivier's *Hamlet*, 'is the story of a man who could not make up his mind.' That is the authentic, over-simplifying demagogic, package-deal tone of mass communications, equally insulting to the audience and to Shakespeare. One of its tendencies has already been to invade the theatre with screen values, screen emphases and even, as in *Henry V in Battledress*, the screen itself. Ultimately, the only defence against it will be informed, responsible criticism, as much at home in the techniques of cinema and television as in Shakespeare's text.

SHAKESPEARE IN THE OPERA HOUSE

BY

WINTON DEAN

There have been so many operas founded on Shakespeare's plays—I know of nearly 200—and the question of what constitutes a good opera, and why, raises so many complex considerations, that I cannot hope to do much more than scratch the surface of the subject. Admittedly the average artistic level is not high. With the exception of a few masterpieces, which can be counted on the fingers of one hand, and a scarcely larger group, mostly based on the comedies, that are good for an occasional airing, you are never likely to hear them in performance. Any interest they possess is historical, and it concerns the history of opera rather than of Shakespeare. Sometimes too they have a certain entertainment value of a type not envisaged by their authors.

The scarcity of masterpieces is hardly surprising. A great opera, depending on a balance between several arts—music, drama, scenery, spectacle, ballet—of which the two most important, music and drama, are notoriously unaccommodating bedfellows, is rare in any circumstances. When one half of the partnership is based on a literary classic, the chances are slenderer still. It is not just a matter of the librettist being faithful to the play and the composer writing agreeable music. A whole series of compromises is necessary if the different time-scales imposed by music and the spoken word are to be reconciled; and the opera, if it is to be worthy of the occasion, must not only rise to the play, musically and dramatically: it must add something of its own. Otherwise there is no point in its existence.

This has not deterred scores of composers of all periods and nationalities from trying conclusions with Shakespeare. They include many of the greatest, though not all of them managed to finish their task. Among the abandoned projects are Beethoven's *Macbeth*, Tchaikovsky's *Romeo and Juliet* and the *King Lear* operas of Debussy, Puccini and Verdi—the last of which was on the stocks for something like half a century. Mendelssohn at various times planned an opera on *The Tempest* with three different librettists, one German, one French and one Italian. Sometimes bad luck seems to have taken a hand. Mozart died immediately after accepting a libretto on the same play, though such a peculiar one that it is difficult to imagine him setting it as it stood. Smetana went mad while composing an opera on *Twelfth Night*. Against these disappointments we have Verdi's three Shakespeare operas and others by Purcell, Rossini, Bellini, Nicolai, Berlioz, Bloch, Holst and Britten. They are not all of equal merit, but none of them deserves to be forgotten.

Before returning to them it may be of interest to take a glance at the whole field and then consider the approach of different periods and countries to Shakespeare as an operatic source. Of the 27 tragedies and comedies, all but two—*Titus Andronicus* and *The Two Gentlemen of Verona*—have inspired at least one opera. There are a few on *Henry IV* and *Richard III*, but for obvious reasons the histories have proved less popular. At the other extreme *Romeo and Juliet* is almost an operatic cliché; it has everything—star-crossed lovers against a background of family feud, duels, dancing, crowd scenes, a wedding and a pathetic finale among the tombs. This was the perfect subject for romantic composers, especially in France and Italy, but its

75

appeal has not been confined to them: *Romeo and Juliet* operas have first seen the light in places as operatically remote as Minorca, Middlesbrough and Mexico City. Quite a number of them enjoyed considerable success in their time, though not many are heard today.

The chief attraction of *The Tempest*, especially for German composers, has been the opening it gives for symbolism and allegory. This is reinforced by the striking resemblance between the characters and those of Mozart's *Magic Flute*. Prospero offers a parallel to Sarastro, Miranda to Pamina, Ferdinand to Tamino, Caliban to Monostatos; Trinculo or Stephano will do at a pinch for Papageno, and Ariel—who moreover plays a magic pipe—for the Three Genii. There is even a potential Queen of Night in Sycorax, who though she is only mentioned in the play appears as a character in several *Tempest* operas. It is no accident that this play sired a whole brood of German operas in the decade after *The Magic Flute*, and quite a lot more during the nineteenth century. Nor is it surprising that they are nearly all very bad—generally because the librettist has deposited such a weight of symbolism on the plot that the characters emerge as caricatures or abstractions or a mixture of the two. This has been an unlucky play in the opera house. With the partial exception of Purcell no composer has managed to translate its essentially lyrical quality into music, and most of them make Prospero preach like a cross between Wagner's Gurnemanz and a Presbyterian divine.

It is a very odd fact that the Germans, who have probably the best translations of Shakespeare, have achieved almost no success in turning him into opera. Of nearly fifty attempts, the only one that comes near to hitting the mark is Nicolai's *Merry Wives of Windsor*—and Nicolai spent an important part of his career in Italy. If I may now plunge into rash generalization, German opera composers have tended to make Shakespeare sententious or sentimental, the French have often made him just sentimental, the English have made him dull, while the Italians have turned him into roaring melodrama. There are of course exceptions in each case. For reasons to which I shall return, the Italian method, when refined, has produced the most satisfactory results.

It has also produced plenty of failures, especially with the great tragedies, which the Italians have set repeatedly, whereas the Germans, wisely, have left them alone. There are no German operas on *Hamlet*, *Lear* or *Othello*, and only one—a singularly tame work—on *Macbeth*. It is the comedies that have inspired the most varied treatment—operas of every conceivable type from a Handelian *opera seria* on *As You Like It* to a modern American musical, from Purcell's Restoration Masques to a German serial setting of *Troilus and Cressida* with overt reference to the last war, from Fibich's portentous Wagnerian music drama on *The Tempest* to sexy French operettas on *Cymbeline* and *All's Well that Ends Well*. Audran's *Gillette de Narbonne*, based remotely on this last play, consists almost entirely of waltzes and polkas in the manner of Offenbach. Of the libretto I will only say that the character corresponding to Shakespeare's Diana, that virtuous Florentine, becomes a promiscuous gipsy who declares that a man has only to whisper the word 'Turlututu' in her ear for her virtue instantly to collapse.

Every age is inclined to see its own reflexion in Shakespeare, to take what it wants from him and leave the rest. This is as true inside the opera house as outside. The idea that a libretto ought to preserve as much as possible of the spirit, plot and characters of the play is comparatively modern. Until about the middle of the nineteenth century, and in some countries much later, the composer and his librettist simply converted the play into the type of opera then in fashion. Shakespeare was no more treated with the respect due to a classic than is the grist that goes into the Hollywood mill today. This was not so very different from the treatment he received in the straight theatre, even in England, where the 'improved' versions of Dryden, Cibber, Garrick and others were still acted in the nineteenth century. People who first made their acquaintance in the theatre, whether here or abroad, probably did not know what was Shakespeare and what was not. It has recently been shown that even such a fanatical Shakespeare-lover as Berlioz based his dramatic symphony *Romeo and Juliet* not on the original text but on Garrick's perversion of it.

There is another reason why we cannot expect to find satisfactory Shakespeare operas before the nineteenth century. Until the time of Mozart's maturity the art of opera was not sufficiently developed to cope with a drama of such complexity and sophistication. Serious opera, an entertainment devised for courtiers and aristocrats whose principal interest was in the singers (and the ballet dancers, if there were any), consisted almost entirely of recitatives and solo arias. Composers of comic opera in Italy were beginning to develop the ensemble, but it was not till Mozart adapted these methods to higher artistic purposes, and the French Revolution altered the whole social basis of opera, that an adequate instrument was available.

There had been Shakespeare operas long before this. The earliest, those of Purcell, are scarcely operas at all in the modern sense. What mattered to the Restoration audience was not the play or the music but the spectacle—the stage machinery and the dancing. To make openings for this, elaborate masques were introduced with mythological characters who had nothing to do with the story; and it was in these scenes that the music was concentrated. Hence there were two separate casts, one for acting and one for singing, and the composer scarcely came into contact with the dramatist at all. In *The Fairy Queen*, based on *A Midsummer Night's Dream*, Purcell never set a line of Shakespeare, even where the poetry seems to cry out for it. The final scene for instance was replaced by an entertainment in a Chinese garden, complete with a chorus of 'Chineses'. In *The Tempest* Shakespeare himself supplied a masque in the scene for the three goddesses; but this was not good enough for the Restoration writers, who substituted a much more spectacular affair for Triton, Amphritrite and other marine deities, and also adorned the play with a whole range of new characters. This time Purcell did set two of Ariel's songs; it is not much, but just enough to give us a glimpse of what this great dramatic composer might have achieved with a tolerable libretto.

In the 1750's J. C. Smith, a pupil of Handel, turned the same two plays into operas, basing himself partly on the Restoration versions. The spectacle has gone, but there is no real attempt to combine music and drama. All that remains is an emasculated play interspersed with songs which are often irrelevant. In his version of *A Midsummer Night's Dream*, called *The Fairies*, Smith omitted Bottom and the rustics altogether. Lysander has a very large part, sung by the famous castrato Guadagni, the creator of Orfeo in Gluck's opera, but Demetrius does not sing at all, probably because only a straight actor was available. Act II of Smith's *Tempest* ends with a bibulous trio for three tenors, and a glance at the score—which names the singers, not the characters—suggests that Prospero has joined the drunken sailors at the bar. It appears however that the same singer doubled the parts of Prospero and Trinculo.

Garrick wrote a prologue to Smith's *Fairies* in which he made a time-honoured point about

English opera by apologizing for a work in a language comprehensible to the audience, and went on:

> This awkward Drama—(I confess th'Offence)
> Is guilty too of Poetry and Sense.

That can scarcely be said of Veracini's Italian opera on *As You Like It*, produced in London in 1744. This too is a succession of arias, but the plot diverges more and more from Shakespeare into the improbable heroic world of Handel's operas. Its climax is a spectacular siege in which Rosalind is rescued from a tyrant's castle. The male parts were mostly sung by sopranos—two of them (including the usurping Duke) by women, and Orlando by a castrato. Veracini based one aria on a Scottish folksong, which the historian Burney regarded as a tactical error, since no self-respecting Scotsman would waste half a guinea on what he could hear better sung by his cook-maid Peggy in his own kitchen. The only other opera I know of based on *As You Like It* was composed by an American contralto who died two years ago; she must be the only opera-composer in history whose legs have been insured for 10,000 dollars.

The earliest Shakespeare opera on the continent seems to have been a setting of *Timon of Athens* by the Holy Roman Emperor Leopold I in 1696. Since this monarch's sole delight, we are told, was 'to compose doleful melodies', the subject at least was a good choice. It was in the last thirty years of the eighteenth century that Shakespeare operas began to appear all over Europe, most of them on *Romeo and Juliet*, *The Merry Wives of Windsor* or *The Tempest*. By far the best of these librettos was a version of *The Comedy of Errors* by Mozart's famous collaborator Lorenzo da Ponte. He wrote it for Vienna in 1786, the same year as *The Marriage of Figaro*. We can only regret that the music was composed not by Mozart but by his English pupil Stephen Storace.

The first *Romeo and Juliet* operas reflect the spirit of the Age of Enlightenment, with sweet reason prevailing at the end. Friar Lawrence or his equivalent—he is often not a priest but a doctor, a chemist or a family friend—always reaches the tomb in time to explain things to Romeo and so ensure a love duet and a happy end. The earliest libretto, set by Schwanenberger in 1773, has only three characters. The third is Benvolio, who supplies the potion and manipulates almost the entire plot offstage. This is another Italian aria-and-recitative opera, with a trio at the end. Georg Benda's German opera of three years later is a *Singspiel*; that is, like all German operas before about 1820, it has spoken dialogue—and far too much of it. The end is again happy, and excruciatingly sentimental: when Romeo proposes to die in the tomb, he weeps copiously over the childless old age of his and Juliet's parents, and looks forward with a certain relish to haunting the place when tourists come to place flowers on his grave.

This play continued to be a popular operatic subject during the French Revolution and its aftermath, when a priest on the stage would probably have provoked a shower of rotten vegetables. In Zingarelli's opera of 1796 Friar Lawrence becomes one Gilberto, a sort of best man who is entrusted with the wedding arrangements and gets them hopelessly mixed up. At the end Romeo dies but not Juliet. Instead of killing herself she soundly rates Gilberto for his incompetence. This is a poor opera, but it was very successful, perhaps because it was a great favourite of Napoleon, whose musical taste was elementary.

A much more interesting opera on this play was produced in Paris in the middle of the Revolution (1793). The composer was Daniel Steibelt, a German pianist whose morals gave such offence in Paris that he had hastily to remove himself to London. This is an *opéra-comique*, with spoken dialogue, but the music has a great deal of energy and makes far more use of choruses and ensembles than any previous Shakespeare opera. It is also richly scored, and is the first opera to employ the gong in the orchestra. But it is the art of opera that is growing up, not the understanding of Shakespeare. Capulet swears that anyone who avenges Tybalt's death by killing Romeo can have Juliet. A Spaniard called Don Fernand undertakes this task; but when all the Capulets have cornered the unarmed Romeo in the tomb, he decides that the odds are too great to satisfy his honour and changes sides—thus affording a classical example of the quixotry expected from operatic Spaniards. The enraged Capulets rush in for the kill, but the noise made by three choruses and all the principals singing at once wakes up Juliet, and all ends happily.

The German *Tempest* operas of this period are almost a study in themselves. There were about a dozen of them, including eight in the two years 1798–9. Four of these were settings of the libretto that had been intended for Mozart, though it was altered later. It presents the play as a struggle between white and black magic: Prospero rules by day, Sycorax by night, and it is Sycorax who invokes the storm. Ferdinand's only companion is a skittish and amorous page, played by a woman, like his obvious model Cherubino in *The Marriage of Figaro*. In order to prevent the lovers from falling asleep and so into Sycorax's power, Prospero keeps them up all night counting corals. The action is a weird compound of spectacle—including a volcanic eruption engineered by Prospero—ballet, ethical humanism and buffoonery. Sycorax and the good spirit Maja are played by dancers, but Ariel is both voluble and sententious and is continually giving Prospero advice, especially on how to control his own daughter. The opera ends with Caliban taking refuge in the sea, after which the entire company sing a hymn in praise of the fatherland. Perhaps the oddest thing about it is that Goethe called the libretto a masterpiece.

The mixture of magic transformation scenes, a high ethical tone in the serious parts and coarse Viennese farce in the rest is typical of German opera at this period, as indeed we can see from *The Magic Flute* itself. All these *Tempest* operas belong to the *Singspiel* type, with fragments of Shakespeare's original dialogue cropping up in the oddest contexts. In Wenzel Müller's opera Stephano has a sister called Rosine, who gets the better of Caliban's improper advances by what can only be called a superior knowledge of judo, and eventually marries Trinculo in order to keep the court supplied with jesters. Miranda—here called Bianka—is so excited by her father's promise of a young man that she throws herself into the arms first of Rosine and then of Trinculo; when she eventually meets Ferdinand she quite upsets his sense of propriety by doing all the wooing. Ariel teases the comics by conjuring up three seductive female shapes, which at the decisive moment change into three bears. In Ritter's opera Ariel himself masquerades in female shape and changes into a tree when embraced. Trinculo has the biggest part here, rather after the manner of Papageno. He steals Prospero's magic robe and convinces Caliban that he is a great magician called Magnus Pumphius Karpunkulus, a descendant of Dr Faust, and that Prospero is an incompetent pupil whom he was compelled to dismiss. Another composer, Hensel, wrote his own libretto and published it with a sour preface denouncing the affectations of Mozart and his school, of which he considered the public were heartily sick.

By the early nineteenth century the literary romantic movement on the continent had welcomed Shakespeare as an exciting if unruly predecessor of their own revolt against the age of reason. His plays were often translated, and like Scott's novels became an increasingly popular operatic source. Hands were laid for the first time on the great tragedies. Rossini's *Otello* of 1816 was the first Shakespeare opera to be acclaimed as a European masterpiece. We are apt today to remember Rossini only as a composer of farcical comedies. In fact he wrote many more serious operas, and virtually abandoned comedy before he was 25. His *Otello* is a landmark, and not only because it was the first Italian opera in which the recitatives were accompanied throughout by the full orchestra instead of the keyboard. In the first two acts the librettist followed the conventions of his day. Iago is a rejected suitor of Desdemona, Roderigo a typical scorned lover who fights a duel with Othello; Othello himself—who never leaves Venice—is little more than an irritable tenor. The handkerchief is replaced by an intercepted love-letter containing a lock of hair; since Desdemona has omitted to address it properly, Iago has no difficulty in convincing Othello that it was intended for Roderigo. But when he reached the last act, the librettist suddenly adhered to the play, including not only the Willow Song and the scene that follows, but the final murder. This was an innovation, and shocked people so much that in some revivals Rossini was compelled to alter it. But the interesting thing is that most of this last act is musically on a far higher level than the rest of the score. Something of Shakespeare's dramatic truth seems to have penetrated to Rossini. Here, perhaps for the first time, we can detect the influence of Shakespeare on a great composer: Rossini's Willow Song and prayer (which probably suggested the Ave Maria in Verdi's opera) are fully worthy of their context.

The most distinguished Italian librettist of the romantic period, Felice Romani, wrote four Shakespeare librettos. His *Hamlet*, set by Mercadante in 1822, has an interesting preface in which Romani calls the play the *Oresteia* of the north and says that he has deliberately emphasized the resemblance between the three chief characters and Orestes, Clytemnestra and Aegisthus, since the English original is too fantastic for the opera house. Thus Hamlet enters for the first time pursued by the Furies, uncertain whether the Ghost is a product of his own imagination. The melodramatic events that follow seem to us far more fantastic than the play. Ophelia is the daughter not of Polonius but of Claudius, who wants to make a diplomatic marriage between her and the Prince of Norway, and Hamlet survives the denouement to mount the throne. Both these refinements occur in other nineteenth-century operas on this play. The part of Hamlet, like that of Romeo in several early romantic operas, was sung by a woman. This was a survival of the castrato hero, before his place had been taken by a tenor.

Romani's libretto on *Henry IV*, again for Mercadante, includes two of the most famous Falstaff scenes, but involves the young Prince Henry in a complicated web of amorous and political intrigue. This is very funny, but I am afraid there is not time to describe it. Both Romani's *Romeo and Juliet* librettos preserve at least the outline of the play, since the tragic end was now acceptable—though of course there had to be a love duet first. Unfortunately the better libretto was set by the lesser composer. In Vaccai's opera of 1825 all the characters are remarkably well drawn, including Juliet's parents and Tybalt, who is in love with Juliet. Vaccai's music is quite pretty, but no one would think of reviving it today. Bellini's opera, on the other hand, five years later, is full of exquisite melody, and I think Covent Garden might have revived it this year instead of Bellini's later opera *I Puritani*. The characters are more the cardboard figures of melodrama, but Bellini does recreate the youth and ardour of the lovers. In this sense the opera takes Shakespeare's point, even if there is a wide difference in the details.

By this time *Macbeth* had made its operatic bow, at the Paris Opéra in 1827. The composer was Hippolyte Chélard, the librettist Rouget de Lisle, otherwise known to fame as the author of the 'Marseillaise'. It is difficult today to take this work as seriously as the authors evidently intended. To begin with, the First Witch rejoices in the good Scots name of Elsie. Banquo, Macduff and Malcolm are left out. Duncan's sole heir is a daughter, Moïna, and Macbeth has a son; but for some reason the librettist does *not* draw the expected conclusion. He gives Moïna a love scene with Douglas, Prince of Cumberland, and a brilliant air in praise of Highland scenery. The murder occurs in the finale of Act II and is not discovered till the very end of the opera, after the sleep-walking scene, which in fact gives the show away since the listeners put two and two together. Among the incidentals—always an important feature of French grand opera—are a chorus of Ossianic bards and an extended ballet. Here Chélard attempted a little local colour by quoting 'Auld Lang Syne'—in a somewhat corrupt text. His score is a strange compound of early German romanticism and the skittish coloratura of Rossini's comedies.

Another curiosity is Wagner's early opera *Das Liebesverbot* (1836), to a libretto of his own based on *Measure for Measure*. Except that one theme reappears later in *Tannhäuser*, it is fairly safe to say that no one would recognize the composer. Wagner does all the things he was later to denounce with particular fury in other people's operas. The score is full of French and Italian tricks and ornaments, many of them again borrowed from Rossini, and sounds rather like the sort of thing Sullivan parodies in *The Pirates of Penzance*. Wagner interpreted the play as an outright attack on Puritanism and a glorification of free love. Angelo becomes the German Viceroy of Sicily, and may, like Beckmesser, have been meant as a caricature of one of Wagner's enemies. All the characters are more or less unpleasant, including Isabella, who is prepared to flirt with Lucio almost before she is out of the convent. Pompey is translated into a buffo tenor called Pontius Pilate, whose chief aim in life is to redeem the name his parents so tactlessly bestowed upon him.

Towards the middle of the century the attitude of librettists to Shakespeare began to change. Instead of manhandling his plots to fit the convention in the same way as they adapted the latest French or Spanish melodrama, they paid him a certain respect. In 1838 the librettist of Balfe's *Falstaff* apologized for his deviations from *The Merry Wives*—although the fact that the opera was written for London—albeit in Italian—may have had something to do with this. Apart from the omission of some characters the libretto does not deviate very much—though Falstaff writes *three* identical love letters, one of them to Anne Page—and the opera, which is full of sparkling Rossini-like tunes, might merit revival if Balfe had any feeling for character. Unfortunately in the scene between Falstaff and the disguised Ford he makes no distinction in mood between their music, which is virtually interchangeable. Ford's jealousy aria is a cheerful and bouncy polacca.

Nicolai's attitude is typical of the changing climate. He first of all said that no composer but Mozart was a fit companion for Shakespeare. Then he himself made a preliminary prose sketch. The finished libretto, by S. H. Mosenthal, borrows hints from three other Shakespeare plays besides *The Merry Wives*. Moreover, where it alters the plot, which is not very often, it preserves its spirit. Although Nicolai's fat knight smacks of the German beer cellar, and is of course overshadowed by Verdi's wonderful creation, the opera successfully combines the sparkle of the comedy with the atmosphere of dawning romanticism that we find in Mendelssohn's *Midsummer Night's Dream* music—clearly one of Nicolai's models. This is particularly true of the Windsor Forest scene, which begins with a real inspiration, a chorus to the rising moon. There is nothing about this in the play, but it sets the mood perfectly for what follows and is a most beautiful piece in its own right. The music is familiar, since Nicolai used it for the first section of his overture.

Almost contemporary with Nicolai's *Merry Wives* is the first version of Verdi's *Macbeth* (1847); and Verdi too began by giving his librettist a prose synopsis. The form in which we hear the opera today is the result of a partial revision in 1865, and presents rather a mixture of styles. Had Verdi first approached the play in his maturity he might have made a superb thing of the Porter's scene, which he left out altogether; on the other hand he would hardly have written the comic-opera choruses of Witches and Murderers, which for some reason he allowed to survive the revision. Yet the sleep-walking scene, also part of the original score, is not only the finest thing in the opera: it is a masterpiece by any standards. And it is an almost literal setting of Shakespeare's words.

Here, as in Act III of Rossini's *Otello*, and all through Verdi's last two operas, we find the contact between Shakespeare and a composer of genius producing great opera. Obviously this could not have happened if Verdi had not been an assiduous student and a passionate admirer of Shakespeare, and in some way peculiarly in tune with him. But another important factor is at work here. There is something about the design of many scenes in Shakespeare that corresponds to the operatic forms current in Verdi's day—to what is called the number opera: that is to say, solo arias, duets and ensembles in closed forms, linked by recitative. The sleep-walking scene, with its watching doctor and gentlewoman, is an example. It does not need to be manipulated for operatic purposes; it can be set as it stands. There is an even more striking instance in Lady Macbeth's first soliloquy, beginning with the reading of the letter and interrupted by the Messenger with news of Duncan's approach. First she reacts to Macbeth's letter

> Hie thee hither,
> That I may pour my spirits in thine ear,

then—much more violently—to the Messenger's news

> Come, you spirits
> That tend on mortal thoughts, unsex me here.

All this exactly corresponds to the almost invariable form of the operatic aria in the first half of the nineteenth century: first a recitative, then a cavatina, then—after some interruption has changed the mood—a rapid and brilliant cabaletta. Shakespeare might have been writing for the opera house.

Of course some plays and some scenes lend themselves to this more than others. *Macbeth* has other operatic advantages in that it is reasonably short, has no subplot, and tells a straightforward story of human passions. *King Lear* is far more difficult, and has defeated every composer who has attempted it. *Hamlet* presents a fascinating problem, which has likewise not been solved but is perhaps not insoluble. The most successful opera on this play is by the French composer Ambroise Thomas (1868). Here we have another libretto that veers between adherence to the play and grotesque travesty of it, and again this proves a touchstone for the composer. Thomas' music is never first rate, but in the passages that fall easily into operatic shape and reflect the action and the language of the play fairly closely—the appearance of the Ghost on the battlements, the ensemble of the play scene, much of the closet scene, and the 'To be or not to be' soliloquy—he reaches a standard far above the rest of the score, and indeed above the rest of his operatic output. A curious point about the play scene is that it includes, in an ironic recitative, the first operatic appearance of the saxophone.

There is one first-rate libretto on *Hamlet*. It was written in 1865 by a young man of 23, Arrigo Boito, and set to music—unfortunately—not by his later collaborator Verdi, but by Franco Faccio. The remarkable thing about Boito's *Hamlet* libretto is how very little he modified the plot or the stature of the characters. Of course the action is contracted, but its spirit is there, waiting for the composer to recreate in terms of his own art. This is equally true of his *Otello* and *Falstaff*, which in Verdi's settings are generally recognized as the greatest of Shakespeare operas—if not the greatest of all operas. They are the only two that rank as works of art with the plays themselves; many people indeed would place *Falstaff* considerably above *The Merry Wives of Windsor*.

To justify this claim in detail would occupy too much time. I can only point to various features that render this collaboration between Verdi, Boito and Shakespeare unique. For it *is* a triple collaboration: on the level of dramatic sympathy, which is what matters most in opera, both librettist and composer had a profound understanding of Shakespeare. But they had to be masters of compression, since music needs so much more time to make its points than the spoken word. Conciseness was always a prominent feature of Verdi's style, so much so that in his early operas he often cut his corners too fine and left out essential links in the story or the dramatic motivation. This is what happens in *Macbeth*, where he reaches the murder too soon without having established the character of Duncan, who comes on but never sings.

Here Boito's double qualifications helped; for he was at once a brilliant and sensitive writer and a distinguished opera composer in his own right. And he had the tact and patience to play the temperamental Verdi like a rebellious salmon. Although he used a great deal of Shakespeare's language, as well as his ideas, characters and situations, he was not afraid to modify the original in the interests of operatic form. The astonishing tautness of design in these two librettos results not merely from cutting things out but from putting things in, and still more from fusing two or three strains into one. In *Falstaff* Boito reconstituted the fat knight of the *Henry IV* plays within the framework of *The Merry Wives*, by means which I think have never been fully analysed. The libretto includes at least eight passages from *Henry IV*, five from the first part, three from the second, and twice combines lines from both parts in a single sentence. Invariably the insertion fits its new context with marvellous aptness. To give an example: Boito attaches the famous speech about honour in *Henry IV, Part I* to Falstaff's dismissal of Bardolph and Pistol for refusing to play the pander (*Merry Wives*, I, iii); and his link is a line taken from a later scene (II, ii), Falstaff's rebuke to Pistol 'You stand upon your honour!'. Some very happy details were invented by Boito, generally with the idea of tightening up the plot: for instance the identification of the 'great lubberly boy' whom Dr Caius marries with his enemy Bardolph, and the brilliant moment in the linen-basket scene when the jealous Ford and his henchmen, after ransacking the house, hear the sound of a kiss behind a screen. Thinking they have caught Falstaff and Mrs Ford in the act, they stalk the screen and after a conspiratorial ensemble throw it down, only to reveal Fenton and Anne. This dovetailing of the various strains of the plot, which goes on all through the opera, has a double advantage; it performs the essential function of saving time, and it opens fresh opportunities for the composer, whose one great advantage over the dramatist is that he can develop two or more ideas simultaneously.

In *Otello* Boito had an infinitely harder task owing to the much greater richness of the play in character, incident and overtone—not to mention the poetry. His bold decision to omit Shakespeare's first act and start the opera with Othello's arrival in Cyprus at the height of the storm was a masterpiece of economy; for the storm, a thrilling opening in itself, presents a physical parallel to the violent psychological upheaval that is soon to follow. But this left very little space in which to establish Othello's stature as a soldier and a man, and the quality, as well as the facts, of his relationship with Desdemona. On these two points of course the proportions of the tragedy depend; and I do not think anyone familiar with the opera would deny that they come across quite as convincingly as in the play. One of Boito's means is the time-honoured convention of a love-duet. But this is like no other love-duet in operatic history. So far from being an unfunctional point of repose, it tells us everything about the past and present relationship of the lovers. Here, as elsewhere in the opera, Boito worked in passages from Act I of the play.

In the short second act he had to demonstrate convincingly the growth of Othello's jealousy from nothing to the savagery of his vow, 'Now, by yond marble heaven', in a fraction of the space available to Shakespeare in the play. To do this he made two small changes; he put in a charming scene in which the Cypriots serenade Desdemona, which at once marks the passage of time and adds a tremendously potent dramatic irony, and he placed Desdemona's first plea for Cassio *after*, instead of before, Iago has roused Othello's jealousy, so that it naturally bursts into more rapid flame. A striking feature of this opera is the way in which the drama and the music play continually into each other's hands, and on several levels at the same time. In Act I Iago sings a brindisi or drinking-song, interrupted by comments from other characters and the chorus—another convention of romantic opera. It corresponds of course to the scene in the play where Iago makes Cassio drunk and provokes the fight leading to his disgrace; but besides doing all this it has to introduce the characters themselves for the first time and set the whole plot in motion while retaining a coherent musical shape.

One of the most pregnant episodes in any opera is the famous quartet in which Desdemona tries to soothe Othello's first outbursts of jealousy while Iago through Emilia gets possession of her handkerchief. Here we have events and characters and their motives, whether explicit or concealed, all developed simultaneously with an economy and a multiplication of irony that is not possible in a play, where there is no orchestra and the characters cannot all speak at once. It is at the same time a piece of music of marvellous beauty and shapeliness. If you read Boito's libretto without the music, you find a good deal of the play missing; but that is rather like reading a prose synopsis of the play instead of seeing it in the theatre. Verdi's music completes the dramatic connexion, and supplies an equivalent for the poetry. The result is a great opera, which is not just a cobbling together of two arts, or a compromise between them; it is a new experience in its own right, and an extraordinarily complex and profound one.

There are I think two special and interlinked reasons why Shakespearian opera reached its climax in late nineteenth-century Italy. The first concerns operatic history. I have mentioned the way in which certain scenes in *Macbeth* lend themselves to the aria-ensemble forms of romantic opera. But in 1847 these forms were too stiff to take all the situations in a Shakespeare play without detracting from its stature. Forty years later the situation was different. *Otello* and *Falstaff* represent the historical climax of the number opera, in its tragic and comic forms, just when it was giving way to a more fluid method of construction. Boito and Verdi contrived to get the best of both worlds. Both operas, while giving an impression of effortless flow, depend on the old fixed forms of aria, duet and ensemble. They possess the structural strength of the set piece without its drawback of holding up the action, and the freedom of continuous arioso without its shapelessness. Everything is in perfect balance—the forward thrust of the plot against the lyrical expansion demanded by the music. This would not have been possible, however great the genius of librettist and composer, had the time itself not been ripe.

The second reason is a quality in Shakespeare himself. Everyone knows that he found many of his plots in Italy and that Elizabethan drama owed a considerable debt to the Italian renaissance; but the similarity in approach, temper and design between his plays and the Italian opera of two and three centuries later is not merely superficial. Nor is it confined to plays on Italian subjects. *The Merry Wives of Windsor* itself has the flavour of an *opera buffa* by Cimarosa or Rossini, for example in the linen-basket scene, an absolute gift for a comic opera finale. Boito seems to have been the first to perceive and exploit this affinity. He wrote after the first performance of *Falstaff*: 'Shakespeare's sparkling farce is led back by the miracle of sound to its clear Tuscan source'—in Boccaccio. Undoubtedly the same Italian roots nourished Shakespeare and his clowns on the one hand and the *commedia dell'arte* and *opera buffa* on the other. If we remember this, and the dramatic detachment characteristic of Italian opera until the late nineteenth century—by which I mean its willingness to allow the story to emerge without smothering it in sentimental, ethical or symbolic encrustations—I think we have the explanation why nearly all good Shakespeare operas have either been written by Italians or have followed Italian methods.

One other nineteenth-century opera might easily have turned out a masterpiece of the same order. This is Berlioz's *Béatrice et Bénédict* (1862). Berlioz, who was his own librettist, was in most respects as good a writer as Boito and as good a composer as Verdi. But he lacked one essential, the ability to subordinate the part to the whole. Like Boito, he cut away much of the play he worked on and added material of his own; and some of this—again like Boito—is not only excellent but Shakespearian. But the rest, instead of binding together what remains of the plot, does the exact opposite. In place of Dogberry and Verges, Don John's conspiracy and the church scene, we have a character of Berlioz's invention, a musical pedant called Somarone, in whom, at quite disproportionate length, he caricatured his enemies at the Paris Conservatoire. This ruined his opera as a work of art. But nothing can dim the beauty of the rest of the score, in which he depicts the sex-war between Beatrice and Benedict with a brilliant wit, an ironic detachment and an underlying sense of the impermanence of human life unlike the music of any other composer. Perhaps the play calls for this last mood less than some others; but it *is* a quality in Shakespeare, and one that Berlioz particularly associated with him. He was very soon to end his memoirs with the lines from *Macbeth* beginning 'Life's but a walking shadow'.

During the last century Shakespeare operas have continued to appear at the rate of at least one a year, and the flow shows no sign of diminishing. With a few exceptions I think the standard has declined rather than improved. For one thing the sharpness—tartness even—of Shakespeare's characters was soon lost when the sugar-content of late romantic opera began to rise. Gounod's *Romeo and Juliet* is a succulent morsel for those with a sweet tooth, but it is idle to pretend that it comes closer to Shakespeare than his *Faust* does to Goethe. Goetz's *Taming of the Shrew*, which contains some charming lyrical music, suffers from the almost painful domesticity of Katharina before the taming even begins. Three German operas on *The Winter's Tale* all omit Autolycus and turn the play into a sentimental romance.

There was a tendency to introduce all the favourite devices of romantic opera whether the context called for them or not. Taubert's *Cesario* (1873), on *Twelfth Night*, has a hunting chorus in Olivia's garden and a naval wedding with a ballet of tritons and sea-spirits. Urspruch's *Tempest* (1888) goes one better with a chorus of huntresses seductively dressed (or undressed) who claim equal prowess in the pursuit of beasts and men. Ariel explains that they are only phantoms, but they enable the composer to offer the attractions of the huntsmen of *Der Frei-schütz* and the flower-maidens of *Parsifal* at one and the same time. The most eccentric opera of this type is Salvayre's *Richard III*, produced at St Petersburg in 1883. This begins with a funeral march followed by a drunken orgy, and ends with Richard interrupting Henry VII's coronation by whipping the crown off his head and falling dead on the steps of Leicester Cathedral. The numerous choruses include large formations of gipsies, huntsmen, clergymen, Welshmen and ghosts. Richard has a court jester called Puck, who sings a song about Queen Mab but is sacked when he breaks down in the middle. A passing minstrel is called in and given his job, and turns out to be the future Henry VII in disguise. Later we meet a band of gipsies living in 'a forest of druidic aspect' near Leicester under the government of a professional soothsayer called 'Madgy', who I need hardly say is Queen Margaret of Anjou. Perhaps the most startling episode is Richard's attempted marriage to his own niece, which begins with a grand wedding march led by Cardinal Bourchier and four bishops to the tune of 'Rule Britannia'.

The decline of the ensemble-opera at the end of the nineteenth century led to types of design less suited to Shakespeare. The Wagnerian music-drama, with its slow-moving action carried chiefly by the orchestra, tends to turn Shakespeare's mercurial and Italianate characters into ponderous abstractions. The results cannot be described as happy. At one point in Fibich's *Tempest* Prospero rides in on a chariot drawn by Caliban and three dragons, gives the courtiers a long moral lecture, and points to the posture of Caliban as a proof of the triumph of mind over matter. The chess game between Miranda and Ferdinand becomes an elaborate and obscure allegory of married life, with the spirits whispering suggestions into their ears. When they are on the point of kissing, Ariel appears behind and knocks their heads together, whereupon the spirits burst out laughing. A complicated leitmotive system does not make this any easier to swallow.

Leitmotive of course can be an asset. By far the best Shakespeare opera that owes any considerable debt to Wagner is Bloch's *Macbeth* (1910), where the leitmotive system is employed with great skill and subtlety to illuminate the drama. For example, when Macbeth takes the lead after the banquet ('It will have blood, they say; blood will have blood'), he appropriates the cruelty motive of his wife; and in the sleep-walking scene ('What's done cannot be undone') she borrows one of his motives, associated hitherto with his guilty conscience. Bloch's motives are musically distinctive (especially in rhythm), which is the first essential; he treats the characters as human beings, not as symbols; and he takes care to retain many features of the number opera. Some of the set pieces, the finales in particular, are very impressive.

The Italian *verismo* method with its emphasis on sensational plots and naked emotion, as in *Tosca* or *Cavalleria Rusticana*, is even less appropriate to Shakespeare and has produced one or two deplorable operas on which there is no need to dwell. A more common cause of failure in the twentieth century is the antithesis of this, a scrupulous respect for Shakespeare's text and a refusal to tamper with it except for a few cuts. This sounds admirable, but it makes the task of the composer very much harder, especially if he sets it in English. The language is so rich in associations and overtones that he may be tempted to bend the music to fit it instead of the other way round. If the music adds little or nothing to the total experience it might just as well not have been written; there is no point in gilding what is already complete. Perhaps the only successful full-length opera of this type is Britten's *Midsummer Night's Dream*; and one of the reasons is that the music, instead of slavishly following the verbal rhythms, does not hesitate to impose its own. Another reason is that Britten has grasped the point about the number opera: although the libretto contains scarcely a word not taken from the play, its design falls constantly into airs and ensembles. Of course this would not be enough without the intense concentration of Britten's style. It has a sinewy quality, a refusal to luxuriate in emotion, which I think is essential for a Shakespearian subject.

Holst's one-act opera *At the Boar's Head*, on the Falstaff scenes in *Henry IV*, has this spareness; Vaughan Williams's *Sir John in Love*, on *The Merry Wives*, has not. Both these operas are built on folksongs and the folk idiom; but where Holst is nimble and preserves the pace and sparkle (if not the style) of *opera buffa*, Vaughan Williams seems to accommodate his music to the mental processes of a country bumpkin. That surely is to mistake the flavour of the play.

Many living continental composers have set the plays in translation, more or less cut: among them Malipiero and Castelnuovo-Tedesco in Italian, Orff, Klebe, Blacher and Frank Martin in German. All seem to me to fail, some completely, some more narrowly, either because the music does not add enough of its own or because it adds the wrong thing. A more successful opera, based on an adaptation rather than a translation, is *The Taming of the Shrew* by the Russian Shebalin. Though produced as recently as 1957, this uses a thoroughly old-fashioned traditional idiom; but at least it hitches on to an appropriate tradition, that of *opera buffa*, and it translates into music a good deal of the high spirits of the play.

There seems no valid reason why good Shakespeare operas should not be written in the future, though the composition of any opera is an arduous task and the mortality rate is and always has been enormous. But the modern composer has very definitely to meet a challenge. Audiences today are more sophisticated than in the past, and will inevitably judge the opera, consciously or not, on how it measures up to the play on which it is based. The final criterion is not the literal fidelity of the libretto, or even the originality of the music, but the creation of a new unity out of the constituent elements. A unity of appropriate stature, needless to say. With the great tragedies this will require an act of rare genius. But I find it surprising that there has never yet been an opera of even the second rank on *As You Like It* or *Twelfth Night*. And there are plenty of opportunities in other Shakespeare plays if the composer and his librettist can discover how to exploit them.

OPERAS BASED ON THE PLAYS

Composer	Title	Librettist	First Performance
	ALL'S WELL THAT ENDS WELL		
E. Audran	*Gillette de Narbonne* (operetta)	H. C. Chivot and A. Duru	1882, Paris
M. Castelnuovo-Tedesco	*Tutto e bene quello che finisce bene*	Composer	1958 (comp.)
	ANTONY AND CLEOPATRA		
J. C. Kaffka	*Antonius und Kleopatra* (duodrama)	—	1779, Berlin
E. F. von Sayn-Wittgenstein-Berleburg	*Antonius und Kleopatra*	J. Mosenthal	1883, Graz
S. V. Yuferov	*Antony i Kleopatra*	Composer	1900 (pub.)
G. F. Malipiero	*Antonio e Cleopatra*	Composer	1938, Florence
	AS YOU LIKE IT		
F. M. Veracini	*Rosalinda*	P. A. Rolli	1744, London
Florence Wickham	*Rosalind* (operetta)	—	1938, Dresden
	THE COMEDY OF ERRORS		
S. Storace	*Gli equivoci*	Lorenzo da Ponte	1786, Vienna
A. Lorenz	*Die Komödie der Irrungen*	—	c. 1890
I. Krejčí	*Pozdvižení v Efesu*	J. Bachtík	1946, Prague
	CORIOLANUS		
A. Baeyens	*Coriolanus*	—	1940, Antwerp
S. Sulek	*Koriolan*	Composer	1958, Zagreb
	CYMBELINE		
R. Kreutzer	*Imogène, ou la gageure indiscrète*	J. E. B. Dejaure	1796, Paris
E. Sobolewski	*Imogene*	—	1833, Königsberg
E. J. L. Missa	*Dinah* (operetta)	M. Carré and P. de Choudens	1894, Paris
A. Eggen	*Cymbelin*	Composer	1951, Oslo
	HAMLET		
L. Caruso	*Amleto*	—	1789, Florence
S. Mercadante	*Amleto*	F. Romani	1822, Milan
M. Mareczek	*Hamlet*	—	1840, Brno
A. Buzzolla	*Amleto*	G. Peruzzini	1847, Venice
A. Stadtfeld	*Hamlet*	J. Guilliaume	1857, Darmstadt
L. Moroni	*Amleto*	—	1860, Rome
F. Faccio	*Amleto*	A. Boito	1865, Genoa
C. L. A. Thomas	*Hamlet*	J. Barbier and M. Carré	1868, Paris
J. L. A. Hignard	*Hamlet*	P. de Garal	1888, Nantes, (pub. 1868)
L. H. Heward	*Hamlet*	—	1916 (comp., unfinished)
J. Kalniņš	*Hamlets*	Composer	1936, Riga

SHAKESPEARE IN THE OPERA HOUSE

Composer	Title	Librettist	First Performance

HAMLET (cont.)

Composer	Title	Librettist	First Performance
M. Zafred	*Amleto*	Composer and L. Zafred	1961, Rome
S. Kagen	*Hamlet*	—	1962, Baltimore
A. Machavariani	*Hamlet*	—	1964, Tbilisi

HENRY IV

Composer	Title	Librettist	First Performance
S. Mercadante	*La gioventù di Enrico V*	F. Romani	1834, Milan
G. Holst	*At the Boar's Head* (1 act)	Composer	1925, Manchester

JULIUS CAESAR

Composer	Title	Librettist	First Performance
J. García Roblez (1839–1910)	*Julio César*		
G. F. Malipiero	*Giulio Cesare*	Composer	1936, Genoa
G. Klebe	*Die Ermordung Cäsars* (1 act)	Composer	1959, Essen

KING LEAR

Composer	Title	Librettist	First Performance
M. Séméladis	*Cordélia*	E. Pacini and E. Deschamps	1854, Versailles
A. Cagnoni (1828–96)	*Re Lear*	—	—
S. Gobatti	*Cordelia*	—	1881, Bologna
A. Reynaud	*Le Roi Lear*	—	1888, Toulouse
G. Cottrau	*Cordelia*	Composer	1913, Padua
Alberto Ghislanzoni	*Re Lear*	Composer	1937, Rome
V. Frazzi	*Re Lear*	G. Papini	1939, Florence

LOVE'S LABOUR'S LOST

Composer	Title	Librettist	First Performance
Z. Folprecht	*Lásky hra osudná*	Capek brothers	1926, Bratislava
A. Beecham	*Love's Labour's Lost*	—	1936 (pub.)

MACBETH

Composer	Title	Librettist	First Performance
F. Asplmayr	*Leben und Tod des Königs Macbeth* (pantomime)	Moll	1777, Vienna
H. Chélard	*Macbeth*	C. J. Rouget de Lisle	1827, Paris
G. Verdi	*Macbeth*	F. M. Piave and A. Maffei	1847, Florence
		C. Nuitter and A. Beaumont	1865, Paris
W. Taubert	*Macbeth*	F. Eggers	1857, Berlin
Lauro Rossi	*Biorn*	F. Marshall	1877, London
E. Bloch	*Macbeth*	E. Fleg	1910, Paris
N. C. Gatty (1874–1946)	*Macbeth*	—	—
L. Collingwood	*Macbeth*	Composer	1934, London

MEASURE FOR MEASURE

Composer	Title	Librettist	First Performance
R. Wagner	*Das Liebesverbot, oder die Novize von Palermo*	Composer	1836, Magdeburg

THE MERCHANT OF VENICE

Composer	Title	Librettist	First Performance
C. Pinsuti	*Il mercante di Venezia*	G. T. Cimino	1873, Bologna
L. P. Deffès	*Jessica*	J. Adenis and H. Boisseaux	1898, Toulouse
J. B. Foerster	*Jessika*	J. Vrchlický	1905, Prague
F. Alpaerts	*Shylock*	H. Melis	1913, Antwerp
A. Radó	*Shylock*	—	1913–14 (comp., unfinished)
O. Taubmann	*Porzia*	—	1915, Frankfurt/Main

Composer	Title	Librettist	First Performance
THE MERCHANT OF VENICE (*cont.*)			
A. Beecham	*The Merchant of Venice*	—	1922, London
F. Brumagne (1887–1939)	*Le Marchand de Venise*	—	Brussels
Beatrice Laufer	*Shylock*	—	1929
R. Hahn	*Le Marchand de Venise*	M. Zamaçoïs	1935, Paris
M. Castelnuovo-Tedesco	*Il mercante di Venezia*	Composer	1961, Florence
THE MERRY WIVES OF WINDSOR			
Papavoine	*Le Vieux Coquet, ou les deux amies*		1761, Paris
F. A. D. Philidor	*Herne le chasseur*	Douin	1773 (comp.)
P. Ritter	*Die lustigen Weiber*	G. C. Roemer	1794, Mannheim
K. Ditters von Dittersdorf	*Die lustigen Weiber von Windsor und der dicke Hans*	G. C. Roemer (altered)	1796, Öls
A. Salieri	*Falstaff osia le tre burle*	C. P. Defranceschi	1799, Vienna
M. W. Balfe	*Falstaff*	S. M. Maggioni	1838, London
O. Nicolai	*Die lustigen Weiber von Windsor*	S. H. Mosenthal	1849, Berlin
A. Adam	*Falstaff* (1 act)	J. H. Vernoy de Saint-Georges and A. de Leuven	1856, Paris
G. Verdi	*Falstaff*	A. Boito	1893, Milan
R. Vaughan Williams	*Sir John in Love*	Composer	1929, London
A MIDSUMMER NIGHT'S DREAM			
H. Purcell	*The Fairy Queen*	?E. Settle	1692, London
R. Leveridge	*The Comick masque of Pyramus and Thisbe* (1 act)	Composer	1716, London
J. F. Lampe	*Pyramus and Thisbe* (mock-opera, 1 act)	Partly based on Leveridge	1745, London
J. C. Smith	*The Fairies*	Composer	1755, London
E. W. Wolf	*Die Zauberirrungen*	F. H. von Einsiedel	1785, Weimar
C. Manusardi	*Un sogno di primavera*	—	1842, Milan
F. von Suppé	*Der Sommernachtstraum*	—	1844, Vienna
L. Mancinelli	*Sogno di una notte d'estate*	F. Salvatori	1917 (comp.)
V. Vreuls	*Un Songe d'une nuit d'été*	P. Spaak	1925, Brussels
D. Arundell (b. 1898)	*A Midsummer Night's Dream*	—	—
J. Doubrava	*A Midsummer Night's Dream*	—	1945 (comp.)
M. Delannoy	*Puck*	A. Boll	1949, Strasbourg
C. Orff	*Ein Sommernachtstraum*	Composer	1952
B. Britten	*A Midsummer Night's Dream*	Composer and Peter Pears	1960, Aldeburgh
MUCH ADO ABOUT NOTHING			
H. Berlioz	*Béatrice et Bénédict*	Composer	1862, Baden-Baden
A. Doppler	*Viel Lärm um Nichts*	—	1896, Leipzig
P. Puget	*Beaucoup de bruit pour rien*	—	1899, Paris
C. Podestà	*Ero*	—	1900, Cremona
C. V. Stanford	*Much Ado About Nothing*	J. R. Sturgis	1901, London
R. von Mojsisovics	*Viel Lärm um Nichts*	—	*c.* 1930, Graz
R. Hahn	*Beaucoup de bruit pour rien*	J. Sarment	1936, Paris
H. Heinrich	*Viel Lärm um Nichts*	—	1956, Frankfurt/Oder

SHAKESPEARE IN THE OPERA HOUSE

Composer	Title	Librettist	First Performance
	OTHELLO		
G. Rossini	*Otello osia il Moro di Venezia*	F. Berio di Salsa	1816, Naples
G. Verdi	*Otello*	A. Boito	1887, Milan
A. Machavariani	*Othello*	—	?1963, Tbilisi
	PERICLES, PRINCE OF TYRE		
G. Cottrau	*Pericle re di Tiro*	—	c. 1915 (comp.)
	RICHARD III		
L. Canepa	*Riccardo III*	Fulgonio	1879, Milan
G. Salvayre	*Riccardo III*	E. R. Blavet	1883, St Petersburg
	ROMEO AND JULIET		
J. G. Schwanenberger	*Romeo e Giulia*	C. Sanseverino	1776, Leipzig[1]
G. Benda	*Romeo und Julie*	F. W. Gotter	1776, Gotha
L. Marescalchi	*Romeo e Giulietta*	—	1789, Rome
S. von Rumling	*Roméo et Juliette*	—	1790, Munich
N. Dalayrac	*Tout pour l'amour, ou Roméo et Juliette*	J. M. Boutet de Monvel	1792, Paris
D. Steibelt	*Roméo et Juliette*	J. A. P. de Ségur	1793, Paris
N. A. Zingarelli	*Giulietta e Romeo*	G. M. Foppa	1796, Milan
B. Porta	—	—	1806, Paris
P. C. Guglielmi	*Romeo e Giulietta*	S. Buonaiuti	1810, London
N. Vaccai	*Giulietta e Romeo*	F. Romani	1825, Milan
V. Bellini	*I Capuleti e i Montecchi*	F. Romani	1830, Venice
M. Morales	*Romeo y Julieta*		1863, Mexico City
F. Marchetti	*Romeo e Giulietta*	M. M. Marcello	1865, Trieste
C. Gounod	*Roméo et Juliette*	J. Barbier and M. Carré	1867, Paris
A. Mercadal	*Romeo e Giulietta*	—	1873, Mahon (Minorca)
P. X. D. (Marquis) d'Ivry	*Les Amants de Vérone*	Composer	1878, Paris
H. R. Shelley	*Romeo and Juliet*	?Composer	1901 (pub.)
C. del Campo	*Los amantes de Verona*	—	1909
J. E. Barkworth	*Romeo and Juliet*	Composer	1916, Middlesbrough
R. Zandonai	*Giulietta e Romeo*	A. Rossato	1922, Rome
H. Sutermeister	*Romeo und Julia*	Composer	1940, Dresden
G. F. Malipiero	*Romeo e Giulietta*[2]	Composer	1950, Italian radio
B. Blacher	*Romeo und Julia* (scenic oratorio)	Composer	1950, Salzburg
E. Gaujac	*Les Amants de Vérone*	—	1955, Toulouse
	THE TAMING OF THE SHREW		
T. S. Cooke and J. Braham	*The Taming of the Shrew*	—	1828, London
H. Goetz	*Der Widerspänstigen Zähmung*	J. V. Widmann	1874, Mannheim
S. Samara	*La furia domata*	—	1895, Milan
A. Maclean	*Petruccio* (1 act)	—	1895, London
C. Silver	*La Mégère apprivoisée*	H. Cain and E. Adenis	1922, Paris
R. Bossi	*Volpino il calderaio* (1 act)	L. Orsini	1925, Milan

Composer	Title	Librettist	First Performance

THE TAMING OF THE SHREW (cont.)

Composer	Title	Librettist	First Performance
M. Persico	*La bisbetica domata*	A. Rossato	1931, Rome
R. Karel	*The Taming of the Shrew*	—	1942–3 (comp., unfinished)
P. G. Clapp	*The Taming of the Shrew*	—	1948, New York
V. Giannini	*The Taming of the Shrew*	Composer and Dorothy Fee	1953, Cincinnati
V. Y. Shebalin	*Ukroshchenie stroptivoi*	A. A. Gozenpud	1957, Kuibyshev

THE TEMPEST

Composer	Title	Librettist	First Performance
H. Purcell	*The Tempest; or, the Enchanted Island*	J. Dryden, W. Davenant and T. Shadwell	1695, London
J. C. Smith	*The Tempest*	?D. Garrick	1756, London
F. Asplmayr	*Der Sturm*	—	1781, Vienna
J. H. Rolle	*Der Sturm (Die bezauberte Insel)* (1 act)	Patzke	1784, Berlin
V. Fabrizi	*La tempesta*	—	1788, Rome
P. von Winter	*Der Sturm*	—	1793, Munich
F. Fleischmann	*Die Geisterinsel*	F. W. Gotter and F. H. von Einsiedel	1798, Weimar
J. F. Reichardt	*Die Geisterinsel*	F. W. Gotter and F. H. von Einsiedel	1798, Berlin
J. R. Zumsteeg	*Die Geisterinsel*	F. W. Gotter and F. H. von Einsiedel	1798, Stuttgart
F. Haack	*Die Geisterinsel*	F. W. Gotter and F. H. von Einsiedel	1798, Stettin
W. Müller	*Der Sturm*	K. F. Hensler	1798, Vienna
P. Ritter	*Der Sturm, oder die bezauberte Insel*	J. W. Doering	1799, Aurich
J. D. Hensel	*Die Geisterinsel*	Composer, based on Gotter and Doering	1799, Hirschberg
L. Caruso	*La tempesta*	—	1799, Naples
F. L. A. Kunzen (1761–1817)	*Stormen*	—	—
A. J. Emmert	*Der Sturm*	—	1806, Salzburg
P. J. Riotte	*Der Sturm*	—	1833, Brno
E. Raymond	*Der Sturm*	—	c. 1840 (comp.)
E. Rung	*Der Sturm*	—	1847, Copenhagen
F. Halévy	*La tempesta*	E. Scribe, tr. P. Giannone	1850, London
E. Nápravník	*Der Sturm*	—	1860, Prague
E. Frank	*Der Sturm*	—	1887, Hanover
A. Urspruch	*Der Sturm*	E. Pirazzi	1888, Frankfurt
Z. Fibich	*Bouře*	J. Vrchlický	1895, Prague
A. Farwell	*Caliban* (Masque)	—	1916
A. M. Hale	*The Tempest*	?Composer	1917 (pub.)
N. C. Gatty	*The Tempest*	R. Gatty and composer	1920, London
F. Lattuada	*La tempesta*	A. Rossato	1922, Milan
H. Sutermeister	*Die Zauberinsel*	Composer	1942, Dresden
K. Atterberg	*Stormen*	—	1948, Stockholm
F. Martin	*Der Sturm*	Composer	1956, Vienna

SHAKESPEARE IN THE OPERA HOUSE

Composer	Title	Librettist	First Performance
	TIMON OF ATHENS		
Leopold I, Holy Roman Emperor	*Timone misantropo*	—	1696, Vienna
	TROILUS AND CRESSIDA		
W. Zillig	*Troilus und Cressida*	Composer	1951, Düsseldorf
	TWELFTH NIGHT		
E. Steinkühler	*Cäsario, oder die Verwechslung*	—	1848, Düsseldorf
W. Rintel	*Was ihr wöllt*		1872, Berlin
W. Taubert	*Cesario*	E. Taubert	1874, Berlin
K. Weis	*Viola (Die Zwillinge)*	B. Adler, R. Šubert and V. Novohradský	1892, Prague
F. B. Hart	*Malvolio*	—	1913 (?comp.)
B. Smetana	*Viola*	E. Krásnohorská	1924, Prague (comp. 1874–84, unfinished)
G. Farina	*La dodicesima notte*	—	1929, Milan
A. Kusterer	*Was ihr wöllt*	—	1932, Dresden
H. Holenia	*Viola*	O. Widowitz	1934, Graz
A. de Filippi	*Malvolio*	—	1937 (?comp.)
C. A. Gibbs	*Twelfth Night*	—	1947 (comp.)
	THE WINTER'S TALE		
C. E. di Barbieri	*Perdita oder ein Winter-märchen*	K. Gross	1865, Prague
M. Bruch	*Hermione*	E. Hopffer	1872, Berlin
J. Nešvera	*Perdita*	J. Kvapil	1897, Prague
H. Bereny	*Das Wintermärchen*	—	1898
C. Goldmark	*Ein Wintermärchen*	A. M. Willner	1908, Vienna

NOTES

1. A printed edition of Sanseverino's libretto dated 1773 (?Berlin) may refer to this or an earlier setting.
2. One section of a composite drama, *Monde celesti e infernali*.

SOME SHAKESPEARIAN MUSIC, 1660-1900

BY

D. S. HOFFMAN

Looking back on Shakespeare's quatercentenary with its exhibitions, performances, scholarly books and all too few concerts, the contemporary musician might be tempted to state, as did Nancy in *The Jubilee* of 1769,

> All this for a poet, O no
> A poet who lived Lord knows how long ago.
> How can you jeer one
> How can you fleer one,
> A poet, o no, 'tis not so
> A poet who lived Lord knows how long ago.
> It must be some great man,
> A prince or a state man.
> It can't be a poet, o no.
> Your poet is poor,
> And nobody sure
> Regards a poor poet I trow.
> The rich ones we prize,
> Send them up to the skies,
> But not a poor poet, o no,
> A poet who lived Lord knows how long ago.

It may be this stress upon Shakespeare as simply a poet that has tempted musicians from the Restoration to the present day to use his texts as convenient pegs on which to hang their music.

Today's casual attitude towards songs from Shakespeare's plays is the result of a trend that began during the Restoration, although 'musical additions were being made to *Macbeth* even before Shakespeare's death'.[1] *Macbeth* was rewritten by Davenant shortly after the Restoration, and in this the operatic trend was manifestly potent. Even more operatic was *The Tempest*, which was altered by Davenant and Dryden in 1667. Some songs like Banister's 'Go thy Way' (known as the Echo Song)[2] were added at this early date, and, within the next ten years, even more music was added. By 1674, *The Tempest*, transformed into an opera by Shadwell, contained songs by Banister, Reggio and Humfrey, incidental music by Locke (who also set 'Orpheus with his lute' in 1673) and a masque in Act II by Humfrey.[3] When Henry Purcell composed his music for *The Tempest*, around 1695, the work was made more operatic still, and, as in the version of 1674, few of the songs are to words by Shakespeare. Purcell's two other Shakespearian works *The Fairy Queen* (1692) and the masque from *Timon of Athens* (1694), which is also an adaptation by Shadwell, do not include a single line by Shakespeare. Indeed, the whole of *The Fairy Queen* bears little or no resemblance to *A Midsummer Night's Dream*, its original model.

About the same time, John Eccles composed a remarkable song which begins, 'A swain long slighted and disdain'd', which was advertised as 'Sung by Mrs Knapp in the Tragedy of Hamlet, Prince of Denmark'. The song itself is dramatic and begins in F minor. The word 'cruel' is underlined by a scotch snap. The entire opening section is more declamatory than melodic with broad leaps for the voice and some florid writing to underline 'scorn', 'friend' and to draw out the phrase 'thus complain'd'. The actual complaint is in F major and the metre changes from duple to triple:

> By long experience have I known,
> And tell you that you need not fear;
> The town that parlays will be won,
> And she will yield who once will hear.

In contrast to the opening section, it is more melodic and less angular. The word 'yield' is underlined by a falling diminished fifth which gives an effect of languour and sensuality.

Few have noticed Jeremiah Clarke's song 'Alas, here lies the poor Alonzo slain' (about 1706), which was advertised as 'Sung by Mrs Hodgson in the Play call'd Timon of Athens'. This song, though not quite so attractive as Eccles' song for *Hamlet*, is thoroughly representative of the theatrical music that was being composed in the late seventeenth and early eighteenth centuries.

From this period, one of the few settings of an actual Shakespearian lyric is John Weldon's 'Take o take those lips away' (*Measure for Measure*), printed in 1702 in his *Collection of New Songs*. Whether or not it was used in a production of *Measure for Measure* is not certain, though its dramatic quality and use of florid writing is similar to that of Eccles and Clarke. The key is B minor, but at the words, 'But my kisses bring again', it changes to D major, and the tempo is indicated as 'brisk'. The music gradually returns to B minor, and at the last statement of 'seal'd in vain', the tempo becomes 'slow' and the word 'seal'd' is underlined by a short florid passage which draws it out.

Between about 1674 and 1710, music composed for Shakespeare's plays, with few exceptions, used non-Shakespearian lyrics, and very little incidental music was composed. There must have been some feeling among playwrights and composers that Shakespeare's works were, in fact, operas without music. An almost unique setting of Hamlet's soliloquy 'To be or not to be...'[4] which is found in a manuscript book, dated 1693, with the title 'Songs and other Compositions Light, Grave, and Sacred For a Single Voice', by Cesare Morelli, serves to illustrate this attitude. By no stretch of the imagination could those lines be considered for music in an ordinary theatrical production. They are far too complex. But if one tended to look for operatic elements in Shakespeare—as almost everyone did in the late seventeenth and early eighteenth centuries, then Hamlet's soliloquy could be regarded as an aria without music.

The eighteenth century carried on the trend begun in the early years of the Restoration, with an ever-increasing movement towards stress on romantic sentiment. 'Sweetest Shakespeare' was regarded in Milton's words, as 'Fancy's child', warbling 'native wood-notes wild'. Milton's lines, slightly modified, appeared in an 'Ode to the Memory of Shakespeare written by Dr Havard and set to music by Dr Boyce':[5]

> Sweetest bard that ever sung,
> Britain's glory, Nature's child,
> Ever may thy witching tongue,
> Warble sweet thy wood-notes wild.

The work is not long nor is it particularly memorable, with the notable exception of Boyce's setting of the lines quoted above. The remainder of the music is fairly commonplace. Its tone may be gauged from its inclusion of a dramatic duet between Mars and Minerva, who sing

> While Britons bow at Shakespeare's shrine,
> Britannia's sons are sons of mine.

It is known that this ode was submitted for use in the Shakespeare Jubilee of 1769, but it was rejected, and Garrick wrote his own 'Ode upon dedicating a Building to Shakespeare', with music by Arne. The opening song ('Rondo')[6] has a verse similar to that by Havard:

> Sweetest Bard that ever sung,
> Nature's glory, Fancy's child;
> Never sure did witching tongue,
> Warble forth such wood-notes wild.

Another song ('Larghetto') 'Thou soft-flowing Avon', perhaps the most famous song from the *Ode*, says of Shakespeare that

> The fairies by moonlight danced round his green bed,
> For hallowed the turf is which pillowed his head.—

lines typical of the atmosphere evoked in this eulogy.

The Shakespeare Jubilee of 1769[7] called for a good deal of music. In addition to his setting of Garrick's *Ode*, Arne's earlier work, 'The Oratorio of Judith', was also performed. Charles Dibdin provided 'Queen Mab, or the Fairies Jubilee', a cantata for soprano and strings, 'The Jubilee or Shakespeare's Garland' (which contains the lilting 'Let beauty with the sun arise' for two sopranos, flutes and a guitar, and songs like 'The Mulberry Tree' and the extremely popular 'Warwickshire Lad') as well as 'XII Country Dances; and VI Cotilions', the titles of the dances being taken from Shakespeare: 'Much Ado About Nothing', 'Doll Tearsheet's Rant' and 'Benedick's Wedding'. Dibdin, it seems, was an astute businessman as well as a successful composer.

Seven years later, in 1776, the younger Thomas Linley composed another 'Ode on the Spirits of Shakespeare', and once more the world of the fairies is evoked:

> None now shall see on yonder plain
> The gambols of Titania's train.

So far as incidental music was concerned not very much appeared in the eighteenth century. A notable exception is Boyce's 'The Music for animating the Statue, in Shakespeare's Play of the Winter's Tale'. It appears to have been co-ordinated with the action of the scene, perhaps after it was composed, for there are two remarks written in the manuscript after the first beat of the twenty-fifth measure: at the top of the page is 'Note, something was spoke in this interval'; at the bottom of the page there is, 'this pause was not originally designed'. The music begins slowly and ponderously and gradually increases in speed as the statue comes to life. Boyce seems to have contributed more music to Shakespearian productions than he is normally given credit for, though it is true that his rival Arne was the more prolific. Charles Burney, who had misgivings about some of the latter's music, declared that these two composers 'were frequently concurrents at the theatres and in each other's way, particularly at Drury Lane'.[8] Both composed masques for *The Tempest* in 1746, Arne for Drury Lane and Boyce for Covent Garden. The two masques are worthy of praise, although they are generally now ignored. One song from Arne's masque, 'Wide o'er this bright aereal scene', was later included in the composer's *Britannia* in 1755. Another song, 'Come unto these yellow sands', has only recently been published.[9] Arne and Boyce each also composed a 'Solemn Dirge' for *Romeo and Juliet* in 1750. Arne's was presented at Covent Garden with great success, and within a few days Garrick, who kept a watchful eye on the box office, commissioned Boyce to compose another for Drury Lane.[10] Arne's music is in A major and, for a special effect, uses a bell which tolls, throughout the 'Dirge', on A. For his 'Dirge', which is in A minor, Boyce uses the same effect; but any similarity to Arne's piece ends there. Arne's is not a good composition, possibly because the text he had to set was rather poor. Boyce's, on the other hand, set to Garrick's words, is a truly fine work, perhaps one of his very best Shakespearian pieces.

In spite of his obvious ability as a theatrical composer, Boyce did not seem to be as popular as Arne, most of whose music for Shakespearian productions was published during his lifetime. Indeed, Arne was so great in his time and so much admired after his death that nineteenth-century compilers of songs to Shakespeare's lyrics gave him credit for works by other, lesser known composers.

One other composer of this period remains somewhat of a mystery. Thomas Chilcot, organist of Bath, set seven of Shakespeare's lyrics. These were included in his *Twelve English Songs*, which was printed about 1755, and are so good that one is convinced they must have been used in the theatre. One would think that they could not have escaped the attention of the directors of his day, and it is conceivable that some of them were used at Bath, which, as is well known, had a very active theatrical life.

John Christopher Smith must also be considered a minor 'Shakespearian' composer because of his opera, *The Fairies*, for which David Garrick spoke a prologue in 1755.

Both this piece and an altered version of *A Midsummer Night's Dream*, which was printed in 1763 and utilized many of Smith's songs, omitted the playlet of *Pyramus and Thisbe*. *Pyramus and Thisbe* had, however, appeared earlier (1745) with music by J. F. Lampe—although his settings are in general mediocre. The only song that succeeds in being funny is 'The Lion's Song' beginning 'Ladies don't fright ye', introducing a kind of musical roar—a vocal vibrato. It is interesting to observe that the comic elements in Shakespearian comedy were apparently considered as ill-suited to the background. One receives the impression that in this age fairies and spirits, part of the romantic image, could not be suffered to live alongside the broad comedy of 'Pyramus' and that these latter scenes had perforce to be acted as a separate farce.

The name of Michael Kelly, who sang under Mozart, is not too well known in connexion with Shakespeare. He had, however, a part in the creation of two pieces: 'To see thee so gentle a creature distrest', described as a 'favorite song, sung by Mrs Crouch with universal applause in *The Tempest*' and 'What new delights invade my bosom'—'A favorite Duett sung by Mrs Crouch and Mr Kelly with universal applause' in the same play; the melodies were by Kelly, the 'Instrumental Parts' were Crouch's. They were composed probably in 1789 when Kelly and Mrs Crouch first acted together in Shakespeare's drama. Both pieces are set out for an orchestra of horns, oboes, and strings; the first song adds a bassoon part, while the second includes a harp. With an orchestra of this increased size, one imagines that a great deal of emphasis must have been placed on music.

There were, then, as many non-Shakespearian lyrics in eighteenth-century productions as there were settings of Shakespeare's own lyrics. The theatrical interpretation of Shakespeare seems to have swung towards the operatic as more professional singers—Lowe, Beard, Reinholt, Mrs Crouch, Kelly and Mrs Jordan—came to assume roles in the plays. For Mrs Jordan, James Hook composed music for a 'Willow' song in *Othello*—sung, says the printed version (about 1798),[11] 'with unbounded Applause. And accompanied by herself on the Lute'. It is typical of much of the music composed towards the end of the eighteenth century in that it lacks substance.

In view of the fact that the songs included by Shakespeare in his plays had a dramatic function which could not be ignored and that the poetry and music were so closely related as to be inseparable elements,[12] it is difficult to explain the decline in the quality of the musical element at this period. Could it have been due, in part at least, to Garrick's retirement from the theatre around 1776?

Whatever the reason, William Linley, whose father and brother had collaborated with Sheridan at Drury Lane in his adaptation of *The Tempest*, was one of the very few in the early years of the nineteenth century to produce important Shakespearian settings. In his introduction to his *Shakespeare's Dramatic Songs* (1815–16), he writes,

Will it not be regretted that so little attention has been paid to those parts of his [Shakespeare's] dramas where the power of music has been called in to heighten the effect of the scene?—The Public is not in possession of any regular series of the characteristic songs in his plays; and although these songs, as they occur, may originally have been sung either to tunes composed expressly for the occasion, or adapted to the popular airs of the day; yet it would be vain to search for them, so as to be certain of their authenticity; and, if the labour of search were even to be crowned with success, the music could not, in the present day, be so shaped as to be palatable to a refined musical ear.

Linley goes on to praise Purcell and to inform the reader that he will take care 'to dramatise, with precision, the music intended by SHAKESPEARE to be introduced in his plays'. He rejects the 'Italian' style and strives to work in that of 'the plain English school'. His collection includes two songs by Purcell—perhaps the only ones Linley knew; the younger Thomas Linley has another two; J. C. Smith, one; T. A. Arne, four; Boyce, three; R. J. S. Stevens, one; Dr Cooke, two; while Linley himself has twenty-two: the second volume ends with 'The Music in Macbeth as it is now performed on the stage—Newly arranged in three parts and a Piano Forte accompaniment by Mr Samuel Wesley', the music attributed to Matthew Locke, Richard Leveridge and Henry Purcell. One notes that Chilcot is not included in this collection, while Arne and Boyce are fairly well represented. Naturally, Linley's purpose was to put his own music before the public; and he shows up very well.

Henry Rowley Bishop constructed some operas based on Shakespearian plays, but these are hardly recognizable as belonging either to Shakespeare or to Bishop: the composer here has, for the most part, merely adapted and arranged. Thus, for example, *A Midsummer Night's*

Dream, which he produced in 1816, quotes or uses music by such composers as Arne, J. C. Smith and Handel, although it must be observed that one of his own contributions, 'By the simplicity of Venus' Doves', is quite pleasing, perhaps among his best compositions of this kind.

Bishop's *Comedy of Errors* appeared in 1819. Its 'Advertisement' states that

The admirers of Shakespeare having long regretted, that most of his lyrical compositions, have never been sung in a theatre, *The Comedy of Errors* (one of the shortest and most lively of his comedies) has been selected as the best vehicle for their introduction.—A few additional scenes and passages were absolutely necessary for this purpose; and however deficient these may be found, it is hoped they will be readily pardoned, as having served to bring on the stage, more of the '*native wood-notes* wild' of our Immortal Bard.

Making use of Shakespeare's name more shamelessly than anyone before him, Bishop produced in this piece even more of a pastiche than his *Midsummer Night's Dream*. Arne was among those quoted, a sure indication of his lasting popularity. Many of the texts were drawn from the sonnets. Others were simply lyrics from other plays such as 'The poor soul sat sighing' (*Othello*), 'Take o take those lips away' (*Measure for Measure*) and 'Come thou monarch of the vine' (*Antony and Cleopatra*), and it may be presumed that those were among the songs which he refers to as never 'sung in a theatre'. Bishop's own setting of 'Lo, here the gentle Lark' is a florid piece for soprano, with a very difficult cadenza for voice and flute, typically operatic. In his alterations of Shakespeare, Bishop thus merely carries on a tradition that had begun in the days of Davenant and Dryden.

Two of his contemporaries are worthy of note. R. J. S. Stevens,[13] whose settings of lyrics like 'Sigh no more, ladies' (*Much Ado About Nothing*) are well wrought, and C. E. Horn, whose setting of 'I know a bank' (*A Midsummer Night's Dream*) is worth a hearing. The latter is set as a duet and was, according to one advertisement, 'introduced into *The Merry Wives of Windsor*'.

About 1825, perhaps in 1827, the year of a Shakespearian Jubilee at Stratford-upon-Avon, there appeared *A Collection of the Vocal Music in Shakespeare's Plays Including the whole of the Songs, Duets, Glees, Choruses, etc.*, 'Revised and Arranged with an Accompaniment for the Pianoforte by Mr Addison, and most respectfully dedicated to the Hon. Mrs George Wrottesley, by John Caulfield'. On its first appearance, Caulfield's collection included only a few plays, but it was evidently popular and was considerably expanded in the later editions of 1864, 1875 and 1898. An even more modern edition appeared in 1922–4, by which time Caulfield's name was no longer mentioned. The editions of 1864, 1875 and 1898, almost identical, contain music for twenty plays. In most cases the composers were given correctly but a few modifications are necessary:

1. 'O bid your faithful Ariel fly' (*The Tempest*), said to be by Stevens, is by the younger Thomas Linley, who composed it for Sheridan's production of *The Tempest* at Drury Lane in 1777.

2. 'Tell me where is fancy bred' (*The Merchant of Venice*), said to be by Sir John Stevenson, is by Arne.

3. 'Haste, Lorenzo' (*The Merchant of Venice*), said to be by Calcott, is by Joseph Baildon.

4. 'My bliss too long my bride denies' (*The Merchant of Venice*), given as anonymous, is by Arne.

5. 'To keep my gentle Jessy' (*The Merchant of Venice*), said to be by Arnold, is by Arne.

6. 'Who is Sylvia?' (*Two Gentlemen of Verona*), said to be by Arne, is by Richard Leveridge.

7. 'Come thou monarch of the vine' (*Antony and Cleopatra*), said to be by Purcell, is by Chilcot.

8. 'On a day, alack the day' (*Love's Labour's Lost*), said to be by Arne, is by Chilcot.

9. 'When icicles hang on the wall' (*Love's Labour's Lost*), said to be by Smith, is by Arne.

10. 'Fear no more the heat of the sun' (*Cymbeline*), said to be by Weldon, is by Arne.

11. 'Orpheus with his lute' (*Henry VIII*), said to be by Purcell, is by Chilcot.

12. 'Sigh no more, ladies' (*Much Ado About Nothing*), said to be by R. J. S. Stevens, is by J. C. Smith.

13. 'Pardon, Goddess of the night' (*Much Ado About Nothing*), said to be by Arne, is by Chilcot.

14. 'Then is there mirth in heaven' (*As You Like It*), said to be by Arne, is doubtful. Stylistically it would appear *not* to be by Arne. It was not published along with Arne's other music from *As You Like It* in 1741.

15. 'The Dirge' (*Romeo and Juliet*), said to be by Bishop, is by Arne.

In the edition of 1922–4, numbers 1, 3, 4, 5, 7, 12 and 13, listed above, are given correctly. But 8 is still said to be by Arne, 10 is given as anonymous, 11 is attributed to Arne and 15 is marked anonymous. It may be observed that this latest edition is the source of the mistaken belief that Arne set 'Orpheus with his lute' (*Henry VIII*).

The *Shakespeare Vocal Magazine* which made its first appearance in 1864 should be mentioned in passing. Many settings of Shakespeare's lyrics were here printed separately and the series included works by Arne and Bishop, both of whom were well represented; included also is Chilcot's 'Pardon, Goddess of the Night', Michael Kelly's 'Hamlet's Letter Versified', Schubert's two well-known Shakespeare settings and Haydn's 'She never told her love'.

It was not until about 1871 that a significant attempt was made to bring music back into the structure of Shakespearian art. In that year Arthur Sullivan's music for *The Tempest* marks a truly great achievement; this composer had an assured sense of the dramatic, and *The Tempest* is one of his finest Shakespeare scores.

A couple of years later Brahms completed his 'Fünf Ophelia-Lieder',[14] and these also show an extraordinary understanding of the requirements of *Hamlet*.

It is obvious that what William Linley wrote in 1815–16 is not true for audiences today. There is no question that the music of Shakespeare's time is, indeed, now 'palatable to a refined musical ear'. Contemporary composers have set Shakespeare's lyrics and much of his poetry merely because they admire the writing, without due consideration of its dramatic significance: in so doing, they have produced admirable concert pieces, but few producers would use a setting such as Stravinsky's 'Full fathom five' in a performance of *The Tempest*.

NOTES

1. Roger Fiske, 'The "Macbeth" Music', *Music and Letters*, LXV (1964), 114–25.

2. Printed in Frederick Bridge, *Shakespearean Music in the Plays and Early Operas* (1923), pp. 81–4.

3. See J. G. McManaway, 'Songs and Masques in *The Tempest*', *Theatre Miscellany*, Luttrell Society Reprints, no. 14 (1953), pp. 69–96, for a complete discussion of this work.

4. Printed in Frederick Bridge, *op. cit.* pp. 85–93. The original accompaniment is for guitar. The piano accompaniment provided by Bridge is very romantic indeed but it is not correct.

5. Boyce composed two odes to Shakespeare. The earlier one to the words of William Havard begins 'Titles and ermines fall behind'.

6. There are nine musical numbers in the *Ode*, which was published in 1769.

7. See J. M. Stockholm, *Garrick's Folly* (1964).

8. Charles Burney, *A General History of Music*, annotated by Frank Mercer, II (1957), 1010.

9. Thomas Augustine Arne, *Nine Shakespeare Songs*, ed. by Percy Young (Chappell, London, 1963), pp. 27–9.

10. The story of these two works is discussed in detail by Charles Haywood, 'William Boyce's "Solemn Dirge" in Garrick's *Romeo and Juliet* Production', *Shakespeare Quarterly*, XI (1960), 173–85. Haywood believes he has found Boyce's missing music in a manuscript in the Library of Congress, but he overlooked a more likely one in the Bodleian Library.

11. 1798, according to the British Museum, is the watermark date. There is no reference in C. B. Hogan's *Shakespeare in the Theatre* to Mrs Jordan's having acted Desdemona at Drury Lane before 1800.

12. See F. W. Sternfeld, *Music in Shakespearean Tragedy* (1963) and *Songs from Shakespeare's Tragedies* (1964).

13. Charles Cudworth, 'Two Georgian Classics: Arne and Stevens', *Music and Letters*, XLV (1964), 146–53.

14. J. Brahms, *Fünf Ophelia-Lieder*, ed. by Karl Geiringer (2nd ed., Vienna, 1960).

SHAKESPEARE IN AMERICA:
A SURVEY TO 1900

BY

ROBERT FALK

Fragmentary records show that the first copies of Shakespeare's works found their way into the libraries of a few wealthy settlers in the New World between about 1675 and 1720. An early performance of *Romeo and Juliet* may have been played in New York in 1730, but it was not until 1750 that we have definite information of a Shakespearian play actually produced in America. On 5 March of that year *Richard III* was advertised in the New York *Weekly Post Boy* to be played 'in the theatre in Nassau St.'—a building identified as the old Rip Van Dam house where rooms were fitted up as an improvised stage. The players may have been the Murray-Kean group which, along with the Hallam company, toured American cities in the early 1750's. Prices for *Richard III* were advertised at 5*s*. for 'the Pitt' and 3*s*. for 'the Gallery'. The play was described as 'Wrote originally by Shakespeare | And altered by Colley Cibber Esqr.'. Cibber's stagey alteration with invented scenes and borrowed lines had been popular at Drury Lane in the 1740's, played by Garrick, and emphasizing spectacular episodes: 'the death of Henry 6th; the artful acquisition of the crown by King Richard; the murder of the princes in the Tower'. In the twenty-five years between this first performance and the closing of the theatres by edict during the war against England, fifteen different Shakespearian plays were played on colonial stages in Charleston, Williamsburg, Annapolis, Philadelphia, and New York, but Cibber's *Richard* seems to have been the favourite in America well down into the nineteenth century.[1]

After 1783, with the theatres once again opened, the canon of Shakespeare plays was further enlarged to include a number of the comedies and other histories. Shakespeare continued to be popular despite Puritan opposition, but more significant than his popularity are certain interesting parallels between early American Shakespearian productions and those of the Elizabethan period. Eighteenth-century Shakespeare-performing in the new world aped that in England, but with exceptions. Audiences were less informed, reading editions were not available, criticism was lacking. The Americans *saw* the plays, for the most part, without having read them. And stage conditions in general were pioneering.

Emerson once observed that the First Folio was printed only three years after the pilgrims landed at Plymouth and that, had Heminge and Condell been a little earlier with their edition of the plays, they might well have stayed home to read them! Instead, the colonists had to wait more than a century for reading copies of Shakespeare to become at all available, and it was not until 1795 that the first American edition was printed in Philadelphia. From that date until 1900 over 150 editions appeared in the United States. The names of Joseph Dennie, Gulian Verplanck, H. N. Hudson, William Gilmore Simms, R. G. White, W. J. Rolfe, and H. H. Furness, editor of the 'New Variorum' (1871–1907), are among the many diligent scholars who helped bring the plays and poems to American readers and students. The editors were likewise the first aesthetic critics.[2] Their work assisted actors to interpret their roles and began the popularizing of Shakespeare among literate Americans—teachers, philosophers, critics, and writers of many different interests. Much of the editing was, necessarily, derivative of English scholarship, but there was independent investigation and much meticulous labour in certain of the editions, especially in those of White and Furness. In widely different ways some of the distinguished names in American literature concerned themselves with Shakespeare —Emerson, Lowell, Whitman, Melville, Mark Twain and Lanier. And a large number of devoted disciples, 'Baconians', and amateur admirers of Shakespeare, added their words to the swelling mass of commentary during the nineteenth century.

The reception of Shakespeare in America becomes an interesting measure of taste and opinion and an accurate barometer of the variable and conflicting elements of the national psyche. If Americans lost much by their distance from the centres of information, they compensated by the enthusiasm of their idolatry. They studied the acting roles with great care, they appropriated Shakespeare's language into the common discourse with an unconscious reverence otherwise reserved only for the Bible, and they managed to convert Shakespeare into a perennial source of torment for recalcitrant schoolboys. Despite anti-British sentiment in the eighteenth century and cultural nationalism in the nineteenth, Americans seem to have been all the more anxious to demonstrate their kinship to Shakespeare and to discover in his plays and poems caviar for the intelligentsia and nutriment for the general.

Indeed, Shakespeare has become many things to Americans. At first he was a source of titillating love scenes and swashbuckling stage effects. Rapidly, however, he became a mark of status to eighteenth-century gentlemen and ladies who attended the plays. He was a source of political wisdom and moral conduct for statesmen like John Adams and Jefferson,[3] a point of departure for transcendental philosophers of Concord, a rich mine for the romantic critics, and a storehouse of apt speech and metaphor for almost every literate citizen. The tragedies struck a chord of sympathy with those few original minds who had inherited the Puritan sense of sin and evil and who sought to transmute this into enduring forms of literature, while the histories appealed to the politically minded who read deep lessons for democracy in the sad stories of the death of kings. Native humorists, punsters, and cartoonists likewise drew upon Shakespeare in their efforts to inform the voters and fill the columns of the newspapers. In the broad panorama of American cultural life, Shakespeare's influence provided a standard of literary accomplishment for native writers to aspire to. His works helped to counteract such cultural deficiencies in America as the effeminization of literature, the 'genteel' mind, the distrust of tradition and the past, and the predilection, as W. D. Howells phrased it, for 'the smiling aspects of life'.

In the East the recognition of Shakespeare by an emerging type of gentleman-scholar-writer helped to establish a class of polite, belletristic *literateurs* like Irving, Cooper, Poe, Lowell and Holmes. It was such democratic-aristocrats who first marked out a significant new path for the intellectual in America. The interest, for example, of Adams and Jefferson in Shakespeare's plays and the beginning of a romantic attitude, first coming through Coleridge, led men like Bryant, R. H. Dana, Sr., Duyckinck and Paulding to follow a literary career in place of the established legal, medical, or clerical professions. The emergence of the man of letters in America was manifest first in the middle states with the Knickerbockers, but it spread to New

England during the 1830's when, among many cultural influences, the romantic criticism of Shakespeare was introduced through the writings of Coleridge. A transition point for the poetic mind in New England is interestingly demonstrated in Emerson's career when, deserting the pulpit, he began lecturing on lay subjects, including literature, and among his enthusiasms Shakespeare was unquestionably placed in the highest rank.

On the western frontier Shakespeare's impact is more difficult to assess. It was expressed in quite different ways from those on the eastern seaboard, yet the degree of reverence implied was scarcely less profound. The plays were performed in villages and the lines were read around the fires in mining camps. They were performed in semi-western costume, on steamboats plying up and down the Mississippi, and in minstrel shows (Hamlet, in 'An Ethiopian Burlesque', is frightened by a ghost 'from the South'; Macbeth is a hen-pecked husband). Shakespeare, in being paid the compliment of parody, was less the butt of such jokes than were the motley spectators and the ungainly surroundings in which he was performed. Indeed, what one begins to realize in these early manifestations of Shakespeare in America is the fact that his language and rhythms had begun to enter deeply into the national consciousness as a source of wit and wisdom for widely different levels of society and divergent cultural groups. Because he was, as Hazlitt put it, the archetypal poet whose genius shone 'equally on the evil and on the good, on the wise and on the foolish, the monarch and the beggar', he provided Americans of all ranks and kinds with a perpetual volume of reference and quotation.

The present effort to summarize a vast subject in small compass is a gesture of recognition toward the poet-dramatist on the 400th anniversary of his birth. Four recognized kinds of reception and influence will be touched upon: the actors of Shakespeare, his editors, the aesthetic critics, and (perhaps the most subtle kind of 'influence') the imaginative use of his themes and language in new forms of literature. Much of the period covered belonged to the Romantic movement when the tradition of criticism from England and Germany exerted a powerful influence in America. Following the lead of Coleridge, Hazlitt, Schlegel, Goethe and others, American critics were prone to moralize over the plays. They read Shakespeare often in the 'closet' way, detaching the characters from the plays and psychologizing them like real persons. In the full sway of romantic idolatry, the commentators reiterated in a hundred ways that Shakespeare could do no wrong.

American actors were slow to make any significant impression in Shakespearian roles. The tradition from Mrs Siddons, Kemble and Henry Irving was too powerful. English actors, like Lewis Hallam, David Douglas and George Frederick Cooke, followed by Edmund Kean, the elder Booth and Macready, played most of the parts in the romantic style of eloquent declamation, stereotyped poses, and strident gestures. Only Forrest, Hackett and Charlotte Cushman established themselves as American actors before 1850. In aesthetic criticism, likewise, the tradition of romantic idolatry was largely taken over from England and Germany with the addition, perhaps, of a stronger note of didacticism in America. The American Baconians were a special group in themselves, seeking in obscure ways to 'discover' Shakespeare's identity. They differed widely in the occultism of their methods and the degree of their apostasy, and we will only have space for a brief notice of this interesting phase of American criticism. Finally, a section must be devoted to *Moby Dick*, where the genius of Shakespeare and that of Melville merged in what was unquestionably the most creative form of Shakespearian influence upon American literature. James Russell Lowell felt that Shakespeare was in some strange way 'unitary with human nature itself', and Emerson pronounced him his 'representative' poet and his works as 'the delight of the nineteenth century'. American literary history during these 150 years was one of experiment, full of cross-currents and self-consciousness, containing both the faults and the freshness of youth. Only a 'myriad' mind such as the romantic critics sensed in Shakespeare could find a generous reception among so many different areas of the American experience.

I

In an interesting and readable book on Shakespeare in America, Esther C. Dunn has recorded many strands of the stage productions and acting of Shakespeare in the nineteenth century and has suggested conclusions which can be drawn from them. Among the most striking is the fact that the conditions of the early American theatre provided a return, in many ways, to those of Shakespeare's time. Uneducated audiences (some unable to read), primitive arrangements for many performances, Puritan and Quaker hostility, the effort to appeal to playgoers of both the Pit and the Gallery, with the resultant emphasis upon declamatory effects and sensational episodes—these factors suggest something like a recapitulation of the spirit and the atmosphere of the original productions. In 1759, for instance, the Hallam company was forced by Quaker opposition in Philadelphia to build a new playhouse on 'Society Hill' which was located 'without the bounds of the city' in order to avoid official interference. A famous incident of another kind occurred in 1752 when the Hallam company opened the season in Williamsburg, Virginia, with *Othello*. Some Cherokee Indians were in town to sign a peace pact, and upon being invited to the play, the Empress (like Partridge in *Tom Jones*) became so astonished by the swordplay on stage that she ordered her warriors to go up and prevent the actors from killing each other! An example of frontier conditions is recorded by Sol Smith in his recollections of theatrical life in the West. A travelling troupe arrived in a small town in 1833, and the local citizens requesting entertainment, a hotel dining-room was hastily fitted up for the leading tragedian to intone 'The Seven Ages of Man' in heavy Mormon accents to the solemnly listening group. Such are only a few instances, but even these tempt one to press the parallel between the circumstances of the early American stage and those of Shakespeare's England.[4]

One of the special ways in which Shakespeare appealed to nineteenth-century Americans was in their love of oratory and declamation. Speechmaking early became one of the national pastimes and an integral part of political contests. From this developed such forms of popular culture as the Lyceum Movement and the Chautauqua Circuit in which speakers vied with each other in intellectual combats and rhetorical flourishes. Mouth-filling periods accounted significantly for the political success of such men as Calhoun and Webster, kept drowsy church-goers awake when intoned from the pulpit, and entered into the very accents of American speech. The part played by Shakespeare in this phase of American life is instanced in various ways. Walt Whitman loved the plays and, as a young man, sat in the omnibuses on Broadway 'declaiming some stormy passage from Julius Caesar or Richard' to passing crowds.[5] Whitman's verse was patterned after operatic rhythms and Shakespearian periods, as well as the Bible, and he was always fascinated by orotund expression. Much of Emerson's appeal derived from oratory, whereas political leaders like John Quincy Adams, Jefferson and Lincoln became thoughtful readers of Shakespeare, drawing from the plays both hints for governing and accents in which to address the public. Like so many Americans of their time, Lincoln and Adams became amateur critics of Shakespeare, debating points of interpretation with their friends and correspondents.

Popular accounts of the early American theatre have emphasized sensational episodes in which patriotic groups like the Sons of Liberty demonstrated against Shakespearian actors. A notorious incident occurred at the Astor Street Theatre in New York in 1849 when police were called to quell a riot over the 'rival' performances of the American actor Edwin Forrest and the English Charles Macready. The two had allegedly insulted each other's acting, the press took up the cause, mobs surrounded the theatre where Macready was acting Macbeth, shouting slogans about 'workingmen' and 'the damned den of aristocracy' until shots were fired and some twenty innocent people were killed. Of such stuff international incidents were made in 1850. The line of demarcation in the public mind between art and patriotism was easily bridged and Shakespeare became the cause of political rivalry.[6]

The American actor James H. Hackett has left us many intimate glimpses of Shakespearian acting during the first half of the nineteenth century.[7] Hackett, whose most popular role was Falstaff, was a serious student of the plays and one of the few actors of the period to submit himself to a scholarly discipline in preparation for his roles, collating texts and studying the opinions of critics on textual problems. He was critical of audiences which preferred cheap effects and of actors who catered to them. He complained that his fellow Americans, Forrest and Charlotte Cushman, were often 'overstrained and unnatural', leaning to 'melodrama *in excelsis*'. He said Forrest's make-up for Lear used over-shaggy eyebrows and a long beard which covered some 'useful and important muscles of the face' and that his expression failed to vary from a stern inflexibility. Conventional costuming for Iago, likewise, employed a black wig with shaggy eyebrows, and he was played without relief as a barefaced ruffian and black-hearted villain. Hackett was often at odds with himself in his attempt to achieve popularity and his struggle to preserve the integrity of Shakespeare's text. In preparing for the role of Hamlet he studied carefully the subtleties of usage and textual commentary, and for the part of Lear he restored the Nahum Tate omissions from certain of the speeches 'in the hope that it might please some lover of Shakespeare in his integrity'. Although Hackett admired and imitated Edmund Kean, Macready and others, he became discouraged with tragic parts after his performance of Iago in 1828 at the Park Theatre because he could not reconcile uncritical audience reactions with his own feeling for textual nuances and his efforts toward innovations of interpretation.

Another first-hand observer of Shakespearian productions in this period was the poet Walt Whitman, who left in his *November Boughs* a reminiscence of his youthful excitements as a spectator of the plays in the Old Bowery and the Park Theatre, where he vividly recalled the acting of Fanny Kemble, Charles Kean, Edwin Forrest, Hackett, Thomas Hamblin, Macready and Ellen Tree.[8] Especially Whitman remembered Junius Brutus Booth in the parts of Richard III, Lear and Iago ('I don't know which was best'). Booth and Forrest always played at the Bowery, rather than the more fashionable Park, probably, as Whitman recalled, because they were taboo'd by the 'polite society' of New York and Boston as being 'too robustuous'. Sitting in his 'good seat in the pit' he could still remember, after fifty years, Booth's quiet entrance as Richard with an abstracted air 'musingly kicking his sword' and making the most of the dramatic 'hush or wait', keeping the audience in 'half-delicious, half-irritating' suspense before pronouncing the opening lines. Although Whitman admitted that Booth was to be classed 'in that antique, almost extinct school, inflated, stagey', his genius was nevertheless 'one of the grandest revelations of my life, a lesson of artistic expression', and without question Booth belonged as 'the royal heir and legitimate representative of the Garrick–Kemble–Siddons dramatic traditions'. Whitman also admired Tom Hamblin in *Macbeth*, John H. Clarke's 'peerless rendering' of the Ghost in *Hamlet*, and Hackett as Falstaff.

Whitman was never a convinced 'Baconian', though in deference to his friend, the ardent Baconian William D. O'Connor, he showed some interest in the theory. Mark Twain, on the other hand, became a vigorous anti-Stratfordian in his later years when he wrote *Is Shakespeare Dead?* Because he employed some of his customary burlesque methods in the early chapters, Twain's book has sometimes been misunderstood. He was quite serious, even ill-tempered, in his attack upon 'these Stratfordolaters, these Shakesperoids' who perpetuated the fetish that an obscure, uneducated butcher's son could have written the plays.[9] His attitude toward Shakespeare was never really distinct from his interest in the authorship problem which began, as he said, with Delia Bacon's book in 1857. Though he attended performances many times, Mark Twain's interest seems not to have extended to a close reading knowledge of the text. Rather, for him Shakespeare was another of those sacred cows, a superstition like many other artistic monuments of the European past which he felt had been inflated by generations of thoughtless worshippers and mouthing tourists. From Missouri, Mark Twain refused to join this throng of believers. Instead, always in the market for burlesque materials, he found in Shakespeare grist for his mill. He wrote a 'news item' on the killing of Julius Caesar for the Territorial *Free Enterprise* on the 300th anniversary of Shakespeare's birth, 23 April 1864. Later, he brought 'Master Shaxpur' as a character into his unpublished pamphlet, *1601, or The Fireside Conversations of Queen Elizabeth*, now a collector's item of sniggering Twainiana. His best-known parody of Shakespeare, however, is the garbled 'to be or not to be' passage in *Huckleberry Finn*. It is mentioned here, not because it is as uproarious as some have thought (it isn't), but because the surrounding context is an amusing and instructive caricature of the way Shakespearian roles must have been played in a small frontier town of the last century. It is also a witty exemplum of Hamlet's advice to the players. As Twain described it, the 'Duke' marched up and down 'frowning horrible', and then

he would hoist up his eyebrows; next he would squeeze his hand on his forehead and stagger back, and kind of moan; next he would sigh, and next he'd let on to drop a tear.... Then he strikes a most noble attitude, with one leg shoved forwards and his arms stretched away up and his head tilted back, looking up at the sky, and then he begins to rip and rave and grit his teeth, and after that, all through the speech, he howled and spread around and swelled up his chest and just knocked the spots out of any acting ever I see before....

Even these two rascally impersonators were too subtle for the audience of Brickville, Arkansas. Only twelve people appeared for their show, prompting the Duke's remark that 'these Arkansas lunkheads' couldn't come up to Shakespeare!

II

The first American edition of Shakespeare was published in Philadelphia in 1795, an eight-volume work under the imprint of 'Bioren and Madan'. Advertised as 'corrected from the latest and best London editions, with notes, by Samuel Johnson L.L.D.' this edition has been described by W. Jaggard as 'the first printed outside the British Isles'. The editor seems to have been either the poet and essayist Francis Hopkinson, or Joseph Dennie, Federalist editor of the *Port Folio* after 1801. Dennie wrote for this magazine a series of articles, which represent the first sustained Shakespeare criticism to appear in America. The text of the Philadelphia edition derived indirectly from the Johnson–Steevens–Reed text of 1785, apparently through the medium of the Dublin Royal edition, by Samuel Ayscough, 1791. The notes came from Johnson and a preface with a life of Shakespeare was appended in which the editor devoted himself largely to a defence of Shakespeare's morality. 'The fools of Shakespeare are always despised', the editor wrote, 'and his villains always hated.' The eighteenth-century opinion voiced by Voltaire that Shakespeare was 'uncouth and abrupt' but at the same time sublime is registered in the preface of this first American edition, now mainly an historical curiosity.

The second edition to appear was printed in Boston in 1802–4, noteworthy if only to indicate that the home of the Puritans was not only early in the field of publishing Shakespeare, but also in dramatic production and criticism. Records of the Boston stage show that *Richard III* and *Macbeth* were first played in the 'tastefully decorated' New Theatre in 1795 by the Hallam company. One other of the early editions must be mentioned here, a work in seven volumes also printed in Boston, and edited by O. W. B. Peabody in 1836. It has been termed 'the first attempt to follow, in general, the readings of the Folio of 1623', though in many cases the notes may have been supplied by Samuel Singer's Chiswick edition of 1826, then the most widely used Shakespeare text in the United States. Peabody was not truly original in his notes or criticism, but he deserves credit for his effort to return to original sources.[10]

From editing to literary criticism was a natural step. In the 1840's Gulian Verplanck's edition contained the first attempt in America to follow Dr Johnson's suggestions of Shakespeare's development. Verplanck grouped the plays 'according to the several progressive stages of their author's style, taste, and general thought'. In this, he was followed by Henry Norman Hudson, schoolteacher, indefatigable lecturer on Shakespeare, later an ordained minister and editor of the *Church Monthly*, an undeviating disciple of the rapturous school of Shakespeare criticism. 'The aesthetic criticism of Coleridge, Schlegel, Hazlitt, and Lamb', he said, 'has probably done more to diffuse and promote the study of Shakespeare than all the verbal criticism in the world put together.' Hudson's lectures were popular in Boston in the 1840's and soon he was speaking in all the large cities from New England to Alabama. Published in 1848, they formed the basis of his eleven-volume edition of Shakespeare (1851–6), where they are condensed into the introductions to the plays. Here and in his textual notes Hudson tended to stray afield into rather laboured explanations of customs and usages of Elizabethan England, often laced with didactic applications. He had absorbed from Emerson and others the language of transcendental idealism which he put to use in a steady defence of Shakespeare as 'the greatest of all poets' and the 'greatest of all dramatic artists'. In 1872 Hudson published his *magnum opus, Shakespeare: His Life, Art, and Characters*. This was an advance upon his earlier criticism in its greater restraint and objectivity and in the corroborative weight of many German and English critics whose judgments were placed in footnotes. But his fundamental assumption, that Shakespeare had no faults, remained unaltered.[11]

Hudson's criticism suffered from a too close attention to the tradition of nineteenth-century romantic Shakespeare-olatry as well as a tendency to 'moralize' the plays in terms of nineteenth-century social and religious ideals. His discussion of Desdemona becomes a diatribe against women's suffrage, and Hamlet's tragedy is due to his inability to transgress 'social justice'. When he differs from Schlegel or Coleridge, he often finds himself involved in unhistorical or inconsistent positions, as his opinion that Hamlet is not weak-willed, but rather heroic and morally righteous so that he cannot kill the king until his crime has been openly revealed to justice. Furthermore, Hudson drew upon studies of Shakespeare's delineations of insanity to prove Hamlet 'really mad', thus largely contradicting his lengthy defence of the moral basis of the play. His lectures today have little intrinsic importance. An historical phenomenon and a genteel Victorian critic, he was an impressive platform speaker and a notable disseminator in America both of Shakespeare's works and (almost equally) of the views of earlier romantic critics upon them.

Unquestionably the most individualistic of the American editors, a man of strong feelings and crotchety opinions, was Richard Grant White, whose *The Works of William Shakespeare* (1857–66) was published in Boston.[12] To his editing White brought a scholarly mind and a professional training in linguistics. In manner and bearing 'altogether aristocratic', White preferred to remain aloof from New York literary circles. He was regarded as snobbish and disagreeable and his dislike of 'nativist' sentiments together with a strong Anglophilism sharpened the authoritarian character of his thinking. Rejecting all schools of opinion, especially the tradition of Coleridge and the German critics, he took his stand with a stalwart agnosticism upon reason and 'common sense' both in personal philosophy and in the solution of complicated textual problems in Shakespeare. Nevertheless, White's knowledge of the history of the field was large enough to gain him great respect. Lowell, for example, said that he possessed 'all the qualifications of a perfect editor', and a recent scholar has described his edition as 'epoch-making ... the most independent and scholarly which had appeared'. White himself defined editing as 'a necessary evil' in which the main function of the editor was to keep out of sight and to place the reader in the position where he can understand Shakespeare as he was understood in his own time.

As a textual critic his reputation rests largely upon his independent position regarding the textual emendations of the so-called 'Perkins Folio' of 1632 which John Payne Collier proposed as a corrective to errors in the earlier editions. In two articles later incorporated into his book *Shakespeare's Scholar* (1854) White carefully examined 1303 alleged emendations and rejected all but 117 as unworthy of attention. This book, according to a recent scholar, represents the first 'purely textual criticism to appear in America' and is still 'one of the best'. In the preface to his edition of Shakespeare White stated that he had avoided as much as possible introducing aesthetic criticism, a position which later solidified into an intransigent form of anti-traditionalism. He came to recommend the reading of 'very little, or better, none at all' of criticism of the 'higher' kind. He attacked Coleridge and the Germans (Ulrici was 'a mad mystic' and Gervinus 'a very literary Dogberry') as 'eulogistic gush'. In his *Studies in Shakespeare* (1874) he rejected, in a fit of militancy, all the commentators: 'Throw the commentators and editors to the dogs. Don't read any man's notes, or essays, or introductions. . . . Don't read mine. Read the plays themselves.'

He was more of an aesthetic critic himself, however, than he admitted to, and in many articles, solicited from him by Lowell for the *Atlantic Monthly*, he continued his sturdy debunking of romantic criticism and gradually substituted a theory of his own in which Shakespeare was portrayed as a man whose personal character and dramatic genius were at odds. He came to feel, in his warfare with the critics who spoke of Shakespeare's 'beauty of soul', that there were two Shakespeare's—the artist and the man, the latter 'a third-rate money-making actor at the Globe theatre, motivated in his writing solely by the desire for filthy lucre'. In his anxiety to destroy the idealized image of the poet, White repeatedly attacked the romantic legend and insisted that the real Shakespeare possessed lapses of character which indicated that there was no necessary likeness between what a man is and what he does. Although White's creation of a new image was almost as fantastic as the one he sought to remove, the direction of his work was to strike at the very basis of the Victorian morality of art, the idolatrous view of Shakespeare's superiority in all things, the concept of ethical unity of the plays, and the romantic theory of genius. Shakespeare always approaches us, he said, 'upon a level of common sense'. His creations came not out of 'an opium dream', but directly from the 'superintendence of his reason and understanding'.

White was too much the individualist to adhere strictly to his own theory of the self-effacing scholar, and it remained for Howard Horace Furness, the editor of the 'New Variorum' *Shakespeare* (1871–1907), to establish himself as both the most thorough and the most eclectic of the American editors. Furness's was technically the fourth Variorum Shakespeare to be undertaken; previous to him and the starting-point for his work was the Boswell Variorum of 1821. However, in 1866 The Cambridge Shakespeare produced a text based upon a thorough collation of folios, quartos, and all subsequent editions and commentaries and included a complete record of collation and the history of emendation. Furness's undertaking, almost at the time of the appearance of the Cambridge text, sought to become even more complete than this. The first of his volumes was *Romeo and Juliet* (1871) wherein, as Karl Knortz put it, Furness exceeded the Cambridge edition by presenting detailed abstracts 'aus den Werken englischer, deutscher, und französischer Kritiken'. Furthermore, he gathered every valuable reading of previous commentators on one page 'und dann dem Leser überlassen, sich ein eigenes Urtheil zu bilden'.[13] In short, every man his own critic. Furness's editions, only recently reissued in paperback, may come to be regarded as first of the 'casebooks' and the most comprehensive of them all.

His two-volume *Hamlet* (1877) divided itself between text and commentary on the play. His text, as stated in the preface, was a 'collation of the texts of the Quartos and Folios, and of some thirty modern editions, together with Notes and Comments from the Editors whose texts are collated'. In his second volume Furness reprinted the 1603 quarto, the source story of the play, *The Hystorie of Hamblet*, the old German tragedy *Der Bestrafte Brudermord*, and a compendious collection of opinions on Hamlet's madness, real and feigned. Furness's prefaces are full of disclaimers. 'Without for one moment wishing to assume the responsibility of umpire', or 'the present editor's opinion which . . . he would be the last . . . to set forth at length', and so forth. Scholarship thus had achieved that stage of objectivity where it is difficult to distinguish between scholarly detachment and critical indecision.

Furness's work, none-the-less, belongs high in the field of Shakespeare editing. For him Shakespeare was a lifelong profession. A man of independent means uncommitted to the winds of doctrine who early in life suffered from deafness, cutting him off from more worldly activities, he devoted himself entirely to his chosen occupation—that is, to know everything possible about Shakespeare. This background explains much about his eclecticism. It is the strength of his work and the fact that makes his Variorum editions still useful, if somewhat dated, today. Of the three important American names in Shakespeare-editing in the nineteenth century—Hudson, White and Furness—we may summarize briefly as follows: Hudson was the critic-popularizer, the indefatigable publicist and romantic salesman of Shakespeare; White the Anglicist, the antidemocratic, independent editor-critic whose major principle was reason and 'common sense'; Furness, the patient, self-effacing, scrupulously judicious editor for whom genuinely ascertainable facts about Shakespeare were rare and to be valued. Although he did not rule out aesthetic criticism (indeed, he regarded it highly) Furness was always sceptical of hasty opinion where information and solid research were lacking.

III

Melville wrote, with pardonable exaggeration, in 1850: 'There are hardly five critics in America, and several of them are asleep.' He was speaking of America's tendency to neglect its own writers, or to expect somehow that when a great genius is born 'on the banks of the Ohio' he will come in the costume of Queen Elizabeth's day and 'be a writer of dramas founded upon old English history'. Criticism in mid-nineteenth-century America, it is true, was imitative of the English tradition, provincial and didactic. After 1850 a gradual effort to provide a native critical tradition may be traced, but its progress was sporadic and uneven, running at times into eccentricity, and at times reverting to conventionalism. The trend from amateurism to professionalism was evident in the last half of the century among Shakespearian commentators, critics, and editors. In White and Furness a genuinely professional attitude replaced the enthusiasms of earlier editors. At the same time there was a greater degree of freshness and originality in the comments on Shakespeare made by a few of America's major writers and creative minds, who were by no means professional critics (with the exception, perhaps, of Lowell), but who possessed distinctive literary philosophies which made their opinions of special interest. However, before discussing the Shakespeare criticism of Emerson, Lowell and Whitman, one should mention the sturdy band of 'Baconians' in America who sought the bubble of reputation by questioning the authorship of the plays.

Delia Bacon's *The Philosophy of the Plays of Shakespeare Unfolded* (1857) first stated for Americans the startling thesis that the great dramas attributed to Shakespeare were in reality an indirect revelation of the New Learning which Bacon and a group of intellectuals sought to transmit to posterity.[14] Her recondite theory, the almost tragic intensity of her dedication to it, the story of her journey to Stratford and her unsettling doubts about the tomb she sought to open in proof of her theory, unbalanced her mind and led to her early death. The theory of Miss Bacon, the New England spinster, became the basic edifice upon which the anti-Stratfordians constructed elaborate designs, some of them inspired by an 'American' point of view. One of the most colourful of her adherents was William D. O'Connor, a journalist, novelist, defender of causes, and a man of high idealisms and great ability, whose pamphlet called *The Good Gray Poet* championed Walt Whitman against the charges of immorality when he was dismissed from his clerkship in Washington. When Richard Grant White referred to Miss Bacon as 'loony' and held that all Baconians should be carried off to madhouses, O'Connor entered the lists in her behalf by calling her 'the splendid Sybil'. In his *Hamlet's Notebook* (1886) he took issue with White's review of Mrs Henry Pott's *Promus*, charging him with misrepresenting her 'parallels' between Bacon and Shakespeare from a newly discovered Bacon manuscript. O'Connor likewise defended the most egregious American Baconian of them all, the gifted writer, orator, politician and abolitionist, Ignatius Donnelly, whose *The Great Cryptogram* (1888) proposed an ingenious 'cipher' method of determining the identity of Bacon in the plays. Donnelly applied an arithmetical system to a page of the Folio edition of *Henry IV, Part I*, where the text reads, 'I have a gammon of Bacon and two razes of ginger', and having derived his formula, he demonstrated a tortuous Daedalian plan winding its way through the plays. This cipher showed that Shakespeare, 'a poor, dull, ill-spirited greedy creature', was incapable of having written the plays and that Bacon, their author, either wrote or inspired the writing of nearly every play in the Elizabethan period with Burton's *Anatomy of Melancholy* and Montaigne's *Essays* into the bargain.

Not all the books belonging to the Baconian heresy were quite as sweeping as Donnelly's. A few expressed moderate views, based for example upon the idea that the playwright's knowledge of the law pointed to Bacon's authorship. Nathaniel Holmes' *The Authorship of Shakespeare*, which went through four editions from 1866 to 1886, and Appleton Morgan's *The Shakespearean Myth* (1881) both sought to destroy the actor-manager theory of authorship and to supplant it with Bacon or a group of men such as Southampton, Raleigh and Rutland surrounding him. The legal argument against Shakespeare penetrated deeply into American controversy, reaching even to Mark Twain, who asserted with vigour that the testimony of Lord Penzance and others was so strong as to convince him 'that the man who wrote Shakespeare's Works knew all about law and lawyers. Also, that that man could not have been the Stratford Shakespeare—and *wasn't*.'

An ironic element suggested by these attacks upon the Stratfordians is in their restatement, in biographical terms, of the much earlier eighteenth-century view, beginning with Voltaire, Dennis, Rhymer and others, that a dual nature was evident in Shakespeare. The neo-classic concept of 'Fancy's child' whereby the poet in his ignorance of dramatic rules and usages managed by a kind of spontaneous 'irregular' genius to produce sublime plays finds a revival in the concept of the uneducated actor-manager from Stratford who either could not have written the plays at all, or who combined the qualities of a stagehand with the genius of a great poet. The paradox was hinted at even by Coleridge in 1811 as between the genius exhibited in the plays and the life that has been attributed to Shakespeare. Emerson's view that the poet 'led an obscure and profane life' carried on the idea, later taken up by the Baconians. And even R. G. White who had attacked 'The Bacon–Shakespeare Craze' voiced the theory, as we have seen, that Shakespeare was a dramatic genius and at the same time a third-rate actor whose works were written in an almost sordid desire for money.

Emerson's interest in Shakespeare, a lifelong preoccupation as his journal entries indicate, rested, as did much of his philosophy, upon a paradox.[15] The man who flouted consistency and who, in his essay 'Shakespeare; or the Poet', could dismiss the Elizabethan as 'the master of revels to mankind', who 'after all shared the halfness and imperfection of humanity', could at the same time elevate Shakespeare to the pinnacle of poetic achievement. 'I delight in persons who clearly perceive the transcendent superiority of Shakespeare to all other writers', he said. The apparent contradiction in these views had several causes. One was Emerson's distrust of the theatre as a place of public amusement. Another lay in Emerson's theory of art and, behind that, in his transcendental, symbolic view of the universe as illusion. As a scholar, a man of letters, a lover of books and the past, Emerson idealized great men and worshipped greatness wherever he found it. Shakespeare was the greatest of poets, but the reality which he so splendidly revealed was finally, like nature itself, secondary. Behind the poet was 'Poetry', just as beneath the evanescent forms of nature lay a divine Oversoul toward which the world of reality aspires. In his moods of highest aspiration Emerson conceived the world of man and of nature as illusion, and therefore even the greatest poet who so brilliantly revealed them was diminished in proportion. Especially was the dramatist expendable, whose vehicle was a public playhouse. In the tradition of his visionary forbears he sought signs of God's meaning in mystic moments of illumination. And what he most wanted to find in the poetry of Shakespeare was just such flashes of insight. When this came to him, he said, 'it sinks the form, as of Drama or Epic, out of notice'.

Shakespeare became for Emerson a symbol and a transcendental abstraction. The mystic in this 'enraptured Yankee' found little enjoyment in the play itself. On one occasion when he attended a performance of Macready in *Hamlet*, he told the critic E. P. Whipple: 'I got along very well until he came to the passage,

> thou dead corse, again, in complete steel
> Revisit'st thus the glimpses of the moon—

and then actor, theatre, all vanished in view of that solving and dissolving imagination, which could reduce this big globe and all it inherits into mere glimpses of the moon'. And, while the play went on, Emerson said, absorbed in this thought he 'paid no heed to it'. Commenting upon this incident Richard Grant White pointed out that such 'nonsensical' speculation, based on a complete misunderstanding of the meaning of the phrase, in which Hamlet is remarking upon the return of the ghost of his father from the spirit world, was characteristic 'of the preposterousness of much of the most pretentious Shakespearean criticism'.

A New England mind of a less speculative and more genuinely historical and scholarly character was that of James Russell Lowell.[16] Lowell was without doubt the most widely read, judicious, and influential critic of nineteenth-century America. His essays on English literature from Chaucer to Keats are a comprehensive and impressive statement of the romantic standards of criticism, and his best work deserves to rank with that of Coleridge, Hazlitt or Lamb. Elements of all three are evident in his writing, as well as a strong infusion of the German romantic critics. He was also well grounded in literary history and critical approaches. His long and scholarly essay, 'Shakespeare Once More', written ostensibly as a review of White's edition of the plays, was Lowell's most complete personal critique of Shakespeare. His approach at first is through the history of the English language, indicating the various stages of its development down to the period in which Shakespeare wrote:

It may be reckoned one of the rarest pieces of good luck that ever fell to the share of a race...that he should have arrived at the full development of his powers at the moment when the material in which he was to work—that wonderful composite called English, the best result of the confusion of tongues—was in its freshest perfection.

Not yet fetlocked by dictionary or grammar-mongers, Shakespeare's language was to a certain extent 'established', yet still malleable in his hands so that he could squeeze meaning into a phrase like an hydraulic press.

Lowell's method as a critic was eclectic, inclined to impressionistic judgments, and studded with literary allusions. Behind his comments on Shakespeare, however, one can make out a loose system of values, drawn from many sources—Coleridge, Lessing, Goethe, Lamb, Schlegel, Carlyle. He appropriated Coleridge's distinctions between talent and genius, fancy and imagination, reason and understanding, but limited their application more strictly to aesthetic problems. He admired Lessing and Goethe, cited Schlegel frequently, and shared Charles Lamb's love of the 'old poets' and dramatists. Like Arnold he tended to rank the great masters, placing Shakespeare among his 'Five Indispensable Authors'. *Hamlet* was his favourite play where, like the Germans, he found a central unity of theme. All grows out of Hamlet's ingrained scepticism and self-doubt, reflected in his 'perpetual inclination to irony'. Following the tradition from Goethe and Coleridge he found irresolution and introversion to be the keys to Hamlet's mind, and saw a parallel in the 'introversion of mind which is so constant a phenomenon of these latter days', divided and weakened by the conflict between science and religion.

Lowell's broad knowledge of Shakespeare and the tradition of criticism reveals little first-hand acquaintance with the stage. He scarcely mentions the famous actors of his time or attendance at the theatre. He belonged to his time in its tendency to ignore the scenic and technical side of playwriting, and when he spoke of 'dramatic structure' he meant the term in the sense of a shaping or plastic power of imagination which welded the plays into organic works of art. It was the poet rather than the dramatic artist which impressed Lowell. The felicitous image and apt metaphor, separate lines and passages rose with amazing ease from Lowell's memory, and he once spoke of Shakespeare's language as possessing that quality of fusing the thought and the word—what Eliot would call the 'association of sensibility'. On the whole, Lowell did much to familiarize Shakespeare to literate Americans and, through his own position of importance as a critic and poet, to transfer to the American mind the principles of romantic criticism which he had absorbed from England and Germany.

Walt Whitman's estimate of Shakespeare included a number of the tendencies we have seen in his contemporaries, but combined in a way which was peculiar to the poet of nineteenth-century democracy.[27] Not a convinced 'Baconian', he flirted with some of the ideas of his friend O'Connor, but absorbed mainly the cultish idea that some great idea 'lurked' behind the plays which needed to be understood. He shared, in his way, the idolizing tradition of romantic criticism with the notable difference, as we have seen, of his experience and knowledge of the stage performances of the plays. Shakespeare was for Whitman much more than closet drama. Later when he came to regard himself as a kind of official spokesman of American democratic ideals, he began to feel reservations in the work of the Elizabethan poet whose work was hostile to 'the pride and dignity of the common people, the life-blood of democracy'. In his late years Whitman spoke of Shakespeare as a poet of 'feudal' history, and he sought ways in which to reconcile his early love of the splendid pageantry and eloquence of the histories and tragedies with his own sense of mission as a poet of a different social order. It seems likely, too, as Clifton Furness suggested, that he considered himself Shakespeare's rival in the New World and was even jealous of his fame.

A key statement of Whitman's attitude was his essay 'What Lurks Behind Shakespeare's Historical Plays' where, elaborating upon a suggestion of O'Connor that 'some ulterior design' lay buried in the histories, he advanced the hypothesis that they were in fact subtle satires upon an outworn age and were really intended to be prophetic of what he described as 'the scientific [Baconian?] inauguration of modern democracy'. By this ingenious argument Whitman sought to confirm his early impressions of the history plays, which he had always preferred, and to explain away the charge that Shakespeare stood for 'the mighty esthetic sceptres of the past' and not for 'the spiritual and democratic' sceptres of the future. Behind such a theory lay an evolutionary reading of history. Yet, after all his statements have been weighed in the balance, Whitman ranked Shakespeare higher even than the poet of common humanity, Burns, because he was 'the poet of great personalities' and his splendid portraits of great men 'are far dearer to me as lessons, and more precious even as models for Democracy, than the humdrum samples Burns presents'. Thus Whitman had come full circle from the years of his youth when he sat enraptured in his seat in the Old Bowery Theatre to his late years when, putting together into a single harmonious theory these various strands of opinion and doctrine, he reached the conclusion that 'If I had not stood before those poems with uncover'd head, fully aware of their colossal grandeur and beauty of form and spirit, I could not have written *Leaves of Grass*'.

IV

If, as Wallace Stevens said, there are thirteen ways of looking at a blackbird, there may be infinite ways of interpreting Shakespeare. To play 'his many parts' is admittedly one of the best. But to do this well depends upon knowledge, editorial and critical interpretation of the plays, and historical knowledge of the period. There is yet another distinguishable form of Shakespeare's impact upon later generations and nations of people. Just as he adapted to his own uses the writings of the classical past or medieval romance, Shakespeare has in turn become a 'usable past' for those who followed. His plots, language, and characterizations have provided materials for later artists to transmute into new forms. This evidence of 'influence' is of a different order from more conventional kinds, and rarer. To embody thematically into a new work of art the essence of another, as, for example, Eugene O'Neill succeeded in doing with the Agamemnon story in *Mourning Becomes Electra* or Mark Twain with the Romeo and Juliet sequence in *Huckleberry Finn*, is to work creatively and originally at a level beyond imitation. O'Neill wanted to revive the tale of revenge and murder of Aeschylus by transposing the Greek idea of 'Fate' into nineteenth-century America, suggesting Hawthorne's sense of the inevitable past affecting the present and replacing the older determinism with a biological and psychological form. Too often in studying literary influence we are diverted into statistical accounts of the use of lines as chapter or book titles, by epigraphs or 'echoes' or 'parallels'. But when a genuinely original writer finds himself moved to emulation by a play or a thematic unit of one of Shakespeare's plays we have, in literary form, the sort of genius which a great actor displays in performing a role.

Herman Melville and Henry James have come to be accepted as perhaps the two most original and subtle literary minds of nineteenth-century America. James never attempted to adapt Shakespeare to his *donnée* in the full sense, but in one story, *The Birthplace*, he did make an interesting study of the nature of genius embodied in a humble worshipper whose duty is to guide visitors around the shrine of the great poet. James, who had frequently cited Shakespeare in his critical writing and who had himself attempted the 'scenic art', attended the plays, and commented upon the actors, here made an oblique approach to the nature of literary greatness by embodying in his story a distinction between the critical mind as illustrated by the American visitors to the shrine and the genuinely artistic mind, as embodied in his central figure, Morris Gedge. Gedge at first is repelled by his assignment of telling lies about Shakespeare to ignorant tourists. But when he is threatened with dismissal for his attitude, he begins to spin elaborate fabrications, lies raised to a level of creativity, until it is clear that James has embodied in him a kind of genius akin to that of Shakespeare himself.[18]

Melville, as is well known, discovered Shakespeare during a decisive stage of his intellectual development in 1850 when he had written the first version of his story of whaling which was later to become *Moby Dick*. At the same time he had recently formed an acquaintance with Hawthorne and had reviewed *Mosses from an Old Manse*, linking together the American writer and the English dramatist by what he called their mutual 'power of blackness' and their 'great art of telling the truth'. The 'touch of Puritanic gloom' in Hawthorne, he saw, was the counterpart of Shakespeare's profound penetrations into the heart of man through 'the dark characters of Hamlet, Lear, Timon, and Iago'. Melville then proceeded to attack the Shakespeare idolaters who extol him without having read deeply and those who simply are impressed by stage manœuvres, 'Richard the third humps and Macbeth daggers'. Melville's comments in this essay led recent scholars like Charles Olson and F. O. Matthiessen to examine the full extent of the impact of Shakespearian themes, images, characters, and other devices upon *Moby Dick*, *Pierre* and *The Confidence Man*. Especially in *Moby Dick* it has become clear that Melville's imagination received a deeply felt impulse toward tragic drama from his reading of *King Lear*. After finishing his first version he apparently rewrote it largely into a tragedy of hate and revenge, employing Shakespearian dialogue, elevated language (close to the rhythms of Shakespearian blank verse), and many echoes and parallels to the Lear–fool scenes in his rendering of Ahab's madness and the insanity of Pip.

To attempt to review the whole story of Melville's use of Shakespeare would be impossible here. *Lear* and *Macbeth* are both written into certain scenes of Melville's masterpiece. Most significant of all the many evidences of influence is perhaps Olson's discovery of what Melville called the 'motto' of *Moby Dick* written on the fly-leaf of his volume of Shakespeare containing *King Lear*, *Othello* and *Hamlet*, a Latin inscription by which Ahab baptizes his lance '*in nomine Diaboli*', suggesting a parallel between the madness of Ahab and that of Lear.[19] F. O. Matthiessen summarizes his long discussion of the Shakespearian influence upon Melville with the statement: '... we are dealing with a rare case in which Shakespeare's conception of tragedy had so grown into the fibre of Melville's thought that much of his mature work became a re-creation of its themes in modern terms'.[20] Above all Melville was obsessed by the evil characters in Shakespeare. He was fascinated by the moral ambiguity of Edmund, for instance, who revealed to him that 'the infernal nature often has a valor denied to innocence', and that love was not the province only of the virtuous, as the relation between Edmund and Goneril showed. When Regan calls Gloucester an 'ingrateful fox', Melville could not restrain a marginal notation: 'Here's a touch Shakespearean—Regan talks of ingratitude!' In *Billy Budd* his exploration into the depths of human depravity in Claggart has suggestions in it of the 'motiveless malignity' that Coleridge saw in Iago.

But we cannot multiply instances. In the last analysis, it is in the composition of scenes and in the structural whole that one discovers Melville's transformation of a whaling epic into a new concept of 'democratic prose tragedy'. The nature of his use of Shakespeare has been compared to that of Eliot's appropriation of thematic elements from Joyce's *Ulysses*, Weston's *From Ritual to Romance* and Frazer's *Golden Bough*. It was a form of adaptation which Eliot described in 'Tradition and the Individual Talent':

No poet, no artist of any art, has his complete meaning alone. His significance, his appreciation is the appreciation of his relation to the dead poets and artists.... What happens when a new work of art is created is something that happens simultaneously to all the works of art which preceded it....

NOTES

1. Accounts of early stage-productions may be found in G. C. D. Odell, *Annals of the New York Stage* (New York, 1927); W. W. Clapp, Jr., *A Record of the Boston Stage* (Boston and Cambridge, 1853); and two more recent studies to which I am indebted throughout my essay: A. V. R. Westfall, *American Shakespearean Criticism, 1607–1865* (New York, 1939), and E. C. Dunn, *Shakespeare in America* (New York, 1939).

2. See A. V. R. Westfall, *op. cit. passim*, and H. R. Steeves, 'American Editors of Shakespeare', in Columbia University *Shakespearian Studies*, ed. Brander Matthews and Ashley Thorndike (New York, 1962), pp. 347–68.

3. Adams found support for his conservative doctrine of an aristocracy of the 'rich, the well-born and the able' in Ulysses' speech on degrees in society from *Troilus and Cressida*. Jefferson copied quotations from Shakespeare frequently into his commonplace book. *Henry IV, Part I, Julius Caesar*, and *Coriolanus* were especially cited. One of them was a speech of Coriolanus deploring the mob and requesting the Senators not to give away their power to the officers of the people (cf. E. C. Dunn, *op. cit.* pp. 88–9 and 95–7).

4. The first of these incidents was reported in the *Virginia Gazette* for November 1751. The second reported in Sol Smith, *Theatrical Management in the West and South for Thirty Years, Interspersed with Anecdotal Sketches* (New York, 1868). Cf. E. C. Dunn, *op. cit.* pp. 65 ff., 175 ff. and elsewhere.

5. The passage occurs in Whitman's *Specimen Days*, where he reminisces over his youthful days of play- and opera-going in New York.

6. The episode is told in various histories of the American stage. The most detailed account I have seen is in Meade Minnegerode, *The Fabulous Forties* (New York, 1924), pp. 187–209.

7. *Notes and Comments upon Certain Plays and Actors of Shakespeare, with Criticisms and Correspondence* (New York, 1863). The book contains a considerable correspondence with John Quincy Adams giving certain of his critical opinions upon the plays. See esp. pp. 95–7, 308–9 and *passim*.

8. *November Boughs* (Philadelphia, 1888), pp. 87–92.

9. His familiarity with some of the famous passages is evident, but there are relatively few references to the plays themselves and to Twain's attendance at performances. His special fondness for *Romeo and Juliet* is indicated in his handling of the feud-scenes in *Huckleberry Finn*. The theory expressed by M. Brashear in *Mark Twain, Son*

of Missouri (Chapel Hill, 1934), p. 218 n., that 'Is Shakespeare Dead?' was an 'exquisite parody' on the Baconians can hardly be accepted in view of A. B. Paine's flat statement: 'Mark Twain had the fullest conviction as to the Bacon authorship of Shakespeare's plays' (*Mark Twain, A Biography*, IV, 1846). The pamphlet itself, despite some burlesquing, leaves little doubt that he was serious, as do many other conversations he had with Paine on the subject in 1908.

10. Most of the information above may be found in A. V. R. Westfall, *op. cit.* chs. 6, 7, and in H. R. Steeves, *op. cit. passim*. Also see Jane Sherzer, 'American Editors of Shakespeare, 1753–1866', *PMLA*, XXIII (1907), 633–96.

11. Hudson's criticism and editing are discussed in both Westfall and Dunn, as well as in my unpublished dissertation, *American Criticism of Shakespeare, 1820–1885*, University of Wisconsin, 1941.

12. See my article, 'Critical Tendencies in Richard Grant White's Shakespeare Commentary', *American Literature* (May 1948), pp. 145–54.

13. Karl Knortz, *Shakespeare in Amerika, Ein Literarhistorische Studie* (Berlin, 1882), pp. 44–5.

14. I am dependent in the following discussion of the authorship theories upon Frank Wadsworth's informative account, *The Poacher from Stratford* (Berkeley, California, 1958).

15. See my article, 'Emerson and Shakespeare', *PMLA* (January 1941), pp. 315–30.

16. Scholarship on Lowell's criticism in general and his commentary on Shakespeare in particular is extensive. One might mention here N. Foerster's *American Criticism* (New York, 1928), pp. 111–56, and J. J. Reilly, *James Russell Lowell as a Critic* (New York, 1915). These two treatments represent opposed views on Lowell. A. Ralli, *A History of Shakespearean Criticism*, 2 vols. (London, 1932), has a section on Lowell's criticism of Shakespeare. G. Wurfl, 'Lowell's Debt to Goethe', *The Pennsylvania State College Studies*, vol. 1 (27 July 1936), treats the German influence in detail.

17. The subject has been treated by R. C. Harrison, 'Walt Whitman and Shakespeare', *PMLA* (December 1929), pp. 1201–38; also by C. J. Furness, 'Walt Whitman's Estimate of Shakespeare', *Harvard Studies and Notes in Philology and Literature*, XIV (1932), 1–33; and by Floyd Stovall, 'Whitman's Knowledge of Shakespeare', *Studies in Philology*, XLIX (October 1952), 643–69. Also see my 'Shakespeare's Place in Walt Whitman's America', *The Shakespeare Association Bulletin* (April 1942), pp. 86–96.

18. James's interest in Shakespeare extended from his youthful attendance at plays to the late prefaces when he discussed his own artistic conceptions, frequently alluding to Shakespearian characters. My brief discussion of the subject is indebted to the essay 'James Examines Shakespeare: Notes on the Nature of Genius', by W. T. Stafford, *PMLA* (March 1958), pp. 123–8.

19. See Charles Olson, *Call Me Ishmael* (New York, 1947).

20. F. O. Matthiessen, *The American Renaissance* (New York, 1941), p. 435. Matthiessen's discussion is detailed and includes parallels, echoes and influences of many of the plays upon Melville's work. He terms *Pierre* 'An American *Hamlet*' and sees a 'mood of Timonism' in *The Confidence Man*. There is also an extended discussion of Melville and Shakespeare in E. H. Rosenberry, *Melville and the Comic Spirit* (Harvard University Press, 1955).

INTERNATIONAL NOTES

A selection has been made from the reports received from our correspondents, those which present material of a particularly interesting kind being printed in their entirety, or largely so. It should be emphasized that the choice of countries to be thus represented has depended on the nature of the information presented in the reports, not upon either the importance of the countries concerned or upon the character of the reports themselves.

Austria

The Shakespeare Quatercentenary was celebrated in Austria both by a number of commemorative festivities and frequent performances of Shakespeare's plays in Vienna and numerous smaller towns.

The series of Shakespeare celebrations was opened at the Burgtheater, Vienna, where Shakespeare has been performed 4505 times since the foundation of the theatre in 1776. The festival address was given by Christopher Fry, and passages from Shakespeare's plays were read by Diana Wynyard and a number of Austrian actors. Other commemorative meetings in Vienna were held at the Akademietheater, at the Theater der Courage, and in the University. The Landestheater of Tyrol commemorated Shakespeare by a performance of *A Midsummer Night's Dream* preceded by an address given by Eugen Thurnher; and the Stadttheater Klagenfurt, Carinthia, also held a Shakespeare week including the performance of two plays and a lecture on Shakespeare's art. Particularly worthy of note is the fact that various smaller provincial towns revealed an increasing interest in Shakespeare and that they introduced their audiences to a number of plays which are not part of the usual repertory of Austrian theatres.

The presentation at the Burgtheater, Vienna, of the complete cycle of the histories, namely *Richard II, Henry IV, Henry V, Henry VI, Richard III* in five successive evenings must be considered the most impressive achievement of the theatrical activities of an Austrian theatre in 1964.

Macbeth was also performed a number of times both at the Landestheater, Linz, and the Burgtheater, Vienna. The Viennese production, so it seems to the reviewer, was alien to the genuine spirit of Shakespeare and through the excessive use of lighting effects in various colours, frequent changes of setting, the interruption of the action, the unjustified attention paid to irrelevant aspects of the tragedy and the purely mechanical and optical effects robbed the production of a good deal of its strength and unity. Schlegel's old translation was used here, with a number of cuts and with undue prominence given to the witch scenes.

In contrast to this production, fundamentally spectacular and operatic in style, the production of *The Merry Wives of Windsor* by Rudolf Steinboeck was an enormous success, indicating the producer's deep understanding of the nature of Shakespeare's art. Here a uniform setting was used and the flow of the action was never noticeably interrupted, the attention of the audience being entirely focused on the action proceeding on the stage. Since the acting was also excellent this production certainly ranks with the best which Austrian theatre-goers have been able to see during the last years. It seems entirely incomprehensible, though it is indicative of the outdated standards by which Shakespearian performances are judged by many in this country, that this Burgtheater production received numerous adversely critical reviews.

Friesach, where every summer a Shakespearian play is performed in the old castle, produced *The Merchant of Venice* (Hannes Sandler), a play which had not been performed in this country during the last twenty years. The Stadttheater Klagenfurt, under the active management of Otto Hans Böhm, produced *Lear* for the first time in the history of the theatre, and, until mid-October 1964, the play saw sixteen performances, which is indeed remarkable considering the small population of the town. *The Taming of the Shrew* saw twenty-three performances in 1963–4, and in 1964 it was played five times. Other productions included those of *Hamlet* in Graz, and *Romeo and Juliet* in Bregenz, Vorarlberg.

It is surprising that the number of comedies performed in 1964 was not at all large and was above all limited in regard to the number of plays produced: *As You Like It*, *Measure for Measure*, *The Comedy of Errors*, and *Twelfth Night*.

Shakespeare has always belonged to the favourite dramatic authors of this country, but through the activities in the Shakespeare Year, including performances of plays, lectures, and newspaper articles, more people than ever before heard of Shakespeare and were introduced to his poetry and his plays. The reviewer feels that in this country Shakespeare was celebrated in a dignified and extensive form and that the quatercentenary has contributed greatly to a wider interest in and esteem of Shakespeare.   SIEGFRIED KORNINGER

Belgium

Throughout the period of 1963–4 Shakespeare has been well to the fore in Belgium, although we must bear in mind that the professional stage in this country, both in the Netherlands and in the French-speaking regions, is limited in numbers and organizational possibilities. Contrary to some of the less lavish productions of the past, many recent presentations lack style and homogeneity. There is a dangerous trend to cut the author's work all too drastically, and to insert sometimes doubtful inventions of the producer. Surely the best kind of production finds its inspiration in and through the text and the dramatic situation. Now it is at the author's cost that many a producer's offering is urged on the audience. The portrayal of the characters themselves shows a craving for outward sound and fury or tends to result in naturalistic mumbling. There seems to be little search for the right dimension in speech and movement. Speed takes the place of rhythm, dreariness and carelessness replace thought and emotion. So it sometimes happens that performances, considerable cuts and speed taken into account, cannot measure up to former well-balanced productions. The most exasperating aspect of these recent performances is the loss of teamwork; we may come across individual work of value, but a high total standard is non-existent.

Summarizing recent Shakespearian activities in Belgium we may note the following:

The Flemish section of the National Theatre (Antwerp) presented *Much Ado About Nothing* (*Veel leven om niets*) and *Othello*. The Royal Flemish Theatre in Brussels gave a limited series of performances of earlier productions of *Hamlet* and *The Merchant of Venice* (*De Koopman van Venetie*), and staged new productions of *As You Like It* (*Elk wat wils*) and *Richard III*. An annual tradition, inaugurated years ago by the Reizand Volks-

teater (Touring), has happily been continued: *The Merry Wives of Windsor* (*De Vrolyke vrouwtjes van Windsor*) and *A Midsummer Night's Dream* (*Midzomernachtsdroom*) were successfully produced in the courtyard and gardens of Rubens's house in Antwerp, joining the already impressive list of Shakespeare plays performed there by this company.

The commemoration of the quatercentenary of William Shakespeare's birth has given the Flemish radio (B.R.T. Third Programme) the opportunity to broadcast an adaptation of *Henry IV, Parts I and II*, and *Henry V*, making Falstaff the central character. A series of lectures on the Bard's work, illustrated by scenes out of *Hamlet*, *Henry V*, *Henry VI*, *Richard III*, and *Antony and Cleopatra*, completed this contribution, whilst Flemish and French television gave excerpts from *Macbeth* and *A Midsummer Night's Dream*.

In recent years several new Netherlands' translations have been tried out, A. L. Burgerdyk's still being the most functional, although the new ones by Willy Courteaux have their own merits.

French–Belgian Shakespearian contributions include a series of performances at the Palais des Beaux-Arts by the Rideau de Brussels of *The Tempest*, *King Lear* and *Love's Labour's Lost* (*Peine d'amour perdue*), as well as the Théâtre du Parc's performances of *Macbeth* under the guidance of Michael Croft as guest producer, using a useful translation by Roger Avermaete.

DOM. DE GRUYTER

Czechoslovakia

Though at the time of writing this report the anniversary year 1964 has not yet ended, it is already safe to say that it may well mean the turning-point in the appreciation of Shakespeare in our country. It would be pointless to count out all the new productions all over Czechoslovakia: they were indeed numerous and have begun to show the new trend in Shakespearian production—vigorous, even controversial underlining of one main idea. Shakespeare is no longer treated as a great classic demanding explanation, he is no longer approached with veneration but courageously (some would even say sacrilegiously) staged as a modern dramatist.

This trend first found expression in Otomar Krejca's *Romeo and Juliet* at the Prague National Theatre, but during 1964 became accepted as a kind of model for contemporary productions. Another stimulus in the same direction was the visit to Czechoslovakia by the Royal Shakespeare Company, especially Peter Brook's *King Lear*. And the third agent were essays of the

Polish scholar Jan Kott which were published here first in magazines and finally in book form. All these new efforts for the modern appreciation of Shakespeare on stage have been enhanced by several new translations.

It is my sad duty to report the death of the best known modern Czech translator of Shakespeare, Erik A. Saudek, who died in the summer of 1963. For a long time his translations held an unchallenged place in the Czech theatres and his influence on both Shakespearian repertory and staging was very pronounced. With him passed away a characteristic period of Shakespearian production in our country and though the new wave of translators tackles almost all the plays not long ago translated by Saudek (especially the tragedies), it will no doubt take some time before his trenchant rendering of *The Merry Wives of Windsor* is ousted from Czech stages by a newer version.

There were naturally several festive occasions commemorating the anniversary, the greatest of which was arranged by the Charles University in Prague on 23 April. A conference on Shakespearian translations and productions brought out many interesting problems and confrontations of controversial ideas. A Shakespeare Exhibition in Prague and a Festival of Shakespeare's plays in Brno were slightly disappointing though they did much for the appreciation of Shakespeare by the general public.

As for books published at the occasion of the anniversary, apart from many editions of Shakespeare's plays, Jan Kott's *Shakespearean Sketches*, Zdeněk Stříbrný's survey *William Shakespeare*, and my anthology of English essays, *Shakespeare and the Modern Stage*, were all favourably accepted. The pride of place, however, should in my mind go to the *Complete Works* of Shakespeare in a classical translation by J. V. Sládek, the last two volumes of which were published in 1964. (Incidentally, the notes and commentary by the editor, Professor O. Vocadlo, if published separately, would make a book of some 500 pages!) Mention should also be made of the issue of a set of Shakespearian records with accompanying surveys of *Shakespeare and Music* by Josef Bachtík and Jiří Berkovec, *Shakespeare on Czech Stages* by Jaroslav Pokorný and *Shakespeare and the Slovak Theatre* by Ladislav Lajcha.

BRETISLAV HODEK

Finland

Since the 1880's twenty-five out of Shakespeare's thirty-six plays have been performed in Finland, both in Finnish and Swedish. Altogether eleven of them were taken up by twenty-two theatres (nineteen Finnish,

three Swedish) to celebrate the festival year. The eleven were: *Hamlet, The Merry Wives of Windsor, A Midsummer Night's Dream, The Taming of the Shrew, Twelfth Night, Macbeth, As You Like It, The Tempest, Othello, Much Ado About Nothing* and *Romeo and Juliet*.

In Helsinki, *Macbeth* was performed by the Finnish National Theatre; *Othello* by the Helsinki Folk Theatre; *Hamlet*, a somewhat Madariaga-influenced approach, by the Swedish Theatre. *The Taming of the Shrew* continued its run, started in 1963, at the National Theatre. At Tampere, *As You Like It* (by the Tampere Theatre) and *Macbeth* (by the Tampere Workers' Theatre) as well as Verdi's *Macbeth* (by the Tampere Opera Society) are appealing to large audiences. The Finnish National Opera in Helsinki celebrated Shakespeare by taking up Verdi's *Otello*. At Turku, *A Midsummer Night's Dream* started its run in 1963; the Åbo Swedish Theatre is performing *As You Like It*.

In April a Shakespeare Festival was arranged by the University of Helsinki. The programme included an address by the Rector of the University, as well as a paper on Shakespeare's changing interpretation by Rafael Koskimies. Two leading artists, Mrs Ritva Ahonen-Mäkelä and Erik Lindström, recited cycles of sonnets, and two of the English lectors of the University, Diana Colman and Kingsley Hart, performed a scene from *As You Like It*. The festival was concluded by Sibelius's suite of music composed for *The Tempest*, played by the Helsinki City Orchestra.

The university section of the Finnish Theatre School are at present working on a project based on an all-round study of *Hamlet*, theory as well as practice, including the Marovidz–Brook version of the play. Several university lectures are being devoted to Shakespeare throughout the academic year. The Drama Studio at Tampere has had a reconstruction built of an Elizabethan stage to celebrate the festival year.

In the theatre journals as well as in daily papers numerous articles on different aspects of Shakespeare have been appearing all through the year. A. L. Rowse's biography as well as the various new books on the sonnets have been reviewed; the Royal Shakespeare Company productions of the histories at Stratford-upon-Avon have been analysed; excursions to Stratford have been arranged.

IRMA RANTAVAARA

France

The Shakespeare Year began with a series of performances of *King John* at the Théâtre de l'Est Parisien. The play had already been presented in 1956 by the same company, which was then called 'La Guilde' (cf. *Shakespeare Survey 11*, p. 119). It was a promising amateur group which has matured, and has acquired professional status. The T.E.P. is now one of the Maisons de la Culture which are being created all over France, and is not unlike that of the Theatre Workshop in the London area. It provides the best type of drama to a new audience, in a part of the world which, until recently, was thoroughly deprived of theatre life. As we have already observed in the case of a number of Centres Dramatiques Régionaux and Maisons de la Culture, Shakespeare is as popular as Molière with the new public. Bernard Guillaumot's setting perfectly suited Guy Rétoré's sober and dynamic style of production, which gave full value to speech and action. Raymond Garrivier as the King, Jean-Jacques Lagarde as the Bastard, and Arlette Tephany as Constance, deserved special praise, but the team work of the whole company was excellent.

Early in the year, Jean-Pierre Granval produced *As You Like It* at Odéon-Théâtre de France. The performance owed a great deal to the translation of Jules Supervielle, which succeeds in recapturing the poetical mood of the adventures in Arden. The simple and attractive settings of Bernard Evein, and the use of banners and emblems, made the change of scenes, always a problem on a traditional stage, as plain as ABC. Perhaps Simone Valère brought unnecessary sophistication to the part of Rosalind, and there were embarrassing moments in the scenes of courtship, with Domenique Paturel as Orlando. J.-L. Barrault was the exiled Duke. Later in the year he was to take, for the last time in his career, the title-part in André Gide's version of *Hamlet*, which he first produced in 1946.

Meanwhile, the company of the Théâtre de la Cité, of Villeurbanne, took possession of the Odéon for a series of performances of *Troilus and Cressida*. This new Shakespearian venture of Roger Planchon's was awaited with curiosity, as his *Henry IV* had raised much controversy (cf. *Shakespeare Survey 13*, p. 127). Planchon had astutely announced a change of position from Brecht to Aristotle. This was obviously calculated to create a stir in the press. Yet he seemed determined, this time, to let Shakespeare speak for himself. He used an unabridged version, and endeavoured to retain all the difficult rhetoric and imagery. Unfortunately this version was based on a literal translation; the final product sounded rather outlandish, and was not very easy for the actors to speak. *Troilus* is one of the longest plays, and André Acquart's mobile setting was interesting but complicated and rather unwieldy. A fair amount of stage business reminiscent of political meeting and sportive competition

was introduced as a topical element and a relief for the audience at Villeurbanne. All this slowed down the performance, and, by way of compensation, the reciting of the text had to be speeded up. Planchon's own reading of the play was that the Greeks and the Trojans alike had nothing but contempt for women's freedom, and that, while pretending to act in the name of honour and courtesy, they behaved not only like war criminals, but like criminals against love. On the stage, allusions to modern warfare were numerous, and soldiers looked rather more like paratroopers than warriors of the *Iliad*. Of course a play like *Troilus*, with a strong satirical element, can, up to a point, stand that sort of treatment. The intrigue, based on the comedy of humours, concerning the rivalry between Ajax and Achilles, came off rather well. But Planchon's error was to make all the Greek chiefs equally ridiculous and despicable. Agamemnon lacked all dignity; Ulysses was unsubtle, and delivered the speech on order and degree like a soap-box orator. By denying his Greeks and Trojans even the appearance of greatness, he deprived himself of the dramatic effect of the collapse of all values, political wisdom, chivalry, and valour in the final scenes. It was a pity because these battle scenes were superbly done, Acquart's mobile setting and Planchon's sense of stage dynamic combining to suggest a world disintegrating and returning to a chaos of primitive violence.

Gabriel Garran produced *Coriolanus* at the Théâtre du Peuple, for the IVth Festival of Aubervilliers (a popular suburb in the north of Paris). He found his inspiration in Brecht's discussion of the play. And while bringing class relationships and conflicts in the foreground, he was careful not to oversimplify the issues, or to sacrifice characterization. Unfortunately the adaptation he used sounded more like a political commentary on the play than a translation of it, and was thoroughly journalistic in tone. And it was rather distressing to observe that the passages from the play quoted by a Brecht expert in the programme notes were missing in the adaptation!

Jean Gillibert used the full text of *Romeo and Juliet*, in Yves Bonnefoy's fine translation, for performances of the play at the Festival open-air du Marais and Cloître St Séverin. The language of Thierry Maulnier's version of *Macbeth* is also beautiful. This could hardly be said of the *mise en scène* by Claude Chabrol, a film producer belonging to what was described, ten years ago, as the *nouvelle vague*. The performances took place in the charming seventeenth-century Théâtre Montansier, at Versailles. In the same theatre, Yves Florenne's smooth and brilliant version of *Romeo and Juliet* (with several lyrical speeches drastically cut, unfortunately) fared better at the hands of Marcelle Tassencourt, the producer, and director of the company. The Tréteaux de France toured the Ile de France, for a second year, under a canvas tent, with *Hamlet*, produced by Morvan Lebesque. Later in the year, the company gave open-air performances of the play at the Arênes de Lutèce. Mention should also be made of *The Taming of the Shrew*, with Pierre della Torre and his Compagnons de Saint-Maur, a promising company doing good work in a suburban area south of Paris. Raymond Hermantier presented his new, much improved, production of Maurice Clavel's version of *Julius Caesar* (cf. *Shakespeare Survey 11*, p. 119), at the Roman Theatre in Lyon-Charbonnières, and later in Paris at the Théâtre Sarah-Bernhardt.

Jean Anouilh presented his new adaptation of *Richard III* at the Théâtre Montparnasse, with Daniel Ivernel in the title-part, and Christiane Minazzoti as Lady Anne. The 'misérabiliste' setting by Denis Maclès, and the caricatural acting of Tsilla Chelton as Queen Margaret, were in keeping with Anouilh's conception of the play as a thoroughly undignified and sordid affair.

Guy Parigot also produced *Richard III* for the Comédie de l'Ouest, while Jacques Fabbri had the rollicking fun he likes with *The Merry Wives of Windsor* (Centre Dramatique du Sud-Est), and Maurice Sarrazin (Grenier de Toulouse) revived his *Twelfth Night* in the Théodore Lascaris version which Jacques Copeau used for his memorable production fifty years ago. The latest addition to this list is André Reybaz's *Romeo and Juliet* for the Centre Dramatique du Nord. On the whole, the suburbs and provinces were far more active than Paris; the capital had to rely, to a large extent, on their contributions for the Shakespeare year. And the abstention of the Comédie-Française and the Théâtre National Populaire was to be regretted. The number of productions, a result of 'décentralisation', is an encouraging sign. But most of the companies have limited resources. And one cannot help longing for Shakespearian performances which, without being lavish, would combine imaginative directorship with financial means that would secure a thoroughly competent cast and the necessary number of rehearsals. Let us wait for the *Hamlet* of the T.N.P. announced for the next year by Jean Vilar's successor, Georges Wilson.

La Société des Anglicistes de l'Enseignement Supérieur was responsible for the formation of a National Committee. Cycles of lectures, exhibitions, performances by student groups, were organized in most university towns, usually in collaboration with the municipalities, libraries, dramatic and cultural centres. On 23 April a simple ceremony took place at the Grand Amphithéâtre of the Sorbonne: a single speech, by André Maurois, followed by scenes from the plays and music inspired by them. The young were in the majority, and the fervour and intensity of the huge audience was impressive.

In this century French scholars have lectured on Shakespeare and commented on his plays for the benefit of generations of students. But apart from editions, translations, and the accompanying apparatus, they have published little. While the whole field of Elizabethan drama was and is still being explored, thesis after thesis, the only two full-length studies to be mentioned are those of Henri Fluchère and Paul Reyher. The IVth Conference of the S.A.E.S., held at Toulouse, might indicate a turn of the tide. It revealed that much work was now in progress on the significance of Shakespeare's work then and now. The Journées internationales d'études organized at the Centre National de la Recherche Scientifique revealed that much research was also devoted to the study of the influence and performance of Shakespeare in Europe in the nineteenth and twentieth centuries. Papers read at both conferences will appear in special numbers of *Etudes anglaises* and *Revue d'Histoire du Théâtre*. A special issue of the *Bulletin de l'Université de Strasbourg* will also be devoted to Shakespeare.

Over the air the anniversary was marked by a series of programmes: a cycle of debates, a presentation of extracts from all the plays in the canon, concerts of Elizabethan music, parallel broadcasts of *Edward II* and *Richard II* associating Marlowe with the commemoration, and, finally, a radio performance of the whole tetralogy, *Henry VI* to *Richard III*.   JEAN JACQUOT

Germany

Although Shakespeare had held the first rank among the popular dramatists on German stages for many years, the year 1964 naturally brought a new climax of Shakespeare productions in Germany. Several large towns arranged for a festival week with a whole series of Shakespeare performances, many universities had their Shakespeare celebrations and the cultural societies and institutions existing in German towns as a rule also devoted one or two nights to the memory of the dramatist. As detailed reports about the new performances of Shakespearian plays have not yet come in, this notice can give only a brief enumeration of the chief events. The most extended Shakespeare festival took place at Bochum, where the Shakespeare Society of Western Germany celebrated the quatercentenary by a series of new productions, lectures, concerts and an exhibition 'Shakespeare and the German Theatre'. Among the new productions *Troilus and Cressida* (produced by Hans Schalla) scored a particularly notable success, but also *All's Well that Ends Well* (produced by Hans Joachim Heyse) and *King Lear* (produced by Hans Fritzsche) maintained the high standard of the Bochum theatre which for many years has been one of Germany's leading Shakespeare stages.

Two famous productions of other German theatres also appeared as guest performances at Bochum, *Othello* (produced by Fritz Kortner of the Kammerspiele, Munich) and *Measure for Measure* (produced by Oscar Fritz Schuh of the State Theatre, Hamburg). In addition there was a French guest performance, *La Vie et la mort du roi Jean* of the Théâtre de l'Est, Paris, and *The Tempest* was shown in a marionette production.

On the morning of 23 April a formal celebration took place at the theatre, where the audience was addressed among others by the British Ambassador Sir Frank Roberts, Cardinal Frings and the Minister of Education, Dr P. Mikat. The anniversary Shakespeare Lecture was given by Wolfgang Clemen. Other lectures on the following days were given by Walter Muschg (Basel) on 'The Romantic Shakespeare Myth', and by Siegfried Melchinger on 'Shakespeare Today'.

Similar Shakespeare-seasons or weeks took place in Stuttgart (with *A Midsummer Night's Dream, Much Ado about Nothing, Measure for Measure* and *The Tempest*), at the Schiller Theatre in Berlin (with *The Taming of the Shrew, Timon of Athens, Twelfth Night,* and *Richard III*), in Munich (with *Macbeth, Much Ado* and *Hamlet* at the Residenztheater; with *Othello* and *Measure for Measure* at the Kammerspiele), at Göttingen (where Heinz Hilpert produced *As You Like It, Twelfth Night, Much Ado, Measure for Measure, The Winter's Tale* and *King Lear*), and at the open-air theatre in the park of Herrenhausen (where *Hamlet, The Comedy of Errors,* and *The Merry Wives of Windsor* were performed during the summer months). Freiburg and Wiesbaden also had their Shakespeare weeks.

Simultaneously with the festival at Bochum, the German Shakespeare Society of Weimar had a week of Shakespeare performances, lectures and concerts at the Nationaltheater in Weimar which showed new productions of *Hamlet* and *Richard III*, while *Troilus and Cressida* was performed by the State Theatre of Dresden. These two theatres also appeared with guest-performances of *Richard III* and of *Troilus and Cressida* on several stages in western Germany.

Altogether 28 plays by Shakespeare were performed on more than 2500 nights in approximately 200 new productions. *Hamlet* alone appeared in 18 different productions. But even plays which so far had rarely been shown on German stages appeared in several new productions, as for example *Troilus and Cressida* of which there were four different productions.

There were several guest performances by foreign théâtres in the course of 1964. The Bristol Old Vic toured Germany with *Henry V* and *Love's Labour's Lost*, and the Theatre de France presented *Hamlet*. An interesting feature of the quatercentenary was the frequency of opera performances and ballets based on Shakespearian plays. Operas like *Macbeth, Falstaff, The Taming of the Shrew, Otello* and *The Merry Wives of Windsor* appeared in altogether 47 new productions, and 11 ballets after scenes from Shakespeare were shown.

In most universities special lectures on Shakespeare were given by visiting professors from England or from other German universities. There was, too, a notable revival of Elizabethan music and also a new interest in films based on Shakespeare plays which were shown in connexion with the Shakespeare celebrations. The 100th volume of the German Shakespeare Jahrbuch was published in April and contained a great variety of contributions not only by scholars but also by actors, producers, translators and critics. KARL BRINKMANN
WOLFGANG CLEMEN

Greece

During 1964, up to October, there have been produced in Greece three Shakespearian plays: on 13 March, the National Theatre of Northern Greece gave in Kavala the première of *Othello*, translated by Kl. Kartheos; on 10 July the 'Greek Popular Theatre' produced in Athens *Julius Caesar*, translated and directed by Minos Volonakis; lastly, the National Theatre of Northern Greece again presented in Kavala *Twelfth Night*, translated by Vassili Rotas. This production was given outdoors and in a place that had not been used before for theatrical presentations—in the courtyard of a church by the sea. The play was presented by the same company on tour in several towns of Macedonia and in Salonica.

ANGHELOS TERZAKIS

Hungary

During the seasons 1962–63 and 1963–64 Shakespeare's plays featured prominently on the Hungarian stage, both in Budapest and in the larger country towns. Fourteen of his plays were produced, a greater number than for many years previously, with some plays achieving remarkably long runs. *Hamlet* was the great favourite, not only in the Budapest Madách Theatre (where Miklós Gábor continued to impersonate the Prince while the rest of the leading roles were taken over by new hands and the entirely new production was directed, as before, by László Vámos), but also in the provincial towns of Pécs and Szeged.

Among the tragedies the production of *Julius Caesar* in the Budapest National Theatre was the most outstanding. The all-star cast of László Ungváry's Caesar, Lajos Básti's Brutus, Ferenc Bessenyei's Mark Antony and Imre Sinkovits's Cassius gave an unforgettable rendering of a play that has not been seen in Hungary for twenty years. In the same theatre Miss Margit Lukács, our great tragic actress, excelled as Lady Macbeth, and a few months later, Lajos Básti as King Lear. His interpretation of the king was, perhaps, not entirely uninfluenced by the performance of the same play, in February 1964, by the Royal Shakespeare Company of Stratford (with Paul Scofield as Lear, directed by Peter Hall) which had an almost frenzied reception in Budapest.

Richard III was a deserved success in the university town of Debrecen, where Károly Bángyörgyi in the title role and Mrs Margit Lontay as Queen Margaret rose to new heights of their distinguished histrionic careers, under the direction of György Lengyel.

Richard II, a play not acted in Hungary since 1925, was revived in the summer of 1963 and was the first Shakespearian drama to be given in a theatre-in-the-round performance in Hungary.

The year 1964 marked a double centenary in Hungary. It was a hundred years ago, in 1864, that *A Midsummer Night's Dream*, ever since that time the perennial favourite of the Hungarian stage, was translated by János Arany and first performed in this country. The fourth centenary of Shakespeare's birth was commemorated this year not only by a very great number of performances of his plays—it is no exaggeration to say that not a week has passed without the presentation of at least one of his dramas in Budapest or elsewhere in this country—but by other events as well. Miklós Borsos, the eminent sculptor, made a powerful portrait-medal of the bard, a Shakespeare commemorative postage-stamp was issued, and a series of sound and television broadcasts were devoted to Shakespeare and his works. The most noteworthy scholarly contribution to Shakespeare studies was made by László Kéry, eminent young critic and assistant professor in Budapest university, who in a recently published volume, the most extensive and scholarly work on Shakespeare in Hungary since the last war, gave a well-balanced Marxist interpretation of all of Shakespeare's comedies.

LADISLAS ORSZÁGH

Israel

The year began with a special evening given at Habimah on the I.T.I. annual theatre day; this was dedicated to Shakespeare. The oustanding actors of the four theatres in Israel (Habimah, Chamber, Ohel and Haifa Municipal Theatres) each gave readings and monologues from the Shakespearian plays they had performed.

In June the Haifa Theatre, under the direction of Joseph Milo, presented a lively and imaginative *Midsummer Night's Dream*, made particularly notable by its novel treatment of Bottom as a youthful and irrepressible figure who became almost the counterpart, in the human world, of the fairy realm's Robin Goodfellow. At Tel Aviv the Habimah is preparing to give its first performances of *The Comedy of Errors*.

REUBEN AVINOAM

Italy

Many countries have issued stamps to commemorate the fourth Shakespearian centenary; Italy has not, notwithstanding a suggestion which came from the same quarters which a few years ago succeeded in persuading the Ministero delle Poste to issue a Byron stamp on the occasion of the inauguration of a Byron Memorial in the Villa Borghese. It would be wrong, however, to conclude from this episode that Shakespeare is less popular in Italy than Byron. On the contrary, to judge from the number of performances and the ever-increasing number of translations, one cannot resist the impression that Shakespeare is extremely popular here.

His latest Italian translator, Gabriele Baldini (*Opere complete*, nuovamente tradotte e annotate, Milan, Rizzoli, 1963, 3 vols.), has tried a compromise in the prose renderings of the plays: Baldini has avoided both the current language and the Italian language of Shakespeare's time; he has found a temperate zone in the speech of the time of Manzoni and Leopardi, which allows for simplicity and clearness, and at the same time has a not too remote classical ring. He says he has followed this principle as far as the 'baroque structure of those dramas allowed it'. In fact what he does may be best illustrated through a parallel from the field of art-history: he treats a baroque surface in a neo-classical way. He frequently reduces a Shakespearian phrase to plain language: for instance Laertes' sentence: 'A sister...whose worth, if praises may go back again, | stood challenger on mount of all the age | for her perfections' becomes in Italian: 'Una mia sorella, i cui pregi—se la lode può applicarsi al passato—esaltati al di sopra di tutti quelli del suo tempo, sfidavano chiunque ad eguagliare la sua perfezione'. In general, Baldini's translation is the nearest approach to a text which actors could successfully adopt without betraying the spirit of the original and at the same time without burdening their memory with turns of phrase and flights of imagery that would not get across to the public. A new edition, augmented with the poems and sonnets, of the complete plays, translated by various hands, which I edited about twenty years ago for Sansoni of Florence, had been prepared for the centenary: originally it was meant to be illustrated by modern artists (Fabrizio Clerici, Leonor Fini and Corrado Cagli), but the inevitable expense this would have involved caused the publishers first to adopt a different plan (to use Delacroix's paintings and drawings inspired by Shakespeare), and finally to drop the idea of an elaborate edition and to issue the revised text in paperback. This ought to be out soon.

Modern translators as a rule are worried about getting their versions accepted by the theatrical companies: therefore they frequently substitute the unfamiliar with the familiar, and give small change for Shakespeare's gold coins. Thus, for instance, Gerardo Guerrieri, in his version of *Hamlet* for the Franco Zeffirelli production (originally staged at the Teatro Edisco in Rome, 1963), which has known an English success at the National Theatre in the summer of 1964 (with Giorgio Albertazzi as Hamlet, Carlo Hintermann as Claudius, Anna Proclemer as Gertrude and Maria Guarnieri as Ophelia) makes the famous monologue begin thus: 'Essere o non essere: è tutto qui'. Both language, setting and costumes in this production aimed at being timeless: after a *Hamlet* in Cranach costumes, another according to the fashions of the Second Empire, and a more epoch-making one in modern dress, Albertazzi wanted to introduce the public to a 'cosmic' *Hamlet*. Another innovation was the disappearance of the ghost, which is only vaguely suggested chiefly by a musical accompaniment reminiscent of vampire films. Italian spectators found Albertazzi much more successful in the second than in the first portion of the play, Maria Guarnieri rather moving and original, and Anna Proclemer somewhat indifferent.

Another notable performance has been *The Tempest* at the Belvedere fortress in Florence in July 1964, produced by Beppe Menegatti, with the actors Glauco Mauri and Vittorio Sanipoli and the famous dancer Carla Fracci as Ariel.

The Shakespeare Centenary was celebrated at the Castle of Bracciano with a lecture by Benvenuto Cellini on 'La personalità di Shakespeare' (30 May 1964), and at the Castel del Poggio di Guardea by the Jimmy Savo Art Center (21 June 1964) with Shakespearian renderings staged on the battlements, and an exhibition.

Articles on Shakespeare have appeared in most reviews and newspapers, most of a purely occasional character; but the Italian bibliography of Shakespeare has been enriched by two remarkable items, Gabriele Baldini's very useful and scholarly *Manualetto Shakespeariano* (Piccola Biblioteca Einaudi), and Nemi D'Agostino's Italian version of D. A. Traversi's *Introduzione a Shakespeare* (Bompiani, Milan, 1964).

MARIO PRAZ

Netherlands

On the initiative of the British Council a committee was set up in the autumn of 1963 to co-ordinate a large variety of 'Shakespeare' projects. These included a number of special manifestations, the most ambitious of which was a nation-wide English-language acting contest of scenes from Shakespeare for secondary schools. Under the auspices of the Genootschap Nederland–Engeland (Netherlands–England Society) this was held in the early months of 1964, 124 schools having entered their teams. The first prize consisted of a trip to England offered by the British Travel Association to the winning team of four; the second of the bronze Shakespeare medal, and the third of books. All participants throughout the country were presented with a copy of the jubilee paperback *Rondom Shakespeare*. The medal had been struck from a highly original design by V. P. S. Esser, as commissioned by the Netherlands Society for Numismatic Art. The pocketbook had been published by Messrs De Haan, and contained over 100 plates to illustrate three Dutch essays. These comprised A. G. H. Bachrach's on Shakespeare's life and times, F. W. S. van Thienen's on Shakespeare in the theatre, and J. Swart's on Shakespeare in translation.

The same subjects were the themes of three exhibitions organized at the Lakenhal Museum in Leiden and at the Museum of Theatre History and the University in Amsterdam, a combined catalogue of which, written to present an overall picture, was published as a result of a generous grant from the Prince Bernhard Fund. The Amsterdam School of Dramatic Art, finally, organized a highly revealing translating contest among a few outstanding professional translators, with a public discussion of the problems involved in the set text chosen.

Among the many periodicals which brought out special numbers, those of *English Studies* edited by R. W. Zandvoort, and *De Gids* edited by W. van Maanen, stand out in particular. Inevitably, one or two inspired visionaries produced new theories about Shakespeare's identity, the most sensational being that the poet was a notorious bigamist who fled to the city of Gouda in 1616, changing his name and turning pipe-maker. The First Folio was, of course, printed at Gouda and its author buried, many eventful years after, in that city's Great Church.

Of amateur performances, *The Taming of the Shrew*, staged by students in a specially erected Elizabethan theatre in the yard of the University of Leiden, attracted full houses for over a fortnight.

Professional productions included *Othello*, *Macbeth* and *King Lear* by 'De Haagse Comedie', *Antony and Cleopatra* by the 'Nederlandse Comedie', *Julius Caesar* by the 'Nieuw Rotterdams Toneel', *The Comedy of Errors* and *Measure for Measure* by 'De Nieuwe Komedie'. The artistic level ranged from disappointing through indifferent to extremely good, as for instance the Othello of Ko van Dijk, with a Iago to match him in Paul Steenbergen, at The Hague.

A few series of radio lectures were broadcast throughout the year, and television's greatest success was undoubtedly the B.B.C. *Hamlet of Elsinore* relayed by special arrangement.

In addition to those mentioned above, various other Dutch cities likewise organized Shakespeare exhibitions, such as Den Helder, Eindhoven, Arnhem and The Hague. At the Museum Boymans-van Beuningen in Rotterdam, an exhibition of Elizabethan needlework attracted huge crowds. Lectures, musical recitals and readings were presented in many places. All in all, the Bard was commemorated lustily, the number of his audiences exceeding many times the combined figures of 'Shakespeare in the Netherlands' from the first visit of the first company of strolling players at the end of the sixteenth century down to 1963.

A. G. H. BACHRACH

Portugal

From the eighteenth century, through the nineteenth century—when the great Portuguese playwright Almeida Garrett, one of the leading figures of the Romantic movement, was deeply influenced by Shakespeare—we may speak quite confidently of a Shakespearian tradition in Portugal. The Quatercentenary celebrations have renewed the interest in Shakespeare. The project of a new Portuguese translation of the works of Shakespeare is becoming a reality. The *Obras de Shakespeare*, published by Scarpa, from Lisbon, began to appear in 1961. The work is still being published in fascicules, of which twenty-eight have so far been issued. The first volume bound up contains *Romeo and Juliet*, *A Midsummer Night's Dream*, *King Lear* and *Macbeth* and has been available since 1963. The second volume is expected to be completed by the spring of 1965: it will include a Portuguese version of J. Dover Wilson's *The Essential Shakespeare*, and a brief study by L. S. Rebelo of *Shakespeare and Our Time*. The editor of the *Obras de Shakespeare* is L. S. Rebelo, whose translation of *Romeo and Juliet* was used by the National Theatre in Lisbon (Teatro Nacional de Maria II) for a very successful production of the play in 1961. The cast was directed by Don Torcuato Luca de Tena, who was especially invited from Spain by the National Theatre.

In 1962 Maria do Céu Saraiva Jorge published her own translation of the *Sonnets* (*Os Sonetos de Shakespeare*), which was received with mixed comments. A new translation of *Hamlet* by the poet José Blanco de Portugal came out in 1964. The well-known Portuguese playwright, Luiz Francisco Rebello, translated also *Measure for Measure* (*Dente por Dente*), which will soon be staged in a Lisbon theatre (before the end of November 1964).

A Shakespeare exhibition organized by the British Council in Portugal lasted from April to May. This displayed 325 items, including 76 translations and adaptations of Shakespeare's plays, 11 biographies and critical studies, 10 essays published in various journals, and a good collection of photographs of Portuguese productions of Shakespeare. A novel feature of this exhibition was the display of dissertations written by Portuguese students of the Universities of Lisbon and Coimbra for the degree of *licenciatura*. In Coimbra Shakespeare and his work have been the subject of 72 dissertations, supervised by Paula Quintela. In Lisbon, 26 theses have been prepared under the guidance of Gonçalves Rodrigues.

In 1964 various articles on Shakespeare and his work were issued in Portuguese magazines, such as *Diário Popular* (Lisbon, 23 April, special supplement), *Diário de Lisboa*, *Comércio de Porto*, *Diário de Notícias* (Lisbon), *Primeiro de Janeiro*, Oporto, *Colóquio* (no. 29, June), *O Ocidente* (Lisbon). LUÍS DE SOUSA REBELO

South Africa

In all the major cities and universities Shakespeare overshadowed in public interest the other centenarians of 1964. *The Comedy of Errors*, *The Taming of the Shrew*,

A Midsummer Night's Dream, Love's Labour's Lost, The Merchant of Venice, Romeo and Juliet, Twelfth Night, Measure for Measure and Hamlet were all performed, mainly by professional companies. Norman Marshall was brought out to direct Romeo and Juliet for the University of Cape Town, and he delivered a number of lectures for Theatre Workshop in Durban, as well as at the Cape, on 'Producing Shakespeare' and other topics. Both Leslie French and Margaret Inglis produced Hamlet, the full-text production in Johannesburg being remarkable for a sensitive performance by Francois Swart of the Performing Arts Council. A Midsummer Night's Dream, artistically produced by Joan Brickhill and Louis Burke, had a long and successful run at the Alexander Theatre, Johannesburg.

In August 1964 the Cambridge University Players presented two memorable performances at South African universities, under the aegis of the English Academy of Southern Africa. The Comedy of Errors, directed by Alexandra Dane with delightful Elizabethan touches, would have pleased Shakespeare himself; the non-stop smoothness of rhythm and polished speaking of the verse were again evident in Stephen Gray's production of Love's Labour's Lost.

Other notable events were the visits in April and August of Peter Quennell, editor of History Today, and Geoffrey Bullough of King's College, London, the latter under the auspices of the British Council. In a strenuous tour of the universities, the leading authority on Shakespeare's sources dealt with a wide range of Shakespearian and modern themes, including his British Academy address on 'The Elizabethan Shakespeare'. The British Council added to this enterprise by offering at the principal centres an exhibition of books and photographs.

A feature of numerous lecture programmes was the attention given to Elizabethan music and madrigals. There were also several attempts to recreate the spirit of the age by means of recitals by contemporary writers, on the lines of 'The Tremendous Ghost' at Stratford-upon-Avon. Verdi's opera Otello was presented by the University of Cape Town Operatic Society in April, and there was a revival in most cities of the important Shakespeare films, including the Russian Othello and Romeo and Juliet performed by the Bolshoi Ballet.

Publications during the year included A Tribute to Shakespeare, 1964, by the English Academy of Southern Africa, Fort Hare Contribution to the Shakespeare Quatercentenary Festival, and A. C. Partridge's Orthography in Shakespeare and Elizabethan Drama. The South African poet Uys Krige made a splendid translation into Afri-

kaans (as yet unpublished) of Twelfth Night. It is an interesting fact that more of Shakespeare's plays have been translated into Bantu languages than Afrikaans.

A. C. PARTRIDGE

Sweden

Before the Jubilee Year two productions from 1963 may be mentioned. In the Malmö Stadsteater The Tempest was performed. From Copenhagen Helge Refn had been invited as a guest-producer. Georg Åorlin read the blank verse excellently in Prospero's role, and Åoke Lindström was an impressive Caliban. Much Ado About Nothing at the Göteborgs Stadsteater (directed by Mats Johansson) was a spectacular piece bordering upon opera with decorations and costumes in the nineteenth-century style. The comedy met with public success. Gun Arvidsson was a pleasant Beatrice and Måns Westfelt a passable Benedick. Othello was given in Uppsala by Frank Sundström in Björn Collinder's new tradition. Gunnar Sjöberg assumed the title-role.

Early in 1964 Richard III was performed at the Malmö Stadsteater; somewhat later in the year As You Like It was produced by Alf Sjöberg in the Stockholm Dramatiska Teatern. A Midsummer Night's Dream was given by the Umeå Shakespeare Society (producer, Margreta Söderwall); Lapland scenery, Lappish attire! The Riksteatern had arranged a 'Shakespeare Cavalcade' for schools; later on it has been touring with Twelfth Night, from Pajala near the Polar Circle to Scania in the south. A small Shakespeare Exhibition has followed the troupe on its touring. Twelfth Night was also given at the Norrköping's Stadsteater. The Comedy of Errors was performed by the Uppsala Stadsteater. Troilus and Cressida was given by the Dramatiska Teatern, Stockholm, a first performance for Sweden (producer, Alf Sjöberg). The Taming of the Shrew is in preparation (October 1964) at Göteborgs Stadsteater.

Sweden's contribution in the all-Scandinavian T.V. programme was Henry IV. There were too many radio performances to be recorded.

Åoke Ohlmarks's translations, Samlade dramatiska arbeten ('Collected dramatic works'), revised by Gunnar Boklund, started with the Comedies (Sthm, Bonniers, 1962), and continued with the Histories, 1964. Björn Collinder published his translations 'De stora dramerna' (Hamlet, Macbeth, King Lear, Julius Caesar, Romeo and Juliet and The Merchant of Venice) in 1964 (Sthm, Natur och kultur), in an edition with English and Swedish texts. Macbeth and Julius Caesar will soon appear in C. A. Hagberg's translation and commentary by Erik Frykman (Sthm, Wahlström and Widstrand). The

Sonnets in a new rendering, with preface and notes, by K. A. Svensson have been edited in Lund (Gleerups).

Among festivals Göteborgs Stadsteater celebrated the Shakespeare Centenary with a special performance at which L. Breitholtz of Göteborg University gave a lecture. There was also a retrospective exhibition, 'Shakespeare in Göteborg 1781–1964', arranged by the local Teaterhistoriska Samfundet.   NILS MOLIN

Switzerland

Switzerland has demonstrated its unflagging interest in, and appreciation of, Shakespeare's work by an unparallelled number of professional and amateur performances, recitals, publications, celebrations and public lectures. Basle offered a specially rich programme with events distributed over the whole year, while Bern and Zürich concentrated their efforts more or less on a Shakespeare Week in October and a festival week in June respectively.

The two major theatres of Basle presented German translations of *As You Like It*, *King Lear* and *The Taming of the Shrew* (in an open-air performance); the Municipal Theatre of Bern staged *Richard II* in German as an auspicious prelude to succeeding productions of the other history plays; Lausanne witnessed performances in French of *Love's Labour's Lost* and *The Merry Wives of Windsor*, and St Gallen had the opportunity to see *Coriolanus* in German. The Schauspielhaus at Zürich presented, after performances of *Henry IV* in January (in German), an Italian rendering of *Hamlet* and a German translation of *The Tempest* in the course of a festival week in June. Two evenings of that week were reserved for the Bristol Old Vic company's brilliant performances of *Henry V* and *Love's Labour's Lost*, which were also warmly applauded by the audiences at Basle, Bern, Geneva and Lausanne. The second English company to tour various Swiss towns (in December) was the Cambridge Experimental Theatre Group, which this year had chosen *The Merry Wives*. Maria Becker, the Swiss actress, recited sonnets at Basle and at Bern.

A great number of schools and societies arranged special Shakespeare celebrations all over the country. Among those organized by universities (in some places together with the local theatre or orchestras), mention may be made of Basle (lecturer: Rudolf Stamm), Bern (on two days, with lectures by Walter Oberer, Robert Fricker and Max Wildi), Lausanne and Neuchâtel (lecturers: Adrien Bonjour, Charly Guyot and René Rapin), St Gallen (lecturer: Raymond Tschumi),

Zürich (lecturer: Heinrich Straumann). The lectures held were or will be published singly or collectively in newspapers or periodicals, or separately. Our principal guest lecturers from the United States and England were A. C. Sprague ('Shakespeare and the Theatre of his Time') and Terence Spencer ('Shakespeare's Women Characters').

Among this year's publications written by Swiss authors pride of place may be given to Ernst Leisi's *Measure for Measure. An Old-Spelling and Old-Meaning Edition* (Heidelberg, Winter). This is not the place to discuss a study which will no doubt be reviewed extensively elsewhere and marks a decisive step in textual criticism and interpretation. Max Lüthi's *Shakespeare. Dichter des Wirklichen und des Nichtwirklichen* (Bern, Francke) contains seven essays devoted to the study of one of the main and most characteristic aspects of the poet's work, while Rudolf Stamm, in four of his ten essays collected under the title *Zwischen Vision und Wirklichkeit* (Bern, Francke), focuses his interest on the Shakespearian drama in the playhouse, including problems of translation. Among the major contributions to the hundredth volume of the *Shakespeare Jahrbuch* no less than five were written by Swiss professors of English (Adrien Bonjour, 'The Test of Poetry'; Robert Fricker, 'Hundert Jahre Shakespeare Jahrbuch'; Ernst Leisi, 'Zur Bestimmung Shakespearischer Wortbedeutungen'; Rudolf Stamm, 'R. A. Schröder als Shakespeare-Uebersetzer'; Heinrich Straumann, 'Der redliche Mensch: Horatio—Kent—Pisanio').

The *Schweizer Theater-Jahrbuch* devoted its thirtieth volume to the poet. It contains eleven essays on what he has meant since the eighteenth century and still means to the Swiss and their theatres both in the French- and German-speaking parts of the country, how he was received and judged by such widely different men as de Chaillet, Ulrich Bräker, Johann Heinrich Füssli, Gottfried Keller and C. F. Meyer, and what the Swiss have contributed to Shakespeare scholarship in our time. Volume VII in the series *Theater unserer Zeit* (Basilius Presse, Basle) will also be devoted to the playwright, with articles written by a variety of authors. Last but not least it may be mentioned that the leading Swiss newspaper, *Neue Zürcher Zeitung*, issued two Shakespeare Supplements on 19 and 26 April, while the Bernese paper *Der Bund* added a corresponding supplement to its number of 17 April.

This dry summary in no way reflects the enthusiasm and devotion that went to the celebration of Shakespeare's quatercentenary in Switzerland, but the number of titles, names and dates may give, however inadequately, an impression of the amount of work that has been done to make it as worthy as possible of its great object.   ROBERT FRICKER

Turkey

Shakespeare's fourth centenary was celebrated in most of the great cultural centres in Turkey. Plays were performed, articles written and lectures given in professional theatres as well as universities, schools and clubs.

The Municipal Theatre of Istanbul, celebrating its own fiftieth anniversary, had an exceptionally rich programme in which Shakespeare was prominent. Each of the six theatres run by the Municipal Theatre joined the celebration on 23 April 1964 with a Shakespearian play.

(1) At Üsküdar Tiyatrosu Avni Givda's version of *Twelfth Night* was produced by Agâh Hün who also took the part of Sir Toby, with Gülistan Güzey and Alev Gürzap as Olivia and Viola respectively.

(2) At Tepebaşi Tiyatrosu Miss Şirin Devrim, who had appeared as Gertrude in last year's *Hamlet*, was responsible for the production of my translation of *The Merchant of Venice* with Nüvit Özdoğru playing Shylock to Mualla Firat's Portia.

(3) Yeni Komedi Tiyatrosu offered *A Midsummer Night's Dream*. The play was produced by a young American producer and designer, David Pursley, who used my translation in Turkish blank verse. In this production where Argun Kinal impersonated Lysander to Birsen Kaplangı's Hermia, and Kâmıran Usluer represented Demetrius to Nur Sabuncu's Helena, Fuat İşhan was Bottom and Ayla Algan Puck. The American producer and his wife presented Oberon and Titania in dumb show, while Puck explained what they meant by their queer gestures.

(4) Hâmit Dereli's version of *Much Ado* was produced by Z. Küçümen at Fatih Tiyatrosu. In this production Turgut Atalay was responsible for the costume and stage designs, and Abut for the music, while dances were prepared by Ferih Egemen, Kemal Güvenç appeared as Don John, Aytaç Yörükaslan as Claudio, Mucip Ofluoğlu as Benedick to Nedret Güvenç's convincing portrayal of Beatrice.

(5) At Yeni Tiyatro Ergun Köknar produced *Romeo and Juliet*. The Turkish syllabic metre of Yusuf Mardin's beautiful version has proved something of a handicap to the actors.

(6) The last play offered by The Municipal Theatre was *Coriolanus*, which started at Yeni Tiyatro and was carried to the open-air theatre within the walls of the fifteenth-century fortress of Mehmet II on the European side of the Bosphorus. Tunç Yalman's *mise-en-scène* was a success with the exception of an unconvincing fire effect. This production was particularly noteworthy for the enormous crowd of actors participating: all the players of the six theatres run by The Municipal Theatre of Istanbul had taken part. These spectacular outdoor performances lasted for a month and were well received; every night, hosts of playgoers drove for miles to the historical citadel. The Turkish text of the play was the co-operative work of the English Seminar at the University of Istanbul.

The Municipal Theatre of Adana in south-western Turkey contributed to the celebrations with Orhan Burian's version of *Othello* produced by Oğuz Bora who also appeared in the title-role.

The National Conservatoire of Ankara offered Avni Givda's version of *Twelfth Night* with the younger group of the Drama Department under Meinecke.

The National Theatre of Turkey under Cüneyt Gökçer produced my text of *Julius Caesar* in Turkish prose at the Grand Theatre in Ankara: opening on 23 April, it was later carried to the second-century Roman theatre of Aspendus in south-western Turkey. Among the huge crowd at the opening performance there were Turkish Cabinet Ministers and several ambassadors representing various countries of Europe, Asia and Africa. In this performance Haluk Kurdoğlu was unusually good as Antony. The miraculous acoustics and stately surroundings of this best-preserved Roman theatre threw the silent audience into the very heart of ancient Rome of the Ides of March in 44 B.C.: the mob, flowing among the occupants of the large amphitheatre in complete darkness, was particularly effective. The same production had seven performances at the modern open-air theatre in İzmir (Smyrna) during the International Fair of İzmir in August.

The National Theatre also produced scenes from Shakespeare at the Yeni Sahne playhouse in Ankara. Mrs Çiğdem Selişik was responsible for the production and explanations during the intervals.

The National Theatre toward the end of the season produced *Twelfth Night* staged by Cüneyt Gökçer, who also appeared as Malvolio.   NUREDDIN SEVIN

U.S.A.

To tell the story of Shakespeare in America in the 400th anniversary year I must borrow 'Gargantua's mouth first'. The account can only be suggestive of the nationwide excitement.

With colleges and universities being in the forefront

of activity and their semesters beginning in September of 1963, many anniversary programmes began early. Probably the first with a major programme was the University of California at Berkeley which opened with Margaret Webster's *Antony and Cleopatra* on 12 September and continued with *The Merchant of Venice, Coriolanus, The Tempest, The Hollow Crown* and Verdi's *Falstaff*.

Never was there such a travelling around of scholarly Shakespearians to fill the demands of celebrating campuses throughout the nation. Foreign dignitaries gave an international flavour. J. E. Gardner, the *Stratford-upon-Avon Herald* drama critic, lectured at more than a dozen colleges and organizations which were happy to have the spirit of Shakespeare brought from Shakespeare's home town. Sir Tyrone Guthrie appeared on campuses from the University of California at Berkeley to The Citadel (Military College) in South Carolina, where a month-long celebration was held. Zdeněk Stříbrný of Prague was at the University of Southern California, Northrop Frye lectured at the University of Denver, Robert Speaight was at Cardinal Stritch College, Peter Alexander spoke at New York University and A. L. Rowse entertained hundreds with accounts of his sonnet scholarship across the nation. Native American professors too were in demand. The present writer, for example, spoke at nineteen commemorative programmes up to October 1964, from Pennsylvania to Oklahoma, and the names of Alfred Harbage, Fredson Bowers, G. B. Harrison, Charlton Hinman, appeared in numbers of programmes.

The present writer's article entitled 'Shakespeare's 400th Anniversary: Suggestions for Commemorative Programs and Activities', listing about three dozen possible programmes for Shakespearian festivals, was simultaneously published in the February issues of *English Journal* and *College English* and evoked rather wide response. But the bardolatrous U.S.A. of 1963–4 needed no special prompting. A survey questionnaire on quadricentennial activities distributed by Kenneth L. Graham, President of the American Educational Theatre Association, had drawn about 400 replies at the time of this writing. Returns indicated that about a thousand different productions, including every play in the canon, would be performed. With 1800 colleges and junior colleges in the country and 29,500 high schools, the actual number of performances must have been enormous. Many schools that staged their own productions invited touring companies as well. Reception was varied. The Canadian Players acted *Henry IV, Part I* at the College of William and Mary and received head-

lines which ranged from 'Bravo' to 'Shakespeare Murdered on Phi Beta Stage'. William and Mary also produced its own version of *Richard III*. The National Players of Washington, D.C., toured widely with *The Taming of the Shrew*.

There were the usual Shakespearian novelties. Birmingham Southern College twisted the tale of Shakespeare by setting its *Much Ado* in the American 'roaring twenties', done in the style of the silent movies and using film clips for parts of the production. A California high school consisting mainly of Mexican-American students performed *Julius Caesar* in the style and period of Pancho Villa, the notorious Mexican bandit leader of the early twentieth century. Rhode Island College cleverly arranged a series of courtship scenes from Shakespeare and other plays and called it *The Comedy of Eros*. Not the least interesting was the *Macbeth* presented by the Jewish inhabitants of the Menorah Home and Hospital for the Aged and Infirm in Brooklyn, N.Y. At one point the 82-year-old Macbeth turned to Lady Macbeth and said: 'A king I had to be? A 15 room castle wasn't good enough for you?' In their 1963 *Romeo and Juliet* the theme was set when the 82-year-old Romeo asked the 75-year-old Juliet, 'You Jewish?'.

New plays for old and young were also featured. Betty Bandel of the University of Vermont wrote *John Bull's Other Playwright* to present in a humorous and informative manner the Shakespearian criticism of George Bernard Shaw. It was produced on 23 April with a cast of faculty, students, and townspeople. The Toledo Repertory Theatre staged a two-act play by Cornel Adam called *Will of Stratford*. At Tufts University an adaptation of *A Midsummer Night's Dream* for children was successfully staged under the title *Puck and the Tinkers*. At Alverno College, Sisters Poverello and Vernon wrote a children's operetta entitled *Under the Greenwood Tree* which proved very stimulating to its young audiences.

Even the very young were caught up in the excitement. A class of third graders in St Mark's Episcopal School (Ft. Lauderdale, Florida) presented a version of *A Midsummer Night's Dream*, and a fourth grade class (Cornita School, Corona, California) did *The Taming of the Shrew*. Teachers, students, and parents were delighted by the performances.

The general pattern of the commemorative programmes put on by the more ambitious schools was the same throughout the country. Virginia State College presents a typical example. Zatella R. Turner had been conducting a 'Shakespeare Hour' to commemorate

Shakespeare's birth every year for the past twenty years, but this year, beginning in February, there was a college production of *Hamlet*, followed five weeks later by the visit of the National Players with *The Taming of the Shrew*, to be followed at later dates by a lecture by Fredson Bowers, an Evening of Elizabethan Music, the planting of a Shakespeare tree, and a Shakespeare Exhibit in the library. Other schools offered Shakespearian operas, a series of Shakespeare films of all vintages, the Folger Shakespeare Library Exhibition, various series of lectures, etc. The summer theatre at Antioch College, where from 1952 to 1956 the complete works of Shakespeare had been staged, this year devoted its entire programme to Shakespeare. *Macbeth*, *As You Like It*, *The Tempest*, *Henry IV, Part I* and *Hamlet* were successfully presented from mid-July to mid-September. Meredith Dallas, Paul Treichler, and David Hooks, who had been members and directors of the original 1952–6 company, participated as directors in the present venture. David Hooks is one of the few people in the world to have been connected with the acting or directing of every play in the canon.

The regular summer Shakespearian festivals, which have been reported here annually, presented longer seasons wherever possible. The Oregon Shakespeare Festival, oldest of the regular festivals in North America, began its twenty-fourth season with a triumphant 12-day engagement at Stanford University in California where it entertained 26,510 playgoers. On its own outdoor Elizabethan stage in Ashland, Oregon, it extended its season by twelve days for a total of fifty-eight. A grand total of 60,939 saw their productions of *The Merchant of Venice*, *Twelfth Night*, *King Lear*, *Henry VI, Part I* and Beaumont and Fletcher's *Knight of the Burning Pestle*.

The Ninth Annual Repertory Season of the American Shakespeare Festival Theatre of Stratford, Connecticut, was distinguished in 1963 by a magnificent production of *King Lear* starring Morris Carnovsky. The tenth season in 1964 featured *Hamlet*, *Much Ado About Nothing* and *Richard III*. Critics were varied in their opinion. *Hamlet* was good, but not great. *Much Ado* was over-exuberantly acted, making it a farce instead of a romantic comedy. I was annoyed greatly by a pouting Don John who stamped his feet, had a tantrum on the floor of the stage, and snapped a whip whenever he was aroused. Typical of the reaction was the laughter of the audience at 'Kill Claudio'. Their *Richard III* was over-dramatized in the early parts of that play because the audience laughed where it should have been shocked, but the play gained power as it progressed.

The New York Shakespeare Festival's eighth annual season in 1963 was animated by a five foot six inch Cleopatra (Coleen Dewhurst) whom most critics found more satisfying than the reclining thirty-foot long Cleopatra (Elizabeth Taylor) in the filmed version. The ninth season, free as usual in the open-air Delacorte Theatre in Central Park, achieved a bad press on opening night not only because Alfred Ryder's Hamlet was plagued by a severe sore throat, but because he did not effectively command the role. Fortunately enough, Richard Burton's understudy was in the audience that night and he was secured to substitute for Ryder. His appearance pulled the cast together and improved the entire play. Remarkably, this *Hamlet* began with a pantomime scene in which we saw Gertrude following the coffin of her late husband. For a moment the procession was halted, giving the Queen an opportunity to embrace the casket in a last show of affection. Their production of *Othello*, in the words of Henry Hewes of *Saturday Review*, was 'memorable because it offered an Othello who suffered not from jealousy but from madness, and an Iago who was not calculatingly evil but merely hotheaded'.

This year, as in the past, the company secured sufficient foundation money to tour a production of *A Midsummer Night's Dream* to thirty-five areas of the city. A mobile stage and 1600 seats accompanied the company. Before some performances, trucks and an open car bearing costumed actors formed a motorcade with placards announcing that 'Free Shakespeare is Here'.

Other regular festivals—almost two dozen of them across the length and breadth of the nation—entertained large audiences, and with the impetus of the quadri-centennial year will probably have greater audiences in the years ahead. Some, like those at Hofstra University in New York and the National Shakespeare Festival at San Diego, California, are celebrating their fifteenth successive season. Hofstra's offering was *Julius Caesar*, the play which opened the Globe Theatre in 1599. Others, like that at the College of Southern Utah, were celebrating their third seasons and making their first bids for national attention. Here A. J. R. Master, director of the East Africa Shakespeare Festival in Kenya, was guest director for a two-and-a-half-week programme of *Twelfth Night*, *Macbeth* and *A Midsummer Night's Dream*.

Most ambitious of the festivals was the Great Lakes Shakespeare Festival which, under the direction of Arthur Lithgow (Producing Director of the complete canon at Antioch College from 1952 to 1956), offered six plays: *The Taming of the Shrew*, *Hamlet*, *Much Ado*, *Henry VI* (the three parts made into one play), *Richard*

III and *Antony and Cleopatra*. The season extended from 30 June to 19 September.

As much as it is possible in a nation about 3000 miles from end to end, New York City remains the dramatic centre. Here, on 4 December 1963, *The Worlds of Shakespeare* opened with two Negro actors (chosen to show the universality of Shakespeare), Vinie Burrows and Earle Hyman. 'The World of Love' offered love scenes as Act I, and 'The World of Music' musical scenes as Act II. Although the actors did well, there was not enough meat in the show to attract large audiences.

On 3 January there was a 'Shakespeare Quattro-Centennial Concert' at Town Hall and in March The Metropolitan Opera House offered Verdi's *Falstaff*. Also in March, a group called Stage 73 offered Fanny Bradshaw's cuttings from five of Shakespeare's histories under the title *The White Rose and the Red*. In April at Philharmonic Hall, Dame Edith Evans, Sir John Gielgud, and Margaret Leighton, whose voices are drama enough, gave readings under the title 'Homage to Shakespeare'; and in the same hall on 25 April Noah Greenberg's Pro Musica group gave an Elizabethan concert in honour of the 400th Anniversary.

From 18 May to 6 June the Royal Shakespeare Theatre of Stratford-upon-Avon presented *King Lear* and *The Comedy of Errors* as the first stage-plays to be given on the stage of The New York State Theatre. Because the theatre was made for musical rather than for spoken performances, Peter Hall engaged in a controversy with the managers over the bad acoustics. New York critics were greatly impressed, though maintaining some reservations, because Lear was so portrayed that the actions of Goneril and Regan were justified. *The Comedy of Errors* was entertaining, but critics, as usual, wondered how far farce could go before it became utterly ridiculous.

The production that will live longest in memory was the Sir John Gielgud production of *Hamlet* starring Richard Burton. Staged in rehearsal clothing on an absolutely bare stage, it was bound to provoke repercussion. Loudest was Alistair Cooke, who declared he was tired of Sir John's 'naïve theory' (which is rather widely held) that to strip the play of all scenery and costume makes, in Sir John's words, 'the beauty of the language and imagery shine through, unencumbered by an elaborate reconstruction of any particular historical period'. Cooke found jeans, corduroy, pullovers, patched-elbow jackets, and so on, filled with more associations than would be the clothing of Elizabethan times: thus the play 'screams for some simple, unpretentious correction', so that the 'richness of the language'

can shine through unencumbered by *modern* associations; it is not true that 'a boy in loafers and a pullover sets us free for the beauty of the English language in its golden age'. Another critic found Burton one of 'the most magnificently equipped actors living', yet cold in this role, and still another said his voice was 'colourless'. The United Press reported that that play was 'vital and compelling...shot through with flashes of brilliance', but the Associated Press reported it as 'uneven, incomplete...a disappointment...Burton apparently has not yet decided just how he wants to interpret the character this time'.

During three performances in June–July, the stage-production was filmed and this film was shown in about a thousand theatres throughout the U.S.A. simultaneously on 23 and 24 September, making for the largest audience ever to see a 'staged' Shakespeare play. The filmed version, however, was deficient in lighting, muted in its sound, and selective in its close-ups—this last fault making for something like a T.V. performance. Stage business performed by other actors was not visible when it should have been. Close-ups do give intimate portraits, but one of the virtues of staged plays is that you see not only the speaking actor but the simultaneous effect he makes on those who hear him.

In New York also there were 'Shakespeare in Art' shows at galleries, exhibits at libraries, dinners, like that of the Shakespeare Association of America at the Pierpont Morgan Library, and series of filmed plays.

In 1963 President John F. Kennedy sponsored a National Shakespeare Committee under the chairmanship of Eugene R. Black of New York City and the American Shakespeare Festival. President Lyndon B. Johnson reconfirmed the Committee, which distributed nationwide a pamphlet on Shakespeare activities, sponsored an American Shakespeare Festival performance for U.N. members, and in June brought its National Committee—scholars and theatre people from throughout the nation—to Connecticut and Washington for performances of *Hamlet* and *Much Ado About Nothing*, for dinners, excursions, a party at the Folger Shakespeare Library, and a reception at the White House, where excerpts of plays were given. It was the second appearance of Shakespeare at the White House this year, the National Players of Catholic University having presented scenes from the *Shrew* on 1 April.

LOUIS MARDER

U.S.S.R.

Shakespeare's popularity among both readers and theatre-goers exceeds that of any other foreign writer.

One need only mention that between 1917 and 1963 nearly five million copies of his plays were printed in twenty-eight different languages. It was natural, therefore, that the 400th anniversary of Shakespeare's birth should be widely observed in the U.S.S.R. There was a gala performance at the Bolshoi Theatre on 23 April; the Institute of World Literature of the Academy of Sciences, the All-Russia Theatre Group, Moscow University, and other establishments of higher education held discussions in Moscow; and there were similar celebrations in Leningrad, Kiev and in many other towns and cities. A large number of articles on Shakespeare were published in the Soviet press.

The Academy of Sciences of the U.S.S.R. published an international collection of essays, with contributions from England, East Germany, Czechoslovakia and Bulgaria, as well as from the U.S.S.R. Leningrad scholars published a collection of articles, entitled *Shakespeare in World Literature*, including one by P. Vykhodtsev on 'Soviet Writers about Shakespeare'. In the jubilee *Shakespeare Yearbook* of the All-Russia Theatre Group there were seven articles on *Hamlet*.

Among the books published in the quatercentenary year was Alexander Anikst's *Shakespeare* in the series 'Lives of Famous People'. This was a sequel for the general public to Anikst's large-scale study *The Work of Shakespeare* (1963) and to the eight-volume *Complete Works* edited by A. Smirnov and A. Anikst (1957–60), which has already sold more than 300,000 copies. (It may be mentioned here that Smirnov's posthumous book *Shakespeare* (1963) was the fruit of half a century's work: his main concern was Shakespeare's mastery as a dramatist, and he found the sources of the poet's humanism in the fact that he was living at the end of feudalism and that he was highly critical of nascent capitalism.)

Three other books, published in 1964, should be mentioned: *Shakespeare—His Hero and His Time*, by Michael and Dimitri Urnov, in which the authors compare Hamlet with 'angry young men'; *The Historical Chronicles of Shakespeare*, by Yury Shvedov, who argues that 1485—not 1640—marked the end of the Middle Ages, that Shakespeare should therefore be regarded as a 'modern' writer, and (as Anikst, too, says) Shakespeare's plays 'were created not under conditions of the middle ages, but during the conflicts of a new age'; and a bibliography, edited by I. Levidov, covering the period 1748–1962, and containing more than 6000 titles of Russian Shakespeariana.

YURY SHVEDOV

Yugoslavia

As a most auspicious prelude to the quatercentenary celebrations of Shakespeare in Yugoslavia, there appeared in Belgrade, in June 1963, a complete Serbo-Croatian translation of all his dramatic and poetic works, issued, in eighteen volumes, in 20,000 sets, and sold at a remarkably low price. As this was the first complete Shakespeare in Serbo-Croatian (so far only about one-half of the plays had been translated, often incorrectly and in language that now sounds obsolete), newly translated by a group of scholars and poets—D. Andjelinović, T. Djukić, H. Klajn, B. Nedić, S. Pandurović, A. Petrović, Ž. Simić, B. Živojinović, and V. Živojinović—it was hailed as a literary event of first-rate importance, and before the end of the year the whole edition was sold out.

Another event that augured well for the 1964 celebrations was the founding of the Belgrade Shakespeare Society, in spring 1963. It is a society of scholars, artists, and writers who are specially interested in Shakespeare and his art, and their aim is: to promote the interpretation, translation, and popularization of Shakespeare's dramatic and poetic works, and particularly to encourage and stimulate presentations of Shakespeare's plays in Yugoslav theatres; to promote Yugoslav Shakespearian scholarship; to collect past and present material—literary, theatrical, and artistic—relating to Shakespeare in Yugoslavia; and to cultivate mutual relations with similar societies abroad. These aims the society realizes by means of regular business meetings of its members, public lectures and conferences, articles in the daily and periodical press, and by issuing its yearly publication, *The Shakespeare Annual*.

Thus, the timely appearance of the *Complete Works*, and the activities of the society, aroused a great deal of interest in the general public and facilitated numerous and various manifestations during the festal year. In schools and universities, in town-halls and theatres, on the radio and the T.V., there were lectures and recitals devoted to Shakespeare. Prominent visitors from Great Britain, like Allardyce Nicoll and Miss Helen Gardner, delivered lectures at the universities of Belgrade, Zagreb and Ljubljana, and the Royal Shakespeare Company gave performances of *King Lear* and of *The Comedy of Errors*, while the Bristol Old Vic Company presented *Love's Labour's Lost* and *Henry V* (in Dubrovnik). There was not one theatre in Yugoslavia that did not produce at least one of Shakespeare's plays during the year. Owing to the fact that all the plays were now available in translation, some of them were now acted for the first time—*Love's Labour's Lost* (Belgrade), *Measure for Measure* (Zagreb), *All's Well* (Kragujevac), *The Merry Wives* (Banja Luka) and *Timon of Athens* (Ljubljana). Also a beautifully dramatized version of *Venus and Adonis*, interlaced with some of the sonnets, was given in Belgrade.

However, the central Yugoslav celebration took place in Sarajevo, and it lasted one whole full and memorable week, 1–8 June. The host was the National Theatre, Sarajevo, and the participants were the best Yugoslav theatrical companies. Each night during the week a play was given by a different company: *A Midsummer Night's Dream* (Dramatic Theatre, Belgrade), *The Taming of the Shrew* (Osijek), *Julius Caesar* (Novi Sad), *Twelfth Night* (Sarajevo), *Love's Labour's Lost* (National Theatre, Belgrade), *Measure for Measure* (Zagreb) and *King Lear* (Ljubljana); besides these, a recital of Shakespeare's sonnets, in a new Slovenian translation by the poet J. Menart, and the dramatic presentation of *Venus and Adonis*, by the actor-members of the Workers' University, Belgrade, were given as matinee performances. During the week, Shakespearian films, *Richard III*, *Macbeth*, *Othello*, *Henry V*, *Julius Caesar* and *Romeo and Juliet* were shown. A conference of scholars and producers, with guests from abroad (Great Britain, the U.S.A., Denmark and East Germany), debated on the problems of the scenic presentation of Shakespeare's plays. Such reports as 'The Elizabethan Stage' (B. Nedić and C. Walter Hodges), 'The Presentation of Shakespeare during the Romantic Period' (S. Bajić), 'Modern Scenic Presentation of Shakespeare' (H. Klajn), 'Rendering Shakespeare's Verse in Serbo-Croatian' (J. Torbarina), *Richard II* (A. Schlösser, Berlin), 'Shakespeare in 19th Century Serbian Drama' (Dj. Radović), 'Joca Savić' (O. Milićević), 'The Integrity of Shakespeare's text and the inviolacy of its dramaturgic structure' (M. Fotez), 'The Breaking of the Classical Unities in Shakespeare's dramaturgy' (V. Petrić), 'One Conception of King Lear' (S. Brkić), 'Death and Corpses in Shakespeare' (B. Drašković) and 'Shakespeare and Bernard Shaw' (H. Krabbe, Copenhagen) provoked much interesting discussion. Also an historical survey of the scenic presentation of Shake-speare in Yugoslav theatres was given by S. Batušić, D. Mihailović and D. Moravec. The exhibition 'Shakespeare on the Yugoslav Stage', in the foyer of the National Theatre in Sarajevo, displayed a wealth of records of Yugoslav productions of Shakespeare's plays in the past hundred years, and another one, 'Shakespeare in Great Britain', held at the National Library, Sarajevo, was kindly placed at the disposal of the Celebration Committee by the British Council. The Committee have also published a beautiful and richly illustrated Memorial Volume, which, besides the detailed programmes of the Sarajevo 1964 Celebration, gives historical records of Shakespearian productions in Yugoslav theatres.

Several periodicals have issued special numbers devoted to Shakespeare and his art. Thus *Filološki Pregled*, organ of the Yugoslav societies for foreign languages and literatures (vols. I–II, Belgrade, 1964), prints much scholarly work on Shakespearian topics by many very distinguished writers from home and abroad. *Pozorište* (Tuzla) and *Pozorišni Život* (Belgrade) have also published special issues dedicated to Shakespeare. But so far there has appeared only one book on Shakespeare written by an individual author, *Šekspirovo Čoveštvo* (*Shakespeare's Humanity*), by Hugo Klajn. The author's résumé, given in English at the end of his book, declares: 'In the enchanted mirror of his dramas Shakespeare reflected his time.... Later centuries sought in them, and found, their own image, but more often only the outward and passing one, that which most obviously distinguished their own age from others and from Shakespeare's. Just as Shakespeare's works were once adapted to suit the tastes of later centuries, so have commentaries, some of them recent, brought us far from the original. It is necessary to return to Shakespeare, heeding in his picture of the world and age, before all else, those aspects which are held in common. It is necessary to give our attention to problems unresolved then as now, to questions whose answers are still being sought, and particularly to that which confronts us in almost every one of these dramas —the question of the essence of man and human-ness.'

B. NEDIĆ

SHAKESPEARE PRODUCTIONS IN THE
UNITED KINGDOM: 1962-4

A List compiled from its Records by the
Shakespeare Memorial Library, Birmingham

1962

JANUARY

10   *As You Like It:* Royal Shakespeare Theatre Company, at the Aldwych Theatre, London. *Producer:* Michael Elliott.

24   *A Midsummer Night's Dream:* English Stage Company, at the Royal Court Theatre, London. *Producer:* Tony Richardson.

29   *Hamlet:* Theatre-in-the-Round, Scarborough, Newcastle-under-Lyme, etc. *Producer:* Stephen Joseph.

FEBRUARY

5   *Othello:* Castle Theatre, Farnham. *Producer:* George Marland.

6   *The Taming of the Shrew:* The Playhouse, Nottingham. *Producer:* Frank Dunlop.

7   *The Merchant of Venice:* Royal Academy of Dramatic Art, London. *Producer:* Derek Martinus.

13   *The Tempest:* Birmingham Repertory Theatre. *Producer:* John Harrison.

13   *Julius Caesar:* Library Theatre, Manchester. *Producer:* David Scase.

18   *Twelfth Night:* Royal Court Theatre, London. *Producer:* George Devine.

19   *Henry IV, Part I:* The Playhouse, Sheffield. *Producer:* Geoffrey Ost.

20   *Henry IV, Part I:* Oxford University Dramatic Society, at The Playhouse, Oxford. *Producer:* Peter Dews.

21   *Henry IV, Part II:* Oxford University Dramatic Society, at The Playhouse, Oxford. *Producer:* Peter Dews.

27   *The Merchant of Venice:* Theatre Royal, Lincoln. *Producer:* K. V. Moore.

28   *Julius Caesar:* Everyman Theatre, Cheltenham. *Producer:* Ian Mullins.

MARCH

5   *Much Ado About Nothing:* Guildford Repertory Theatre. *Producer:* Eric Jones.

6   *Much Ado About Nothing:* Belgrade Theatre, Coventry. *Producer:* Graham Crowden.

6   *Richard III:* Old Vic Company, at the Old Vic Theatre, London. *Producer:* Colin George.

6   *Othello:* The Playhouse, Salisbury. *Producer:* Desmond O'Donovan.

7   *Julius Caesar:* Fylde College Theatre Group, at the Tower Circus, Blackpool. *Producer:* Frank Winfield.

9   *Romeo and Juliet:* Norwich Players, at the Maddermarket Theatre, Norwich. *Producer:* Ian Emmerson.

12   *Macbeth:* Marlowe Society, at the Arts Theatre, Cambridge. *Producer:* Trevor Nunn.

SHAKESPEARE PRODUCTIONS IN THE UNITED KINGDOM

MARCH

12   *Romeo and Juliet:* Colchester Repertory Theatre. *Producer:* BERNARD KELLY.

12   *Much Ado About Nothing:* Perth Theatre. *Producer:* DAVID STEUART.

13   *The Merchant of Venice:* Repertory Theatre, Dundee. *Producer:* PIERS HAGGARD.

APRIL

2   *Julius Caesar:* Theatre Royal, York. *Producer:* DONALD BODLEY.

10   *Measure for Measure:* Royal Shakespeare Theatre, Stratford-upon-Avon. *Producer:* JOHN BLATCHLEY.

17   *Julius Caesar:* The Old Vic Company, at the Old Vic Theatre, London. *Director:* MINOS VOLANAKIS.

17   *A Midsummer Night's Dream:* Royal Shakespeare Theatre, Stratford-upon-Avon. *Director:* PETER HALL.

23   *The Taming of the Shrew:* Royal Shakespeare Theatre, Stratford-upon-Avon.

MAY

1   *All's Well that Ends Well:* Bristol Old Vic Theatre Company, at the Theatre Royal, Bristol. *Producer:* VAL MAY.

7   *Othello:* A.D.C. Theatre, Cambridge. *Producer:* GORDON MCDOUGALL.

14   *The Taming of the Shrew:* Living Theatre, Leicester. *Producer:* DAVID GOODWIN.

22   *Julius Caesar:* The Playhouse, Nottingham. *Producer:* FRANK DUNLOP.

29   *A Midsummer Night's Dream:* Queen's Theatre, Hornchurch. *Producer:* DAVID PHETHEAN.

29   *The Tempest:* The Old Vic Company, at the Old Vic Theatre, London. *Producer:* OLIVER NEVILLE.

JUNE

   Love's Labour's Lost: Royal Academy of Dramatic Art, London. *Producer:* NOEL ILIFF.

1   *Henry V:* Harrow School. *Producer:* RONALD WATKINS.

4   *A Midsummer Night's Dream:* Regent's Park Open-Air Theatre, London. *Producer:* DAVID WILLIAM.

5   *Macbeth:* Royal Shakespeare Theatre, Stratford-upon-Avon. *Producer:* DONALD MCWHINNIE.

12   *King Lear:* Repton School. *Producer:* R. M. CHARLESWORTH.

16   *Henry IV, Part I:* Cheltenham College. *Producer:* K. H. VIGNOLES.

18   *Macbeth:* White Rose Company, Opera House, Harrogate. *Producer:* EDGAR METCALFE.

26   *Twelfth Night:* Ludlow Festival Company, at Ludlow Castle. *Producer:* DENIS CAREY.

JULY

4   *Romeo and Juliet:* Birmingham University Guild Theatre Group. *Producer:* JOHN BROWN.

JULY

9 *Much Ado About Nothing:* Marlowe Society, at the A.D.C. Theatre, Cambridge. *Producer:* TREVOR NUNN.

11 *Twelfth Night:* Open-Air Theatre, Regent's Park, London. *Producer:* DENNIS CAREY.

17 *Cymbeline:* Royal Shakespeare Theatre, Stratford-upon-Avon. *Director:* WILLIAM GASKILL.

19 *The Winter's Tale:* Polesden Lacy Open-Air Theatre. *Producer:* ELSIE GREEN.

27 *Twelfth Night:* Stowe School. *Producer:* J. BAIN.

AUGUST

12 *Love's Labour's Lost:* Hovenden Theatre Club, London. *Director:* VALERY HOVENDEN.

20 *King Lear:* Prospice Players, Hull Training College, at the Edinburgh Festival. *Producer:* T. G. MARTIN.

20 *Troilus and Cressida:* Royal Shakespeare Theatre Company, at the Edinburgh Festival. *Director:* PETER HALL (revival of the Stratford production of 1960).

21 *Love's Labour's Lost:* Open-Air Theatre, Regent's Park, London. *Producer:* DAVID WILLIAM.

21 *Twelfth Night:* Elizabethan Theatre Group, at the Edinburgh Festival. *Producer:* BOBBY BROWN.

27 *Henry V:* The Youth Theatre, at Sadlers Wells Theatre, London. *Director:* MICHAEL CROFT.

30 *Julius Caesar:* The Youth Theatre, at Sadlers Wells Theatre, London. *Director:* MICHAEL CROFT.

SEPTEMBER

11 *Comedy of Errors:* Royal Shakespeare Theatre, Stratford-upon-Avon. *Producer:* CLIFFORD WILLIAMS.

11 *Macbeth:* Haddo House Choral Society, Aberdeen. *Producer:* RONALD WATKINS.

14 *The Taming of the Shrew:* Invercauld Theatre Festival, Braemar. *Producer:* ANNIE H. LOUDON.

15 *Love's Labour's Lost:* Crescent Theatre, Birmingham. *Producer:* PAULINE SMITH.

17 *A Midsummer Night's Dream:* Citizens Theatre, Glasgow. *Producer:* PIERS HAGGARD.

OCTOBER

2 *Twelfth Night:* The Playhouse, Nottingham. *Producer:* JOHN NEVILLE.

9 *Hamlet:* Repertory Theatre, Dundee. *Producer:* JOHN HENDERSON.

9 *The Merchant of Venice:* The Playhouse, Salisbury. *Producer:* PETER GREGEEN.

17 *The Merchant of Venice:* The Old Vic Company, at the Old Vic Theatre, London. *Producer:* MICHAEL ELLIOTT.

30 *Twelfth Night:* Library Theatre, Manchester. *Producers:* DAVID SCASE and BRYAN STONEHOUSE.

NOVEMBER

6 *Hamlet:* Repertory Theatre, Colchester. *Producer:* BERNARD KELLY.

6 *King Lear:* Royal Shakespeare Theatre, Stratford-upon-Avon; afterwards at the Aldwych Theatre, London. *Producer:* PETER BROOK.

13 *Julius Caesar:* Bristol Old Vic Company, at the Theatre Royal, Bristol. *Producer:* TOBY ROBERTSON.

17 *Twelfth Night:* Questor's Theatre, Ealing, London. *Producer:* ALAN CHAMBERS.

26 *Twelfth Night:* Gateway Theatre, Edinburgh. *Producer:* KENNETH PARROTT.

DECEMBER

5 *Henry V:* Fylde College Theatre Group, at the Tower Circus, Blackpool. *Producer:* FRANK WINFIELD.

10 *Twelfth Night:* People's Theatre Arts Group, at the Arts Centre, Newcastle-upon-Tyne. *Producer:* CATHERINE BRANDON.

1963

JANUARY

No date given *Henry V:* Oldham Repertory Theatre Club. *Producer:* CARL PAULSEN.

28 *Romeo and Juliet:* Castle Theatre, Farnham. *Producer:* JOAN KNIGHT.

30 *Othello:* Old Vic Company, at the Old Vic Theatre, London. *Producer:* CASPAR WREDE.

FEBRUARY

5 *Henry V:* Arts Theatre, Ipswich. *Producer:* ROBERT CHETWYN.

11 *Hamlet:* Empire Theatre, Sunderland, for the North-east Theatre Festival. *Producer:* JOSEPH O'CONOR.

12 *Henry VIII:* Birmingham Repertory Theatre. *Producer:* DAVID BUXTON.

19 *Troilus and Cressida:* Birmingham Repertory Theatre. *Producer:* JOHN HARRISON.

19 *Henry V:* Library Theatre, Manchester. *Producer:* DAVID SCASE.

19 *King Lear:* Playhouse, Sheffield. *Producer:* COLIN GEORGE.

25 *Othello:* Gateway Theatre, Edinburgh. *Producer:* KENNETH PARROTT.

26 *Othello:* Oxford University Dramatic Society, at the Playhouse, Oxford. *Producer:* ADRIAN BRINE.

27 *Antony and Cleopatra:* Royal Academy of Dramatic Art, at the Vanbrugh Theatre, London. *Producer:* DAVID GILES.

MARCH

No date given *Richard II:* Dulwich College. *Producers:* D. M. FITCH and Dr P. J. B. TUCKER.

4 *Twelfth Night:* Her Majesty's Theatre, Barrow-in-Furness. *Producer:* DEREK GOLDBY.

5 *Much Ado About Nothing:* Bristol Old Vic Company, at the Theatre Royal, Bristol. *Producer:* COLIN GRAHAM.

5 *Twelfth Night:* Belgrade Theatre, Coventry. *Producer:* ROGER JENKINS.

5 *As You Like It:* Leatherhead Repertory Theatre. *Producer:* EDGAR WREFORD.

5 *As You Like It:* Theatre Royal, Lincoln. *Producer:* KAY GARDNER.

MARCH

6 *Twelfth Night:* Fylde College Theatre Group, in the College Hall, Blackpool. *Producer:* FRANK WINFIELD.

11 *As You Like It:* Marlowe Society, at the Arts Theatre, Cambridge. *Producer:* NICHOLAS BARTER.

11 *Henry V:* Guildford Repertory Theatre. *Producer:* RICHARD MARLIN.

11 *Macbeth:* Perth Theatre. *Producer:* WILFRED BENTLEY.

11 *Twelfth Night:* Empire Theatre, Sunderland, for the North-east Theatre Festival. *Producer:* GEORGE HARLAND.

12 *Titus Andronicus:* Birmingham Repertory Theatre. *Producer:* RONALD EYRE.

12 *As You Like It:* Everyman Theatre, Cheltenham. *Producer:* IAN MULLINS.

12 *Cymbeline:* The Playhouse, Nottingham. *Producer:* ANDRÉ VAN GYSEGHEM.

18 *Twelfth Night:* White Rose Company, at the Opera House, Harrogate. *Producer:* EDGAR METCALFE.

25 *Henry V:* Theatre Royal, York. *Producer:* DONALD BODLEY.

APRIL

2 *The Tempest:* Royal Shakespeare Theatre, Stratford-upon-Avon. *Producers:* CLIFFORD WILLIAMS and PETER BROOK.

3 *Measure for Measure:* Old Vic Company, at the Old Vic Theatre, London. *Producer:* MICHAEL ELLIOTT.

9 *Julius Caesar:* Royal Shakespeare Theatre, Stratford-upon-Avon. *Producer:* JOHN BLATCHLEY.

15 *The Comedy of Errors:* Royal Shakespeare Theatre, Stratford-upon-Avon. *Producer:* CLIFFORD WILLIAMS.

22 *Twelfth Night:* Royal Academy of Dramatic Art, at the Southwark Shakespeare Festival; and on tour. *Producer:* JUDITH GICK.

30 *King Lear:* Playhouse, Liverpool. *Producer:* BERNARD HEPTON.

MAY

10 *Measure for Measure:* The Norwich Players, at the Maddermarket Theatre. *Producer:* IAN EMMERSON.

13 *Henry V:* Richmond Theatre. *Producer:* ALEXANDER DORE.

14 *Macbeth:* Playhouse, Salisbury. *Producer:* PETER CREGEEN.

21 *Much Ado About Nothing:* The Magdalen Players, at Magdalen College, Oxford. *Producer:* MICHAEL CHESNUTT.

31 *Much Ado About Nothing:* Harrow School. *Producer:* JEREMY LEMMON.

JUNE

4 *Measure for Measure:* The Wadham Players, at Wadham College, Oxford. *Producer:* ADRIAN BENJAMIN.

10 *Much Ado About Nothing:* The New Shakespeare Company, at the Regent's Park Open-Air Theatre, London. *Producer:* DAVID WILLIAM.

JUNE

13   *A Midsummer Night's Dream:* Royal Shakespeare Theatre Company, at the Aldwych Theatre, London. *Producer:* PETER HALL.

20   *As You Like It:* Royal Academy of Dramatic Art, London. *Producer:* NOEL ILIFF.

25   *Richard II:* Ludlow Castle Festival. *Producer:* PETER DEWS.

JULY

1   *A Midsummer Night's Dream:* Birmingham University Guild Theatre Group. *Producer:* DAVID BRADFORD.

12   *The Winter's Tale:* Exeter University Dramatic Society. *Producer:* DAVE LAMBERT.

17   *A Midsummer Night's Dream:* Regent's Park Open-Air Theatre, London. *Producer:* DAVID WILLIAM.

17   *The Tempest:* Oxford Council for Music and Drama, at St John's College, Oxford. *Producer:* DAPHNE LEVENS.

17   *Henry VI, Edward IV:* Royal Shakespeare Theatre, Stratford-upon-Avon. *Producer:* PETER HALL.

31   *A Midsummer Night's Dream:* Windsor Theatre Guild. *Producer:* CHARLES HUNT.

AUGUST

12   *Richard II:* Dryden Society, at the A.D.C. Theatre, Cambridge. *Producer:* JONATHAN FRASER.

12   *Henry VI, Part III:* Hovenden Theatre Club, London. *Producer:* VALERY HOVENDEN.

19   *Richard III:* The National Youth Theatre, Scala Theatre, London. *Producer:* MICHAEL CROFT.

20   *Richard III:* Royal Shakespeare Theatre, Stratford-upon-Avon. *Producer:* PETER HALL.

SEPTEMBER

2   *Hamlet:* National Youth Theatre, Scala Theatre, London. *Producer:* MICHAEL CROFT.

9   *Macbeth:* Citizens Theatre, Glasgow. *Producer:* IAIN CUTHBERTSON.

OCTOBER

8   *Much Ado About Nothing:* The Playhouse, Salisbury. *Producer:* PETER CREGEEN.

16   *Richard III:* Marlowe Theatre, Canterbury. *Producer:* PETER JACKSON.

21   *Twelfth Night:* Little Theatre, Bristol. *Producer:* DAVID PHETHEAN.

22   *Hamlet:* National Theatre, London. *Producer:* LAURENCE OLIVIER.

NOVEMBER

No date given   *The Winter's Tale:* A.D.C. Theatre, Cambridge. *Producer:* PHILIP MANSELL.

4   *The Merchant of Venice:* Perth Theatre. *Producer:* DAVID STEUART.

5   *The Merchant of Venice:* Library Theatre, Manchester. *Producer:* OLIVER NEVILLE.

11   *The Merchant of Venice:* Flora Robson Playhouse, Newcastle-upon-Tyne. *Producer:* JULIAN HERINGTON.

NOVEMBER

19 *The Merchant of Venice:* University Dramatic Society, at Marischal College, Aberdeen University. *Producer:* R. BARRETT-AYRES.

22 *As You Like It:* Norwich Players, at the Maddermarket Theatre, Norwich. *Producer:* IAN EMMERSON.

25 *The Merry Wives of Windsor:* Gateway Theatre, Edinburgh. *Producer:* VICTOR CARIN.

DECEMBER

12 *Coriolanus:* The Playhouse, Nottingham. *Producer:* TYRONE GUTHRIE.

17 *A Midsummer Night's Dream:* London Academy of Music and Dramatic Art. *Producer:* NORMAN AYRTON.

1964

JANUARY

24 *Twelfth Night:* Tavistock Repertory Company, at Canonbury Tower, London. *Producer:* ROBERT PENNANT JONES.

28 *Twelfth Night:* Oxford University Dramatic Society, at the Playhouse, Oxford. *Producer:* MICHAEL RUDMAN.

FEBRUARY

3 *Julius Caesar:* Shakespeare for Schools, at the Comedy Theatre, London. *Producer:* JOHN FRANKLYN ROBBINS.

4 *A Midsummer Night's Dream:* Arts Theatre, Ipswich. *Producer:* ROBERT CHETWYN.

11 *The Merchant of Venice:* Shakespeare Festival Company, at the Theatre Royal, Brighton; and on tour in South America and Europe. *Producer:* DAVID WILLIAM.

11 *Love's Labour's Lost:* Glasgow University English Department. *Producers:* J. F. ARNOTT and P. DREW.

12 *Hamlet:* Her Majesty's Theatre, Barrow-in-Furness. *Producer:* DONALD SARTAIN.

18 *A Midsummer Night's Dream:* Shakespeare Festival Company, at the Theatre Royal, Brighton; and on tour in South America and Europe. *Producer:* WENDY TOYE.

18 *The Merchant of Venice:* Theatre Royal, York. *Producer:* PETER SCHOFIELD.

19 *The Merchant of Venice:* Her Majesty's Theatre, Barrow-in-Furness. *Producer:* DONALD SARTAIN.

21 *King Lear:* Empire Theatre, Sunderland, for the North-east Theatre Festival. *Producer:* MICHAEL ALDRIDGE.

25 *A Midsummer Night's Dream:* Birmingham Repertory Theatre. *Producer:* JOHN HARRISON.

25 *Macbeth:* Everyman Theatre, Cheltenham. *Producer:* IAN MULLINS.

25 *A Midsummer Night's Dream:* The Playhouse, Liverpool. *Producers:* DAVID SCASE and TONY COLEGATE.

25 *Twelfth Night:* Guildhall School of Music and Drama, London. *Producer:* LEIGH HOWARD.

25 *A Midsummer Night's Dream:* Library Theatre, Manchester. *Producer:* OLIVER NEVILLE.

25 *Macbeth:* Welsh Theatre Company, on an Arts Council tour of Wales. *Producer:* WARREN JENKINS.

FEBRUARY

25   *The Merchant of Venice:* Empire Theatre, Sunderland, for the North-east Theatre Festival. *Producer:* JOSEPH O'CONOR.

26   *King Lear:* Bristol University Drama Society. *Producer:* DAVID WILLIAMS.

MARCH

2   *Macbeth:* Flora Robson Playhouse, Newcastle-upon-Tyne. *Producer:* JULIAN HERINGTON.

2   *The Merchant of Venice:* The Coliseum, Oldham. *Producer:* CARL PAULSEN.

3   *Richard III:* Sheffield University Theatre Group. *Producer:* MIKE JOHNSON.

5   *Twelfth Night:* The Playhouse, Salisbury; and the Nuffield Theatre, Southampton University. *Producer:* NOREEN CRAVEN.

5   *As You Like It:* Royal Academy of Dramatic Art, Vanbrugh Theatre, London; and at Tucson, Arizona. *Producer:* ROGER JENKINS.

7   *Twelfth Night:* Citizens Theatre, Glasgow; and at Greenock. *Producer:* JOHN BRYDEN RODGER.

7   *Macbeth:* Royal Academy of Dramatic Art, Vanbrugh Theatre, London; and at Tucson, Arizona. *Producer:* JOHN FERNALD.

9   *Troilus and Cressida:* Marlowe Society, at the Arts Theatre, Cambridge. *Producer:* ROBIN MIDGELY.

10   *Julius Caesar:* Colchester Repertory Theatre. *Producer:* DAVID FORDER.

10   *Twelfth Night:* Dundee Repertory Theatre. *Producer:* DERRICK GOODWIN.

16   *King John:* The University Theatre Group, at the Nuffield Theatre, Southampton. *Producer:* RICHARD SOUTHERN.

17   *Hamlet:* Belgrade Theatre, Coventry. *Producer:* ANTHONY RICHARDSON.

30   *Henry V:* Theatre Royal, Bristol; and on tour in Europe and England. *Producer:* STUART BURGE.

APRIL

6   *The Merchant of Venice:* The White Rose Company, at the Opera House, Harrogate. *Producer:* DEREK GOLDBY.

7   *Richard II:* Theatre Royal, Lincoln. *Producer:* KAY GARDNER.

10   *Richard III:* Norwich Players, at the Maddermarket Theatre, Norwich. *Producer:* IAN EMMERSON.

13   *Othello:* Bristol Old Vic Company, at the Theatre Royal, Bristol. *Producer:* DAVID SCASE.

14   *Much Ado About Nothing:* Citizens Theatre, Glasgow. *Producer:* ERIC JONES.

15   *Richard II:* Royal Shakespeare Theatre, Stratford-upon-Avon. *Producers:* PETER HALL, JOHN BARTON and CLIFFORD WILLIAMS.

16   *Henry IV, Parts I and II:* Royal Shakespeare Theatre, Stratford-upon-Avon. *Producers:* PETER HALL, JOHN BARTON and CLIFFORD WILLIAMS.

18   *Twelfth Night:* Pitlochry Festival Theatre. *Producer:* PETER STREULI.

20   *Love's Labour's Lost:* Bristol Old Vic Company, at the Theatre Royal, Bristol. *Producer:* VAL MAY.

APRIL

20   *Romeo and Juliet:* Perth Theatre. *Producer:* DAVID STEUART.

21   *Macbeth:* Castle Theatre, Farnham. *Producer:* JOAN KNIGHT.

21   *Twelfth Night:* Queen's Theatre, Hornchurch. *Producer:* JANE HOWELL.

21   *Othello:* National Theatre, London; and at the Chichester Festival Theatre. *Producer:* JOHN DEXTER.

21   *Antony and Cleopatra:* The Playhouse, Sheffield. *Producer:* COLIN GEORGE.

22   *Macbeth:* Mermaid Theatre, London. *Producer:* JULIUS GELLNER.

27   *Richard II:* Phoenix Theatre, Leicester. *Producer:* CLIVE PERRY.

MAY

3   *Twelfth Night:* Century Theatre, Chester. *Producer:* HEINZ BERNARD.

5   *King John:* Northampton Repertory Theatre. *Producer:* KEITH ANDREWS.

20   *Macbeth:* Shakespeare for Schools, Ltd., at the Shaftesbury Theatre, London. *Producer:* ROBERT TRONSON.

28   *Julius Caesar:* Harrow School. *Producer:* RONALD WATKINS.

JUNE

3   *Henry V:* Royal Shakespeare Theatre, Stratford-upon-Avon. *Producers:* PETER HALL and JOHN BARTON.

4   *Fortunes of Falstaff:* Norwich Players, at the Maddermarket Theatre, Norwich. *Producer:* IAN EMMERSON.

5   *Henry V:* New Shakespeare Company, at the Open-Air Theatre, Regent's Park, London.

10   *Sir Thomas More:* Nottingham Playhouse. *Producer:* FRANK DUNLOP.

30   *The Merchant of Venice:* Ludlow Castle, for the Ludlow Festival. *Producer:* COLIN GEORGE.

JULY

7   *Measure for Measure:* Royal Academy of Dramatic Art, at the Holland Park Court Theatre, London. *Producer:* JUDITH GRICK.

8   *The Two Noble Kinsmen:* Bristol University Drama Department, at Dartington Hall; and the Royal Fort, Bristol. *Producer:* WILLIAM ROYSTON.

8   *Twelfth Night:* Hampton Court Palace, London. *Producer:* LESLIE FRENCH.

15   *A Midsummer Night's Dream:* Oxford University Dramatic Society, at Alveston Manor Hotel, Stratford-upon-Avon. *Producer:* VINCENT GUY.

15   *The Taming of the Shrew:* New Shakespeare Company, at the Open-Air Theatre, Regent's Park, London. *Producer:* VLADEK SHEYBAL.

16   *The Taming of the Shrew:* The Coliseum, Oldham. *Producer:* not known.

16?   *The Taming of the Shrew:* Oxford Stage Company, at the Shakespeare Institute, Stratford-upon-Avon. *Producer:* CHRIS PARR.

16   *Hamlet:* Southampton University Theatre Group, Nuffield Theatre, Southampton University. *Producer:* JOCELYN POWELL.

SHAKESPEARE PRODUCTIONS IN THE UNITED KINGDOM

JULY

20   *A Midsummer Night's Dream:* Marlowe Society, at the Arts Theatre, Cambridge. *Producer:* SHAUN CURRY.

22   *The Taming of the Shrew:* City of Oxford Theatre Guild. *Producer:* DAPHNE LEVENS.

29   *Henry VI:* Royal Shakespeare Theatre, Stratford-upon-Avon. *Producers:* PETER HALL and JOHN BARTON.

AUGUST

12   *Henry VI, Parts II and III [Edward IV]:* Royal Shakespeare Theatre, Stratford-upon-Avon. *Producers:* PETER HALL and JOHN BARTON.

12   *Richard III:* Royal Shakespeare Theatre, Stratford-upon-Avon. *Producers:* PETER HALL and JOHN BARTON.

17   *Henry IV, Parts I and II:* Theatre Workshop, London, at the Assembly Hall, Edinburgh. *Producer:* JOAN LITTLEWOOD.

18   *Coriolanus:* National Youth Theatre, at the Queen's Theatre, London. *Producer:* MICHAEL CROFT.

24   *The Tempest:* Cambridge University Theatre Company, Lauriston Hall, Edinburgh. *Producer:* CAREY HARRISON.

31   *A Midsummer Night's Dream:* National Youth Theatre, at the Queen's Theatre, London. *Producer:* MICHAEL CROFT.

SEPTEMBER

2   *The Merchant of Venice:* Nottingham Playhouse. *Producers:* JOHN NEVILLE and COLIN GEORGE.

13   *The Merchant of Venice:* Unity Theatre, London. *Producer:* LISA GORDON SMITH.

14   *Hamlet:* Derby Playhouse. *Producer:* IAN COOPER.

21   *A Midsummer Night's Dream:* Bristol Old Vic Company, at the Theatre Royal, Bristol. *Producer:* DENIS CAREY.

21   *Much Ado About Nothing:* Byre Theatre, St Andrews. *Producer:* DAVID BENSON.

28   *Henry V:* Queen's Theatre, Hornchurch. *Producer:* not known.

      Henry IV, Part I: Everyman Theatre, Liverpool. *Producer:* MARTIN JENKINS.

29   *Julius Caesar:* National Youth Theatre Company, at the Empire Theatre, Sunderland.

OCTOBER

11   *A Midsummer Night's Dream:* Marlowe Theatre, Canterbury. *Producer:* not known.

12   *A Midsummer Night's Dream:* Richmond Theatre. *Producer:* ROBERT PEAKE.

27   *King Lear:* Victoria Theatre, Stoke-on-Trent. *Producer:* PETER CHEESEMAN.

NOVEMBER

2   *A Midsummer Night's Dream:* Gateway Theatre, Edinburgh. *Producer:* VICTOR CARIN.

2   *As You Like It:* Perth Theatre. *Producer:* DAVID STEUART.

3   *The Tempest:* The Playhouse, Liverpool. *Producer:* TONY COLEGATE.

NOVEMBER

9   *The Tempest:* Civic Theatre, Chesterfield. *Producer:* BARRY J. GORDON.

26   *Julius Caesar:* Royal Court Theatre, London. *Producer:* LINDSAY ANDERSON.

DECEMBER

7   *Much Ado About Nothing:* Repertory Theatre, Dundee. *Producer:* DERRICK GOODWIN.

8   *Much Ado About Nothing:* Lincoln's Inn Hall, Bar Theatrical Society, London. *Producer:* GREVILLE POKE.

17   *The Merry Wives of Windsor:* Aldwych Theatre, London, by the Royal Shakespeare Theatre Company. *Producer:* JOHN BLATCHLEY.

THREE KINDS OF SHAKESPEARE

1964 Productions at London, Stratford-upon-Avon and Edinburgh

BY

JOHN RUSSELL BROWN

At the National Theatre, in 1964, those fortunate or persistent enough to obtain a ticket saw a starred performance by Sir Laurence Olivier, an Othello whose words could startle and whose actions were inventive and sensuous. His last speech can serve as an image for the whole production. Othello, naked beneath a simple white gown, closed only at the waist, kneels on a low bed placed down-stage centre with tall hangings around it disappearing into the 'flies' behind the top of the proscenium arch. He clasps Desdemona's dead body to his chest, as if she knelt with him, and he raps out a loud: 'Soft you!' After the following pause his voice is surprisingly quiet, almost soft: 'a word or two before you go'. And then without break, continuing the impulses that had changed his voice, Othello kisses Desdemona on the neck, sensuously engrossed. Then the speech follows with recollected formality: 'I have done the state some service...'.

For the production of seven history-plays in a series at the Royal Shakespeare Theatre, Stratford-upon-Avon, in 1964 (the three parts of *Henry VI* freely adapted to form two plays only), a representative image might be a scene change. There is music and a slow, purposeful filing off-stage, nicely judged to illustrate the political factions and the concerns of the characters. The lights change and two large, dark, triangular-based structures turn before a dark, trellised background. And the stage is now a battlefield, with instruments of war, care-worn soldiers, and the slow yet alert tempo of battle. Other notable features could be chosen to represent the Stratford productions, especially the acting of Peggy Ashcroft and Hugh Griffith, but the deliberate scene-changes are demonstrative of the originality and distinction of this season as a whole.

At the 1964 Edinburgh Festival, Joan Littlewood's production of *Henry IV, Part I* by the Theatre Workshop Company (with re-arrangements and cuts and some interpolations from *Part II*) can be represented by the conclusion of its first half. Hal is backing away on the bridge stage that was constructed across the Assembly Hall of the Church of Scotland. Poins remains in the centre. He wears a trim, black velour bowler hat, a single ear-ring, high heeled, blue suede boots, and dark ski-pants. He bends forward as he listens to Hal's words (addressed to Peto in both quarto and Folio texts): 'We must all to the wars, and thy place shall be honourable. ... Be with me betimes in the morning; and so good morrow, Poins.' The delivery of the words is not remarkable and in the centre of the picture is the listener, not the speaker. Poins is smiling; puzzled; embarrassed, perhaps; ingratiating; there is a servility in his jaunty appearance, an insecurity in his knowing manner.

One element common to these three images is a determined realism, of sensuous embodiment in Sir Laurence Olivier's Othello, of the side-effects of power politics in the Stratford Histories, of psychological observation in Joan Littlewood's *Henry IV*. This element is realistic in the sense that it is meant to awaken in the audience a recognition of actuality. And the realism is determined because it is continuously attempted in contrast to unrealistic elements: the undoubted showiness of the star actor; the simplification of the motives of men involved in power politics; the witty vitality of the highway, tavern and rustic scenes of the Workshop production.

Eccentricity is another feature found in the three productions. But Shakespeare is so large that any enactment tends to seem odd; even those rare productions, that seem on first viewing to fill a play to its very limits, will be thought in ten years' time to have missed whole areas of Shakespeare's invented world. And with eccentricity these 1964 productions had a further object in common: a strenuous search for a 'way to do Shakespeare'. For more than sixty years English directors have been engaged on this quest, but their efforts have recently been intensified and multiplied. (Financial help from the State for two competitive theatres may be a cause of this, or new influences from contemporary dramatists and from theatre directors of other countries, or, perhaps, the thought that a distinctive brand of Shakespeare, a production with a clear image, would gain more attention from the general public.) Today theatre directors are convinced of the need to make Shakespeare 'come alive'. They search, experiment, debate, justify and try to learn.

The stage-settings at Stratford represent only one part of that theatre's obvious and advertised experimentation. The isolating effect of John Bury's cross-stage platform for *Measure for Measure* in 1962 or the dwarfing effect of his spacious flats, steps and ramp for *Julius Caesar* in 1963, have given way to a more variable design. Sometimes a vast background without local emphasis is seen behind a completely empty, level stage, marked with rectangles in a perspective that enhances the impression of space. At other times, one or two large pieces of scenery, with steps, recesses, doors or windows to choice, come in from either side, giving intimate and localized settings. Trees, greenery, thrones, prison-bars also vary the setting, but large steps or rostra are seldom introduced so that movement can always be free and often wide-ranging. For battles, group entries or spectacular opportunities (like the lists at Coventry in *Richard II* or the embarkation of Henry V at Southampton) the stage is filled with nimble and well-drilled supernumeraries giving, by action, costume, properties and make-up, an extraordinarily complete attempt at verisimilitude. This mixture of the vast and localized, with this reliance on actors to 'dress' the stage, is a useful solution to the problems of providing a decor for Shakespeare; it is capable of sustaining the audience's interest through most of the seven plays. At present it is used too indulgently, in that too many items are introduced to support the actors—especially torches, carts and animals; and scene changes or fairly simple entries often take up thirty to sixty seconds before the play can proceed. The scenery accounts in part for the slow tempo of the Stratford productions.

In colour the set has small variations of a basic brown, black and grey, and simple sharp contrasts for costumes and properties. The variations are shrewdly used and associated with differing textures (not unlike a fashionable mode of interior decoration): wood, various metals, gloss, matt and stippled surfaces, coarse fabrics and smooth, leather and silk. By apparently economical (though probably expensive) means the stage can vary as widely in tone as in form. Particularly memorable was the austere use of black and white for the Archbishop Scroop scenes or the black and dull tones for Henry IV's bed-chamber. The French court was distinguished from the English by the usual means of colour contrast, but in this neutral set the details of peacock blue and gold were more than usually effective. The only conspicuous omission in the range of effects was wealth and assured regality; Henry IV's words:

> the perfum'd chambers of the great,
> Under the canopies of costly state...

bore no relation to what the audience had seen.

The directors of the plays—Peter Hall, John Barton and Clifford Williams, working in collaboration—would not be likely to judge this omission to be important. For another of the experiments of the Stratford season was a continuous emphasis of violence and of the shallowness of politicians' pretensions. The plays became a high-class cartoon, a relentless horror comic. An elevated tone was sustained by restrained colour in the setting, slow tempo and deliberate utterance. And, with this, horror and violence were presented by liberal splashes of blood, and by inventive business that elaborated every opportunity for the exhibition of cruelty and pain that the text suggested, and more that were foisted on to the text. Joan of Arc cut her own wrist like a Tamburlaine with a very large sword; Young Clifford's head was cut off on stage and carried around upon a spear; Clarence was drowned in the malmsey-butt at the back of the stage, rather than 'within' as the words of the text direct. Going beyond the requirements of the stage-directions and dialogue, action was realized as horribly as possible: Richard II struck the dying Gaunt with a whip repeatedly; when he smashed the looking glass he did so with his bare fist and so inflicted pain upon himself; in prison he was tethered by a huge, noisy chain that had to be flung aside to allow movement and which he used as a weapon that threatened to pull himself down in the last struggle with his warders—the sound and apparent weight of that chain may well have been the dominating impression given by the prison scene. Fights were arranged with persistent ingenuity, important ones with disparity of weapons to heighten interest, as Hotspur with a two-handed sword against Hal with sword and buckler, or Douglas using a spiked mace against a sword. Deaths were thoroughly painful; sack was thrown around and splashed liberally; Hotspur and Lady Percy rolled on the floor in their love-fights; Henry IV was given a foul-tasting potion to drink after its ingredients had been ground in a mortar by a monk-like doctor clothed in black. Repetition lessened the effect of these devices, but they were placed importantly at dramatic crises: *Henry IV, Part I* did not end with the king's deceitful and dramatically ironic exhortation:

> And since this business so fair is done,
> Let us not leave till all our own be won

but with Vernon in death agonies, swinging in a noose; he was then cut down and Worcester climbed to take his place. This experiment had a slight connexion with current talk of a 'theatre of cruelty' and the Royal Shakespeare Theatre's experimental programme of that name shown to the public in the L.A.M.D.A. studio in 1963; but it lacked the severity of Peter Brook's innovating production of *Titus Andronicus* or the emotional depth and rigour required by Artaud in his newly translated *The Theatre and its Double*. Its most obvious effect was a grand-guignol grip on the audience (especially in the first four or five plays that each member had seen), and its most assured the verisimilitude given to certain horrible episodes in the text of *Henry VI*, the earliest in date of composition. The most interesting achievements were the mob-violence that accompanied Bolingbroke's judgment on Bushy and Green, building that into a scene of general social interest rather than a further revelation of the emergent ruler, and, more surely within the scope of the text, the very ample provision of exhibits for Falstaff's discourse on a dead man as a counterfeit. Thus the directors' exaggeration of violence served to accentuate one vein in the text of these plays that has often been obscured by another picturesque indulgence, the accentuation of pageantry and royal panoply.

The shallow, cartoon-like presentation of the major political characters was another continuous feature of these productions, and it, too, was most satisfactory in the plays written earliest. Sharp verbal juxtapositions were pointed for comic effect without concern for the loss in dignity. Burgundy's

> I am vanquished; these haughty words of hers
> Have batt'red me like roaring cannon-shot
> And made me almost yield upon my knees.   (*1 H VI*, III, iii, 78–80.)

so relished the rapidity of his change of sides that the audience was encouraged to laugh. So too, the multiple throwing down of gages before Aumerle in *Richard II*, IV, i, quickly deflated the pretensions of the newly loyal nobles. Wars and rivalries became what Shakespeare once called them: a 'comic sport'. Edward IV wooed the widow so slowly that his lechery was foolish as well as his government; and later when Warwick surprises him, '*bringing the King out in his gown, sitting in a chair*' (IV, iii, S.D.), the directors had him dragged out on a mattress where he was lying with a whore and sent both off-stage as nearly naked and foolish as possible —a rhetorically impressive scene was made to seem like a notorious comic strip. Equally, Henry VI's ineffective attempts at friendship and love were comically played. David Warner in this role, and in the first half of his Richard II, used nervous smiles and a loose-limbed awkwardness to suggest anxious timidity. Richard's commands were under-played so that even these gave an impression of weakness:

> Think what you will, we seize into our hands
> His plate, his goods, his money, and his lands

was said with neither assurance nor effort. Later, when York remarks on his eye 'bright as is the eagle's', Richard's 'We are amaz'd' was very quiet and flat.

For the central political characters of the later plays, Hotspur, Hal, Henry IV and Henry V, and for the virtuoso role of Richard III, the lack of psychological subtlety deprived the productions of long-valued qualities. Ian Holm's Richard was childish in his humour; he sat alone after the scene with the two religious men—here soldiers comically disguised—and kicked his heels. At the end, he was more concerned with his own importance than with his fear, stressing, for example, the second personal pronoun in: 'I fear . . . *I* fear'. His character did make a changing impression as the play proceeded, but in one direction only; towards violent fury, expressed by vocal power and tremendously taxing fights. At the end a monster died: he had struck Catesby a blow when he offered help, but his voice began to fail so that 'A horse! a horse!' was weak as well as terrible and mad; and his death pangs were prolonged close to the audience at the centre of a vast empty stage. Here was little intimation of a tragedy, little scope for any reaction to Richard besides aversion.

Hotspur was comic and coarse, so that Lady Percy's praise of his 'chivalry' seemed wholly fantastic (and out of keeping with her own hoydenish behaviour in the first part of the play); and Henry IV's envy of his character, wishing Hal were like him, seemed absurdly misplaced. Henry IV was nettled and sour, with little indication of his ability to rule and his strength of spirit. Hal was coldly played, as if the actor's main task were to prepare the audience for the 'rejection' of Falstaff. When this point was reached it was easily reached, so that the new king's speech was neat and wholly controlled. The major impression of the last scene of this play was left for Falstaff and his fellows to make in the succeeding episode. Henry V was shallow in another way. He was so obviously thoughtful, careful and, occasionally, sharp, that he never attempted to enter the outline depicted by the Chorus of 'cheerful semblance and sweet majesty . . .' or 'A largess universal, like the sun'. The Chorus was allowed to orate and make flourishes about a quite different play, as if the directors thought that all he said had to be ironically wrong.

Although simplification of character was not the most noticed feature of the Stratford productions, it was probably the most regrettable because it obscured deeply observed and imaginative elements of Shakespeare's art. The directors indulged and supplemented the horrible and the curiously picturesque; and they neglected the humane, the psychologically true, the emotional and affective. The rivalries of the Wars of the Roses were presented clearly and relentlessly as kid's stuff.

A further objective of the whole season—an attempt at a uniform vocal style that respects the poetic qualities of the text—was potentially a safeguard against this sort of simplification. Peter Hall can justly claim in the pamphlet, *Crucial Years* (1963): 'There is no question that the verse-speaking of this Company has improved. It has started to be noticed . . .'. Gone are almost all the glossy tones and meaningless pomposities that could be heard twenty, ten or five years ago. The speaking often echoes 'ordinary speech', and can be both alert and pedestrian. David Warner and Ian Holm have these qualities abundantly, and almost all the company seem to strive to follow them. But, as Peter Hall is aware, this is a noticeable beginning rather than a maturing of the company's style that could lead them into Shakespeare's imaginative world. The early achievements have brought unhelpful side-effects. First, there is a lack of sustained line or rhythm, and a would-be impressive slowness. Long speeches are broken with pauses and far too frequently short speeches are prepared for with silent business, or followed by some such invention. The aim, here, is not psychological subtlety or depth of feeling but effectiveness and psychological actuality for each simplified moment; the broken and slow delivery at Stratford is an aspect of the company's determined realism. And, unfortunately, it combats the excitement of Shakespeare's writing, its ability to draw the audience like a kite in the wind.

Besides rhythm, music and forward pressure, rhetorical energy is lost, and the effectiveness of emphasis and climax. The new style is, in fact, uneconomical. And it is self-important in that the actors seem to think the audience will always wait for them. Hamlet's was good general advice for acting Shakespeare's plays: 'speak the speech . . . trippingly on the tongue'. An actor must, of course, rehearse in slow tempo and study the phrases of his part one by one, but in performance he should not expect the audience to share this trouble. Within a strongly paced production the necessary moments of slow speaking will grow in power, and the whole design gain in eloquence. So, too, the production will gain the subtle influence of a continuous metrical control.

The second side-effect of the new vocal style is a sacrifice of affectiveness to effectiveness. The actors seem to lack temperament and size, as if they tried to be clever at the cost of developing an impression of great feeling. Of course, this is apt for the directors' denigrating attitude to the characters of the plays but two performances that outshone all others were reminders of the limitations elsewhere in the productions of both acting and direction.

These interpretations—acclaimed by rapt and heightened attention and by press-notices—were achievements of temperament and bold psychological conception. Hugh Griffith, as Falstaff, occasionally took his time too much in common with others and resorted to repetitive hand movements to sustain interest, but using an individual and comparatively florid delivery he played up his role. Although the production demanded a Falstaff ripe for rejection, a 'sink of iniquity', he added a visionary's temperament, the surprise, wealth and endurance of an imaginative life. 'The rogue fled from me like quicksilver' (*Part II*, II, iv, 217) was not simply an empty boast, irresponsible and slick, but a ruminative and beloved indulgence, played as if Falstaff for the moment believed in a long-past valour. When he acted Henry IV to Hal's Falstaff in the play-within-the-play, Falstaff became Harry's benevolent father indeed—in his imagination—and peacefully touched the prince's head and face on the concluding: 'And tell me now, thou naughty varlet, tell me, where hast thou been this month?' (*Part I*, II, iv, 416–17). Occasionally the general style of the production hampered his performance; the sherris-sack soliloquy was held back from its natural rhythm by realistic business with a tun of wine and a drinking cup, and the Orchard Scene (v, iii, of *Part II*) was interrupted by a dim-witted three-man band fussing around on stage. But this Falstaff had size and a consistent and inventive complexity: at the end of *Part II*, when the new king has left the stage, Hugh Griffith showed the struggle for an imaginary and imaginative survival; and there was a last breakdown as he allowed Pistol to help him to his feet, so accenting the silent exit that Shakespeare has given him.

Peggy Ashcroft's Margaret, in the two parts of the re-arranged *Henry VI* and in *Richard III*, started with an intrusive lisp. (At times it seemed as if this was intended to be a 'funny' foreign accent.) But in the Paper Crown Scene (*Part III*, I, iv) her portrayal of weakness in cruelty, helplessness in victory, brought depth of understanding and a sustained beauty of phrase to the rhetoric; other barbarous episodes seemed trivial and shocking in contrast. The cruel humour of the lines was played close to hysteria: 'I prithee grieve to make me merry' (line 86) was an almost necessary request to excuse Margaret's impulse towards helpless laughter, a physical and emotional relief and a breakdown of control. Margaret was constantly changing her stance and position as if instinctively; her taunts were controlled and insistent so that only her body, moving repeatedly, could show the inward instability. As York replied in pain and passion, Margaret was silent, after one last, and now forced, laugh. When she stabbed him it was with a quick movement, and then she wept. And then the tears stopped with a wild, painful cry. In this scene the violent was emphasized as much as anywhere, but there was also rhetorical and musical control and a daring, emotional performance.

In *Richard III*, Margaret's long scene with the mourning Queen Elizabeth and the Duchess of York (IV, iv) lacked the consistency of style for its shared (or concerted) rhetoric. But Peggy Ashcroft's first scene, entering alone to Edward's divided court as an old, vindictive woman, was compelling. She spoke from compulsion ('I can no longer hold me patient') and caught the strange verbal exaggerations of her speeches, accentuated them, and added the physical deformities of extreme age and spite. She was crazed and helpless. No one could effectively speak to her except Richard, and he resorted to shock and surprise. She talked to herself as well as to her victims, and to the heavens: 'Can curses pierce the clouds and enter heaven?' she *actually* asked, and with 'Why then, give way' she clapped her hands for attention. She entered, too, into the cruelty she described: 'Look when he fawns, he bites', she warned Buckingham, and then acted the biting and gave a mad laugh. The scene was held back only by the inability to show on the stage a commensurate response: 'My hair doth stand on end to hear her curses', says Buckingham, but this in his performance seemed untrue after the sharp reality, deep feeling and persuasive rhetoric of this Margaret.

A director's shaping hand has great influence over a production; but psychological truth, emotional, ambitious acting, and Shakespeare's rhetoric and poetry can be more powerful. In Joan Littlewood's witty and intelligent *Henry IV* much of what she had devised to demonstrate her reading of the play seemed slight tricks beside some superbly right and sustained performances she encouraged among the comparatively minor characters. She saw the king and nobles as cold politicians, uniform in dress and clipped and unemotional in speech. Only Hotspur, played by Julian Glover in a manner reminiscent of Stratford performances of five years ago, was allowed to make flourishes and he, lacking any answering voice, seemed to beat the air. The director permitted no uncertain effect here. A neurotic reading of the letter scene (II, iii) where added emphasis and quickening tempo turned assurance into an expression of fear—'a good plot, good friends, and full of expectation; an excellent plot, very good friends'—indicated that Hotspur's grandiloquence was *meant* to sound empty. A single, huge cannon, awkwardly pushed into position behind Henry IV for the battle of Shrewsbury, showed that the king was *meant* to lack stature on his own account. So half the play dwindled at the director's command; through manner of speech and action, costume, stage-movement, this half became a demonstration of inadequacy.

It was hardly surprising that newspaper critics, uncompensated with the picturesque and horror-seeking realism of the current Stratford production, castigated Miss Littlewood. But they rightly excepted from censure the actors of some minor characters to whom she had given more rewarding roles. In the highway, tavern and rustic scenes (including the recruiting episode from *Part II*) there was music and abundant activity to make them generally entertaining and here the characterization was more ambitious. Victor Spinetti, the most accomplished actor in the company, was Poins, and there were inventive and strong performances from Murray Melvin as Gadshill and Shadow, and Brian Murphy as Bardolph. Costumes throughout the production were modern, with hints of the 'historical' in cloaks, hats and accessories, and this appearance was matched with modern ways of speech and behaviour. While the politicians suffered by these devices—they were given the fixed poses and grey-and-black colour of newspaper photographs—other characters gained: there was no verse to combat the modern inflexions, and lines and incidents normally guyed in performance were acted so that they gave new recognitions of meaning and truthfulness. The wide range of Poins's responses to Hal was revealed. Gadshill's boast that he has nothing to do with 'landrakers, ... six-penny strikers, ... purple-hu'd malt-worms' shed all its footnote fustiness to become the compensating gloss of a slight-bodied rogue, a cheap, street-corner exquisite. His 'Tut', his negative constructions, his eagerness ('She will, she will'), reliance on a group-image ('We steal ... we have ... we walk'), and scorn of others, concern with others, posh airs, and scornful dismissals, all ceased to be unusable lumber from Elizabethan London, and became amusing and revealing dramatic lines: 'Go to; "homo" is a common name to all men. Bid the Ostler bring my gelding out of the stable. Farewell, you muddy knave' (*Part I*, II, i, 96–7). At Stratford, Francis was a gormless lout, kicked around for broad comic effect, but in the Theatre Workshop production, played by Jeremy Spenser, his scene with Hal revealed honesty, loyalty, ambition, ignorance—a small, conventional and intense imagination; and all this was given by a performance taking much less acting-time than at Stratford. Richard Gurnock as Feeble, the woman's tailor, was mincingly polite, nervously pulling down his jerkin and smiling with each speech. Not only was this character more 'recognizable' and funnier than at Stratford but the scene as a whole was more lively and complete; instead of trying to make Feeble's philosophy sound impressive by an answering pause after 'we owe God a death', Joan Littlewood turned Bardolf's 'Well said; th'art a good fellow' into a quick, smirking response to make everything easy again, after this rather too smug and tactless facing of facts. Feeble's good nature was as firmly established, but his philosophizing was not produced as if it were philosophy; he was the sort of man who might quote Patience Strong in the barrack-room. 'Faith!, I'll bear no base mind' spoke of inexperience as well as bravery, self-concern as well as honesty; it was of a piece with the whole characterization.

Falstaff, without the traditional whiskers and ruddiness, was an unsentimental picture of a public-bar soldier. His bulk, high-living and capacity for friendship were as much a part of his fantasy as his valour. But here the dialogue Shakespeare has provided leapt ahead of the characterization; the verbal energy and colour of the text bore little relationship to the physical image or the tone and rhythm of speech. The search for a contemporary portrayal of Falstaff is not finished; a realism depending on the accurate observation of human behaviour and a general vitality and invention has not filled out this role.

The production of *Othello* at the National Theatre, undertaken by John Dexter, aimed at grandeur; except for its sombre colours and wide groupings it was reminiscent of a Stratford production five or ten years ago. But it also gave an impression of uncertainty; on recollection, it might seem that the current trend towards realistic stage-movement was represented by some awkward entries and exits, but in performance they often looked like clumsiness. So time was wasted in repeated backward turns for Emilia after giving Iago the handkerchief, or the drunken scene was staged in a corner of a largely empty stage so that the actors had to work too hard to give an impression of conviviality.

Characterization also seemed uncertain. Or perhaps some roles were deliberately scaled down in confident expectation that Laurence Olivier's Othello could best succeed as a solo performance. Ian Finley as Iago so neglected the verbal dexterity required by the technical difficulties of his speeches that he was often hard to hear from centre-stalls. This looked like miscalculation until it became clear he was not suggesting the danger, evil or, even, energy under his 'honest' appearance; perhaps he wished to seem wholly ruthless and blunt. Maggie Smith as Desdemona may have intended to be cold and doll-like, responding to danger and loss by tension and then simplicity. Either of these interpretations would have been more successful within their own terms by added scale or intensity.

The interpretation of Othello was not as remarkable as the artistry which presented it. Here was a sensuous man of primitive culture breaking through social propriety and making a great misjudgment. (A conception reminiscent of Alfieri's summing-up of Eddie in Arthur Miller's *View from the Bridge*: 'even as I know how wrong he was, and his death useless, I tremble, for I confess that something perversely pure calls to me from his memory—not purely good, but himself purely. ... And so I mourn him—I admit it—with a certain ... alarm.') In token of a movement back to primitive responses, this Othello tore from his breast the crucifix he had always worn and sometimes fondled.

In execution the most original element was Olivier's persistent sensuousness: a full-lipped make-up, cat-like walk, soft and low-pitched passages, caressing movements. In his first scene he entered carrying and smelling a red (twentieth-century) rose. This emphasis continued to the end: in Shakespeare's text Lodovico says:

> Look on the tragic loading of this bed.
> This is thy work.—The object poisons sight; ...

and immediately commands 'Let it be hid'; but here the implicit stage-direction was not followed; rather there was a very slow fade with lights focused on the two dead bodies, Othello's chest naked. Olivier also gave a sustained impression of physical power even in relaxation, as if Othello practised weight-lifting weekly in a gymnasium.

His verbal delivery was equally accomplished and more ambitious. At first his speech had remarkable ease, allowing a low, self-amused and quick laugh on 'Upon this hint I spake'. But in 'Farewell the tranquil mind ...' which was given immediately before the single interval, two hours after the play began, Olivier revealed a tremendously increased range of voice. He spoke the repeated 'Farewells' with lengthened and varied vowels, and gave an illustrative expressiveness to the succeeding evocations of 'big wars ... shrill trump ... rude throats ... dread clamours'. Olivier strongly marked a rhythm that grew more insistent throughout the sustained passage so that vocal virtuosity was combined with a compelling performance. At this point, too, his postures became more studied or artificial, often held for several lines and occasionally restraining Iago in an unmoving grip. With 'ne'er ebb to humble love', there was a long silence after 'humble' while Othello forced himself to say the word 'love' that had stuck in his throat; this silence was full with the impression of physical struggle and when at last the word came it was, convincingly, quiet. This device was similar to the many pauses in the Stratford productions, but Olivier used time more sparingly, worked hard to deserve each split second, and by controlling the tempo and shape of each speech and episode counteracted an occasional slowness with a display of both temperament and art.

The central performance of the National Theatre's *Othello* was a demonstration of the huge opportunities Shakespeare has provided for an actor who is at once realistic and histrionic. While several small performances at Edinburgh brought a more immediate recognition of psychological truth, and the Stratford Falstaff and Margaret more imaginative reach and emotional depth, Olivier's performance was supremely inventive, sustained and astonishing. As so often in the past, an actor rather than a director had created his own kind of Shakespeare.

THE YEAR'S CONTRIBUTIONS TO
SHAKESPEARIAN STUDY

1. CRITICAL STUDIES

reviewed by NORMAN SANDERS

It is a presumption to believe that dramatic experience can be fully described in terms of pattern and symbol.... To speak of Shakespeare's plays in symbolic terms reveals a unity, but it does not necessarily follow that the plays are wholly harmonious, or that this unity is the only one. Such criticism may seem to clarify our appreciation, but it does not necessarily follow that the plays are without other aspects important to author and audience.

So writes John Russell Brown[1] in an important article which is indicative of the re-appraisal which Shakespearian criticism is undergoing. The symbolist-imagist orthodoxy is being questioned as too narrow, even as its exponents questioned its Bradleian predecessor. The plea is for a more inclusive view of the plays with greater emphasis on what Brown calls, in another article,[2] 'the expression of character in subconscious existence and in the deeper recesses of consciousness'. But these aspects of the plays are also to be seen in terms of the theatre—'of repetitions, silences, sudden intensities and insistences that are apparently without motive', devices that we may now perceive with greater clarity owing to our exposure to the 'new' drama of Pinter, Beckett and Ionesco.

Other pleas have been made on similar lines by V. Y. Kantak[3] and Norman Holland.[4] The former claims that 'there is...something wrong in the approach that considers Shakespeare's realism of character as a sort of technical proficiency valuable in its way but not at all very essential to his tragic vision'. He laments too the lack of a balanced approach to the functioning of images, and suggests that everything in a play, 'even a poetic play, [is] cast in the shape of human activity making it an image of men in action. The poetic pattern aids the plausibility of that image.' Holland takes a fresh look at psychoanalytic criticism and lists the two steps necessary if it is to have any real value: the establishing of a congruity between a work of literature and some general psychoanalytical proposition, and the relating of this proposition to some mind in particular, either the author's, a character's, or the audience's. He defines a 'new' psychoanalytical approach to Shakespeare as one which would come to a work of literature 'not as a single unconscious wish, but as a totality or *gestalt* of competing unconscious wishes, the showplace of an interior drama in the minds of the playwright or his audience'. The direction of the fledgling new orthodoxy is perhaps already perceptible.

Some of the criticism produced in 1962 and 1963 reflects this desire for wider or newer lines

---

[1] 'Mr Beckett's Shakespeare', *Critical Quarterly*, v (1963), 310–26.

[2] 'Mr Pinter's Shakespeare', *Critical Quarterly*, v (1963), 251–65.

[3] 'An Approach to Shakespearian Tragedy: The "Actor" Image in *Macbeth*', *Shakespeare Survey 16* (1963), 42–52.

[4] 'Shakespearean Tragedy and the Three Ways of Psychoanalytic Criticism', *Hudson Review*, xv (1962), 217–27.

of approach. H. M. V. Matthews[1] has produced an excellent book which seems in general alignment with Brown's viewpoint. Her basic thesis is that Shakespeare must be read in terms of 'both individual characterisation and individual symbolism' and 'the tension between the particular and the universal'. These matters are difficult to write about, but Matthews navigates the course between them with some success and displays some fine critical insight. The 'symbol' of her book's title is really limited to a group of symbolizations in Christian myth and doctrine either in specifically Christian formulations or in secularizations of them. She traces such themes as: Lucifer (hubris, rebellion, and usurpation) in characters like Claudius, Richard III, Henry IV, Macbeth and Edmund; revenge; death; the saviour; justice and mercy; redemption and salvation. As the author's method is to move from one group of plays to another, the impression often conveyed is that Shakespeare was working through a pre-arranged orderly progression. This is perhaps a result of a too rigid adherence to her thesis which occasionally leads her to push her analogies too far (e.g. the comparison of the Edgar–Edmund duel with both Childe Roland and Lucifer and Michael), and which also prompts her to condemn a play when it does not fit the myth rather than question the validity of her thesis when applied to the play under discussion. One is brought up short by such a judgment on the handling of Brutus as, for example, 'Already perhaps Shakespeare was aware of some inadequacy to his purposes in the Luciferian myth on which he was depending'. However, such disagreements only slightly detract from the value of her excellent handling of topics like *Julius Caesar*, the ambiguity of Shakespeare's treatment of Henry V, or the difference in degree of dramatic coherence between *Hamlet* and *Macbeth*.

In rather a different way C. J. Sisson[2] casts his net wide over topics dealt with in some of Matthews's chapters. He considers justice in its various aspects—divine, private, poetic, as well as the related ideas of revenge and mercy. The tragedies are examined with these ideas in mind and difficulties of interpretation are frequently elucidated by reference to real-life contemporary law processes. The essays are full of perceptive interpretations of character and situation, and valuable remarks on audience reaction; for example, the play scene in Hamlet is viewed as a juryless trial, and *Othello* seen in part as a revenge play. Even where they provoke disagreement (e.g. is not the stress on Hamlet's ambition for the crown too heavy?), these discussions stimulate thought and suggestive lines of approach.

Anne Righter[3] takes a theatrical orientation for her reading of the plays. She considers Shakespeare's use of the stage metaphor, which has frequently been used previously only in analyses of single plays, as a means of perceiving his changing attitudes to life and art. In the early part of the book Righter traces the changes in relationship between audience and player from medieval drama to the Elizabethan professional stage. She argues that at a mystery play the spectators were witnesses of a ritual world 'more real than the one which existed outside its frame', whereas by the time the morality plays were being acted, the play was subjected to the 'tyranny of the audience'. Thus she sees the challenge presented to the dramatists of the 1590's as being the establishing of the self-contained wholeness of the stage world. With this historical perspective, the second section of the book is devoted to an examination of the

---

[1] *Character and Symbol in Shakespeare's Plays* (Cambridge University Press, 1962).
[2] *Shakespeare's Tragic Justice* (Methuen, 1962).
[3] *Shakespeare and the Idea of the Play* (Chatto and Windus, 1962).

Shakespearian canon under the various aspects of the stage metaphor: the play image in the early plays, the player king, the power of illusion, disguise and deceit, its extension in dreams and shadows, etc. All are treated with great penetration and are full of, to me, genuinely fresh and fecund ideas, particularly those passages on the player king and the play-within-the-play. In the two final chapters, however, the reader's rapture is modified, for here Righter goes biographical on us, claiming that, in the work from *Hamlet* to *Timon* and *Coriolanus*, the increasing derogatory references to plays and players indicate that Shakespeare's 'faith in the power of illusion [was] seemingly gone' and that he has 'a tendency to insult the theatre'. Surely such references may be seen to carry a quite different interpretation: namely, that Shakespeare was so sure of his art, he could afford to draw the distinction between good and bad actors, weak and strong theatre. Allusions like Cleopatra's to the quick comedians and the squeaking boy suggest a writer so confident that he is willing to shatter his illusion only to reinforce it. One questions too whether Righter's concept of the self-contained play is not an oversimplification; the very use of the play-within-the-play and extensions of it like the letter scene in *Twelfth Night* or the gulling of Benedick may be seen as examples of Shakespeare's stepping across the imaginary barrier between audience and actors. The final chapter is full of individually good judgments and subtle perception, but the biographical thesis is obtrusive. Righter sees Shakespeare in his final phase turning 'the world itself into a theatre, blurring the distinction between art and life' and 'restoring the dignity of the play metaphor'. This is true only in part, for this final blurring could just as well be the last logical step in a process which was only partially complete in the tragedies and middle comedies.

Another general essay, smaller in scope but every bit as suggestive as Righter's book, is Mary Lascelles's British Academy Lecture.[1] This is a sensitive and gracefully written attempt to grasp the elusive essence of Shakespeare's comic view. It contains among other things a fine analysis of Falstaff and the perception of the two-way traffic in the theatre across what Lascelles calls the 'fourth wall':

Surely it is significant that Shakespeare should allow the fourth wall to be crossed, as it were, in both directions—and by such diverse fugitives, all of whom this device of soliloquy compels us to admit, even while we laugh, to sanctuary. This traffic indeed creates a sort of fellowship between those who are found out, and those who are witty enough to find themselves out....Could we, and would we, claim exemption from this fellowship?

All of these books are provided with a context by a most useful article by Robert Hapgood,[2] who surveys the work of critics whose approach to Shakespeare has been through myth and ritual under conveniently basic headings: Elizabethan ceremonies, Elizabethan theatre, dramatic and literary traditions and dramatic genres. He defends the ritualistic approach against such critics as Levin, Brooks and Wimsatt, and while admitting its weaknesses of 'mistaking analogies for identities, of making claims far in excess of evidence, of trying to reduce literature to myth, of oversolemnity', prognosticates a future productiveness.

Shakespeare's comedy in general and particular has received rather more than its usual share

---

[1] *Shakespeare's Comic Insight* (British Academy Annual Shakespeare Lecture, 1962; Oxford University Press, 1963).
[2] 'Shakespeare and the Ritualists', *Shakespeare Survey* 15 (1962), 111–24.

of critical attention. G. K. Hunter[1] in a useful British Council booklet, which maintains the high standards of its predecessors, provides an introduction to the middle comedies. While designed for the general reader, the account possesses a welcome clarity to the scholar peering through the wood of mounting Shakespearian criticism, and is good on such topics as the comic judgment in *A Midsummer Night's Dream*, the structure of *As You Like It*, the mood of *Twelfth Night*, and the delicate balance only just preserved in *Much Ado About Nothing*. John Dover Wilson[2] also considers the comedies as a group. His book is an outgrowth of his labours on the New Cambridge Shakespeare, and comprises the revised versions of essays on individual comedies, which were originally delivered as lectures in the 1930's, together with two general chapters on the nature and origins of Shakespeare's comedy, and a 1961 postscript on *A Midsummer Night's Dream*. Wilson sees Shakespearian comedy as descended from Terence and Plautus by way of the comedies of sixteenth-century Italy, with the enhancement of the love interest as one of Shakespeare's special contributions to the form. All of the essays contain the qualities for which Wilson is justly celebrated: quickness and ingenuity of mind, a gusto of style which conveys the enjoyment originally aroused by the plays, the sudden shafts of insight into single phrases and whole situations, and the occasional unblushing waywardness of learned and informed speculation. The approach to the plays certainly reflects that the author 'has refrained from reading anything else on the subject' since 1944; however, one must be grateful for the way in which the elements that go to make up the comic fabric of the plays are skilfully isolated and illuminated by a well-stocked and humane mind.

Many of the comedies individually have been the subjects of articles of varying quality and scope. There are some useful critical asides in T. W. Baldwin's[3] examination of Shakespeare's adaptation of homiletic material in *The Comedy of Errors*, II, i, 7–25, 104–15; II, ii, 132–48. On *The Two Gentlemen of Verona* two good papers are offered by Stanley Wells[4] and Harold Brooks.[5] With little reverence, Wells subjects the plot to a rigorous examination and demonstrates that Shakespeare's dramatic technique in the play is limited exclusively to three devices: soliloquy, duologue, and aside as comment. Admitting the well-known virtues of the piece, Wells concludes that Shakespeare 'fails, partly because he puts more into the framework than it can hold, and partly because he still has much to learn about the mechanics of his craft'. Brooks examines one of the excellences of the play mentioned by Wells: namely, the functional roles of the clowns as common-sense commentators and parodists.

Both Cecil Seronsy[6] and E. M. W. Tillyard[7] argue for a closer relationship between the two plots in *The Taming of the Shrew* than is usually allowed. The former bases his case on the grounds that Shakespeare, working under the influence of Gascoigne's play, had his interest shifted from the shrew-taming theme to the idea of 'supposes' as a unifying idea. He shows

[1] *Shakespeare: The Late Comedies* (Longmans, Green and Co., 1962).

[2] *Shakespeare's Happy Comedies* (Faber and Faber, 1962).

[3] 'Three Homilies in *The Comedy of Errors*', *Essays on Shakespeare and Elizabethan Drama in Honor of Hardin Craig*, ed. Richard Hosley (University of Missouri Press, 1962), pp. 137–47.

[4] 'The Failure of *The Two Gentlemen of Verona*', *Shakespeare Jahrbuch*, XCIX (1963), 161–73.

[5] 'Two Clowns in a Comedy (to say nothing of the Dog): Speed, Launce (and Crab) in *The Two Gentlemen of Verona*', *Essays and Studies*, XVI (1963), 91–100.

[6] '"Supposes" as the Unifying Theme in *The Taming of the Shrew*', *Shakespeare Quarterly*, XIV (1963), 15–30.

[7] 'Some Consequences of a Lacuna in *The Taming of the Shrew*', *English Studies*, XLIII (1962), 330–5.

how this is worked out in the induction and the two plots, and suggests that the piece is concerned with the 'interplay of love and illusion, and transformation on varying levels', a view with which Tillyard agrees. Deeper issues are also detected in *Love's Labour's Lost* by Cyrus Hoy[1] and Philip Parsons.[2] Hoy claims that in addition to the recognized butts of satire, there is 'the infirmity of human purpose'. He sees in the play the basic pattern of Shakespeare's comedy as a whole 'which consists in a movement from the artificial to the natural always with the objective of finding oneself'. In this particular play the perspective for viewing man's frailties is provided by the context of the seasonal variations of the natural world wherein they are adumbrated. Parsons concentrates his attention on the 'masks' in the play which he sees as 'one of love's dark images' and also 'an element in the creative pattern of self-discovery'. *A Midsummer Night's Dream* has stimulated three notes on special aspects of the play. Dorelies Kersten[3] sees Puck as a combination of hobgoblin and refined fairy, the only character never to become the object of an action against his will and who can, therefore, act as commentating mediator between audience and play. John Cutts[4] attempts to identify the two love potions by reference to Gerard's *Herball*, and details the satirical functions of the Pyramus and Thisbe playlet at various levels. The play-within-the-play is also examined by Madeleine Doran[5] who contrasts it with the principal medieval and Renaissance versions of the story and comes to the wry conclusion that Shakespeare perpetrated the outrage on the tale and its absurd incidentals that it 'had always been asking for'.

An interesting and original reading of *As You Like It* is that by Jay L. Halio,[6] who sees the tensions in the play as residing in the contrast between the timelessness of the Forest of Arden and the time-ridden occupations of court and city life. Since neither extreme affords a balanced view of time, Shakespeare makes Rosalind the link between the two worlds and thus 'a primary agent for the synthesis of values that underlies regeneration in Shakespeare's comedy'. With regard to time she moves with Orlando by the agency of the forest, the repository of natural life, 'to a proper balance of unharried awareness' in love. In the same play Angus McIntosh[7] marks a grammatical clue to the characters of Celia and Rosalind in the uses of 'thou' and 'you'. In a curiously uneven piece, Lydia Forbes[8] makes some interesting observations on the unity, character relationships, and juxtaposition in *Twelfth Night*; it is a pity, however, that she should take so much notice of Kenneth Tynan's and Harold Clurman's facile journalistic condemnations of the play. The troublesome inscription on Malvolio's letter is looked at again in a, to me, rather obscure article by Lee Sheridan Cox,[9] who argues that Maria expected Malvolio to take 'M, O, A, I' to mean 'I AM O (Olivia)' and that Malvolio's misinterpretation only underlines his self-importance. At some points I think his idea leads him to place on certain lines interpretations they will not bear. An implicit warning against such attempts to take

---

[1] 'Love's Labour's Lost and the Nature of Comedy', *Shakespeare Quarterly*, XIII (1962), 31–40.

[2] 'Shakespeare and the Mask', *Shakespeare Survey 16* (1963), 121–31.

[3] 'Shakespeare's Puck', *Shakespeare Jahrbuch*, XCVIII (1962), 189–200.

[4] 'The Fierce Vexation of a [Midsummer Night's] Dreame', *Shakespeare Quarterly*, XIV (1963), 183–5.

[5] 'Pyramus and Thisbe Once More', *Essays on Shakespeare and Elizabethan Drama*, pp. 149–61.

[6] '"No Clock in the Forest": Time in *As You Like It*', *Studies in English Literature*, II (1962), 197–207.

[7] '"As You Like It": A Grammatical Clue to Character', *Review of English Literature*, IV (1963), 68–81.

[8] 'What You Will?', *Shakespeare Quarterly*, XIII (1962), 475–85.

[9] 'The Riddle in *Twelfth Night*', ibid. p. 360.

I A   Henry IV in his palace, with his doctor and Prince Hal

I B   Henry V with his army and Montjoy
THE ROYAL SHAKESPEARE THEATRE'S 1964 PRODUCTIONS OF THE HISTORIES
Directed by Peter Hall, John Barton and Clifford Williams, settings and costumes
by John Bury

II   Peggy Ashcroft as Queen Margaret in *3 Henry VI*
THE ROYAL SHAKESPEARE THEATRE'S 1964 PRODUCTIONS OF THE HISTORIES

III   Peggy Ashcroft as Queen Margaret in *Richard III*
THE ROYAL SHAKESPEARE THEATRE'S 1964 PRODUCTIONS OF THE HISTORIES

IV A   Hugh Griffith as Falstaff
THE ROYAL SHAKESPEARE THEATRE'S 1964 PRODUCTIONS OF THE HISTORIES

IV B   George A. Cooper as Falsta
with Victor Spinetti as Poins
THEATRE WORKSHOP
PRODUCTION, EDINBURGH, 196.
Directed by Joan Littlewood

V   Hugh Griffith and Ian Holm as Falstaff and Prince Hal in the 'play' scene
THE ROYAL SHAKESPEARE THEATRE'S 1964 PRODUCTIONS OF THE HISTORIES

VI David Warner as Henry VI, on his throne

THE ROYAL SHAKESPEARE THEATRE'S 1964 PRODUCTIONS OF THE HISTORIES

VII   Roy Dotrice as Edward IV, with a whore. Brewster Mason as Warwick

THE ROYAL SHAKESPEARE THEATRE'S 1964 PRODUCTIONS OF THE HISTORIES

VIII A   Roy Dotrice as Hotspur

VIII B   Ian Holm and Eric Porter as Richard III and Richmond in the last scene of *Richard III*
THE ROYAL SHAKESPEARE THEATRE'S 1964 PRODUCTIONS OF THE HISTORIES

A

B

C

D

E

F

G

H

I

IX A Edmund Kean; B Salvini; C Forbes-Robertson; D Frederick Valk; E Paul Robeson;
F Orson Welles; G Godfrey Tearle; H John Gielgud; I James McCracken
THE VISUAL PRESENTATION OF OTHELLO

X   Mario del Monaco and Raina Kabaiwanska as Otello and Desdemona in the death scene
'OTELLO', ROYAL OPERA HOUSE, COVENT GARDEN
Setting and costumes by George Wakhevitch

XI Othello dead with Desdemona: Laurence Olivier and Maggie Smith
'OTHELLO', NATIONAL THEATRE, 1964
Directed by Laurence Olivier, settings and costumes by Jocelyn Herbert

XII A   Laurence Olivier as Othello

XII B   'What would you with her, sir?'
'OTHELLO'

Shakespeare's comedies too realistically is delivered by C. J. Sisson[1] in an examination of the treatment of 'mad' Malvolio, which leads him to deduce that everything in Malvolio's exper-ience is at complete variance with Tudor practice in life and the legal process.

The Merchant of Venice is a play which shares with *Hamlet* the power to stimulate some of the best as well as the most wrong-headed Shakespearian criticism. Bernard Grebanier's[2] book on the play is fascinating and well worth the reading, but is also unsatisfactory and occasionally irritating in some respects. Like its title, the tone is altogether too positive. One wonders also what purpose exactly is served by the old trick of transplanting characters (e.g. on Portia and Hamlet married: 'What a lively time the two of them would have passing the world in review with their merry but compassionate tongues!'). Yet despite such irritants, the book is a close and able reading of the play. Grebanier works from the historical background of the play and sees Shylock as a villain rather than the comic-cum-heroic figure of some critics. Even his adherence to his religion is to be viewed with some scepticism, and in fact, as Grebanier acutely remarks on the Leah speech, Shakespeare

gives Shylock the one softening touch allotted him in the entire play.... It is a wonderfully simple human touch, and it reminds us that Shylock, before he gave in to his passion for accumulating money, was once a human being too.

He rightly notes that any attempt to sentimentalize the character by projecting him outside the limits of the play must be eschewed so that we begin 'with no preconceptions concerning Shylock's character and start gauging him from the moment we first meet him in the play'. Antonio tends to emerge from this interpretation as rather nobler than he ever appears in the theatre, and Bassanio receives a well-argued defence. The chapters on the trial and the lovers are lively and informative and there is a selective account of the play's theatrical fortunes. Two other papers make significant contributions to our understanding of the play in quite different ways. Sigurd Burckhardt[3] offers a sensitive and well-written examination of the handling of the plot, and argues that it is 'circular' and most exactly structured:

The Merchant is a play about circularity and circulation; it asks how the vicious circle of the bond's law can be transformed into the ring of love. And it answers: through a literal and unreserved sub-mission to the bond as absolutely binding.

Burckhardt, however, goes much further than this: he gives a new interpretation of the Jessica–Lorenzo plot, speculates legitimately on the lost play, *The Jew*, and links the working out of the play with Shakespeare's own development in wrestling with the conditions under which he practised his art. This is an important essay and deserves to be used alongside John Russell Brown's work on the play. Barbara K. Lewalski,[4] in a well-documented article, notes rightly that over-ingenuity and special pleading have marred some 'Christian' criticism of Shakespeare, and makes a plea for 'rigorous standards of evidence and argument in such investigations'. She lists the many parallels of idea and wording between *The Merchant of Venice* and the Bible,

---

[1] 'Tudor Intelligence Tests: Malvolio and Real Life', *Essays on Shakespeare and Elizabethen Drama*, pp. 183–200.
[2] *The Truth About Shylock* (Random House, New York, 1962).
[3] '*The Merchant of Venice*: The Gentle Bond', *English Literary History*, XXIX (1962), 239–62.
[4] 'Biblical Allusion and Allegory in *The Merchant of Venice*', *Shakespeare Quarterly*, XIII (1962), 327–43.

and argues that her study uncovers 'patterns of Biblical allusion and imagery so precise and pervasive as to be patently deliberate', and that Shakespeare is ultimately concerned with the nature of Christian living and love. Her contention is persuasive, but she tends to stress rather too heavily the equation between Antonio and Christian love.

One of the more remarkable shifts in critical interest in the past thirty years has been in the amount of consideration given to *Measure for Measure*. No less than eight articles have recently appeared concerned with some aspect of this puzzling work. D. R. C. Marsh[1] attempts to ascertain the dominant mood of the play, the clue to which he sees in Isabella's speech about 'proud man' who lives in a world of his own making, tailored to fit his own desires and prejudices. Marsh remarks that the mood also depends on our attitude to the duke and the justice he dispenses, and claims that our confidence in both are subtly undermined from the first scene. He concludes that 'it is a mood of wry clear-sightedness that seems to characterize this play'. Wilbur Dunkel,[2] Robert Hapgood[3] and John W. Dickinson[4] all discuss the theme of equity in the play. Dickinson and Dunkel agree in seeing equity as one of the themes; both deal with the theory and practice of equity in Elizabethan England and reflect upon Shakespeare's own probable acquaintance with its workings in the Court of Chancery. They agree too that Escalus is the upholder of equity in contrast to Angelo's injustice, and that the lesson of the play is that equity is an inferior principle to Christian mercy. Hapgood would place the shadowy figure of the Provost alongside Escalus as one of the characters who seeks to moderate the law for the sake of equity instead of attempting to alter its strict course as some of the others do. S. Narajan[5] also handles one of the prime sources of difficulty in the play—how to interpret the betrothals. He contests Ernest Schanzer's claim[6] that the play can only be interpreted in the light of Elizabethan moral tenets, and states that all that is necessary is to be found in the text: namely, that Claudio's betrothal to Juliet is a *de futuro* engagement and Mariana's to Angelo *de praesenti*. His conclusion that ignorance of the various types of marriage contracts in Shakespeare's day is not likely to lead a modern reader astray hardly stands scrutiny in the light of the technical nature of his own discussion. Warren D. Smith[7] has a rather different approach to the problem inherent in the play, and argues that what Shakespeare accomplishes will only be perceived if we realize that all the principals are dynamic, and are intended to change as the plot develops, in calculated contrast to the minor characters whose static quality serves as a backdrop helpful to the understanding of the audience. Edward L. Hart[8] also takes a character approach and defends Shakespeare's motivation and understanding of Angelo as a man whose habitual suppression of his passions has made Isabella a necessary property for the accomplishment of a ritual defilement; and one whose experiences in the play enable him to be rehabilitated rather than painfully punished. Two very very different solutions to the play's overall difficulties

---

[1] 'The Mood of *Measure for Measure*', *Shakespeare Quarterly*, XIV (1963), 31–8.
[2] 'Law and Equity in *Measure for Measure*', *Shakespeare Quarterly*, XIII (1962), 275–85.
[3] 'The Provost and Equity in *Measure for Measure*', *Shakespeare Quarterly*, XV (1964), 114–15.
[4] 'Renaissance Equity and *Measure for Measure*', *Shakespeare Quarterly*, XIII (1962), 287–97.
[5] '*Measure for Measure* and Elizabethan Betrothals', *Shakespeare Quarterly*, XIV (1963), 115–19.
[6] *Shakespeare Survey 13* (1960), 81–90.
[7] 'More Light on *Measure for Measure*', *Modern Language Quarterly*, XXIII (1962), 309–22.
[8] 'A Mixed Consort: Leontes, Angelo, Helena', *Shakespeare Quarterly*, XV (1964), 75–84.

are put forward by Eileen Mackay[1] and S. Musgrove.[2] The former suggests that a staging of the play, which would allow Isabella to stand out against the carefully drawn background of ecclesiastical corruption, would make 'the troublesome play…stand foursquare'. Her demonstration certainly displays how such a production as she envisages would solve a good many problems, but it also shows how it would be imposing a reading *upon* the play for which there is only minimal evidence in the text. Musgrove's textual explanation of some of the cruxes is persuasive. By analyses of II, i, and III, i, he argues that there is evidence that there are two strata in the play, and that parts of the text as we have it have been made up from a combination of originally separate elements. He also suggests that the last act which has attracted so much critical comment was written as a unit to give an allegorical rounding off to a botched play.

Ernest Schanzer[3] also discusses *Measure for Measure* among his 'problem plays'. However, he reverses the procedure of other writers on this subject, such as Boas, Tillyard and Lawrence, in that he defines the term first and then considers 'which…of Shakespeare's plays this definition fits'. His definition of the term is: a play in which we find a pre-occupation with a central moral problem 'which will inevitably take the form of an act of choice confronting the protagonist', and in relation to which 'we are unsure of our moral bearings, so that uncertain and divided responses to it in the minds of the audience are possible or even probable'. When this definition is tested against the various possible candidates, I find some of Schanzer's conclusions dubious. For example, in rejecting *Troilus and Cressida*, he posits that the only moral problem posed is that concerning the return of Helen to the Greeks. Although he goes on to admit that the question of value is also raised in the play, he claims that to the audience it is metaphysical rather than moral. But surely the question has moral implications for the characters and by extension for the audience too? *Hamlet, Coriolanus* and *Henry IV* are all rejected for, to me, unsatisfactory reasons. However, in spite of disagreement with his limiting procedure one must be grateful for the real insights Schanzer provides into the three plays which pass his test: *Measure for Measure, Julius Caesar* and *Antony and Cleopatra*. In the chapter on *Julius Caesar* he is excellent on Caesar in Renaissance writing, on Plutarch, and on the presentation of Brutus' dilemma and the analysis of his character. However, I would question whether the play is quite so ambiguous in not offering evidence for a plain and clear-cut answer to the moral problem of the justifiability of the murder. Herbert R. Coursen[4] sees the ambiguity of the play as residing in Shakespeare's divided interest between the political and tragic aspects of the story which caused him to 'achieve something less than a tragedy'. Schanzer's section on the other Roman play is less satisfying although it does present some new lines of approach to the piece. Of *Measure for Measure* the theme is seen to be 'a common reprobation of legalism in favour of a more humane, more truly just interpretation of the Law, whether man-made or divine' which is evident 'in the field of public ethics…with the nature of Justice and Good Rule; in the field of private ethics…with the choice of Isabel'. This essay is full of fine things, including the discussions of the nature of Claudio's guilt and Shakespeare's use of the contradictions surrounding the Elizabethan marriage contracts (*pace* Mr Narajan).

[1] '*Measure for Measure*', *Shakespeare Quarterly*, XIV (1963), 109–13.
[2] 'Some Composite Scenes in *Measure for Measure*', *Shakespeare Quarterly*, XV (1964), 67–74.
[3] *The Problem Plays of Shakespeare* (Routledge and Kegan Paul, 1963).
[4] 'The Fall and Decline of *Julius Caesar*', *Texas Studies in Literature and Language*, IV (1962), 241–51.

The other non-Schanzerian problem plays have also claimed some attention. R. A. Foakes[1] queries the conclusions of those critics who have tried to label *Troilus and Cressida* as comedy or tragedy and suggests that the two endings are not 'opposed, but complementary, and together establish an "open ending"', which he sees as being in harmony with both the emphasis of time in the play and the audience's knowledge of the whole myth. He goes further and claims that the play does not damage the larger myth, but may rather be viewed as 'an heroic farce, in which the comedy and satire finally reinforce those noble values envisaged in the action'. Mary Ellen Rickey[2] refuses to see that the same play is about any pair of abstract concepts such as love and war, or love and honour, or policy and emotion, and insists it deals rather 'with the single problem of corruption and its causes;…the war story and the love story simply manifest different aspects of the same essential decay'. She makes a close analysis of the play and well illustrates her point that it is pride and appetite mistaken for honour and glory that corrupt both nations and individuals; but she is far too certain that her view holds the 'answer' to the play. Jay L. Halio[3] lists the problems that still need attention in *All's Well* such as: dramatic emphasis, the rhetoric, the function of the minor characters, and the underlying unity of the structure; and admonishes that they should not be dealt with as separate entities. He proceeds to demonstrate, mainly by an examination of Bertram's role in the play, how his method may be used, and gives a reading of the role which is one of the most convincing I know. He argues that the weakness of the part derives from Shakespeare's too heavy emphasis on the young man's faults which forces us to depend more than usual on the implications of structural relationship to locate the meaning of the play. The theme of 'self-treason' in most of the main characters is well worked out and the central paradox isolated as 'what is often a worthy or lawful objective may have to be obtained through a somewhat dubious means'. Taking his cue from the play's title, James L. Calderwood[4] asks what is it exactly that ends well. By concentrating upon Helena's two main soliloquies and her actions, he contends that there is both an element of self-deception, and a subconscious sexual drive in her character which is given direction by her conversation with Parolles. The marriage failure-to-success progression reflects the mixed nature of her desires and the bed-trick is seen as 'not only lawful…but chaste as well. She has found the one irreproachable use for virginity and, at the same time, the way in which innocence can accompany action'. Margaret Loftus Ranald[5] looks at the betrothals of the same play in the light of what is known about Elizabethan practice and finds that both the betrothal ceremony in II, iii, and the exchanges of the final scene are illuminated by their close correspondence to contemporary requirements.

Among the tragedies both *Lear* and *Hamlet* have received their usual lion's share of comment. Russell A. Fraser[6] devotes a book to the former play in relationship to 'Shakespeare's poetics', by which he means 'the underlying principles which sustain Shakespearean drama', or to be more specific, the moral patterns of the plays. Fraser's approach to the play is that of an iconologist

---

[1] '*Troilus and Cressida* Reconsidered', *University of Toronto Quarterly*, XXXII (1963), 142–54.
[2] "Twixt the Dangerous Shores: *Troilus and Cressida* Again', *Shakespeare Quarterly*, XV (1964), 3–15.
[3] '*All's Well That Ends Well*', ibid. pp. 33–45.
[4] 'The Mingled Yarn of *All's Well*', *J.E.G.P.* LXII (1963), 61–76.
[5] 'The Betrothals of *All's Well That Ends Well*', *Huntington Library Quarterly*, XXVI (1963), 179–92.
[6] *Shakespeare's Poetics in Relation to 'King Lear'* (Routledge and Kegan Paul, 1962).

who musters 'many documents—poems, sermons, proverbs, ballads, pictures—concurrent in time with the work he has chosen to discuss, and revealing, in their use of like symbols, pretty much the same notion of the way the world goes'. Although such an approach is somewhat limiting to the play's scope, every student must be grateful to the author for his analysis of the materials he has gathered and his perspicacious relating of it to the poetic imagery. In chapters 2 to 9 he discusses certain 'governing imperatives': the role of Providence, the function of Kind, the nature of Fortune, the opposition of Anarchy and Order, the conflict of Will and Reason, the confusion of appearance and reality, and the question of redemption. But all of these chapters go beyond a mere coupling of image and illustration, for Fraser lays before us the complicated mass of ideas, connexions, and visual associations which stocked the minds of Shakespeare and his audience. The final chapter is devoted to an unsatisfactory discussion of Shakespeare's 'poetics' and his practice in tragedy and comedy. It is not a worthy conclusion to such a book, for the remarks on one genre are commonplace and on the other inadequate. The lavish and expertly chosen illustrations should be mentioned as one of the values of this stimulating book.

Other writers have considered *Lear* from more specialized viewpoints. Francis G. Schoff[1] is uncomfortable about the frequency with which Lear is seen as a morality figure, and suggests that there is no evidence in the text for such an interpretation. He performs a valuable corrective function in tracing a very human Lear as father, king and man, but tends to go too far and over-idealize the character who, among the noblest and wisest, through a mis-step or accident places himself in the fearful power of evil. The nature of this evil is defined by Eleanor N. Hutchens,[2] who notes its seeming dynamism in contrast to the passivity of good. The transfer of power from its good or lawful possessor, she argues, is brought about by a power vacuum which forms when either legal or moral right fails to function and is filled with a force generated by the negative behaviour of right itself. Manfred Weidhorn[3] traces Lear's progress initially through the use of exclamatory questions in the first two acts, the shocks of which become his 'school-masters'. He considers the nature of Lear's transformation under the various functions of father, king, judge, proud man and deceived man. Josephine W. Bennett[4] asserts the need for a decision concerning the exact moment when Lear succumbs to madness, and fixes upon the Hovel Scene of which 'the chief function is to establish that Lear is mad'. Bennett stresses the inner conflict in the character, the causes of his madness, his responsibility for suffering and 'his want of insight…which constitutes his tragic flaw'. However, in her admirable attempt to see the significance in Lear's displays of madness, she rather underestimates the insight in his speeches to Edgar. John P. Cutts[5] takes issue with Bennett's account and contends that madness should be assessed by the consideration of 'how much, and what special kind of, pertinency Lear's remarks hold even when dismissed by his stage hearers'. He takes the 'learned Theban' reference to be to Oedipus and appropriate in Lear who 'learns the riddle of man'. His working out of this idea is not convincing, particularly in his rejection of a similar allusion in *Pan's*

[1] 'King Lear: Moral Example or Tragic Protagonist?', *Shakespeare Quarterly*, XIII (1962), 157–72.
[2] 'The Transfer of Power in *King Lear* and *The Tempest*', *Review of English Literature*, IV (1963), 82–93.
[3] 'Lear's Schoolmasters', *Shakespeare Quarterly*, XIII (1962), 305–16.
[4] 'The Storm Within: The Madness of Lear', *ibid.* pp. 137–55.
[5] 'Lear's "Learned Theban"', *Shakespeare Quarterly*, XIV (1963), 477–81.

Anniversary. John C. McCloskey[1] illustrates how Lear's recognition of man as 'a poor, bare forked animal' is prefigured by the descending levels of animal imagery in the play, the climax of which descent he sees as coinciding with the climax of the play. Lear's re-ascent to reason and humanity is also charted in animal images before 'it is arrested by the resurgence of tragedy —the death of Cordelia'. Robert F. Fleissner[2] has some interesting comments on Cordelia's role, seeing her as the reflexion of many of the issues considered, particularly in her early exchanges with Lear and its subsequent echoes throughout both plots. The subtleties of the first scene are also dealt with in Angus McIntosh's[3] note on the emotional changes implied by Lear's use of 'thou' and 'you' to his daughters. Huntington Brown[4] contends that the evidence in the play points to the Fool's part being played by a boy actor rather than a man—a casting, he suggests, that would heighten the pathos. He does not mention the possibility of Armin's playing the role, nor does he consider that 'knave' and 'boy' seem perfectly appropriate in the theatre when the part is played by adult actors like Alan Badel or Ian Holm.

Hamlet is certainly the most perplexing and possibly the most real of Shakespeare's characters —a fact which is underlined in an interesting note by G. Wilson Knight[5] who sees a remarkable correspondence between Byron and Shakespeare's hero. Many of the apparent inconsistencies in the prince's actions are attributed by Charles O. McDonald[6] to Elizabethan rhetoric rather than psychology. Working from Aphthonius' *Progymnasmata*, he suggests that Shakespeare appears to have borrowed one of the work's central rhetorical concepts: 'ethos a consistent habit of mind, pathos a transient, passionate compulsion'. Hamlet's delay, McDonald argues, is due to a stalemated ethos-pathos until the moment Fortinbras's expedition to Poland supplies the final objective-correlative necessary to raise the hero's pathos irrevocably. For Sidney Warhaft[7] Hamlet's reluctance to act is moral rather than rhetorical in that he cannot do so until he becomes an instrument of justice instead of an agent in his own right. This he becomes when he ceases to play God, awaits the divinity that shapes his end, and leaves Claudius' soul to heaven. Fredson Bowers[8] takes a fresh look at Hamlet's soliloquy at III, ii, 406–17, and argues that Hamlet is prepared to kill Claudius but before doing so must carry out 'an important part of the revenge as it applies to Gertrude', namely to force her to recognize her sin; this Bowers sees as a clearly planned attempt at the redemption of Gertrude in which Hamlet is successful. I think some of his evidence tends to force certain lines in the play. Also on the subject of action in the play is a good article by Jean S. Calhoun[9] who starts with the Sartrean pronouncement:

What the characters are determines what they do, but what they do no less significantly determines what they are...they are seen in the process of creating themselves through their actions, as each character carries with him into the play's future the heavy legacy of the present responsibility for his deeds in the past.

---

[1] 'The Emotive Use of Animal Imagery in *King Lear*', *Shakespeare Quarterly*, XIII (1962), 321–5.

[2] 'The "Nothing" Element in *King Lear*', ibid. pp. 67–70.

[3] '*King Lear*, Act I, Scene i. A Stylistic Note', *Review of English Studies*, new series, XIV (1963), 53–6.

[4] 'Lear's Fool: A Boy, Not a Man', *Essays in Criticism*, XIII (1963), 164–71.

[5] 'Byron and Hamlet', *Bulletin of the John Rylands Library*, XLV (1962), 115–47.

[6] '*Decorum, Ethos,* and *Pathos* in the Heroes of Elizabethen Tragedy, with Particular Reference to *Hamlet*', *J.E.G.P.* LXI (1962), 330–48.

[7] 'The Mystery of *Hamlet*', *English Literary History*, XXX (1963), 193–208.

[8] 'Hamlet's Fifth Soliloquy, III, ii, 406–417', *Essays on Shakespeare and Elizabethan Drama*, pp. 213–23.

[9] '*Hamlet* and the Circumference of Action', *Renaissance News*, XV (1962), 281–98.

She sees Shakespeare exploring the three motivational sources of action in Hamlet: passion, reason and role, and produces a pessimistic reading of the play in which there is nothing to define the nature and intention of the special providence in the fall of a sparrow, and in the world of which man has no guarantee of either success in action or even of the preservation of life. In direct opposition to Calhoun's view, Miriam Joseph[1] views *Hamlet* 'in the strict sense a Christian tragedy'. She sees the whole play imbued with a Christian atmosphere on both verbal and conceptual levels: the Ghost is a good spirit sent by God (from purgatory?) to command Hamlet to punish Claudius, which is not possible until the prince measures up to the heroic Christian virtues demanded of him by a moral situation and purges himself of his hatred. Paul N. Siegal[2] takes up one of the many points of disagreement provoked by Joseph's essay and points out that scholastic texts are no real indication of how an audience would respond to the Ghost in the play. Charles R. Forker[3] and Arthur Johnston[4] consider various aspects of the theatrical metaphor within the play. The former provides a clear examination of the interactions between the theatre symbol, the actor idea, and the themes of appearance and reality. The latter closely analyses the function and form of the Player's speech, which he places in the context of the references to Jephtha and Dido and sees these as allusions to Ophelia's situation. He argues that the speech presents the audience with a mirror of the revenge motif in order to force it away from a stock response. William A. Ringler[5] also considers the theatrical allusions in the play and suggests that it contains a far more detailed reply to attacks on the stage than is usually conceded; he supports his case with an analysis of the functional use of drama in the play scene. He sees Shakespeare as using some of the conventional Elizabethan arguments in favour of the stage, in asserting that a play is the image of truth, 'but he was also aware that knowledge of the right does not necessarily lead a person to righteousness'. Adrien Bonjour[6] disputes effectively Lily B. Campbell's contention that Hamlet was the slave of excessive grief, and stresses that evidence such as Hamlet's contemplation of suicide should be viewed in the perspective of Ophelia's death and Horatio's offer at the end of the play. To Linda Welsheimer Wagner,[7] however, Ophelia and her death are 'a condescension to the audience, who were expecting some romance and pathos'—presumably not the same audience as witnessed *Macbeth* and *Lear*? Toshikazu Oyama[8] has an interesting note on the cloud imagery in the play and relates its dramatic presentation in I, ii, with the line in II, ii, showing how the theme is connected with 'the basic undertone of the whole play'. A well-organized and brief summary of the various good, bad, and plain insane opinions that have grown up around the play is provided by Margarita Quijano.[9] Her introductory chapter deals with the 'symphonic themes', and subsequent sections are devoted to Claudius, Polonius, Laertes, Gertrude, Horatio, Ophelia and

[1] 'Hamlet, a Christian Tragedy', *Studies in Philology*, LIX (1962), 119–40.
[2] 'Discerning the Ghost in *Hamlet*', *PMLA*, LXXVIII (1963), 148–9.
[3] 'Shakespeare's Theatrical Symbolism and its Function in *Hamlet*', *Shakespeare Quarterly*, XIV (1963), 215–29.
[4] 'The Player's Speech in Hamlet', *Shakespeare Quarterly*, XIII (1962), 21–30.
[5] 'Hamlet's Defense of the Players', *Essays on Shakespeare and Elizabethan Drama*, pp. 201–13.
[6] 'The Question of Hamlet's Grief', *English Studies*, XLIII (1962), 336–43.
[7] 'Ophelia: Shakespeare's Pathetic Plot Device', *Shakespeare Quarterly*, XIV (1963), 94–7.
[8] 'The Cloud Theme in *Hamlet*', *Shakespeare Studies* (Japan), I (1962), 47–60.
[9] 'Hamlet' y sus Criticos (Universidad Nacional Autonoma de Mexico, 1962).

the dramatic evolution of Hamlet's character. For Quijano the main theme of the play is Hamlet's struggle with the undermining corruption in life.

A good general essay on *Macbeth* is provided by Dolores G. Cunningham,[1] who sees the basis of the tragedy in the hero's deliberate repudiation of his human role by a series of decisions to release himself from mortal bonds while never escaping them. Out of her discussion of the play grow some speculations on the nature of tragedy and comedy: 'a helpful distinction might be drawn between Shakespearian comedy and tragedy in terms of the effective operation of grace as one method of organizing the happy ending and its rejection or delay as a formative principle of the tragic ending'. Ruth L. Anderson[2] looks at the play rather more politically as a 'highly conventionalized' pattern common in Elizabethan thought of nobility-ambition-crime-fear-tyranny-brutishness-destruction. Miguel A. Bernard[3] considers the tragedy under five headings: a physical fall from high estate, the disintegration of two splendid personalities, the downfall of moral order, of social order, and the theological implications of the hero's damnation. The essay evokes some strange responses to the play, however, such as the comparison of Lady Macbeth with 'the broken-hearted little girl sitting on the doorstep weeping over her broken doll'. A case is put by Peter Dyson[4] for the banquet scene as the watershed through which the action must pass: he sees it as the moment marking the movement from order to chaos, and the turning point for Macbeth himself as he perceives that he is living in an ambiguous world where he has chosen 'nothingness'.

By re-examining John Wilson's 'dual time scheme' in *Othello*, Arthur McGee[5] offers a new motive for the murder. Citing many contemporary real-life parallels to incidents in the play, he argues that Othello was betrothed to Desdemona *de praesenti*, and that Iago's insinuations are to an extended pre-marital affair between her and Cassio in Venice. Iago's power over Othello is seen to have a different source by Margaret Loftus Ranald[6] who tests Desdemona's behaviour against the common Elizabethan attitudes to women and concludes that she flouts many of the strictures embodied in the courtesy books of the time, and that Othello would have appeared less gullible to a seventeenth-century audience than he does to its twentieth-century counterpart. Peter Milward[7] cites Shakespeare's obvious interest in the Judas story throughout his works and claims that 'the base Judean' is also a reference to it. *Titus Andronicus* has been the subject of some recent apologia. A. C. Hamilton[8] suggests that it is wrong to see the excesses of the play as a sign of weakness, for the 'concept of tragedy which Shakespeare inherited is complete by the end of the first act, while the remaining acts show an extension of the tragic form through language which is uniquely Shakespearian'. He claims that the play is a vision of fallen nature in which it is the archetype of the mature tragedies. Judith M. Karr[9] also finds more control in the play than is usual. She isolates the six scenes of pleading, seeing them as

---

[1] 'Macbeth: The Tragedy of the Hardened Heart', *Shakespeare Quarterly*, XIV (1963), 39–47.

[2] 'The Pattern of Behaviour Culminating in *Macbeth*', *Studies in English Literature*, III (1963), 151–73.

[3] 'The Five Tragedies in *Macbeth*', *Shakespeare Quarterly*, XIII (1962), 49–61.

[4] 'The Structural Function of the Banquet Scene in *Macbeth*', *Shakespeare Quarterly*, XIV (1963), 369–78.

[5] 'Othello's Motive for Murder', *Shakespeare Quarterly*, XV (1964), 45–55.

[6] 'The Indiscretions of Desdemona', *Shakespeare Quarterly*, XIV (1963), 127–39.

[7] 'The Base Judean', *Shakespeare Studies* (Japan), I (1962), 6–14.

[8] '*Titus Andronicus*: The Form of Shakespearian Tragedy', *Shakespeare Quarterly*, XIV (1963), 201–13.

[9] 'The Pleas in *Titus Andronicus*', *ibid.* pp. 278–9.

deliberately placed; parallel in content, visual effect and verbal echoes; and mirroring the decline or ascendancy of the two political powers. David Cook[1] discusses *Timon of Athens* in terms of the characters in the two halves of the play. He claims that Timon isolates himself from his fellows in the first half by indiscriminate God-like generosity, and in the latter by his equally indiscriminate hatred.

Shakespeare's early history plays appear to be undergoing a critical revaluation as well as a theatrical *succès d'estime*. Ronald S. Berman[2] holds that Shakespeare's grasp of the tragic act within the historical process was already certain in the *Henry VI* plays. He perceives it as 'emanating from guilt of the past, and affecting the family and the state', to show itself in the treatment of such themes as the question of birthright, the persecution of kindred, the rights of inheritance, blood relationships as hindrances to ambition, and the pattern of inheritance which can become the transmission of spiritual evil. Shakespeare's historical awareness is also traced in *Richard II* by Robert Hapgood,[3] who shows that the play looks towards both the past and the future so that three distinct areas can be distinguished corresponding to the reigns of Edward III, Richard and Henry IV, with different methods being employed to convey the special characteristics of each. Peter G. Phialas[4] concentrates on the character of Richard in the same play and holds that the play was a milepost in Shakespeare's career in so far as it was the first tragedy to go beyond the *de casibus* explanation and make 'human causality the chief tragic force'. There are two interesting papers on *King John*. William H. Matchett[5] sees the unity to be derived from the question of the right to the throne. Focusing his attention on the character of the Bastard, he argues that when Faulconbridge kneels to Henry, he becomes 'the best of subjects in a unified England, and this, in the logic of the play, is more important than the character of the king'. The scene with Arthur and Hubert in the same play is closely inspected by Robert D. Stevick[6] who shows how the impact is made by a synthesis of poetic and dramatic imagery.

The gradual renewal of the king's role is demonstrated by Joan Webber[7] through the mature history plays. She concentrates on the modes of speech typical of each ruler, and concludes that Hal, prepared by his years as a prince, expresses a world view more complete than that of Richard, who seeks to make verbal tableaux out of life, and more meaningful than that of Henry, who distrusts 'the rhetoric appropriate to the design he has destroyed'. As Henry V makes himself the 'center of his people's dreams', England seems to speak through him whether he wills it or not. Roy Battenhouse[8] has a rather different attitude to the final play of the tetralogy, and one which upsets traditional labels. He argues that *Henry V* comments ironically, at the levels of character, plot and situation, on the very heroic and patriotic values it seems to applaud—that it is an heroic comedy of which the theme is 'a pitiful history of "foiled" cupidity'. I find

[1] 'Timon of Athens', *Shakespeare Survey 16* (1963), 83–94.

[2] 'Fathers and Sons in the *Henry VI* Plays', *Shakespeare Quarterly*, XIII (1962), 487–97.

[3] 'Three Eras in *Richard II*', *Shakespeare Quarterly*, XIV (1963), 281–3.

[4] '*Richard II* and Shakespeare's Tragic Mode', *Texas Studies in Literature and Language*, V (1963), 344–55.

[5] 'Richard's Divided Heritage in *King John*', *Essays in Criticism*, XII (1962), 231–53.

[6] '"Repentant Ashes": The Matrix of "Shakespearian" Poetic Language', *Shakespeare Quarterly*, XIII (1962), 366–70.

[7] 'The Renewal of the King's Symbolic Role: From *Richard II* to *Henry V*', *Texas Studies in Literature and Language*, IV (1962), 530–8.

[8] '*Henry V* as Heroic Comedy', *Essays on Shakespeare and Elizabethan Drama*, pp. 163–83.

Battenhouse's handling of the evidence not altogether satisfactory, particularly in his reading of the prologue to Act IV. Two excellent introductions to the history plays are provided by Clifford Leech,[1] who considers *Henry VI, Henry IV* and *Henry VIII*, and L. C. Knights,[2] who deals with *Richard III, King John, Richard II* and *Henry V*. Both provide good accounts of the individual plays, with Knights noting that Shakespeare was using historical material as a means of exploring the fundamental principles of man's moral and political life. Leech has some wise words to say on the topic of 'History for the Elizabethans', and his discussions illuminate his point that, in the plays dealt with, Shakespeare was writing 'open-textured' history—'the kind of drama in which there is not a persistent consciousness of an ineluctable march of events'.

The different appeals exercised by the Roman plays are reflected by the topics considered in the year's batch of articles on them. *Coriolanus* is viewed as a political play by H. Gordon Zeeveld[3] and one of topical interest when written. Against a background of the views of men like Elyot, Fulbecke, and Thomas Smith, and the parliamentary debates on purveyance, he considers the play as 'above all the story of the dismemberment of the commonwealth' owing to a lack of mutual co-operation. In a valuable article, G. Thomas Tanselle and Florence W. Dunbar[4] analyse the way in which the legal motif is carried by the language of the play, which invests it with a 'stern and uncompromising quality'. The hero of the play is seen by William R. Bowden[5] in the light of a rather simplified version of other virtuous but unattractive characters such as Shylock (*sic*), Malvolio, Isabella, Cordelia and Hal. He suggests that our difficulty in seeing Coriolanus as a tragic hero is due to our current social values rather than any weakness in the play. Far more than *Coriolanus, Antony and Cleopatra* attracts the imagery approach. David Daiches[6] isolates the player image and argues that Shakespeare, in attempting to build 'a moral universe out of non-moral materials', stresses the different roles a man can play and the relationship of these roles to the player's true identity. Antony, after a variety of 'roles', unites in his suicide both warrior and lover, and Cleopatra 'brings together in her death in a great vindication the varied meanings of her histrionic career and temperament'. Katherine Vance MacMullen[7] examines the death imagery of the play which she sees as being used with that of sleep and love, darkness and light, to display the natures of the central figures, their influences upon each other and 'the continuity of their fates'. Three critics concentrate on Cleopatra's end. Richard C. Harrier[8] views her death as a moment of revelation when she can at last perceive what she has lost, as well as 'feel the reality of Antony's ideal and his heavenly reality'. Mary Olive Thomas,[9] however, sees the event in a larger context: she interprets Cleopatra's management of the asps as being a poetic acceptance of both life and death, and an illustration of Shakespeare's interest in human love as 'a paradoxical mixture of *concupiscentia* and *caritas*, the source of life and its value in the perfect symbol of the serpent at the breast'.

[1] *Shakespeare: The Chronicles* (Longmans, Green and Co., 1962).
[2] *Shakespeare: The Histories* (Longmans, Green and Co., 1962).
[3] '*Coriolanus* and Jacobean Politics', *Modern Language Review*, LVII (1962), 321–34.
[4] 'Legal Language in *Coriolanus*', *Shakespeare Quarterly*, XIII (1962), 231–8.
[5] 'The "Unco Guid" and Shakespeare's Coriolanus', *ibid.* pp. 41–8.
[6] 'Imagery and Meaning in *Antony and Cleopatra*', *English Studies*, XLIII (1962), 343–58.
[7] 'Death Imagery in *Antony and Cleopatra*', *Shakespeare Quarterly*, XIV (1963), 399–410.
[8] 'Cleopatra's End', *Shakespeare Quarterly*, XIII (1962), 63–5.
[9] 'Cleopatra and the "Mortal Wretch"', *Shakespeare Jahrbuch*, XCIX (1963), 174–83.

James G. McManaway[1] compares the final scene in the play with Anouilh's *The Lark*, and suggests that Shakespeare is in fact allowing us to leave the theatre with a vision of the Cleopatra for whom Antony gave up half the world. The imagery of the sea, and games of chance which require a combination of skill and chance is assessed by Michael Lloyd[2] to convey Shakespeare's attitude to Fortune in the play as the reward of the man whose own initiative in 'sea peril' is timely. A good introduction to all the Roman plays and *Titus Andronicus* has been written by T. J. B. Spencer[3] with excellent short essays on 'Roman History in Elizabethan Literature' and 'North's translation of *Plutarch*'.

The miraculous nature of the last plays continues to exercise its growing fascination on the products of a disrupted and scientific century—an aspect which finds its way into the title of D. R. C. Marsh's book.[4] For Marsh the 'miracle' of all the Romances, and of *Cymbeline* in particular, is the constant renewal of life, and his Shakespeare is one who asserts the value of earthly life outside of Christian doctrine with its entailed belief in a life beyond the grave. I think this aspect of Shakespeare's vision has been understressed in recent years, but Marsh almost totally ignores the suggestions of a divine ordering of life which are surely present—albeit vaguely—in such speeches as Prospero's Epilogue. The bulk of the essay is devoted to a scene-by-scene reading of *Cymbeline* which demonstrates that the play has a unity not always appreciated. Despite the frequent dullness due to the method adopted, the analysis is a rewarding one particularly in its tracing of the idea that it is the rising above preoccupations with self that makes recognition of life's value possible. In opposition to Marsh's view, Robin Moffet[5] will have none of the non-Christian Shakespeare in his discussion of the same play. He argues that 'the fact that Jesus was born during the period of Cymbeline's reign was what made it unique', and locates in the play a reflexion of the central truths of the theatre of the world:

the straits into which men have fallen as a result of sin, error, and misfortune, followed by a supernaturally effected restoration and reconciliation which will be both an imperfect analogue of the full restoration to come and a fitting preparation and greeting for the divine child soon to be born.

This is an interesting article as much for the disagreement it provokes as for the suggestive interpretation of the play it offers. A rather different approach to the unsatisfactory features of the play is given by F. D. Hoeniger.[6] Admitting the play to be a romance, he suggests that it is of a kind that involves a highly ironic perspective towards the characters which ends only in the final scene where 'mockery yields to vision, the world of appearance to the world of reality and joy, and irony dissolves in romance'.

The problems of *The Winter's Tale* are also in part due to the genre and in part to the characterization. While the pastoral tradition may be seen, by William O. Scott,[7] as providing Shakespeare with a pattern derived from 'Renaissance seasonal myth and floral symbols', Jerry

---

[1] 'Notes on Act v of *Antony and Cleopatra*', *Shakespeare Studies* (Japan), 1 (1962), 1–5.
[2] 'Antony and the Game of Chance', *J.E.G.P.* LXI (1962), 548–54.
[3] *Shakespeare: The Roman Plays* (Longmans, Green and Co., 1963).
[4] *The Recurring Miracle: A Study of 'Cymbeline' and the Last Plays* (Natal University Press, 1962).
[5] 'Cymbeline and the Nativity', *Shakespeare Quarterly*, XIII (1962), 207–18.
[6] 'Irony and Romance in *Cymbeline*', *Studies in English Literature*, II (1962), 219–28.
[7] 'Seasons and Flowers in *The Winter's Tale*', *Shakespeare Quarterly*, XIV (1963), 411–17.

H. Bryant[1] notes that Shakespeare also transformed it into an 'involved and subtle commentary on appearance and reality', in which evil lies not in appearance itself but in the mind of Leontes which 'insists that appearance is reality'. Leontes' sudden change is subjected to scrutiny by Edward L. Hart,[2] who contends that the jealousy is made believable by the fierce poetic concentration of the language that conveys it. Hallett Smith[3] suggests that the soliloquy at I, ii, 138–46 is simplified if we take 'Affection' to mean not 'lust' but 'Affectio' in the sense of 'a sudden mental seizure'. Examining the final scene of the play and its implications, Northrop Frye[4] notes that in the whole piece 'nature is associated, not with the credible, but with the incredible' and that the revival of Hermione is 'appropriately that of a frozen statue turning into a living presence' where we sense the 'reviving power of nature identified with art, grace, and love'.

Unlike *The Winter's Tale*, *The Tempest* is a play that responds better to a thematic than to a character approach. Frank Davidson[5] reads the play in the light of philosophical and psychological thinking of the Tudor period, principally as it is reflected in Prospero and those aspects of himself represented by Ariel (the sensible soul) and Caliban (the reproductive level of life) which, by the end of the play, he has brought into the perfect balance that will make him an ideal Tudor prince. The form of the play is discussed by Erika Flamm[6] with a view to ascertaining whether it is an 'open' or 'closed' drama (according to Volka Klotz's definition of the terms), and she deduces that while there are evidences of both modes present *The Tempest* is basically an 'open' drama. Frank Kermode[7] gives us general essays on the four final plays and *The Two Noble Kinsmen*. He rightly states that the plays are best considered singly, and is epigrammatically forthright on such topics as the Christian elements in *The Winter's Tale*, the importance of the theme of recognition, the authorship of *The Two Noble Kinsmen*, and excellent on *The Tempest* and *Pericles*.

In a good survey of work done on the Sonnets since 1900, A. Nejgebauer[8] notes that their language, stanzaic structure, metre, and imagery 'demand the full tilth and husbandry of criticism'. Hilton Landry,[9] in a knotty little book, attempts a little deep ploughing by examining some twenty sonnets in detail, and discusses their relationship with about twenty-five others. He is concerned primarily with what these poems are about and how they make their effects. He assumes that the sonnet order found in the 1609 quarto 'is generally and essentially right', a view not shared by Brents Stirling,[10] who suggests that Thorpe's copy 'was not a single manuscript, and that his materials represented various histories of disarrangement, copying, and recopying'. Stirling's arguments are too complex to be gone into here, but the article is

[1] '*The Winter's Tale* and the Pastoral Tradition', *ibid.* pp. 387–98.
[2] See p. 161, n. 8.
[3] 'Leontes' Affectio', *Shakespeare Quarterly*, XVI (1963), 163–6.
[4] 'Recognition in *The Winter's Tale*', *Essays on Shakespeare and Elizabethan Drama*, pp. 235–46.
[5] '*The Tempest*: An Interpretation', *J.E.G.P.* LXII (1963), 501–17.
[6] 'Offener und Geschlossener Dramenstil in Shakespeares *Tempest*', *Shakespeare Jahrbuch*, XCIX (1963), 142–60.
[7] *Shakespeare: The Final Plays* (Longmans, Green and Co., 1963).
[8] 'Twentieth-century Studies in Shakespeare's Songs, Sonnets, and Poems. 2. The Sonnets', *Shakespeare Survey* 15 (1962), 10–18.
[9] *Interpretations in Shakespeare's Sonnets* (University of California Press, 1963).
[10] 'More Shakespeare Sonnet Groups', *Essays on Shakespeare and Elizabethan Drama*, pp. 115–35.

required reading for any worker on the poems. Landry's book, however, is most valuable for its scrupulous weighing of possible emendations and interpretations, its subtle tracing of the ironic tone of Sonnet 94, and its explication of multi-level connexions between the individual poems. M. M. Mahood[1] singles out Sonnets 33–124 and argues that they illustrate Shakespeare's various methods of coming to terms with the fear of betrayal of trust, which is a strong element in such plays as *Twelfth Night* and *The Merchant of Venice*. In two perceptive essays, Anton M. Pirkhofer[2] and David Kaula[3] respectively examine Shakespeare's use of unpointed alliterative techniques and 'varying time perspective, both objective and subjective'. E. C. Evans[4] has a note on 'summer's time' in Sonnet 97, and John Doebler[5] on a submerged 'compass' emblem in Sonnet 116. The longer poems have also received some detailed consideration. J. W. Lever[6] provides a well-balanced summary of scholarship and criticism produced in the twentieth century; and also a view of *Venus and Adonis* which deplores the modern puritanism of some recent critics of the poem, suggesting that our responses should proceed from the recognition that Venus is essentially a mythical being. He notes how many of the themes of the poem are taken up again in *Antony and Cleopatra* where the myth receives its full explication in human terms. This similarity between poem and play is also noted by A. Bonjour[7] who analyses the echoes from the poem in Enobarbus' speech describing Cleopatra. E. B. Cantalupe,[8] approaching the poem iconographically, considers that Shakespeare was 'parodying not only the myth but also the traditional interpretations, literary and pictorial', fulfilling the requirements of the Ovidian genre, and demolishing the Neo-platonic formula. D. C. Allen[9] provides a learned and well-documented gloss on certain passages in *Lucrece* in the light of traditional Christian controversy about the nature of Lucrece's guilt, and concludes that Shakespeare saw her action as 'rare and wonderful, but a little beyond forgiveness'. Equally learned is Robert Ellrodt's[10] paper on *The Phoenix and the Turtle*, which posits that 'the deeper meaning of the poem' lies in Shakespeare's contemplation of 'Love and Constancy, Truth and Beauty', and his straining after the highest poetic intensity.

One of the advantages of Shakespeare's having exercised so permanent a fascination through the centuries is that the writings which have him as their subject provide an insight into their authors' intellectual attitudes, and the special preoccupations of the ages in which they lived. Many good articles furnish evidence for such insight. A welcome issue of a revised edition of

---

[1] 'Love's Confined Doom', *Shakespeare Survey* 15 (1962), 50–61.
[2] '"A Pretty Pleasing Pricket"—On the Use of Alliteration in Shakespeare's Sonnets', *Shakespeare Quarterly*, XIV (1963), 3–14.
[3] '"In War with Time": Temporal Perspectives in Shakespeare's Sonnets', *Studies in English Literature*, III (1963), 45–57.
[4] 'Shakespeare's Sonnet 97', *Review of English Studies*, new series, XIV (1963), 379–80.
[5] 'A Submerged Emblem in Sonnet 116', *Shakespeare Quarterly*, XV (1964), 109–10.
[6] 'Twentieth-century Studies in Shakespeare's Songs, Sonnets, and Poems. 3. The Poems', *Shakespeare Survey* 15 (1962), 18–30.
[7] 'From Shakespeare's Venus to Cleopatra's Cupids', *ibid.* pp. 73–80.
[8] 'An Iconographical Interpretation of *Venus And Adonis*, Shakespeare's Ovidian Comedy', *Shakespeare Quarterly*, XIV (1963), 141–51.
[9] 'Some Observations on *The Rape of Lucrece*', *Shakespeare Survey* 15 (1962), 89–98.
[10] 'An Anatomy of *The Phoenix and the Turtle*', *ibid.* pp. 99–110.

D. Nichol Smith's[1] work on eighteenth-century criticism of Shakespeare discusses and illustrates those aspects of the canon which occupied so many of the best critical minds of the period. However, Sailendra Kumar Sen's[2] description of Walter Whiter's *A Specimen of a Commentary*, *etc.* shows that at least one critic of that time anticipated in many ways modern imagery study. Across the channel at the same period Voltaire was, according to Claude Pichois,[3] focusing interest on Shakespeare by the very attacks he was making on the tragedies. German criticism has also been subjected to scrutiny in a recent *Jahrbuch*. Hans Georg Heun[4] traces Goethe's opinion of *Romeo and Juliet* as it is reflected primarily in his partial rewriting of Schlegel's translation in 1812, and notes a general tendency towards a moderate and dignified manner of speech at the expense of vividness. Heinrich Wilhelm von Gerstenberg's criticism is seen by Karl S. Guthke[5] to embody many of the most important tenets of both Classicism and Romanticism as well as the main currents of German Shakespearian critical ideas. Friederich Gundolf's criticism is assessed, by Eudo C. Mason,[6] which he finds to be full of incidental excellences, while dismissing some of its basic theories about the poet. Eric A. Blackall[7] analyses Ulrich Bräker's use of Johann J. Eschenburg's translation of Shakespeare, and draws a comparison between the two critics.

One book and a group of papers look at Shakespeare's relationship to our own century. Jan Kott,[8] in a brilliant and stimulating book, sees a remarkable resemblance between Shakespeare's age and our own, and claims that his work, like that of some modern dramatists, is permeated with disillusionment, with the awareness of man's inhumanity, and with the overpowering knowledge of political excesses. At the heart of Shakespeare's vision, Kott sees the inescapable driving force of history,

un grand escalier que monte sans trève un cortège de rois....Les souverains changent. Mais l'escalier est toujours le même. Et les bons, les méchants, les courageux et les poltrons, les vils et les nobles, les naïfs et les cyniques continuent de le gravir.

With this belief as his platform, he ranges over many of the plays, relating them to each other, providing fresh and exquisitely phrased opinions, and forcing us to see plays like *The Tempest*, *Macbeth* and *King Lear* in a totally new light. As one would expect, Kott is at his best on those plays, like *Troilus and Cressida* and *Coriolanus*, in which the individual conscience and 'le grand mécanisme' of history are at war, and those which may be seen as an exemplification of his view, like *Richard II* and *Richard III*. Yet, while all Kott writes demands to be pondered and tested against the text, certain strong doubts arise after even a first reading: Can an interpretation of *Lear* which all but omits Cordelia be other than very one-sided? Was Shakespeare *really* not concerned with the legitimacy of a king's right? Are *Macbeth* and *The Tempest* so totally historically orientated? And what kind of a Shakespeare was it who wrote comedies which are

---

[1] *Eighteenth Century Essays on Shakespeare* (2nd ed., Oxford University Press, 1963).

[2] 'A Neglected Critic of Shakespeare: Walter Whiter', *Shakespeare Quarterly*, XIII (1962), 173–85.

[3] 'Voltaire et Shakespeare, un Plaidoyer', *Shakespeare Jahrbuch*, XCVIII (1962), 178–88.

[4] 'Goethes Kritik an Shakespeares *Romeo und Julia*', *ibid.* pp. 201–15.

[5] 'Richtungskonstanten in der deutschen Shakespeare-Deutung des 18. Jahrhunderts', *ibid.* pp. 64–92.

[6] 'Gundolf und Shakespeare', *ibid.* pp. 110–77.   [7] 'Ulrich Bräker und Eschenburg', *ibid.* pp. 93–109.

[8] *Shakespeare Notre Contemporain*, translated by Anna Posner (René Julliard, Paris, 1962) from *Szkice o Szekspirze* (Państwowy Instytut Wydawniczy, Warsaw, 1961).

apparently only peripheral to his vision of life? J. P. Brockbank,[1] with a glance at the attitudes of earlier centuries, notes that each generation can add to current perceptions only what the special awareness of our age, 'controlled by our experience of modern literature and thought', allows us. He illustrates his point with wide-ranging ideas and perceptive observations on such matters as Leontes' soliloquy, and the impact of *The Merchant of Venice*. R. B. Parker[2] would rather we use our limitations to illuminate certain aspects of the works and suggests a two-way benefit might follow if we consider Shakespeare's use of certain devices in such areas as character portrayal and the building of dramatic unity in the light of Brecht's clear statement of his intention when using similar devices. Wolfgang Clemen[3] defines what he sees as the modern contribution to the understanding of Shakespeare, and singles out our greater ability to accept perplexing apparent contradictions in character behaviour and their thematic implications, and the questioning of traditional values. Noting also the modern *penchant* for appearance and reality motifs, ambiguity and ambivalence, he casts doubts on the fashionable search for irony which he sees as an idiosyncrasy of our generation due to the influence of the techniques of much twentieth-century poetry. Two pleas are made by Louis B. Wright[4] and John Russell Brown[5] for some of the directions that future work on Shakespeare might take: the former for a greater degree of efficiency and organization in assessing work done, and a recognition of the experts' responsibility to the general reader; the latter for far greater use to be made of theatre research which would lead literary critics to a consideration of the 'full theatrical life of the plays they study'. A plea along the same lines is also made by Clifford Lyons,[6] 'who, by means of skilfully chosen and analysed illustrations from the plays, demonstrates that, in our study of imagery, it may be helpful to remember that the whole play is a dramatic image, and that we should pay more attention to the 'interplay of the imagery-discourse with the stage imagery, what the spectators hear the actors speak with what they see on the stage'.

Certain special aspects of Shakespeare's work have been given detailed consideration. Two dramatic techniques are isolated by Maynard Mack[7] and Robert Hapgood[8] in two stimulating articles. Hapgood analyses three scenes in detail: the rejection of Falstaff, the deposition of Richard II, and the assassination of Caesar. He illustrates by what methods the playwright manages a shift of audience sympathy with regard to the central figures. Mack also discusses the manipulation of audience response in the light of Shakespeare's use of the complementary elements of engagement and detachment in his employment of such techniques as the interplay of fact and dream, on-stage recapitulation of theatrical matters, and personal commitment. Matthew Black[9] examines Shakespeare's repetition of favourite situations, and shows how there were successive stages in their use so that they were transformed rather than simply repeated.

---

[1] 'Shakespeare and the Fashion of these Times', *Shakespeare Survey 16* (1963), 30–41.

[2] 'Dramaturgy in Shakespeare and Brecht', *University of Toronto Quarterly*, XXXII (1963), 229–46.

[3] 'Shakespeare and the Modern World', *Shakespeare Survey 16* (1963), 57–62.

[4] 'An Obligation to Shakespeare and the Public', *ibid.* pp. 1–9.

[5] 'Theater Research and the Criticism of Shakespeare and his Contemporaries', *Shakespeare Quarterly*, XIII (1962), 451–61.

[6] 'Stage Imagery in Shakespeare's Plays', *Essays on Shakespeare and Elizabethan Drama*, pp. 261–74.

[7] 'Engagement and Detachment in Shakespeare's Plays', *ibid.* pp. 275–96.

[8] 'Shakespeare's Delayed Reactions', *Essays in Criticism*, XIII (1963), 9–16.

[9] 'Repeated Situations in Shakespeare's Plays', *Essays on Shakespeare and Elizabethan Drama*, pp. 247–59.

Michel Grivelet[1] passes some interesting observations on Shakespeare's use of language. Starting from the position that all word-play is a form of word-corruption (with tragic utterance as the wildest), he claims that such 'corruption' is made in hope, despair, and confusion 'to relieve the mind from the pressure of its own conceit'. Paul A. Jorgenson[2] examines certain key words or word clusters to discover their exact meaning both in their dramatic context, and against a background of their use in Renaissance literature such as sermons, moralities, courtesy books and military textbooks. The words he treats are: 'honesty' in *Othello*, 'nothing' in *Much Ado About Nothing* and other plays, 'redeeming time' and 'bright honour' in *Henry IV* and 'noble' in *Coriolanus*. There is also a final chapter on Hamlet's 'world of words' which explores not a single master word but the various aspects of speech itself, noting that 'what is frequently *talked* about in *Hamlet* is not so much disease as speech'. Although occasionally limiting to the plays considered, the book is full of suggestive ideas, with those contained in the chapter on 'Much Ado About *Nothing*' especially so. Shakespeare's use of the most conventional language is the subject of Charles G. Smith's book[3] on proverb lore. He lists some 346 proverbs found in the works which have parallels with Leonard Culman's *Sententiae Pueriles* and/or Publius Syrus' *Sententiae*, and some twenty-five parallels found in Cato. The listing is impeccably arranged and indexed with full citations and translations, and useful cross-references to Erasmus, Udall, classical sources, as well as standard works like Tilley and Smith. Altogether a well-produced book to ponder with pleasure.

The philosophical and religious attitudes of a dramatist are always puzzling matters, and never more so than in the case of Shakespeare. Rolf Soellner[4] surveys the allegedly antiphilosophy pronouncements in the plays in their dramatic context and against the background of Renaissance thought, and concludes that, while one misses an awareness of the significant developments of Ramus and Bacon, the evidence 'points strongly to [Shakespeare's] curiosity and concern in contemporary philosophical problems, such as the methods of consolation, the limits of knowledge, and the wisdom of folly'. Roland Mushat Frye[5] tackles the whole problem of Shakespeare's knowledge and use of Christian doctrine. To this formidable task he brings an obviously wide and expert knowledge of Renaissance theology, and, after discussing what sources of religious ideas would have been available to the playwright, settles down to consider the theories of the 'Christianizers' of Shakespeare and of their opponents. Both groups are taken to task, with the former coming out of the examination rather worse, particularly those of their number who find proliferating Christ figures. Among Frye's conclusions are: that no single play or extended passage from one is framed to present Christian doctrine in either a literary or allegorical form, even though there are many incidental references which indicate Shakespeare's interest in the subject; that Shakespeare is a secular playwright in so far as he is concerned with his characters' lives upon this earth and is unconcerned with their fate after death; and that to postulate Shakespeare's 'own personal position within so broad a range of

[1] 'Shakespeare as "Corrupter of Words"', *Shakespeare Survey 16* (1963), 70–6.
[2] *Redeeming Shakespeare's Words* (University of California Press, 1962).
[3] *Shakespeare's Proverb Lore* (Harvard University Press, 1963).
[4] '"Hang Up Philosophy". Shakespeare and the Limits of Knowledge', *Modern Language Quarterly*, XXIII (1962), 135–49.
[5] *Shakespeare and Christian Doctrine* (Princeton University Press, 1963).

possibilities would at worst be a task for rationalizing speculation and at best for personal surmise'. The arguments leading to these convictions may—and certainly will—be disputed at many points, but they are a useful corrective to those critics who too often make a Shakespeare in their own doctrinal image. The third section of the book is devoted to a classified listing of the theological topics with which the playwright appears to have been familiar. There is also a fascinating appendix which analyses the censoring of a 1632 Folio by a Jesuit, William Sankey, for use in the English College at Valladolid. In view of some of the recent interpretations of *Measure for Measure*, it is interesting to note that this was the only play that Sankey rejected *in toto*.

2. SHAKESPEARE'S LIFE, TIMES AND STAGE

reviewed by STANLEY W. WELLS

The most restrained among recent attempts to tell the story of Shakespeare's life is Gerald Eades Bentley's *Shakespeare: A Biographical Handbook*.[1] Documentation is generous; comment, concise and tart in its refusal to indulge in speculation. This is an eminently useful book which assumes a care for scholarship in its readers, yet succeeds too in mediating between the scholar and the student. Another, more recent book in which Shakespeare's career is narrated with scholarly rigour is Peter Alexander's *Shakespeare*.[2] In the section concerned with the life, Alexander is at pains to show how false beliefs have developed, thus enabling the reader to disentangle truth from legend. This part of the book is distinguished by much hard thought and a refusal to accept easy assumptions. No evidence derived from the Sonnets is admitted: indeed, the book includes little about them or the other poems. The chapters on the plays are inevitably limited in scope, but they tell much in little space, with notable learning and sympathy; the author frequently uses the relationship between play and source as the basis of his remarks. This is a hard-headed but not unattractive volume which presupposes in its readers a serious interest in its subject.

Heralded with strident fanfares of publicity, A. L. Rowse's *William Shakespeare: A Biography*[3] proved a disappointment. In his preface, the author declares himself 'overwhelmed by what historical investigation, by proper historical method, has brought to light'. But none of Rowse's 'discoveries' is supported by evidence that would bear close examination. The 'historical method' (nowhere defined) appears to consist in a willingness to accept with acclamation any guess that suits one's purposes. All is inductive. It is the old method of 'discovering' that historical circumstances could have been referred to in terms employed by Shakespeare, and thence asserting that they are. And it produces the same old results. The pity of it is that so long as he is following the traditional outlines of Shakespeare's life and environment, Rowse is a vigorous, lively, and informative writer. He has read the right secondary sources; and he popularizes them well, vividly sketching the background examined in detail by, for example, T. W. Baldwin and Caroline Spurgeon. To make this material attractive for a wide circle of readers (the book has already had a large sale) is no negligible achievement. And Rowse's

[1] Yale University Press, New Haven, 1961.   [2] Oxford University Press, 1964.
[3] Macmillan and Co. Ltd., 1963.

literary responsiveness is more vital and intelligent than that of many more pedestrianly careful writers on Shakespeare. He searches the plays for evidence of Shakespeare's formative years in Stratford, and of his personality. We need not believe everything he tells us, but the image he produces is in many ways acceptable. Yet one cannot but wish that what will perhaps be the most popular biography of Shakespeare of our time should have been less arrogant in its claims, less aggressive in its manner, that it should have shown more of an historian's respect for fact, less for fiction, and that it should in general have been more worthy of 'gentle' Shakespeare.

Published at the same time as Rowse's book, and somewhat overshadowed by it, was Peter Quennell's *Shakespeare: the Poet and his Background*,[1] less sprightly but more temperate in tone, notably well illustrated, and offering a sound historical background. Like Rowse's, this is a book by an historian obliged by his subject to treat of literary matters. Though Quennell is a critic of some sophistication, he nevertheless shows survivals of generally outdated attitudes: for him, for instance, *Love's Labour's Lost* is 'not an adult work', and Malvolio 'deserves to rank among the dramatist's tragic characters'.

The title of J. Dover Wilson's admirable *Shakespeare's Sonnets: An Introduction for Historians and Others*[2] suggested that this paperback issue of a version of the introduction to a forthcoming edition of the Sonnets might not have been unconnected with the publication of Rowse's views. Rowse shows to his total satisfaction that the Sonnets were addressed to the earl of Southampton, and that 'Mr W. H.' was Sir William Harvey, the earl's stepfather. Quennell had less clamorously drawn attention to an important earlier statement of the same theory (which is about a century old). Wilson comes out in favour of William Herbert, earl of Pembroke, as both friend and dedicatee. The question remains open. Hugh A. Hanley has published an interesting article on 'Shakespeare's Family in Stratford Records',[3] based on documents in the Kent Archives Office, Maidstone, and having special reference to the marriage of Judith Shakespeare and Thomas Quiney. This is a real find. Christopher Whitfield's *Robert Dover and the Cotswold Games*[4] includes some speculations on possible links between Dover and Shakespeare.

An important re-interpretation of an episode in Shakespeare's life often adduced as evidence of his character is offered by Raymond Carter Sutherland,[5] who points out firmly that it was John, not William, who applied for a grant of a coat of arms, and argues that he may well have had good practical reasons for desiring one. The handsome 'Soest' portrait of Shakespeare (*c.* 1660–80) is reproduced with a note by Levi Fox.[6] William H. Moore[7] writes on a possible early allusion to *The Taming of the Shrew* and its implications on the date of that play. Also concerned with dating is Arthur Freeman,[8] who has written on the date of *Solyman and Perseda* in relation to *Romeo and Juliet* and *King John*, both of which appear to him to echo it. Paul

---

[1] Weidenfeld and Nicolson, 1963.
[2] Cambridge University Press, 1963.
[3] *The Times Literary Supplement*, 21 May 1964, p. 441.
[4] Distributors: Henry Sotheran Ltd., London; William Salloch, Ossining, New York, 1962.
[5] 'The Grants of Arms to Shakespeare's Father', *Shakespeare Quarterly*, XIV (1963), 379–85.
[6] *Shakespeare Survey 15* (1962), 130.
[7] 'An Allusion in 1593 to *The Taming of the Shrew*?', *Shakespeare Quarterly*, XV (1964), 55–60.
[8] 'Shakespeare and *Solyman and Perseda*', *Modern Language Review*, LVIII (1963), 481–7.

Morgan[1] adds to our knowledge of Shakespeare's reputation among his contemporaries by his discovery of a manuscript note by Leonard Digges comparing Shakespeare with Lope de Vega as a sonneteer. A full-length study of Shakespeare's reputation is essayed by Louis Marder in *His Exits and His Entrances*.[2] His concern is with Shakespeare as a social and cultural phenomenon rather than as an artist. This readable book is the work of a real enthusiast, and assembles a great deal of interesting and curious information about Shakespeare's posthumous career. A particular episode that has been studied in great (possibly excessive) detail is the Garrick Jubilee of 1769. Christian Deelman's *The Great Shakespeare Jubilee*[3] is a full, well-researched account which makes an entertaining piece of social and cultural history. More economical of space, and more objective in presentation, is Johanne M. Stochholm's *Garrick's Folly*.[4] A later celebration is described in Isabel Roome Mann's 'The Royal Gala of 1830'.[5]

In the amassing of fascinating historical details, especially of Shakespeare's Stratford background, no recent biography can compete with E. I. Fripp's *Shakespeare, Man and Artist*, newly re-issued.[6] Fripp may have been overconfident in seeing connexions between life and art, and inevitably his book, first published in 1938, is dated in some respects, but it remains a splendid monument and an inexhaustible repository.

Source studies have tended to a concern with verbal detail rather than narrative structure. In *Shakespeare's Proverb Lore*[7] Charles G. Smith discusses Shakespeare's 'use of the *Sententiae* of Leonard Culman and Publilius Syrus'. He adduces many parallels, and adds to our awareness of Shakespeare's echoing of proverbial wisdom, though not necessarily by way of the writers mentioned in his title. This is useful as an adjunct to Tilley's great dictionary. T. J. B. Spencer's edition of *Shakespeare's Plutarch*[8] makes readily accessible the four main lives in modernized texts, and prints at the foot of the page those passages from the plays that show direct verbal influence. T. W. Baldwin discusses 'Three Homilies in *The Comedy of Errors*',[9] and Madeleine Doran interestingly surveys pre-Shakespearian versions of the Pyramus and Thisbe story, concluding that in *A Midsummer-Night's Dream* Shakespeare 'brought it to the absurd extreme its accidental features—its Wall, its Lion, and its Moonshine—had always been asking for'.[10] 'Shakespeare and the Fairies' by Roger Lancelyn Green[11] is a pleasantly discursive essay concerned with both the background and the influence of Shakespeare's conception of fairies. Harold F. Brooks[12] suggests some possible influences on Shakespeare of Elyot's *The Gouernour*. Background

[1] '"Our Will Shakespeare" and Lope de Vega: An Unrecorded Contemporary Document', *Shakespeare Survey 16* (1963), 118–20.

[2] John Murray, 1964.

[3] Michael Joseph, 1964.

[4] Methuen and Co. Ltd., 1964.

[5] *Shakespeare Quarterly*, XIV (1963), 263–6.

[6] Oxford University Press, Second Impression, 1964.

[7] Harvard University Press, Cambridge, Massachusetts, 1963.

[8] Penguin Books, 1964.

[9] *Essays on Shakespeare and Elizabethan Drama*, ed. Richard Hosley (Routledge and Kegan Paul Ltd., 1963), pp. 137–47.

[10] 'Pyramus and Thisbe Once More', *ibid.* pp. 149–61.

[11] *Folk Lore*, 73 (1962), 89–103.

[12] 'Shakespeare and *The Gouernour*, Bk. II, ch. XIII. Parallels with *Richard II* and the *More* Addition', *Shakespeare Quarterly*, XIV (1963), 195–9.

and analogous material to *Love's Labour's Lost* is provided in an article by John L. Nevinson.[1] There have also been notes on the sources of *The Two Gentlemen of Verona*,[2] *As You Like It*,[3] *Hamlet*,[4] *The Tempest*[5] and Sonnet 30.[6] A more general background of the Sonnets is provided in Joan Grundy's clear, well-phrased article 'Shakespeare's Sonnets and the Elizabethan Sonneteers'.[7] She examines some conventions of the Elizabethan sonneteers, and discusses Shakespeare's relation to them, concluding that, while in some of the sonnets Shakespeare 'is merely playing the fashionable game', in others 'he both re-examined the sonneteers' "poetic", and gave it, through his practice, a philosophical and critical depth that it had not possessed before'. Muriel C. Bradbrook[8] sees *Venus and Adonis* as having been designed to obliterate the impression made by Greene's famous attack on Shakespeare. In the narrative poem 'the player has shown his capacity to move in a world of gorgeous paganism, to write upon a noble model, and to deal with love in aristocratic boldness and freedom'.

On the plays again, E. W. Talbert's *The Problem of Order*[9] is a specialized study which stresses the complexity of the political background, with particular reference to *Richard II*. T. J. B. Spencer[10] usefully explores the development of popular prejudices about the Greeks current in Shakespeare's time. William A. Ringler, Jr.,[11] considers the reflexions discernible in *Hamlet* of attacks on, and defences of, the stage. He further maintains that these parts of the play are essential to its structure, not of merely topical interest. Also relevant to *Hamlet* is Alfred Harbage's 'Intrigue in Elizabethan Tragedy',[12] which argues that intrigue was only with great difficulty assimilable within a truly tragic pattern; *Hamlet* succeeds partly because the hero fails as an intriguer. C. J. Sisson[13] has added to the background of *Twelfth Night*, and Gustav Ungerer,[14] suggesting that 'Armatho' and 'Chirrah' in *Love's Labour's Lost* may represent Shakespeare's attempt 'to record the sounds of Spanish speech', interestingly investigates the background of the Elizabethans' knowledge of Spanish. Shakespeare's influence on a minor contemporary is subtly studied by J. M. Bemrose,[15] and Donald K. Anderson, Jr.,[16] has drawn attention to a

---

[1] 'A Show of the Nine Worthies', *Shakespeare Quarterly*, XIV (1963), 103–7.

[2] Jim C. Pogue, '*The Two Gentlemen of Verona* and Henry Wotton's *A Courtlie Controuersie of Cupids Cautels*', *Emporia State Research Studies* (June 1962), pp. 17–21.

[3] William E. Miller, '"All the World's A Stage"', *Notes and Queries*, X (1963), 99–101.

[4] James O. Wood, '*Hamlet* and the first Epistle of John', *ibid.* 413.

[5] Paul F. Cranefield and Walter Federn, 'A Possible Source of a Passage in *The Tempest*', *Shakespeare Quarterly*, XIV (1963), 90–2.

[6] Ralph Aiken, 'A Note on Shakespeare's Sonnet 30', *ibid.* pp. 93–4.

[7] *Shakespeare Survey* 15 (1962), 41–9.

[8] 'Beasts and Gods: Greene's *Groats-worth of Witte* and the Social Purpose of *Venus and Adonis*', *ibid.* pp. 62–72.

[9] The University of North Carolina Press, Chapel Hill, 1962.

[10] '"Greeks" and "Merrygreeks": A Background to *Timon of Athens* and *Troilus and Cressida*', *Essays on Shakespeare and Elizabethan Drama*, ed. Richard Hosley (Routledge and Kegan Paul Ltd., 1963), pp. 223–33.

[11] *Ibid.* pp. 201–11.

[12] *Ibid.* pp. 37–44.

[13] 'Tudor Intelligence Tests: Malvolio and Real Life', *ibid.* pp. 183–200.

[14] 'Two Items of Spanish Pronunciation in *Love's Labour's Lost*', *Shakespeare Quarterly*, XIV (1963), 245–51.

[15] 'A Critical Examination of the Borrowings from *Venus and Adonis* and *Lucrece* in Samuel Nicholson's *Acolastus*', *Shakespeare Quarterly*, XV (1964), 85–96.

[16] '*Richard II* and *Perkin Warbeck*', *Shakespeare Quarterly*, XIII (1962), 260–3.

possible influence of Shakespeare on Ford. Macdonald P. Jackson,[1] pointing to the presence of a 'Shakespearian' image-cluster in *Edmund Ironside*, also casts doubt on the validity of image-clusters as evidence of authorship. And Roland Mushat Frye[2] has recorded 'Three Seventeenth-Century Shakespeare Allusions'.

In *Elizabethan Taste*,[3] John Buxton vividly surveys Elizabethan attitudes to architecture, painting, sculpture, and music; a final section offers more detailed studies of particular works of literature, including *Venus and Adonis* and *Hamlet*. Throughout, the author insists that knowledge is necessary to understanding; and he himself employs learning in the service of criticism. This is a delightful book—erudite, intelligent, sometimes brilliant—which should do much to increase understanding of the artistic climate in which Shakespeare worked. It would be difficult to come away from it without a more alert appreciation of those manifestations of Elizabethan taste that survive. A darker side of life is briefly illuminated by F. P. Wilson's[4] selection of plague pictures, with notes making connexions with passages in Shakespeare's plays and other Elizabethan writings.

David M. Bevington's *From 'Mankind' to Marlowe: Growth of Structure in the popular Drama of Tudor England*[5] is an original and convincing study of certain aspects of pre-Shakespearian drama. He is concerned particularly with the popular professional drama, and with the relationship between the composition of acting troupes and the structure of plays written for them. His findings have important implications for the later drama; thus, his conclusions as to the versatility of Elizabethan actors ('Renaissance dramatists were remarkably free from the need to conform in the creation of character to company capabilities or types') are opposed to those arrived at by T. W. Baldwin and taken for granted in for instance Richard David's British Academy Lecture for 1961, 'Shakespeare and the Players'.[6] That the interludes may be more significant than the mysteries as a background to the Elizabethan stage is suggested by Richard Southern.[7] A corollary of his study is a comparison between the Tudor hall and the de Witt drawing of the Swan Theatre—a comparison also made by Glynne Wickham in his new volume, mentioned below. Another branch of drama that has Shakespearian affinities is the *Commedia dell'Arte*, studied in Allardyce Nicoll's *The World of Harlequin*,[8] a book as elegant in style as it is sumptuous in appearance.

The native dramatic tradition, explored in detail by Bevington, is also emphasized in the second volume of Glynne Wickham's important and wide-ranging survey, *Early English Stages*.[9] The first part of the present volume is concerned particularly with external influences on the development of drama, tracing the imposition of state control, and discussing both its causes and its effects. 'Reformation' and 'Renaissance' are the key terms here. Wickham sees

---

[1] 'Shakespeare and *Edmund Ironside*', *Notes and Queries*, X (1963), 331–2.
[2] *Shakespeare Quarterly*, XIII (1962), 361.   [3] Macmillan and Co. Ltd., 1963.
[4] 'Illustrations of Social Life. IV. The Plague', *Shakespeare Survey* 15 (1962), 125–9.
[5] Harvard University Press, Cambridge, Massachusetts, 1962.
[6] Oxford University Press, 1962.
[7] 'The Contribution of the Interludes to Elizabethan Staging', *Essays on Shakespeare and Elizabethan Drama*, ed. Richard Hosley (Routledge and Kegan Paul Ltd., 1963), pp. 3–14.
[8] Cambridge University Press, 1963.
[9] *Early English Stages, 1300–1660*. Vol. II, *1576 to 1660*, part I (Routledge and Kegan Paul Ltd., 1963).

'Renaissance' influences as having been, at least partially and temporarily, stifled by pressures of 'Reformation'. In his later chapters he deals with the structure and stage-conventions of the earlier Elizabethan public playhouses. Rejecting a progressivist view, he sees the changes observable during the period in terms of a transition from an emblematic theatre to one providing images of actuality. Readers of his first volume will be aware of the range of Wickham's learning, the thoughtfulness of his approach. This is no easy resurvey of well-trodden ground. He has new evidence to offer; but more important is his re-appraisal of the familiar. He impels us, for instance, to reconsider the influence of the inn-yard on theatre design, for he believes that most performances in inns were given indoors, not in the yard. And he re-examines for us the de Witt drawing, with interesting results. This is a rich and rewarding book. One looks forward to the concluding volume, not in the expectation that a definitive work on the Elizabethan stage will have been achieved—that would be unreasonable—but in the knowledge that a great deal of precise evidence will have been set in a background that will suggest many illuminating connexions.

More restricted in scope, and consequently even more detailed in presentation, is Bernard Beckerman's study of the Globe during Shakespeare's greatest decade.[1] This is based on the fifteen Shakespearian and fourteen non-Shakespearian plays performed there between its opening and the opening of the Blackfriars. While thus limiting the sources of evidence (so avoiding the dangers of argument by analogy) the author goes much beyond the use normally made of such sources in studies of the Elizabethan theatre. Instead of restricting himself—as so many writers on staging do—to the evidence provided by the plays about the physical facts of staging—the setting, properties, machinery, etc.—he extends his investigation to such matters as the dramaturgy, the acting, and the grouping of characters. He denies the assumption that 'the stage-structure and its machinery played the decisive role in the presentation of an Elizabethan drama'. He rejects the notion that mansions were employed on the stage of the Globe, and feels that 'it is time to reassert that the Globe stage *was* bare'. And (like Bevington) he believes that roles were distributed 'without attention to personal traits of the actors'. Naturally, he is led into a lengthy (and interesting) discussion of Elizabethan acting, in the course of which he finds that it was neither 'formal' nor 'natural' but 'romantic'. Bertram Joseph, who is usually cited as the main believer in the 'formal' style, hits back in the substantially revised edition of *Elizabethan Acting*[2] at his critics in what he calls 'the futile and really quite unnecessary controversy on the subject'. He insists that he does not and did not think that Elizabethan acting was 'formal'; 'in every case, and whatever the interpretation, the actor was identified'. Joseph's views appear to have been considerably modified over the years; he puts forward his case here with learning, apt illustration, and economy. On a particular actor—Edward Alleyn—A. J. Gurr[3] has replied to an argument advanced by W. A. Armstrong.[4] Gurr argues that Hamlet's remarks on acting can be applied to Alleyn, and show that Shakespeare regarded the acting of Burbage and other members of his company as more restrained than that of Alleyn and his men. Armstrong replies in a review.[5]

[1] *Shakespeare at the Globe, 1599–1609* (The Macmillan Co., New York, 1962).
[2] Oxford University Press, 1964.
[3] 'Who Strutted and Bellowed?', *Shakespeare Survey 16* (1963), 85–102.
[4] *Shakespeare Survey 7* (1954), 82–9. [5] *Theatre Notebook*, XVIII (Spring, 1964), 108–9.

F. W. Sternfeld's *Music in Shakespearian Tragedy*[1] is a major contribution to the study of one aspect of the plays. The author's learning is immense; his bibliographies are invaluable; he is aware of the practical needs of producers; and he is sensitive to overall dramatic effect. But the book's organization leaves something to be desired; it is an uneasy compromise between a work of reference and a critical study; furthermore the title is misleading, since chapter V is mainly about the comedies. Nevertheless, this book is indispensable to all concerned with the authentic presentation of the plays, and has much to offer to anyone interested in the music and drama of the period. Also of practical value to producers is Frances A. Shirley's *Shakespeare's Use of Off-Stage Sounds*.[2] The author draws some useful parallels with other dramatists, and is well-versed in the post-Commonwealth stage-history of the plays. Her book should make producers and others usefully aware both of the practical need for off-stage sounds at many points where they are often omitted, and also of the part that these can play in the deeper patterns of performance. An appendix listing sounds necessary for each play enhances the book's practical value; this should be a standard reference work for producers of Shakespeare. The probability that the original producer of the plays was Shakespeare himself is demonstrated by David Klein.[3]

The location of The Curtain has been investigated by Lucyle Hook.[4] Hal H. Smith's 'Some Principles of Elizabethan Stage Costume'[5] is an admirable assessment of a difficult topic. William E. Miller[6] has persuasively countered Leslie Hotson's objections to his theory that the early Blackfriars was furnished with one or more *periaktoi*. Albert B. Weiner[7] has suggested that *Richard III* V, iii, was originally staged 'with one tent against the tiring house wall for Richmond, and a table and chair on the platform for Richard'. Herbert E. Childs bases his article 'On the Elizabethan Staging of *Hamlet*'[8] firmly on performances of the play on the reconstructed Elizabethan stage at Ashland, Oregon. 'The Staging of the Dover Cliff Scene in *King Lear*' is discussed by Waldo F. McNeir.[9] Richard Hosley employs detailed statistical evidence in writing about 'The Staging of Desdemona's Bed'.[10] He argues that the bed was not discovered, but brought on to the stage; 'the original staging of *Othello* did not require the use of a discovery-space'. This is one of those scrupulous examinations of particular points of staging which are gradually modifying long-held opinions about the Elizabethan stage.

It is coming increasingly to be realized that, just as our views of Shakespeare's plays are inevitably if unconsciously influenced by what many generations of critics have written about them, so too are they influenced by the ways they have been presented in the theatre. No one

---

[1] Routledge and Kegan Paul Ltd., 1963. Of more strictly practical value is Alan Boustead's *Music to Shakespeare. A practical catalogue of current incidental music, song settings and other related music* (Oxford University Press, 1964).
[2] University of Nebraska Press, Lincoln, 1963.
[3] 'Did Shakespeare Produce His Own Plays?', *Modern Language Review*, LVII (1962), 555–60.
[4] 'The Curtain', *Shakespeare Quarterly*, XIII (1962), 499–504.
[5] *Journal of the Warburg and Courtauld Institutes*, XXV (1962), 240–57.
[6] '*Periaktoi*: Around Again', *Shakespeare Quarterly*, XV (1964), 61–5.
[7] 'Two Tents in *Richard III*?', *Shakespeare Quarterly*, XIII (1962), 258–60.
[8] *Ibid.* pp. 464–74.
[9] *Studies in English Renaissance Literature*, ed. W. F. McNeir (Louisiana State University Press, Baton Rouge, 1962), pp. 87–104.
[10] *Shakespeare Quarterly*, XIV (1963), 57–65.

has done more to further our knowledge and understanding of this process than Arthur Colby Sprague, whose *Shakespeare's Histories, Plays for the Stage*[1] is characteristic in its combination of sense with sensitiveness, lucidity with learning. Marvin Rosenberg[2] has done something similar, though on a larger scale, for a single play: *Othello*. His is a thoughtful and well-informed study; in its way, a pioneering book. Anyone interested in the stage-history of *Othello*, the critical history of *Othello*, or just *Othello*, could learn much from it. It may seem a shade laboured beside Sprague's book; but that has the ease of the master. The new edition of Granville-Barker's *Prefaces to Shakespeare*[3] is graced by illustrations, and annotations to them, provided by Muriel St Clare Byrne, which in themselves constitute an original contribution to Shakespearian stage history. It is to be hoped that they may be incorporated into later reprints of the hard-cover edition, since the paper-back volumes, though unquestionably a bargain, are not over-durable.

Nahum Tate's adaptation of *King Lear*, so important in the critical history of the play, has been the subject of two articles, one by Margareta Braun,[4] another, more sympathetic, by Christopher Spencer.[5] A. E. Kalson[6] has shown that Colley Cibber drew on sources other than Shakespeare for his even more popular version of *Richard III*. Joseph G. Price[7] has traced the fortunes of *All's Well That Ends Well* from the first revival of the original, in 1741, in which the comic element was emphasized, through Garrick's adaptation, which simplified the play and focused attention on Parolles, then Pilon's even more farcical version (which has not survived), and finally to Kemble's influential alteration from farce to romantic melodrama, presenting a sentimentalized Helena. Thomas Sheridan's *Coriolanus*, based on both Shakespeare's and James Thomson's plays of the same name, is studied by Esther K. Sheldon.[8]

Outstanding among scholars concerned with the stage-history of the nineteenth century is Charles H. Shattuck, who has edited two of Macready's prompt-books.[9] Both are splendidly produced and meticulously annotated; both deserve to be taken as models of theatrical scholarship. The present writer, in commenting on 'Shakespeare in Planché's Extravaganzas',[10] has suggested a rather more influential place for Planché in the history of Shakespearian production than he is usually credited with. Claris Glick[11] has sketched William Poel's theory, practice, and influence in an article mainly intended for those unfamiliar with his work. Forbes-Robertson's *Hamlet* is best known through Bernard Shaw's brilliant review of it; W. A. Armstrong[12]

[1] The Society for Theatre Research, 1964.

[2] *The Masks of Othello: the Search for the Identity of Othello, Iago and Desdemona by Three Centuries of Actors and Critics* (University of California Press, Berkeley and Los Angeles, 1961).

[3] B. T. Batsford Ltd., 1963.

[4] '"This is Not Lear"—Die Leargestalt in der Tateschen Fassung', *Shakespeare Jahrbuch*, XCIX (1963), 30–56.

[5] 'A Word for Tate's *King Lear*', *Studies in English Literature*, III (1963), 241–51.

[6] 'The Chronicles in Cibber's *Richard III*', ibid. pp. 253–67.

[7] 'From Farce to Romance. *All's Well that Ends Well* 1756–1811', *Shakespeare Jahrbuch*, XCIX (1963), 57–71.

[8] 'Sheridan's *Coriolanus*: An 18th-Century Compromise', *Shakespeare Quarterly*, XIV (1963), 153–161.

[9] *Mr William Charles Macready Produces 'As You Like It': A Promptbook Study* (University of Illinois, 1962); *William Charles Macready's 'King John'. A facsimile promptbook* (University of Illinois, 1962).

[10] *Shakespeare Survey 16* (1963), 103–17.

[11] 'William Poel: His Theories and Influence', *Shakespeare Quarterly*, XV (1964), 15–25.

[12] Ibid. pp. 27–31.

has interestingly shown that Shaw had a considerable influence on the production, so that his review is 'a happy blend of critical objectivity and justifiable delight in the success of his own ideas'. The same writer has made an admirable brief survey[1] of trends in Shakespearian production from the time of Tree and Poel to the present day. A much fuller survey of London and provincial performances in roughly the same period is essayed by J. C. Trewin in *Shakespeare on the English Stage, 1900–1964*.[2] This is so comprehensive as to become sometimes rather sketchy, relying too often on lists of names and the exaggeratedly 'evocative' phrase. Yet it is sometimes genuinely illuminating (e.g. on Olivier's Titus) and unquestionably remarkably well-informed. Trewin conveys a good quick impression of changing styles of production. His detailed appendices of performances in the West End and at the Old Vic and Stratford give the book permanent value as a reference work. Would that we had something similar for the nineteenth century!

'Shakespeare en France: mises en scène d'hier et d'aujourd'hui'[3] is a learned and superbly illustrated survey by Jean Jacquot, who also writes the foreword to the excellent catalogue of the exhibition 'La Vie Théâtrale au temps de la Renaissance'.[4] Some of Max Reinhardt's Shakespeare productions, and Jean-Louis Barrault's *Hamlet*, have been the subject of articles in *Shakespeare Jahrbuch*.[5] David William's 'Hamlet in the Theatre'[6] looks at the role from the point of view of the modern actor, who, he feels, should be more willing than he often is to take 'emotional risks'. Rudolf Stamm, writing on 'Modern "Theatrical" Translations of Shakespeare',[7] has concentrated on German versions by Hans Rothe and Richard Flatter. Eleanor Prosser[8] is readier to approve the rewriting of Shakespeare; studying a production of *Henry IV, Part II* at San Diego in which the play had been 'completely rewritten', she somewhat dismayingly defends the principle of 'rearranging Shakespeare's own material in an attempt to present Shakespeare's play to the modern audience in terms it could understand', while finding fault (justifiably, it would seem) with many features of this particular version. She also attempts to draw some general conclusions about effective methods of revision. There are others who would still prefer Shakespeare to be caviare to the general than that he should be turned into fish paste. Alan S. Downer may perhaps be counted among them, on the evidence of his vigorous analysis[9] of several productions of the present 'great age of Shakespeare Improved Again'. N. J. Sanders,[10] studying the repertory of the Royal Shakespeare Theatre, comes to the consoling conclusion that audiences 'possess a basic good sense and an intuitive feeling for dramatic propriety which enables them to detect gimmickry and elaboration which destroys

---

[1] 'The Art of Shakespearean Production in the Twentieth Century', *Essays and Studies*, xv (1962), 74–87.

[2] Barrie and Rockliff, 1964.

[3] Paris, 1964.

[4] Paris, 1963.

[5] Edmund Stadler, 'Reinhardt und Shakespeare, 1904–1914', *Shakespeare Jahrbuch*, xcix (1963), 95–109; Elisabeth Brock-Sulzer, 'Barraults Hamlet', *ibid.* 123–32.

[6] *Stratford-upon-Avon Studies 5: 'Hamlet'* (Edward Arnold Ltd., 1963), pp. 29–43.

[7] *Shakespeare Survey 16* (1963), 63–9.

[8] 'Colley Cibber at San Diego', *Shakespeare Quarterly*, xiv (1963), 253–61.

[9] 'For Jesus' Sake Forbear: Shakespeare *vs.* the Modern Theater', *Shakespeare Quarterly*, xiii (1962), 219–30.

[10] 'The Popularity of Shakespeare: An Examination of the Royal Shakespeare Theatre's Repertory', *Shakespeare Survey 16* (1963), 18–29.

a play's excellence'. The present state of popular journalism does not encourage rigorous and well-informed theatre criticism of any scope, but that of John Russell Brown in *Shakespeare Survey* and of some of the contributors to *Shakespeare Quarterly* has more than day-to-day value. Some of the finest productions of our time are recalled by John Gielgud in *Stage Directions*,[1] which includes interesting essays on some of his greatest roles and adds in an appendix his fascinating rehearsal notes of Granville-Barker's production of *King Lear*.

3. TEXTUAL STUDIES

reviewed by JAMES G. MCMANAWAY

The primary intention of forty years of a bibliophile's life and the bibliographical persistence and acumen of a scholar have come to rich fruition in *The Printing and Proof-Reading of the First Folio of Shakespeare*,[2] which Charlton Hinman tells us could never have been written unless Henry Clay Folger had hunted out and brought together an unprecedented number of copies for scholarly use. Nor could it have been written unless Hinman had invented his now famous collating machine and devoted nearly two decades to the study. Announcing his most important discoveries as they were validated, Hinman removed the element of surprise from his book while simultaneously making the new methods of research available to other scholars. Now we know that the First Folio was not put into type seriatim but by formes; we have a printing schedule that is unlikely to be greatly modified; we know where interruptions occurred in composition and press work, that five men were engaged, and what pages, columns and parts of columns they set. Further refinements are needed, as Hinman points out, particularly in recognizing and tabulating the spelling preferences and other characteristics of compositors *C* and *D*. Although the collation of more than fifty copies of the Folio has produced few substantive variants, it has indicated which compositors need to be checked most carefully and has given editors a true understanding of many short or otherwise abnormal lines and greater leeway in rectifying them.

Henry VIII is the last play in the New Shakespeare. Its editor, J. C. Maxwell,[3] follows Spedding and his successors in attributing the play to Shakespeare and John Fletcher, not only because he finds two styles in the play, or because metrical tests support Spedding's attribution, but because the vocabulary tests of Thorndike, Partridge, Oras and others give strong confirmation. Though Maxwell would like to consider the matter settled, there is contrary evidence. Some hitherto neglected evidence against Fletcher's participation in *Henry VIII* is offered by John P. Cutts,[4] who maintains that Shakespeare and Fletcher use song in very different ways and for different purposes. He compares the situation of Queen Katherine with that of Mariana and Desdemona and concludes that the same hand is at work; then he illustrates Fletcher's quite

[1] Heinemann, 1963.

[2] C. K. Hinman, *The Printing and Proof-Reading of the First Folio of Shakespeare* (Oxford University Press, 1963).

[3] J. C. Maxwell, ed., *King Henry the Eighth*, New Shakespeare (Cambridge University Press, 1962). It may be noted that Hinman agrees with Maxwell and, earlier, Foakes, in assigning part of the play to Jaggard's compositor *B* but identifies the man who paired with him as probably *C*, not *A*.

[4] John P. Cutts, 'Shakespeare's Song and Masque Hand in *Henry VIII*', *Shakespeare Jahrbuch*, XCIX (1963), 184–95.

different use of song—even a song about Orpheus—in *The Captain* and *The Bloody Brother*. Then, turning to Queen Katherine's vision, he shows that the masque of the angelic visitors has deeper significance than has been recognized and that the masque itself conforms to Shakespearian usage. Strongly in support of Fletcher's participation in *Henry VIII* is the concluding section of Cyrus Hoy's study of Fletcher and his collaborators.[1] This diminishes greatly the number of scenes assigned to Fletcher and uses vocabulary tests to show that there are Fletcherian interpolations in scenes that are essentially Shakespeare. He is not at all sure that there is justification for 'attributing to Fletcher the superb speeches made by Wolsey after his fall'. Hoy's study is based solidly on linguistic evidence and the way compositors *A* and *C* deal with copy, and he makes his inferences only after considering all the possibilities of authorial and scribal copy.

Pending his completion of the edition of the Sonnets, the final volume of the New Shakespeare, John Dover Wilson[2] has paid quatercentenary tribute to his author by publishing the introduction, an urbane book, whose relative informality permits a charming directness of statement. Marshalling expertly the evidence accumulated from Tyler, Beeching, Dowden, Wyndham and others, Wilson makes a strong case for William Herbert, earl of Pembroke, as the Fair Youth and for a late dating of the sonnets, 1597–1606. Wilson's belief that some at least of the sonnets were secured in manuscript by Thorpe from the Dark Lady, after she realized the poet had made a final break with her, introduces a new factor into the calculation of how the sonnets came to be printed. And his inclusion of the descriptions of Pembroke by Clarendon and Aubrey helps to an understanding of how the young earl might win and command the abnegating love of a great poet, though I find it difficult to reconcile the character described by Clarendon with that depicted in Sonnets 87 ('Farewell! thou art too dear for my possessing') and 94 ('They that have power to hurt and will do none').

It is regrettable that when the out-of-print early volumes of the New Shakespeare are reissued the venerable editor has not the leisure to bring all portions of the apparatus up to date. In *The Comedy of Errors*,[3] 'the Text, Notes, and Glossary have been revised throughout' with help from J. C. Maxwell. The Note On the Copy is left untouched except for a cautionary paragraph. Wilson continues to insist upon the importance of 'auditory misprints', which he interprets as evidence that the Folio text was printed from a dictated transcript of Shakespeare's foul papers. Another work long out of print, Wilson's *The Manuscript of Shakespeare's 'Hamlet' and the Problem of its Transmission*,[4] has been reissued with a foreword by G. I. Duthie, who recognizes the historical importance of the work and traces the course of more recent bibliographical and textual study of the play. Time has modified or reversed some of Wilson's conclusions, many of which were revolutionary, for like his volumes in the New Shakespeare this study of *Hamlet* has stirred readers passionately to confirm or confute it.

The Winter's Tale, which has been the object of harsh criticism since the days of Ben Jonson,

---

[1] Cyrus Hoy, 'Fletcher and his Collaborators', *Studies in Bibliography*, xv (1962), 71–90.

[2] John Dover Wilson, *An Introduction to The Sonnets of Shakespeare for the Use of Historians and Others* (Cambridge University Press, 1964).

[3] John Dover Wilson, ed., *The Comedy of Errors*, New Shakespeare (Cambridge University Press, 1962).

[4] John Dover Wilson, *The Manuscript of Shakespeare's 'Hamlet' and the Problem of its Transmission* (Cambridge University Press, 1963).

finds a resolute defender in J. H. P. Pafford.[1] He deals even-handedly with expositors that find myth or allegory or Christian doctrine behind every bush and takes just account of multiple sources and literary influences, except perhaps the indebtedness to the Greek romances.[2] In a conservative text, why was it considered necessary to follow F 2 at IV, iv, 98? 'Then make you [for yourself] gardens rich in gillyvors' is a perfectly good reading.

The amply annotated edition of *The Comedy of Errors* by R. A. Foakes[3] gives a conservative text and a judicious discussion of the problems of date of composition and of the staging. His reproductions of two woodcuts from the *Comedies* of Terence (Lyons, 1493) will be helpful to readers who think habitually of an Elizabethan stage in terms of the Swan drawing. Foakes emphasizes the use Shakespeare made of New Testament references to witchcraft in Ephesus and to the proper relations between husband and wife, master and servant.

Pericles is one of the most difficult of the plays to edit. The only text is a quarto that has no transcriptional relation to the original manuscript, that is, it is a reported text. It contains verse printed as prose and prose as verse; words and lines are omitted, and superfluous words are inserted; there are passages of nonsense. In addition, there is such a difference in literary quality between the first two acts and those that follow as to encourage a belief in divided authorship. In the last decade, Philip Edwards has argued that two reporters of unequal capacity produced the report, with the implication that Shakespeare was sole author and that the unevenness in literary quality is chargeable to the reporters. These ideas are rejected by F. D. Hoeniger,[4] who attributes Acts I and II to one or more writers other than Shakespeare. Rejecting Rowlands and Heywood, and demonstrating the difficulty in accepting George Wilkins as the collaborator, he produces parallels in II, i, and II, iii, to lines found in plays by John Day and suggests that Day may have written these two scenes and possibly I, ii. Because of the conjectural history of the text, Hoeniger emends chiefly when the error may reasonably be considered compositorial or when the accepted reading is supported by the wording of the corresponding passage in *The Painfull Adventures of Pericles Prince of Tyre* (1608), a novelistic report of the play by George Wilkins. Quite properly, Hoeniger makes many changes in the lineation of the verse.

As long ago as 1931, Leslie Hotson announced his belief that *The Merry Wives of Windsor* was first performed at Windsor at the Feast of the Order of the Garter celebrated on St George's Day, 1597. Now William Green publishes the results of his testing of that thesis.[5] The play is sprinkled with allusions to Windsor, to the gathering of nobles, to a grand affair in prospect. One of the nobles to be honoured—the prospect of his election seems to have been an open secret—was Henry Carey, second Lord Hunsdon, a kinsman to the queen and the patron of Shakespeare's company. Green believes that Hunsdon more than anyone else was responsible for the writing and acting of the play, and he points to the exact spot in the festivities where he thinks the performance took place. The vast differences between the Bad quarto text and the longer and better Folio version arise from the fact that Q was printed from an abridgement

---

[1] J. H. P. Pafford, ed., *The Winter's Tale*, New Arden (Methuen, London; Harvard University Press, 1963).
[2] Cf. J. H. Bryant, 'The Winter's Tale and the Pastoral Tradition', *Shakespeare Quarterly*, XIV (1963), 387–98.
[3] R. A. Foakes, ed., *The Comedy of Errors*, New Arden (Methuen, London; Harvard University Press, 1962).
[4] F. D. Hoeniger, ed., *Pericles*, New Arden (Methuen, London; Harvard University Press, 1963).
[5] William Green, *Shakespeare's 'Merry Wives of Windsor'* (Princeton University Press, 1962).

made for provincial use—all the references to the Court or the Order of the Garter have been removed—whereas the Folio text represents changes that were made between the first, 'occasional', performance and the adaptation of the play for public production in London during the next twenty-odd years. Green believes that Q's version is too bad to have been prepared by Shakespeare's company for a provincial tour or reconstructed by them by memory while on tour. It must be a reported text; and since it borrows from *Henry V*, a later play, and was entered in the Stationers' Register by John Busby, one of the publishers of the Bad quarto of *Henry V* (1600), he suggests that the same actor may have been involved in both reports (according to Greg, this would have been the man who played the part of Host of the Garter Inn). The change of Brooke's name to Broome, the 'Duke de Jarmany', and the horse-stealing incident are treated sensibly.

Two hundred and fifty-five years have passed since the publication of Rowe's edition of Shakespeare's plays, but scholars are not yet satisfied that the text is established. A non-specialist that thinks they are straining at gnats will discover in an essay by Fredson Bowers[1] why textual scholars are compelled to live laborious days. Using very few technical terms, he describes the chief problems to be solved and illustrates typical decisions that must be made in the choice of a reading. Not until a reader knows the many different ways by which the text of a Shakespearian play could get into print and the subtle tests by which an editor attempts to decide its relative authority can the complexity—and excitement—of textual study be appreciated. The essay is a fine introductory statement, one that will bear frequent reading.[2]

The choice between variants of apparently equal authority and the emendation of difficult lines must not be made, writes F. W. Bateson,[3] until full consideration has been given to the objective (Bateson calls it 'external') evidence, the dramatic propriety, and the literary evidence. His first illustration, the Hostess's 'a Table of greene fields' (*Henry V*, II, iii, 18), is presented persuasively: what Shakespeare intended was 'a talkd of greene fields'. Too many imponderables are introduced, it seems to me, in the comparison of Hamlet's 'quietly interr'd' with 'quietly inurned'. The preference for the latter, almost wholly subjective, is only shakily supported by the possibility that Shakespeare made a spot revision—or that Burbage or someone else may have altered words in a prompt-book.

One of the very welcome quatercentenary volumes is the attractive facsimile edition of the Poems published by the Elizabethan Club at Yale.[4] It consists of the unique Bodleian copy of *Venus and Adonis*, the Elizabethan Club's own *Lucrece* and *Sonnets*, the Huntington Library *Passionate Pilgrim* (second edition), and the Folger Shakespeare Library copies of *Passionate Pilgrim* (first edition, fragment), and *Phoenix and Turtle*. The facsimiles are clear, but it was an

---

[1] Fredson Bowers, 'What Shakespeare Wrote', *Shakespeare Jahrbuch*, XCVIII (1962), 24–50.

[2] For a more general and wider-ranging discussion of textual and editorial problems, see Bowers's 'Textual Criticism', in *The Aims and Methods of Scholarship in Modern Languages*, ed. James Thorp (Modern Language Association of America, 1963).

[3] F. W. Bateson, 'Shakespeare's Laundry Bills: The Rationale of External Evidence', *Shakespeare Jahrbuch*, XCVIII (1962), 51–63.

[4] The Publications Committee of the Elizabethan Club, James M. Osborn, *Ch.*, Louis L. Martz and Eugene M. Waith, edd., *Shakespeare's Poems: Venus and Adonis, Lucrece, The Passionate Pilgrim, The Phoenix and Turtle, The Sonnets, A Lover's Complaint, A Facsimile of the Earliest Editions* (Yale University Press for the Elizabethan Club, 1964).

error in judgment to reprint only portions of the unique fragment of the first printing of *Passionate Pilgrim*. The editors give a precise account of the first editions of the poems and provide a selected bibliography. 'Familiarity breeds consent', the editors say. 'The effect of moving easily into the presence of the poem [in a modernized text] is in part an illusion: what we read is not quite the poem, but something that includes spellings, punctuation marks, and even emendations that may keep us at some distance from the original poem' (p. xi). They are aware of the obstacles interposed by early scribes and compositors and by erratic spelling and inconsistent punctuation and ask, if i-j, u-v, and -s are modernized, whether it is 'mere sentimentality to urge the retention of spellings that offer no service to pronunciation, rhythm and meaning'. Then they illustrate the way in which modern punctuation can spoil the flow of lines and break the natural unity of a quatrain and point to further advantages provided by the original capitalization and spelling. The modern spelling and pointing give an 'illusion of familiarity' that may be narcotic. Sometimes the old spellings give just sufficient pause to suggest multiple meanings, and the old pointing may permit the association of phrases with either what precedes or follows, or with both, where modern punctuation closes the door on fluency and interpenetration.

Reference should be made to the unpretentious reprint of the Trinity College, Cambridge, copy of *Passionate Pilgrim*,[1] the only one known until the Britwell–Huntington copy came to light. The book belonged at some time about 1740 to one W.B., who noted of his purchase: 'Not quite perfect, see 4 or 5 Leaves back; so it cost me but 3 Halfpence'.

Working independently on the printing of *Much Ado*, John Hazel Smith[2] finds confirmation of W. C. Ferguson's statement that only one compositor set the type for Valentine Simmes. Then tracing the recurrence of running-titles and the patterns in which identifiable pieces of type appear throughout the play, he attempts to do for *Much Ado* what Hinman has done for the First Folio. He observes an interruption in press work between sheets A and B and another between G and H. The first interruption remains inexplicable—possibly a piece of job printing to be done in a hurry—but the second, Smith believes, was caused by the need to print a cancel for Q 1 of *Henry IV, Part II*. This play, it will be remembered, was first printed by Simmes without Act III, Scene i; to repair the omission, leaves E 3 and E 4 were cancelled and their text was reset as the first part of a cancellans signed E 3–6, with III, i, filling out the sheet. Smith's evidence is the use in the cancel of one identifiable type used in G (o) of *Much Ado* and two from G (i)—types that do not appear in the next forme H (i), though each occurs in a later forme.[3] Thus is answered the vexing question about when the missing scene of *Henry IV, Part II*, was printed. Though a quarto forme uses a small amount of type in comparison with a folio, Smith thinks he has found enough identifiable types to warrant the belief that *Much Ado* was composed by formes from cast-off copy, and he argues that miscalculations in casting off produced open and crowded pages, the stretching out of text and the compressing of it to the point that stage-directions are positioned abnormally, and the setting of more or fewer than the normal thirty-seven lines to a page. These and attendant abnormalities are,

---

[1] *Passionate Pilgrim* (E. and E. Plumridge, Cambridge, 1964).

[2] John Hazel Smith, 'The Composition of the Quarto of *Much Ado About Nothing*', *Studies in Bibliography*, XVI (1963), 9–26.

[3] Smith provides a Type Chart on pp. 25–6.

then, casual results of printing house adjustments, not evidence of textual revision by the author.

Hamlet, The First Quarto 1603 by Albert B. Weiner reprints[1] the text with modern spelling and punctuation. The original part of the book is largely an attempt to prove that there is no clear-cut case of a pirated play and that the theory of reported texts is silly. Weiner suggests, as if for the first time, that the text of Q 1 was vamped up for performance; then he argues that the cuts are judicious and the scenes between Horatio and Gertrude are ingenious simplifications devised to accommodate the play to a touring company of twelve (sharers, hirelings, and boys). He believes that Shakespeare's foul papers were adapted and abridged by an unidentified agent of the Globe company and that after the accession of James this very foul touring version was offered by the King's Men to Ling and Trundell for use in printing Q 1, for which '*favor* [italics mine] they would give Ling their London version after just one more season'. Weiner continues: 'By Autumn [1604] *Hamlet* was no longer popular enough for the King's Men to retain the prompt copy. The complete *Hamlet* was turned over to Ling, and this time Roberts agreed to print the text.' Other statements about the text are, to me, equally preposterous. As a by-product of this book, Weiner offers a suggestion about the location of the 'To be or not to be' soliloquy in Q 1, which is different from that in Q 2 and F 1.[2] This passage of some 94 lines is about what is required to fill one leaf of dramatic manuscript and he suggests that, in fact, the leaf bearing the passage was by accident shifted from its right place, as established by Q 2 and F 1. This may have happened, but *Der bestrafte Brudermord*, which is likewise based on performance of Shakespeare's play, agrees with Q1 in the ordering of this scene.

Since bibliographers began to analyse the spelling of Elizabethan texts and construct tables of preferential spellings of the compositors who set them, there has been spectacular progress. This was one of the most heavily used tools, for example, in Hinman's study of the printing of the First Folio. Much more could be done if more manuscripts had survived that served as printer's copy, but there are few survivors like the fragment of Sir John Harington's translation of *Orlando Furioso*. Much more will be done when there has been time to study, not just a few Shakespeare quartos and the First Folio, but the output over a period of years of the shops that printed them, and when works of many other authors have been examined similarly. This time-consuming research is particularly liable to error originating in human frailty, and it may be hoped that techniques will be perfected for the use of electronic computers, which are speedy and tireless. T. H. Hill's[3] attempt to formulate a rationale of the study of Elizabethan spelling proposes some useful technical terms (spelling-habit, spelling-pattern) and warns against facile assumptions. One may question whether the average Elizabethan printer's shop had as clear a concept of a 'rule of the house' as Hill seems to take for granted. Until the major output of many shops has been studied in depth, will it be possible to characterize a change in spelling by the corrector of the press as an application of the 'rule of the house'?

In the enumeration of the nobles who returned to England with Bolingbroke (*Richard II*, II, i, 277–82), a line has obviously been lost after line 279. Editors have produced from Holinshed

---

[1] Albert B. Weiner, ed., *William Shakespeare: 'Hamlet', The First Quarto 1603* (Barron's Educational Series, New York, 1962).

[2] Albert B. Weiner, 'Evidence of a Stray Sheet in the Q 1 "Hamlet" Manuscript', *AUMLA*, no. 19, 88–92.

[3] T. H. Hill, 'Spelling and the Bibliographer', *The Library*, 5th ser., XVIII, 1–28.

the omitted name, that of 'Thomas Arundell, sonne and heire to the late earle of Arundell beheaded at Tower Hill', and have devised various emendations. It has been supposed hitherto that a scribe or compositor was at fault. William J. Griffin[1] argues persuasively that the Master of the Revels probably struck out the offending name because young Thomas Howard, son to the late Earl of Arundell (who had been executed in 1595), was deep in the shadow of Queen Elizabeth's displeasure.

[1] William J. Griffin, 'Conjectures on a Missing Line in *Richard II*', *Tennessee Studies in Literature*, VII, 109–11.

BOOKS RECEIVED

[Inclusion of a book in this list does not preclude its review in a subsequent volume.]

ALEXANDER, P. *Shakespeare* (London: Oxford University Press, 1964).

BAILEY, HELEN P. *Hamlet in France from Voltaire to Laforgue* (Geneva: Librairie Droz, 1964).

BLOOM, E. (ed.). *Shakespeare 1564–1964* (Providence: Brown University Press, 1964).

BOUSTEAD, A. *Music to Shakespeare* (London: Oxford University Press, 1964).

BOWERS, FREDSON. *Bibliography and Textual Criticism* (Clarendon Press: Oxford University Press, 1964).

BRENNECKE, E. (ed.). *Shakespeare in Germany* (Chicago University Press, 1964).

BROWN, J. R. and HARRIS, B. (eds.). *Stratford-upon-Avon Studies 5: Hamlet* (London: Arnold, 1963).

BULLOUGH, G. (ed.). *Narrative and Dramatic Sources of Shakespeare*. Vol. v. *The Roman Plays* (London: Routledge and Kegan Paul, 1964).

BUXTON, J. *Elizabethan Taste* (London: Macmillan, 1963).

DEELMAN, C. *The Great Shakespeare Jubilee* (London: Michael Joseph, 1964).

DUTHIE, G. I. (compiler). *Papers Mainly Shakespearian* (Aberdeen University Studies, 1964).

EASTMAN, A. M. and HARRISON, G. B. *Shakespeare's Critics: From Jonson to Auden* (Ann Arbor: Michigan University Press, 1964).

FRIPP, E. I. *Shakespeare, Man and Artist* (London: Oxford University Press, second impression, 1964).

FRYE, R. M. *Shakespeare and Christian Doctrine* (Princeton University Press, 1963).

GIELGUD, J. *Stage Directions* (London: Heinemann, 1963).

GRANVILLE-BARKER, H. *Prefaces to Shakespeare* (London: Batsford, revised edition, 1963).

HARTNOLL, PHYLLIS (ed.). *Shakespeare in Music* (London: Macmillan, 1964).

HINMAN, C. K. *The Printing and Proof-Reading of the First Folio of Shakespeare* (London: Oxford University Press, 1963).

KRIEGER, M. *A Window to Criticism: Shakespeare's Sonnets and Modern Poetics* (Princeton University Press; London: Oxford University Press, 1964).

LANDRY, H. *Interpretations in Shakespeare's Sonnets* (University of California Press, 1963).

LASCELLES, MARY. *Shakespeare's Comic Insight* (British Academy Annual Shakespeare Lecture, 1962; London: Oxford University Press, 1963).

MARDER, L. *His Exits and His Entrances* (London: Murray, 1964).

MARTZ, L. *Shakespeare's Poems: a facsimile* (Yale University Press, 1964).

NICOLL, ALLARDYCE. *The World of Harlequin* (Cambridge University Press, 1963).

PARTRIDGE, A. C. *Orthography in Shakespeare and Elizabethan Drama* (London: Arnold, 1964).

QUENNELL, P. *Shakespeare: the Poet and his Background* (London: Weidenfeld and Nicolson, 1963).

ROWSE, A. L. *William Shakespeare: A Biography* (London: Macmillan, 1963).

SCHANZER, E. *The Problem Plays of Shakespeare* (London: Routledge and Kegan Paul, 1963).

SHAKESPEARE, WILLIAM

Pericles, New Arden Shakespeare, edited by F. D. Hoeniger (London: Methuen; Harvard University Press, 1963).

BOOKS RECEIVED

The Winter's Tale, New Arden Shakespeare, edited by J. H. P. Pafford (London: Methuen; Harvard University Press, 1963).

The Passionate Pilgrim (Trinity College, Cambridge, copy: E. and E. Plumridge, Cambridge, 1964).

SHIRLEY, FRANCES A. *Shakespeare's Use of Off-stage Sounds* (Lincoln, U.S.A.: Nebraska University Press, 1963).

SMIDT, K. *Iniurious Impostors and Richard III* (Norwegian Universities Press, 1964).

SMITH, C. G. *Shakespeare's Proverb Lore* (Harvard University Press, 1963).

SMITH, D. NICHOL (ed.). *Eighteenth Century Essays on Shakespeare* (London: Oxford University Press, second edition, 1963).

SPENCER, T. J. B. (ed.). *Shakespeare's Plutarch* (London: Penguin, 1964).

SPRAGUE, A. C. *Shakespeare's Histories, Plays for the Stage* (London: The Society for Theatre Research, 1964).

STAMM, R. *Zwischen Vision und Wirklicheit* (Bern: Francke, 1964).

STERNFELD, F. W. *Music in Shakespearian Tragedy* (London: Routledge and Kegan Paul, 1963).

STOCHHOLM, J. M. *Garrick's Folly* (London: Methuen, 1964).

SUTHERLAND, J. and HURSTFIELD, J. (eds.). *Shakespeare's World* (London: Arnold, 1964).

TALBERT, E. W. *Elizabethan Drama and Shakespeare's Early Plays* (Chapel Hill: North Carolina University Press; London: Oxford University Press, 1964).

TREWIN, J. C. *Shakespeare on the English Stage, 1900–1964* (London: Barrie and Rockliff, 1964).

WEIMAN, R. *Dramen der Shakespearezeit* (Leipzig: Dieterich'sche Verlagsbuchhandlung, 1964).

WICKHAM, G. *Early English Stages, 1300–1660*. Vol. II, *1576 to 1660*, part I (London: Routledge and Kegan Paul, 1963).

WILSON, J. DOVER. *Shakespeare's Sonnets: An Introduction for Historians and Others* (Cambridge University Press, 1963).

WILSON, J. DOVER. *The Manuscript of Shakespeare's 'Hamlet' and the Problem of its Transmission* (Cambridge University Press, 1963).

INDEX

Acquart, André, 122
Adam, Cornel, 131
Adams, John, 103
Adams, J. Q., 105
Ahonen-Mäkelä, Mrs Ritva, 121
Aiken, R., 180
Ainley, Henry, 73
Albertazzi, Giorgio, 126
Alexander, Peter, 24, 43, 44, 131, 177
Algan, Ayla, 130
Allen, D. C., 173
Alleyn, Edward, 182
Altick, Richard, 19, 20
Anderson, D. K., 180–1
Anderson, Ruth L., 168
Andjelinović, D., 134
Anouilh, J., 123, 171
Åorlin, Georg, 128
Aphthonius, 166
Arany, János, 125
Aristotle, 36, 122
Armin, Robert, 166
Armstrong, Edward A., 54, 55
Armstrong, W. A., 182, 184–5
Arne, T. A., 96, 97, 98, 99, 100
Arnold, 99
Arnold, Matthew, 114
Artaud, A., 61, 149
Arundell, Earl of, 192
Arvidsson, Gun, 128
Ashcroft, Dame Peggy, 147, 152–3
Atalay, Turgut, 130
Aubrey, John, 187
Audran, E., 76
Austria, Shakespeare productions in, 119–20
Avermaete, Roger, 120
Ayscough, Samuel, 17, 108

Bachrach, A. G. H., 126
Bachtík, Josef, 121
Bacon, Delia, 107, 111–12
Bacon, Francis, 176
Baconians, American, 111–15
Badel, Alan, 166
Baildon, Joseph, 99
Bajić, S., 134
Baldini, Gabriele, 125, 126
Baldwin, T. W., 159, 177, 179, 181
Balfe, M. W., 81
Bandel, Betty, 131
Bángyörgyi, Károly, 125
Banister, J., 94

Barrault, J.-L., 122, 185
Barrymore, John, 71
Barton, John, 149
Baskerville, J., 17
Básti, Lajos, 125
Bateson, F. W., 189
Battenhouse, Roy, 169–70
Batusić, S., 134
Beaumont, Francis, 46, 132
    The Woman-Hater, 35
Becker, Maria, 129
Beckerman, Bernard, 62, 182
Beckett, Samuel, 61, 156
Beeching, H. C., 187
Beethoven, L. van, 75
Belgium, Shakespeare productions in, 120
Bell, J., 17
Bellini, V., 75, 80, 81
Bemrose, J. M., 180
Benda, Georg, 78
Bennett, Josephine W., 165
Benson, Sir Frank, 72
Bentley, G. E., 36, 177
Bergner, Elizabeth, 73
Berkovec, Jiří, 121
Berlioz, H., 75, 77, 85
Berman, R. S., 169
Bernard, M. A., 168
Bessenyei, Ferenc, 125
Bethell, S. L., 57 n.
Betterton, Thomas, 35, 36
Bevington, David M., 181, 182
Bible, The, St Mark's Gospel, 49
Bishop, Henry Rowley, 98, 99, 100
Blacher, B., 87
Black, Eugene R., 133
Black, Matthew, 175
Blackall, E. A., 174
Blair, Hugh, 16
Bloch, E., 75, 86–7
Boas, F. S., 39
Boccaccio, 85
Boden, Nicholas, 17
Böhm, Otto Hans, 119
Boito, Arrigo, 83–4, 85
Boklund, Gunnar, 128
Bonjour, A., 129, 167, 173
Bonnefoy, Yves, 122
Booth, Junius Brutus, 104, 106–7
Bora, Oğuz, 130
Borsos, Miklós, 125
Boswell, James, 37

INDEX

INDEX

INDEX

INDEX